THE GANG PARADOX

STUDIES IN TRANSGRESSION
Editor: David Brotherton
Founding Editor: Jock Young

The Studies in Transgression series will present a range of exciting new crime-related titles that offer an alternative to the mainstream, mostly positivistic approaches to social problems in the United States and beyond. The series will raise awareness of key crime-related issues and explore challenging research topics in an interdisciplinary way. Where possible, books in the series will allow the global voiceless to have their views heard, offering analyses of human subjects who have too often been marginalized and pathologized. Further, series authors will suggest ways to influence public policy. The editors welcome new as well as experienced authors who can write innovatively and accessibly. We anticipate that these books will appeal to those working within criminology, criminal justice, sociology, or related disciplines, as well as the educated public.

Terry Williams and Trevor B. Milton, *The Con Men: Hustling in New York City*
Christopher P. Dum, *Exiled in America: Life on the Margins in a Residential Motel*
Mark S. Hamm and Ramón Spaaij, *The Age of Lone Wolf Terrorism*
Peter J. Marina, *Down and Out in New Orleans*
David C. Brotherton and Philip Kretsedemas, editors, *Immigration Policy in the Age of Punishment*

THE GANG PARADOX

Inequalities and Miracles on the U.S.-Mexico Border

Robert J. Durán

Columbia University Press   New York

Columbia University Press
Publishers Since 1893
New York   Chichester, West Sussex
cup.columbia.edu
Copyright © 2018 Columbia University Press

All rights reserved
Library of Congress Cataloging-in-Publication Data

Names: Durán, Robert J., author.
Title: The gang paradox : inequalities and miracles on the U.S.-Mexico border /
    Robert J. Durán.
Description: New York : Columbia University Press, 2018. | Includes
    bibliographical references and index.
Identifiers: LCCN 2018019751 | ISBN 9780231181068 (cloth) |
ISBN 9780231181075 (pbk.) | ISBN 9780231543439 (e-book) Subjects:
LCSH: Gangs—Mexican-American Border Region. |
    Crime—Mexican-American Border Region. | Youth—Mexican-American Border
    Region—Social conditions. | Mexican-American Border Region—Social conditions.
Classification: LCC HV6439.M58 D87 2018 | DDC 364.106/609721—dc23
    LC record available at https://lccn.loc.gov/2018019751

Cover design: Milenda Nan Ok Lee

Cover art: Mural by Francisco Delgado. Director: Mauricio Olague
and Bowie High School Students.

To the residents of Aztlán, particularly those living in Nuevo Mexico and El Chuco, and the struggle for justice!

Contents

List of Illustrations   ix

Acknowledgments   xi

Introduction   1

PART I   A REVISIONIST HISTORY   21

ONE   The Context for the Origination of Gangs: Double Colonization   23

TWO   The Formation of Gangs in El Chuco   40

THREE   Moral Panic Under a Research Microscope: The Organizational Scene Prior to Arrival   69

PART II   AN ETHNOGRAPHIC FOUNDATION   95

FOUR   How Youth of Mexican Descent Encounter Criminalization   97

FIVE   Contradictions in Law Enforcement   129

SIX   Participatory Action Research Teams at a Minority-Serving Institution   157

SEVEN   Empirical Miracles and Where Do We Go from Here?   188

Conclusion   217

Appendix 1: Methods   229

Appendix 2: Development of Gangs Timeline in the
New Mexico/Texas Region   235

Notes   239

References   261

Index   289

Illustrations

Figures

1.1 Viceroyalty of New Spain Map, 1810   26
1.2 U.S. Territorial Acquisitions Map   28
1.3 Historical Trade Route Map   31
2.1 El Paso Gangs in the 1950s   59
2.2 El Paso Gangs in the 1970s   65
4.1 Hispanic or Latino Relative Rate Index (RRI) Compared to Whites   104
4.2 Levels of Concentration of Latinos in Southern New Mexico and El Paso   106
5.1 Border Region: Border Enforcement Enhanced 100 Miles North of the Border   131

Tables

3.1 Official Reports of Number of Gangs and Gang Members Compared to the Population   84
4.1 7-Year Averages (2002–2008) for the State of New Mexico by Race and Ethnicity   102
7.1 Number of Homicides per Year in the City of El Paso and Rate per 1,000   195
7.2 Number of Homicides per Year in Las Cruces and Rate per 1,000   196
7.3 Estimated Number of Homicides per Year in Ciudad Juárez, Mexico, and Rate per 1,000   196

Acknowledgments

I'd like to first thank the residents of Anthony, Chaparral, Columbus, Deming, Doña Ana, El Paso, Hatch, Las Cruces, Lordsburg, Silver City, and Sunland Park for providing me a space to learn about issues of colonization, border politics, crime control, gangs, and the struggle to improve the lives of our children. I'd like to express my gratitude to Jennifer Perillo, Stephen Wesley, Eric Schwartz, Lowell Frye, Milenda Nan Ok Lee, Marielle Poss, and Columbia University Press for supporting this second book project. My thanks go to the blind reviewers and their feedback in improving this final product. I am indebted to several gang scholars who have studied gangs for decades and have continued to provide me individualized mentorship (John Hagedorn, Joan Moore, Avelardo Valdez, David Brotherton, and James Diego Vigil). I thank my scholarly mentors at Weber State University (Brenda Marsteller Kowalewski, Daniel T. Gallegos, Marjukka Ollilainen, Robert Reynolds, and Huiying Wei Hill) and at the University of Colorado (Patti Adler, Joanne Belknap, Arturo Aldama, Tom Mayer, and Robert Regoli). My admiration goes to the activists of Denver (Ernesto Vigil, Shareef Aleem, Rudy Balles, Leroy Lemos, Earl Armstrong, Doug Vaughan, Steve and Vicki Nash), and my appreciation goes to my friends in graduate school who kept me sane (Marcos Martinez, Robert Muñoz, Lori Peek, Patrick De Walt, and Ted Young).

I stand in solidarity with my colleagues from New Mexico State University (NMSU), where I lived and worked for eight years. I am grateful to Carlos and Mayra Posadas, Cynthia Bejarano and Jeff Shepherd, Spencer and Jessica Herrera, Romina Pacheco and Pierre Orelus, RJ Maratea, Dulcinea Lara, Christina Medina, William Eamon, Rudolfo Chávez Chávez, Hermán García, Cristobal Rodriguez, Christina Chavez

Kelley, Viola Fuentes, Daniel Villa, William Quintana, Antonio Lara, René Casillas, Louí-Vicente Reyes, Luis Vázquez, Jennie Luna, Rodrigo Mora, Breeana Sylvas, Tom Winfree, Larry Mays, David Keys, and Waded Cruzado. I thank my graduate research assistants at NMSU (Samantha Slim, Wesley Patterson, Lisa Wright, Seitu Porter-Robinson, Israel De La Rosa, and Steven Gregory). Several graduate students, including Maria Bordt (University of Tennessee-Knoxville), Wesley Patterson, Seitu Porter-Robinson, and Charlene Shroulote Durán (New Mexico State University), served as assistant editors for the gang update technical reports, from which excerpts were provided in chapter 6. I thank my social justice–oriented and critical colleagues at the University of Tennessee (2014–2018) and Texas A&M University (2018–present) in the Departments of Sociology. Much respect and gratitude goes to my mentoring networks, including the Racial Democracy Crime and Justice Network, Latina/o Criminologists, Division on People of Color and Crime, Hispanic Faculty and Staff Caucus at NMSU, Interdisciplinary Research Training Institute, National Hispanic Science Network, and the Law and Society Association. I thank the scholars who have reviewed and given me feedback and support for my scholarship over the years, ensuring that I could remain in academia (David Brotherton, John Hagedorn, Aaron Kupchik, Ramiro Martinez, Jody Miller, Alfredo Mirandé, Wilson Palacios, Anthony Peguero, Ruth Peterson, Martín Urbina, and Avelardo Valdez).

I am thankful for the primary data resources housed at El Paso Public Library, NMSU Library, University of Texas at El Paso Library, and from professional associates in District Three, District Six, and from those with the State of New Mexico, for data involving schools, law enforcement, juvenile probation, and district attorney offices. Partial funding for the research developed in this book came from NMSU's College of Arts and Sciences, University of Tennessee start-up research funds, and consulting contracts obtained from District Three, District Six, and the Children, Youth and Families Department of the State of New Mexico. All appreciation goes to Judge Fernando Macias for advocating on behalf of the importance of these studies and for securing grant funding. I'd like to thank the artist Francisco Delgado, Director Mauricio Olague, and Bowie High School students for the "Sagrado Corazon" mural image on the book's cover. A section of chapter 4 previously appeared in *Journal of Ethnicity in Criminal Justice*. A section of chapter 5 appeared in *Race and Justice: An International Journal*.

The original articles were written with my friend and colleague Carlos Posadas.

Finally, none of this work could occur without the support of my wife Charlene and our four children: Jazmine, Doroteo, Jocelyn, and Justice. My familia and my ancestry in Nuevo Mexico continues to inspire me, as well as my parents' efforts to ensure I received the encouragement to push forward with my education. Here is to challenging generations of exclusion![1]

THE GANG PARADOX

Introduction

As a former gang member, and someone who had devoted more than a decade studying gangs in two different southwestern states, my introduction to gangs along the U.S.-Mexico border began qualitatively differently than my previous research. On September 30, 2007, my field notes highlight the inquisitiveness I feel as I reentered my familial homeland of New Mexico. At this point in time, I have only been living in southern New Mexico for 13 months, and I have been curiously observing and listening to the stories and experiences of those around me. I walk into a community center where an audience of nearly 50 individuals, of whom many are elderly, wait patiently for a gang expert to speak on the topic titled "Signs Your Child Might Be Involved in a Hispanic Youth Gang." The gang expert's name is David, and he is a middle-aged "Hispanic" man who runs a faith-based organization focused on gangs.[1] In the front of the room, newspaper articles are organized in a manner to highlight David's work, along with shirts and clothing described as gang-related. David stands in the front of the room along with two teenagers and begins his presentation:

> One of the complaints that was made recently about the presentation in Anthony [a small town along the border] was because we called it Hispanic gangs. There is a very good reason why we call it Hispanic gangs because Hispanic gangs are growing and all the gangs that you see here in Chaparral are Hispanic. It would be incorrect to talk about black gangs in Chaparral. [A woman in the back asks, 'What about the white gangs?']. They are not youth gangs. Please hold your questions until the end if you wouldn't mind, it would make it a lot easier otherwise we lose the flow of what is going on with our presentation.[2]

Questioning the over-labeling of Latinos and blacks as gang members was key in Denver, Colorado, and in Ogden, Utah, but here individuals of Mexican descent were the majority of the population, and I wonder whether a similar level of stereotyping occurs. David introduces two teenagers who are current gang members working to reform, but due to their problematic mindsets and behaviors are incapable of changing.

> We have a lot of kids who believe that we owe them something. I don't owe them a darn thing. Everyone by their own merit has to come up here, earn their way, and change their past until they get to where they are going. This country is a great country, but let me tell you, it's giving too much to too many people and too many people believe that they are entitled to more than what they have already been given. It's a very sad situation. I like to tell parents that our very great importance is to instill discipline. I'm not saying spankings at home. What I am saying though is many parents are very lax when it comes to rules. When I go to a child's home and see a child who does not have chores to do, when I see a child who is able to stay up on a school night until one o'clock in the morning, when I see a child who is texting on his cell phone until three in the morning, that gives you a very clear idea of who has the pants on in that household.

David's reasoning taps into a common ideology used to explain youth misbehavior in the area: blaming parents and, in particular, mothers.[3] As he continues, David criminalizes hip-hop clothing and youth attitudes. He states how at 12 years of age, young Hispanic males possess a gene that makes them want to be gang members, and by the age of 14 there is no way out of that lifestyle. Audience members inquire whether David's shirt could be considered gang-related, or his short-cropped hair. David side-steps these questions. "No, no, it's these types over there," as he too inadvertently fit the appearance of a gang member as he had outlined it. Unexpectedly, David begins telling a hypothetical story and points to me in the audience, giving me a moniker of "Rabbit." He is quickly challenged by a fellow Mexican American colleague in the audience, who states that I am a professor at the university and should not be given the nickname. David responds, "He looks like a rabbit," and then he sidetracks a little and says that he is joking, but continues his presentation. David asks the young men to speak, then he critiques their responses, similar to a theatrical street performance. My initial reaction is shock. How could a Hispanic man present such a negative depiction of *gangs, and why would teenagers with this identity facilitate such a portrayal for individuals of Mexican descent? I wonder whether gangs are different here than Denver and Ogden. Could I say David is wrong in providing such negative characterizations? I am perplexed by the change in brown versus brown dynamics, and I decide that I needed to do more local research. And so the journey began in the state of my ancestral homelands and in the nearby city, where many claim gangs of Mexican descent first began: El Paso.*

A month later, I returned to Chaparral to march with residents protesting federal and county immigration raids. Once again, my field notes captured the uniqueness of this geographic region:

> *I attended the counter rally to Otero County Sheriff Department's participation in the federal program called "Operation Stonegarden" in Chaparral. I was amazed to see more than 250 people walking together and shouting in Spanish for President Bush to listen to the plight of the people in this community. We marched for three miles through the community until we reached the park to hear several speakers. I felt like I was in Denver again, but here many individuals were speaking in Spanish and the momentum felt historical. Has there ever been a march of this size down this street? Instead of walking between skyscrapers, we were walking along a quiet two-lane road bordered by small homes and trailers, surrounded by desert. The participants carried a variety of signs and flags for the United States and Mexico. The news media made a visible presence, and my Mexican American colleague gave an excellent interview, telling the camera person how the United States is a nation of immigrants. He was later shown on the evening news. Several of his students marched proudly alongside their professor. I observed my friend, a Mexicana professor, conduct one memorable interview after another with her video camera and microphone. I had an opportunity to see my colleagues as leaders of the future. Yesterday I was the student who came to learn about border issues. I learned a lot about this community and how it has the energy and desire for justice. I have a new respect and admiration for the struggle in this area. I met people from the American Civil Liberties Union (ACLU), Border Network for Human Rights, Las Americas Immigrant Advocacy Center, and Paso Del Norte Civil Rights Project. I saw how they all organized the community to fight for their rights as human beings. I observed senior Chicano professors and community organizers. I can only wonder what stories they have to share.*

Early on, the gang presentation and protest highlighted a difference between Colorado and Utah. Most people assume individuals of Mexican descent are the same, wherever they are, but the border region and New Mexico challenged the notion of racial kinship due to different experiences with immigration (generational) and the ability to use skin color as a marker of who is white or nonwhite. Residents were divided by the U.S.-Mexico border, deportation, incarceration, and death, all of which destabilized many families.

The scholarly literature is consistent regarding several patterns involving gangs. Gangs originate in problematic areas encountering a wide variety of marginality, including class and race and ethnicity.[4] Individuals who join gangs are lower in societal social power, and they experience multiple risk factors that increase the likelihood of running into groups with a similar combination of adversity, which sets the stage for heightened levels of delinquency, crime, and violence. The dominant narrative, that of gangs as criminals, holds that gang members commit more crime than those who do not join gangs, although they don't necessarily specialize in any type of crime, such as homicides or the drug trade.[5] Most members spend time hanging out and socializing rather committing illegal acts, but many people assume that delinquent and criminal behavior causes the increased attention from various forms of social control. Researchers from a wide variety of perspectives have examined whether the policies, legislation, and punishment focused on these groups and the individual members can reduce criminal offending, as well as the reasons why these gangs exist in the first place. My work has continued to question the relationship between gangs and crime, the reasons why gangs exist, and the response they receive from formal institutions. In this book, I ask what social conditions increase the creation of gangs as an identity and as a group for belonging, and I investigate whether such belonging increases levels of delinquency, crime, and violence. What if there is a paradox in which the community conditions alone are not enough to lead to the development and maintenance of gangs? What if the groups that formed didn't encounter the same type of punishment as other locations, which ensured that these groups did not increase in size, presence, or participation in illegal forms of activity? What if the stereotypical views of Mexicans, the border region, and gangs were incorrect? The U.S.-Mexico border region and its residents, the majority of whom are of Mexican descent, provide an opportunity to examine some of the most accepted scholarly findings of gang research during the past ninety years.

I was part of an increasing number of Chicano/a faculty who were recruited to New Mexico State University. Nationwide, the number of Latinos with doctoral degrees hovers around 5 percent, and we had become a 12 percent constituency in a state where at least 47 percent of the residents were of this ethnic group. Latina/o faculty claimed underrepresentation, whereas administrators claimed success. According to the U.S. Department of Education, Latinos comprised 5 percent of all doctoral degrees in 1999 to 2000 and 6 percent of all doctoral degrees in 2009 to 2010.[6] Nevertheless, the university's version of success resulted in very little attention devoted toward retention or instituting a culturally empowering atmosphere.[7] Latinos existed in a state of historical ambivalence, never treated as white despite being given this designation through conquest.[8] Nationwide, many see race relations primarily through the lens of a black and white binary, molded by centuries of slavery and conflict between the North and the South.[9] In this paradigm, Latinos don't exist. Nevertheless, an examination of history and ongoing social relations will argue that individuals of Mexican descent were discriminated against not only through citizenship but also through ancestral heritage, culture, and skin color.

Analyzing the U.S.-Mexico Border and How State Violence Impacts Youth of Mexican Descent

My focus will be primarily concentrated on understanding youth experiences in the community and with various forms of institutionalized punishment that were designed around a perception of "help" as offered through school discipline, law enforcement interaction, and juvenile justice programming. Such a focus will provide an opportunity to examine the notion of hierarchy reinforcing institutions outlined by psychologists Jim Sidanius and Felicia Pratto, the youth control complex by sociologist Victor Rios, and whether youth of color were ever intended for inclusion in the juvenile justice outlined by criminologist Geoff Ward.[10]

Similar to my first book, *The Gang Paradox* will contribute to a counter-gang paradigm by challenging the "gang as criminal" framework popularized by the media, the criminal justice system, and most criminologists.[11] More importantly, it disputes the fear-mongering claims regarding Mexicans, Mexican Americans, immigration, and the threat of spillover violence along the border region. I have utilized several methodological and theoretical alternatives to mainstream criminology and sociology. In terms of methodology, I incorporate ethnography, collaboration, and comparison. Theoretically, I build upon the role of settler colonialism and critical race theory under the framework of racial oppression in shaping the formation and response to marginalized racial and ethnic groups. Finally, I advocate the importance of social movements focused on civil rights to challenge the root causes of colonized social control. Moreover, my interviews with practitioners inform us that inclusion alone does not fix structural problems. In this book, I analyze a section of the U.S.-Mexico border that is considered the Ellis Island for Mexicans and the birthplace of Chicana/o resistance, as well as the area that had the largest Mexican population prior to becoming a territory of the United States, and I outline the factors that led to differing patterns of gang formation. Despite such an early presence of groups identified as gangs, these areas developed along a trajectory that was very different from that of Chicago and Los Angeles (the cities considered by many to be the gang capitals of the United States). This geographic area did, however, maintain lower levels of violence alongside a border city in Mexico that occasionally encountered periods of perhaps the highest levels of violence in the world (Ciudad Juárez).

As important scholarly and societal corrections have begun to highlight the work of black sociologists, social movements such as Black Lives Matter, along with criticism of the underrepresentation of blacks in many professional fields and in giving of awards, so too should scholars recognize the struggles of other marginalized groups in U.S. society, including Chicanas/os.[12] My goal is to unite these differential historical precedents under a common theme of racialized oppression. In *Gang Life in Two Cities*, I outlined how the concept of racialized oppression involved a process of socially constructing power differences through excessive regulation, differences that were enhanced through separation and segregation. I described how dominant groups in two communities in the Southwest created a moral panic regarding gangs of Mexican and African descent. Individual and group resistance to unequal starting points and treatment often led to increased punishment, but the ability to provide alternatives depended upon the success of grassroots civil rights organizations and dominant group allies. Neither strategy completely removed gangs from the community, because the structural conditions ruled, but they did provide insight into ways to challenge racialized social control. This study builds on my previous work by looking toward the center of the Mexican numerical presence and political influence in a geographic area now considered part of the United States.

Ethnography as a Foundation for Social Activism and Collaboration

Methodologically, ethnography has been key in providing insight into a wide variety of social problems. Ethnography can provide insight into undiscovered processes of hidden, exclusive, or closed-off groups in society.[13] The strategy of listening and observing individuals in their social environment provides an opportunity to learn firsthand the lived experiences of marginalized communities.[14] It provides an avenue for the voiceless, oppressed, or the underdog to reveal their experiences.[15] In the *Handbook of Ethnography*, sociologist Paul Atkinson and colleagues defined ethnography as ". . . grounded in a commitment to the firsthand experience and exploration of a particular social or cultural setting on the basis of (although not exclusively by) participant observation."[16] Sociologists Paul Gellert and Jon Shefner argued that not only does ethnography ". . . lay bare the meanings of social life to individuals," but it also outlines the "real dynamics and processes of power."[17] The methodology has the ability to provide historical context and illuminate activities that macro studies obscure, such as various forms of resistance to structural inequality.

The beginnings of ethnography can be found in the Du Bois-Atlanta School and the Chicago School during the early 1900s.[18] Contrary to anthropological studies of visiting a foreign country, the Du Bois-Atlanta School and Chicago School leaders encouraged students to go out into the city and use that setting as a laboratory for understanding human interactions, behaviors, and cultures. The earliest urban ethnographer, W.E.B. Du Bois, studied the condition of blacks in the city of Philadelphia.[19] Du Bois utilized a similar racial background when canvassing the community and talking with residents from 1896 to 1897. Throughout his career, Du Bois developed a form of reflexivity, ". . . this sense of always looking at one's self through the eyes of others, . . ." for which his standing, along with blacks in America, formed into a concept he described as double consciousness.[20] An implied objective of the Atlanta Sociological Laboratory was to influence social and public policy, whereas proponents of the Chicago School encouraged researchers to remain detached and objective.[21] The University of Chicago was primarily white, and the Atlanta school was primarily black; both schools differed in social acceptance in the United States and thus their ideas differed about whether social science should be detached compared to being oriented to influence social policy.

It is through this divide between the Du-Bois Atlanta School and the Chicago School that we encounter one of the major obstacles facing the methodology of ethnography: relational distance involving insider or outsider research. The crux of this argument is similar to colonization in that a researcher enters a community and takes from residents while personally benefitting and simultaneously increasing the level of stigmatization for the residents. Although many ethnographers from marginalized backgrounds have commented on individuals with very different backgrounds in terms of the communities they are studying as a form of colonialism, cowboy ethnography, or jungle-book tropes, these outsider ethnographic studies continue to be the most mainstream and widely accepted.[22] Ethnographers from underrepresented backgrounds must negotiate difficult boundaries between conducting research projects with marginalized populations and agents of the state while at the same time surviving primarily white institutions of higher education.[23] Success in academia is built, in many ways, from maintaining the social capital that exists in these white spaces, which differ greatly from poor, inner-city social environments with heavy criminal justice involvement.[24] Despite insider studies of methodological and theoretical value, these works were often ignored because white academics who exemplify the privileges of the system are able to maintain hierarchical advantage. Such issues of neglect and omission have plagued social science disciplines from their beginnings.[25]

One of the earliest forms of urban ethnography focused on the topic of gangs. As a doctoral student at the University of Chicago, Frederic Thrasher produced the first recognized systematic study on gangs.[26] Thrasher collected data on 1,313 gangs for a period of about seven years. He found that no two gangs were alike, and the setting in which these groups developed were key to developing solutions. Since this time, several excellent studies utilizing field observations and interviews have occurred in many communities across the nation.[27] There have been thousands of publications involving gangs, many of which have been very problematic. In response, gang scholar David Brotherton challenged the hegemonic versions of gangs and gang members as pathological and decried how such a negative message had been adopted by mass media, social science, and professionals engaged in intervention.[28] He set out to provide a way to think about these groups differently, outline improved methodological standpoints, and develop a counter-narrative to the traditional deficit viewpoint of gangs in his book *Youth Street Gangs: A Critical Appraisal*.

The source of data for the *Gang Paradox* is based on ten years of analysis consisting of seven years of ethnography (2007–2014) with follow-up visits during a portion of the summers in 2015 and 2016. It includes 76 interviews with community members and practitioners. More than a hundred student research projects were incorporated of which, 78 percent were done by students of color and 48 percent of the participants were women. My access to the community was produced by living in the East Mesa section of Las Cruces, having my children attend public schools, and then receiving increased access to formal sources of social control (law enforcement, courts, and juvenile probation) made possible through several projects involving the study of disproportionate minority contact and evaluating juvenile justice programs. Moreover, each chapter utilizes official data sources and primary documents to broaden the empirical argument. More detail on my methods will be provided in specific chapters and in appendix 1.

Comparative Research and the Importance of Geographic Settings

C. Wright Mills, a highly esteemed critical sociologist, argued that developing a sociological imagination required examining the distinction between personal troubles and larger structural issues.[29] Mills stated:

> Comparisons are required in order to understand what may be the essential conditions of whatever we are trying to understand, whether forms of slavery or specific meanings of crime, types of family or peasant communities or collective farms. We must observe whatever we are interested in under a variety of circumstances. Otherwise we are limited to flat descriptions.[30]

Mills believed such a process involved the integration between comparative study and historical study. Nationwide, politicians and criminal justice stakeholders have become infatuated with targeting alleged gang members through deportations, enhancements, injunctions, and differential law enforcement.³¹ Thus, conducting comparative research, particularly between different geographic settings, has become more important to determining the reasons that these groups exist and what policies or responses may be the most practical.

In their book, *Divergent Social Worlds*, sociologists Ruth Peterson and Lauren Krivo found whites, Latinos, and blacks often lived in communities with differing levels of equality. Blacks lived in neighborhoods with the highest levels of disadvantage and violent crime. Latinos lived in highly disadvantaged neighborhoods, although less extremely disadvantaged compared to areas where blacks lived, and Latino communities reflected unexpectedly lower rates of violence. Whites lived in areas with the lowest violence rates and the best neighborhood circumstances. Peterson and Krivo's analysis found that removing disadvantage would make black neighborhoods have an average rate of violence only 65 percent greater than white neighborhoods, compared to 327 percent higher at the time of study. The average rate of Latino neighborhood violence would be decreased to 29 percent higher than white neighborhoods rather than 149 percent higher at the time of the study. This analysis explained a large portion of the gap in violent offending, but the authors were still curious as to why rates of violence weren't higher in Latino neighborhoods despite living in disadvantage. These scholars drew on the research of criminologists María Vélez and Ramiro Martínez, whose research studies have pointed toward the role of immigration and living in more integrated neighborhoods.³² Ramiro Martinez analyzed homicide data in six cities with a higher proportion of Latinos (i.e., Chicago, El Paso, Houston, Miami, San Antonio, and San Diego).³³ His work confirmed the lower rates of violence, as measured by homicide, but he acknowledged the uniqueness of each community, stating, "Local conditions matter; each research setting has a unique history, shaped by micro- and macro-processes and has national implications."³⁴ Although several of these cities benefitted from immigration, San Antonio did not, and this emphasized a difference between Latinos who were both old and new. In other words, although Latinos may have experienced demographic changes because of immigration, they were still primarily of Mexican origin, native-born, and residing in a border-state region. Therefore, additional factors such as employment differences and higher levels of social integration must also play a role. Analyzing variables larger than poverty alone was required to understand the reasons for higher levels of violence among certain populations. Sociologist María Vélez analyzed homicide data alongside census tract data in the city of Chicago and found that Latinos lived in relatively advantageous structural positions (i.e., neighborhoods with lower levels of concentrated disadvantage and segregation, more immigrants, and better ties to economic officials, police departments, and local politicians) compared to blacks. Thus, her research was guided by the racial invariance thesis, which argues that criminological processes are the same for all neighborhoods regardless of racial composition.

In addition to these two studies cited by Peterson and Krivo, other researchers have sought to understand Latino neighborhoods. Sociologists Edward Telles and Vilma Ortiz had the opportunity to build upon a previous survey conducted in 1965 and 1966 of Mexican-origin residents from Los Angeles, California, and San Antonio, Texas.[35] Telles and Ortiz re-interviewed the original respondents three decades later, as well as their children. The outcome was their book titled *Generations of Exclusion: Mexican Americans, Assimilation, and Race*, in which they wrote that public education continued to serve as the greatest source of Mexican exclusion, and this continued to affect jobs and involvement in politics. Thus, third- and fourth-generation Mexican Americans were not necessarily better off in terms of levels of success. Generational differences based on immigration were also highlighted in anthropologist Daniel Dohan's ethnographic research in two barrios, where he found that a community composed primarily of first-generation Mexicanos struggled for legal employment, whereas the community consisting of second- and third-generation Mexican Americans maintained gangs and drug-distribution networks.[36] Thus, like the Latino Paradox argument, assimilation or greater acculturation into the United States did not necessarily improve the access to good and services, i.e., life chances.[37]

The U.S.-Mexico border and the local residential neighborhoods were a central place for socio-economic inequality. The border demonstrated a socially constructed political line (i.e., the ground itself cannot tell you which part is Mexico and which part is the United States) that continued to enhance a militarized physical geographic separation.[38] This heightened level of enforcement has required an extensive amount of funding devoted to increased security.[39] Political and media attention has shaped enforcement efforts along the border region, and often by individuals who do not and have never lived on the border.[40] Despite such important issues of societal concern, there has been a major gap in the scholarly literature on this section of the country.[41] Historian David Romo argued that residents who live on the border are frontizeros, or in other words hybrids for being neither of the United States nor of Mexico.[42] Divisions based on citizenship, generation, levels of poverty, and fluctuating levels of propaganda targeted against Mexicans and the U.S.-Mexico border area continues to keep this population constantly working to gain equal treatment. Social scientists Edward Herman and Noam Chomsky outlined in *Manufacturing Consent* the propaganda model that has continued to shape ideologies regarding how we think about issues.[43] Ideologies provide a set of cultural beliefs, values, and attitudes for understanding our social world.[44] This is a structural framework that shapes how we think about, discuss, and reinforce our understanding of race.[45] In addition, there has been increased interest among criminologists as to why there has been so little research on Latinos and their experiences with the law and law enforcement.[46] Latinos have become the largest minority group in the country, and research data indicate differential treatment by the police in many ways similar to blacks.[47]

Contrary to those who portray the U.S.-Mexico border as a narco-culture with pervasive drug trafficking, stash houses, delinquency, violence, and danger because of immigration, I argue the data indicate the opposite conclusion.[48] Trade from Mexico into the area now considered the United States has existed for centuries before colonization, and the demand for illegal drugs continues to be extremely high. However, residents who live along the border have lower rates of violence and gang membership than many urban locations around the country. My research will highlight the structural obstacles of this geographic region, and it will emphasize how residents themselves continue to work hard to raise their children and support their families through patriotic allegiance to the United States, school involvement, sports commitment, and participation in Catholicism.

Racialized Social Control as a Theoretical Explanation

To explain these patterns of inequality based on race and ethnicity, I have incorporated critical race theory, minority group threat, colonization, and social dominance theories. According to law professors Richard Delgado and Jean Stefancic, critical race theory includes four basic tenets. First, racism is the ordinary way society does business, making it difficult to eradicate. Legal scholar Derrick Bell argues that "we are imprisoned by the barriers of racism."[49] Law professor Ian Haney-López (2003) reinforces this tenet using the term "common sense" to describe how racism has become ordinary and pervasive, and how it thereby legitimates much social knowledge. Second, white-over-color ascendancy serves psychic and material purpose (interest convergence). The tenet of white-over-color ascendancy argues that racism is difficult to cure or address because it provides both psychic and material benefits to whites, regardless of class, gender, sexual orientation, and other forms of structural hierarchies.[50] Third, race and races are socially constructed in different ways throughout history. Haney-López outlined the changing definitions of racial categories and how certain people were defined as white and nonwhite.[51] Finally, because people of color have different histories and experiences, they offer a unique voice. Critical race theorists, particularly Richard Delgado, have utilized storytelling to bridge the gap between persons of good will with those whose backgrounds were radically different from people of color, thus giving people of color the power to describe how everyday experiences involve how Americans see and are controlled the by social constructions of race.[52]

Another theory of minority group relations, the racial threat hypothesis, concentrates on a power framework involving numerical population numbers, resources, and social organization.[53] The theorist, Hubert M. Blalock, posited that in situations where the minority group is small, it could result in political discrimination, symbolic segregation, and threat-oriented ideologies. However, in an area with a larger minority group presence, it was unclear whether residents could gain greater political and socio-economic inclusion in society or simply become middle-man minorities (i.e., minority entrepreneurs who serve as intermediaries between dominant and subordinate groups). Blalock particularly focused on the role of geographic context in shaping minority group relations by his interest in comparing the South with the North and looking to other countries around the world, such as South Africa and Brazil, which achieved differing outcomes with larger numbers of minority group members compared to the dominant group.

Chicana/o theorists have used the concepts of colonialism, internal colonialism, neocolonialism, and settler colonialism from the 1970s to the present to explain the Mexican experience with unequal neighborhoods, schools, and police brutality in the Southwest.[54] Several Chicano scholars have reported that Mexican Americans were a colonized people in the United States.[55] Sociologist Edward Murguía outlined the ideal colonial model as encompassing a foreign military taking over a territory of residents from a different cultural background; the individuals conquered were expected to serve as laborers rather than as a skilled workforce; the colonized were held at the bottom of the society, whereas the colonizers controlled resources of power; and finally, while the colonizers live in finer residential areas and a small number of colonized in the community were granted privileges to maintain the façade of equality, the colonized masses remained segregated in ghettos.[56] Historian Kelly Hernández stated that settler colonialism differs from other forms of colonization because it is not based on resource extraction but rather on a desire for land, a model in which settlers invade "to remove, dominate, and, ultimately, replace the indigenous populations."[57] Racialized outsiders were never intended to be incorporated politically or to be treated equally, and institutions of social control such as poor labor conditions and incarceration maintain the societal separations while upholding an ideology that such inequality and disproportionality was legal, fair, and achieved through problematic behavior. Most of these studies focus on the violence exerted by the state in creating the conditions for intraracial violence.

Sociologist Alfredo Mirandé emphasized how the United States has formed a gringo system of justice that continues to treat whites and Chicanos differently.[58] As the Southwest shifted from indigenous, Spanish, Mexican, and then United States political control, it has heightened the perception that Latinos possess a foreign-residency status. The intertwining of race and citizenship has been used throughout settler colonialism. Legal scholar Haney-López reported how obtaining the classification as white was central to gaining citizenship in the United States.[59] Individuals of Mexican descent walked an ambiguous line. Legal scholar Laura Gómez outlined three key themes that highlighted the Mexican experience in New Mexico: the centrality of colonialism for the Mexican American experience; the paradoxical legal construction of Mexicans as racially white and the social construction of Mexicans as racially inferior; and the inclusion of a middle group for subordination (Mexican Americans) between the white-over-black racial order that created a more complicated racial hierarchy.[60] Combined, the wide array of scholarship on the Mexican and the Mexican American experience is saturated with stories of inequality and unequal treatment.

Rather than emphasize the contextual nature of geographic of racial differences, psychologists James Sidanius and Felicia Pratto argued through social dominance theory that all societies develop group-based hierarchies based on age, gender, and socially constructed arbitrary sets such as clan, class, ethnicity, race, etc.[61] Dominant groups in society seek to hold onto these powers and privileges at the expense of subordinate groups; however, control requires the participation of all human actors. Some institutions reinforce such hierarchy, whereas others limited or attenuated the hierarchy. The differences were primarily based on whether the institution increased or maintained group-based hierarchies. Law enforcement was a hierarchy-reinforcing institution, and it recruited and hired individuals who held anti-egalitarian beliefs.[62] Educational and juvenile justice institutions also serve as hierarchy-reinforcing institutions despite an ideological philosophy that advocates greater levels of equality and interest in reformation.

In this book I examine four theoretical themes involving the centrality of race, numerical presence, power, and universal patterns that maintain group domination. These four theories are not traditional explanations for the disciplines of criminology or sociology, but the theoretical absence of these perspectives continues to hinder the social sciences from acknowledging societal inequality based on the intersection of race, class, gender, citizenship, and geographic setting.

The Concept of a Miracle

There are excellent forms of inspiration to explain how religion can help oppressed groups cope with colonization and domination.[63] For example, René Laurentin's book titled *Miracles in El Paso? The Amazing Story of God's Work Among the Poor of El Paso-Juarez*, documents the religious success along the border.[64] Residents were reportedly healed of sickness, but the primary accomplishment was the spiritual and "material reclamation" of the poor. There are also important studies of how organized religion can provide an alternative form of social control in urban neighborhoods, providing accepted forms of transition for gang members to leave behind criminal lifestyles or to reduce levels of violence.[65] Sociologist Cid Martinez, in his book *The Neighborhood Has Its Own Rules*, outlines several proactive strategies for which parishioners in a Catholic church in South Los Angeles have adopted counternarratives for how to respond to incidents that could result in violence.[66] However, in this book I am particularly drawn to the conceptual notion of a miracle similar to a paradox in that the expectation would be much higher levels of problematic responses (e.g., gang activity and violence) but in actuality the opposite outcome is attained.[67] Such an idea coincides with the Latino paradox that has often found Latinos, especially first generation immigrants, were less likely to use drugs and alcohol or engage in violence compared to native-born residents.[68] In this area of deep Catholicism, we encounter contradictions that are central to these paradox arguments.

Organization of the Book

The Gang Paradox begins chronologically after *Gang Life in Two Cities*. The focus shifts to a different region of the Southwest, where individuals of Mexican descent were the majority and whites were a numerical minority. In such a context, the racialization process continued to shape colonization and state power. The book is divided into two parts. Part One is devoted to historical revisionism and includes chapters 1, 2, and 3. Part Two uses ethnography as a base to collect and analyze data collected from official sources and includes chapters 4 and 5. By taking a critical race theory methodology, an insider voice of color thesis and a solutions-oriented approach is provided in chapters 6 and 7.

Chapter 1 outlines the historical origination of New Mexico, El Paso, and the U.S.-Mexico border region from 1598 to the struggles for adjustment occurring until the first reporting of gangs between 1915 and 1919. The geographic region includes territory that was once part of Spain and Mexico, and since 1848 it had been a colony and later a state of the United States. The border region and New Mexico have been some of the longest continually inhabited areas in North America. Mexicans living in New Mexico were granted federal citizenship and designated as "white," but they were treated as socially inferior. El Paso residents of Mexican descent received federal citizenship but were segregated in schools, housing, and work environments. White perceptions of Mexican inferiority impacted the entire territorial area. Despite whites taking political control much earlier, it took until 1912 for New Mexico to achieve statehood; sixteen other states achieved this designation more quickly. I trace the social history of this region, and I provide an outline of the social issues that resulted in cultural resistance in the form of pachuquismo and later gangs developing out of the Mexican Revolution. This chapter contextualizes the structural challenges of this geographic area.

Chapter 2 provides the early history of pachuquismo and later the development of gang activity in El Paso, Texas. In this time frame, prohibition, the depression, and the Ku Klux Klan merged to create conditions along the U.S.-Mexico border that allowed smuggling and resistance to serve as a means to provide for the needs of residents of Mexican descent. Gangs became more formalized in the 1940s and 1950s, and to counteract these groups, community leaders and church organizations developed athletic programs to provide alternative activities. The police launched wars against "rat packs" and initiated "clean-up campaigns" to remove certain residents. Residents in the 1970s were impacted by these historical conditions as gangs shifted toward reduced levels of violence and increased drug use for residents coming back from Vietnam and prison, shifts that altered the relationships between various social groups. Throughout this period, South El Paso (Chihuahuita and El Segundo Barrio) played a dominant role.

In chapter 3, I begin to explore contemporary organizational group activities in El Paso and Southern New Mexico prior to my arrival in 2006. These patterns overlap with various fears, such as El Paso being the number one gang city in Texas and the institutionalization of gangs in New Mexico through contradictory data claims. During this time, we see the development of gang units and data collection regarding the number of gangs and gang members which resulted in increased law enforcement practices against gangs. We encounter other groups beyond gangs that traffic drugs and engage in violence, such as motorcycle clubs and family members engaging in drug trafficking. In addition, I explore how incarceration and deportation can transform a traditional street gang into a different type of organization. Finally, an examination of the issues occurring in Ciudad Juárez in Mexico, such as cartels and increasing violence.

In chapter 4, I emphasize the concept of disproportionate minority contact to provide a model for examining racial and ethnic differences in neighborhoods, schools, and the juvenile justice system. Throughout these crises we see the impact of deportation, incarceration, and drugs and alcohol upon the family. Several researchers have written about the school-to-prison pipeline and youth exposure to various forms of social control at a young age. One of the key factors mentioned by practitioners of disparities by race and ethnicity was gang membership. Thus, coming from a minority background increased reasons for gang membership, attributed negative reactions to group behavior, and enhanced penalties to target these perceived groups, further widening the levels of inequality. The label of "gangs" became a mechanism to request increased resources, justify overrepresentation of Latino youth in the juvenile justice system, and allow for the implementation of additional school policies and juvenile probation punishments. I will analyze county, judicial, and state data to present an overview of how the youth of Mexican descent become criminalized.

Chapter 5 explores law-enforcement practices, including U.S. Border Patrol, U.S. National Guard, sheriffs, local police departments, the presence of several military bases, and barriers such as fences, surveillance, and checkpoints. The policing of immigrants was intertwined with rationalizations to target gangs and drugs. This chapter focuses on how law enforcement influenced the lives of residents and how the drug-cartel violence and fears of Mexico continued to push a heightened level of enforcement despite these communities having many shared relationships on both sides of the border. In addition, my interviews with law enforcement officers and observations highlight how these different jurisdictions and internal hierarchies created division. Thus, rather than being united as hierarchy-reinforcing institutions, they expressed frustration and limitations as to what they could realistically change and thus exhibited what appeared to be high levels of burnout.

Chapter 6 explores the findings from exploratory research utilizing participatory research teams, which provided perspectives for learning about gangs and expanding the level of understanding of the role of gender and the experiences of young women who are involved with gangs or are caught up in the juvenile justice system. A total of 111 students contribute their insights based on three undergraduate and two graduate courses that I taught from 2008 to 2012. Although my students had only been working to apply their sociological imagination to the topic of gangs for three months, they were able to utilize their lived experiences and backgrounds to provide new levels of insight. Most of my students were first-generation college students from the same communities we were studying, and they were overwhelmingly of Mexican descent. They covered themes that I neglected in my research, such as graffiti and the military, along with networks that went beyond my contacts. They demonstrated excellence in attempting to achieve success at a minority serving institution.

Chapter 7 examines how the central arguments used to negatively portray the U.S.-Mexico border region, New Mexico, and El Paso, along with residents who were of Mexican descent, were inaccurate. The data I obtained indicate lower levels of gang involvement and interpersonal violence in the form of homicide by civilians. Thus, although this region of the country was experiencing significant structural challenges produced through colonization, the residents themselves struggled to obtain an opposite outcome, thus the chapter's title. The success stories involve two Chicanas who have overcome adversity and how they have encountered obstacles that question the inclusiveness of the miracle framework. The third section of this chapter shifts towards possible solutions to the issues of gangs, juvenile delinquency, and the lack of resources along the border region.

Chapter 8 offers a concluding analysis of how settler colonialism has affected residents along the U.S.-Mexico border in a region of the country that has maintained one of the longest and largest numerical populations of individuals of Mexican descent. In a national climate that is increasingly anti-Mexican, anti-gang, anti-drug, and pro-border enforcement, the rhetoric of the past has become re-energized. The ongoing war against gangs, drugs, and immigrants varied throughout the past 150 years. I will outline how punishment is not a solution and how propaganda rhetoric does not address structural problems. This will then allow us to examine why a gang paradox exists in these communities and where such a paradox leaves our youth. The goal of this book is to educate using research, to counter sensational propaganda, and to develop internal solutions.

PART ONE
A Revisionist History

Critical race theories' notions of a revisionist history will be incorporated to explore the multifaceted role for which the contested border region of New Mexico and Texas has had on gang formation and, more importantly, on political inclusion. According to critical race theory scholars Richard Delgado and Jean Stefancic:

> Revisionist history reexamines America's historical record, replacing comforting majoritarian interpretations of events with ones that square more accurately with minorities' experiences. It also offers evidence, sometimes suppressed, in that very record, to support those new interpretations. Revisionist historians often strive to unearth little-known chapters of racial struggle, sometimes in ways that reinforce current reform efforts.[1]

In graduate school, my dissertation advisor trained me to immerse myself in a setting to learn about social groups. However, my experiences merged into a history-based form of immersion. In doing so, I attempt to be more conscious and aware of the structures that shape interactions. My goal in these next three chapters will be to provide plenty of detail that future researchers can use to follow up on the empirical trail uncovered.

CHAPTER ONE

The Context for the Origination of Gangs
Double Colonization

In 2006, my family and I moved to Las Cruces, New Mexico, from Denver, Colorado. Las Cruces sits in the Chihuahua desert, so grass or anything green is rare and expensive. Las Cruces is a quiet, laid-back community with amazing food and nice people. The city ranks highly as a location to retire, play youth sports, and experience more days with sunshine. We had a lot of friends, bought roasted green chile, attended our kids' athletic games and practices, and participated in the social life of the community. We were friends with our neighbors and looked out for the residents living in our community, and they did the same for us. It is, however, one of the economically poorest areas of the country, and it suffers from a tremendous lack of resources. My previous research had been focused on poor neighborhoods within relatively prosperous counties and states. Thus, lower structural resources on a larger scale was a change for thinking about poverty and solutions. Every year, Annie E. Casey Foundation's Kids Count database has ranked the State of New Mexico last or second to last in terms of overall child well-being based on a wide variety of indicators such economics, education, family and community, and health. Southern New Mexico is situated along the U.S.-Mexico border, and if it were a state, analysts argue it would rank as fifty-first. According to the Bureau of the Census, from 1969 to 2015 New Mexico has ranked between 44 and 50 as the poorest state in the country.

For eight years, my wife and I lived, worked, and shared in the struggle to raise our four children. We moved into a new housing development with a lot of military families interspersed in a subdivision surrounded by several trailer parks on a poorer side of town (East Mesa) that, at the time, didn't have many services, such as stores or restaurants, but it was rapidly growing. The local gas station included a mix of laborers in construction or other types of manual labor. Alcohol was a popular item for purchase, and tattoos were the norm. I fit in perfectly. Most faculty members lived closer to the college campus, about 10–15 minutes away from the freeway. However, the newer housing area offered lower rental prices and more rental units. For my young family, this was the opportunity we dreamed about.

For well over 400 years, a contested tri-cultural relationship developed between Spanish, Native American, and Anglo populations. New Mexico's race relations made this geographic region historically complex for at least four reasons: double colonization (Spain and United States); a social construction of race beyond the black and white binary (Native American and mestizo); political notions of federal and state citizenship; and a numerical minority majority population that has retained an established presence but has been unable to completely uproot the sociological implications of a marginalized experience. Columbia University anthropologists Charles Wagley and Marvin Harris defined a minority group as 1) experiencing unequal treatment, 2) sharing physical or cultural characteristics, 3) having an ascribed status rather than an identity chosen voluntarily, 4) maintaining a strong sense of group solidarity, and 5) generally marrying within the group.[1] Thus, utilizing revisionist history, I have developed an outline of how marginality continued to keep individuals of Mexican descent within a racialized minority group experience.

Native American and Spanish Influences

For at least 10,000 to 12,000 years, Native Americans have lived in the Americas. The earliest people in the Southwest consisted of a variety of pueblo and nomadic groups, including the Anasazi, Mimbres, and later Acoma, Jemez, Hopi, Taos, and Zuñi pueblos, with early archeological sites including Chaco Canyon, Gila Cliff Dwellings, Mesa Verde, and Sky City. Historian Ramón Gutiérrez estimated the Pueblo Indians may have numbered as many as 248,000 at the beginning of the sixteenth century, with seven different languages.[2] Pueblo Indians preserved egalitarian societies with tribal differences based on age and personal characteristics. They avoided violence and war as they defied the moral orders of pueblo society. It was only in the past half millennium did Europeans begin exploring North and South America. After Christopher Columbus set sail in 1492, arriving in the region of the Caribbean, many additional European nations soon followed.[3] These colonial adventures resulted in large numbers of indigenous deaths as cultures experienced tremendous devastation to their way of life. Historian David Stannard described the conquest of the new world as an American holocaust because violence was a major tool for gaining power.[4] England, France, Netherlands, and Spain created empires and colonies in the Americas by 1700.[5] For the Spanish, conquest primarily entailed spreading Catholicism and attaining precious resources. Gutiérrez describes how male Spanish conquistadors encountered a variety of pueblo and nomadic Native Americans as they surveyed the region.[6] From the beginning, Spanish explorers conflicted with the indigenous populations, whom they viewed as inferior, from Hernán Cortés's overthrow of Aztecs in 1523 to Don Juan de Oñate's establishment of the Nuevo Mexico colony in 1598. Sociologist Thomas Hall, who examined social change in the Southwest from 1350–1880, stated, "The name 'Nuevo Mexico' reflected a hope that the new area would be another Mexico, full of mines, Indians, and wealth."[7] Despite the ongoing terror, native resistance continued and culminated in the 1680 pueblo revolt against religious leaders and missions that led the Spaniards to temporarily flee the area.[8] In addition, nomadic Native Americans inspired fear and threatened the Spaniards' ability to safely occupy or control the land.[9] For these reasons, Hispano society remained weak and precarious during the Spanish colonial era.[10]

Critical race theorist Laura Gómez describes how the colonial experience from Spain brought a five-tier racial hierarchy.[11] At the top of the hierarchy were a very small number of residents descending from Spain. This small population intermarried to maintain land and economic control. The second group was known as mulato or mestizo (having mixed Spanish and Native American ancestry). This was the majority of the population, but most of these families used Spanish surnames and attempted to claim more Spanish blood than Native American blood. The third group in this stratification consisted of Native Americans who were kept as servants within elite Spanish homes. Fourth were the pueblo Indians, whose culture, civilization, and community were the most stable and longest lasting before the arrival of the Spanish. Fifth were other nomadic tribes including the Apaches, Comanches, Navajos, and Utes.

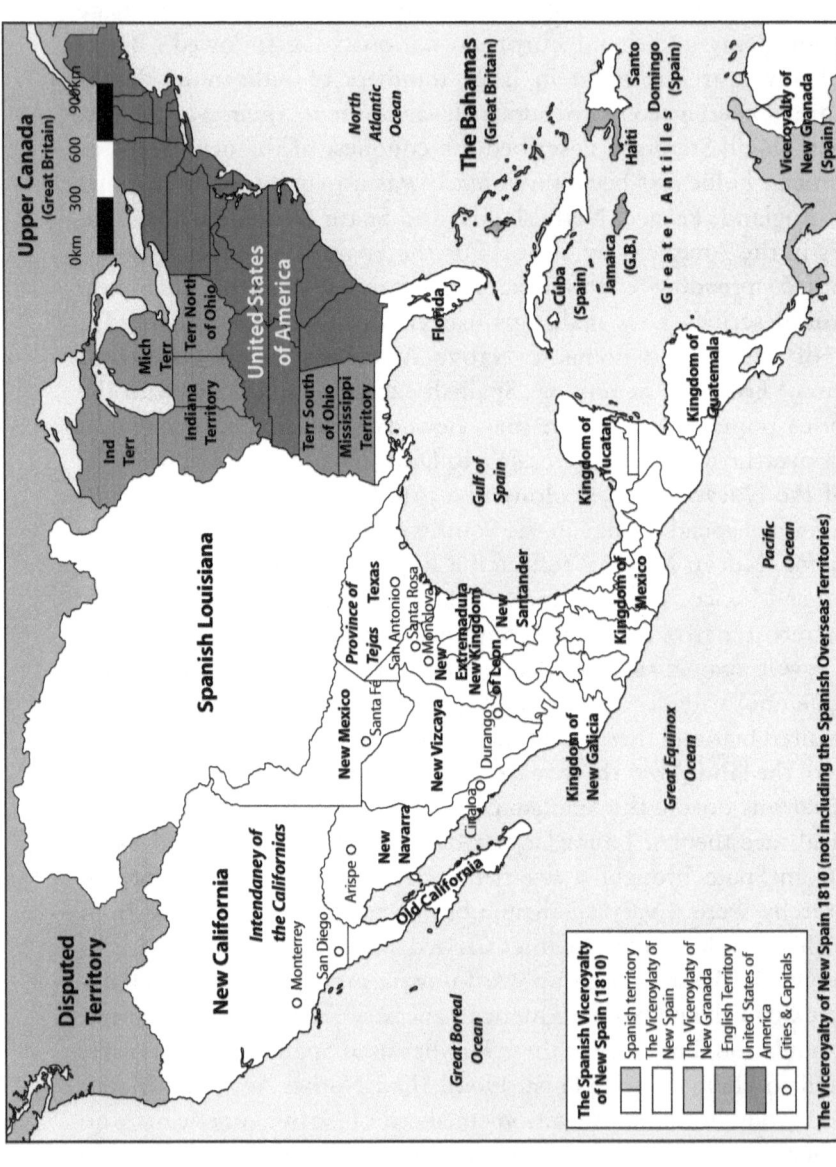

FIGURE 1.1 Viceroyalty of New Spain Map, 1810.
Courtesy of the United State Geological Survey. Image available on the Internet (https://tshaonline.org/handbook/online/articles/nps01) and included in accordance with Title 17 U.S.C. Section 107.

Gutiérrez reported how the scarcity of Spanish women and abundance of native women resulted in the characterization of New Mexico's colonists in 1631 as "mestizos, mulattos, and zambohijos."[12] The continued abuse of native women often resulted in their stigmatization and the abandonment of children who were born fair-skinned. The New Mexico form of slavery valued female slaves twice as much as male slaves. Gutiérrez elaborated on the role of race: "Whereas before 1760 racial labels accounted for less than 10 percent of total observations, after 1760 and into the beginning of the nineteenth century, race became the dominant way of defining social status."[13] The two main labels were *español* (Spaniard) and *indio* (Indian). The lighter skin color was associated with Spanish blood and an individual's social status and occupation. Men could possess honor, while shame was an attribute intrinsic to females, which resulted in an insistence on keeping them sheltered. This served to enforce the earliest forms of Spanish patriarchy.

Mexico's Independence

In 1820, the population in New Mexico was estimated to be 38,359, of which 74 percent (28,436) were Spanish and 26 percent (9,923) were Native American.[14] During the war for Mexican independence in 1821, the original small number of Anglos attempted to coexist with the Spanish elite by living, marrying, and working together. This produced a society in which racial power-sharing was evident. The numerical minority of Anglos existed in a social world where Spanish language, jury involvement, and police representation of Hispanos was fully evident.[15] Racial labels were legally abolished in favor of nationality labels of ciudadano, mexicano, or "no mention."[16] Sociologist Thomas Hall stated that there was an increase of Native American attacks during the 1830s and 1840s, possibly due to the increased trade in alcohol and guns.[17] Mexican governors in the states of Chihuahua and Sonora enacted a policy of Apache extermination by offering money for scalps. In 1843, residents established the Doña Ana Bend Colony Grant, but due to fears of Apache attacks the area remained sparsely populated with possibly as few as 47 families and 22 single men.[18] The city of Las Cruces would later develop in this area. The other regions of southern New Mexico, including Grant, Luna, and Hidalgo Counties, also remained sparsely populated.

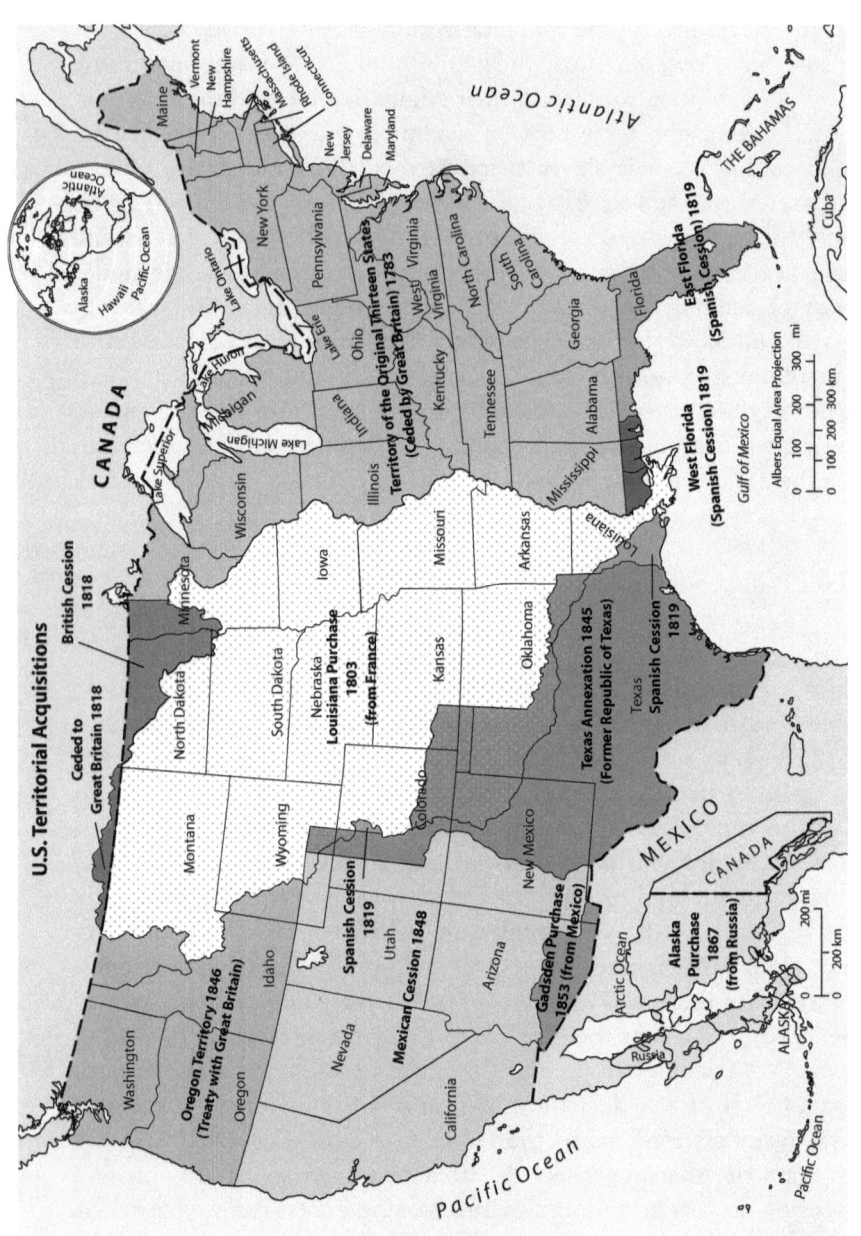

FIGURE 1.2 U.S. Territorial Acquisitions Map.
Source: http://www.thomaslegion.net/americancivilwar/mexicancessionlessonstudentsandkids.html.

The United States Influence

As the United States used the U.S.-Mexican War (1846–1848) to seize the entire Southwest, nearly half of what was then Mexico, one researcher described the war as defining white, Anglo-Saxon supremacy.[19] While the Treaty of Guadalupe Hidalgo granted the mestizo population a white identity for having one drop of Spanish blood, this did not result in equal treatment.[20] Hall reported that New Mexico differed from California and Texas by three important distinctions: a large Mexican and Native American population that had been established for centuries, a slower population growth, and the only non-elite organized rebellion. New Mexico was the most populated section of the region.[21] It was reported that there were at least 60,000 residents living in New Mexico compared to 7,500 in California, 5,000 in Texas, and 1,000 in Arizona.[22] Most of these residents (91 percent) were Nuevomexicanos with Spanish names, 5 percent were Native American, and less than 3 percent were Anglo American.[23] The Rio Grande became the separating line between Mexico and the United States, in the process splitting the land of the original El Paso del Norte into what is now known as El Paso in the United States and Ciudad Juárez in Mexico.[24] Gómez described how Mexicans living in the area were given three options: move south of the newly created U.S.-Mexico border, keep their homes but retain Mexican citizenship, or keep their homes and after one year acquire U.S. federal citizenship.[25] Federal citizenship granted protection of the Constitution but did not offer political rights until statehood was achieved.

The Hispano lifestyle in New Mexico was a culture largely described as ricos and peones, with no middle class during the early colonization by the United States. The agrarian and Catholic ways of life quickly changed to one of commercial, technological, and industrial emphases with the arrival of the railroad. Residents of New Mexico quickly encountered a new group of foreigners claiming superiority and racial purity: Anglos, or English-speaking Protestants of primarily northern European ancestry. Historian Daniel Montgomery estimated less than 4 percent of the residents of New Mexico were Anglo, and this number remained relatively small until the railroad increased the numbers of Anglos to one third of the population by 1900.[26] The small number of Hispano families and the slowly increasing Anglos came to dominate the state. They saw both Mexicans and those proclaiming Spanish identity as the same: nonwhite.[27] Montgomery described how Anglo success was built from their conceptualization of race, "In other words, Anglos conquered ethnic Mexicans by taking their resources while defining them as racially inferior and properly marginal to white society."[28] New Mexico was considered the most geographically isolated state, which allowed social and cultural isolation to ensure a greater level of preservation of its cultural heritage.[29]

El Paso: The Queen City of the Southwest

Contrary to the isolation and lack of federal political rights in New Mexico, Historian Mario T. García described El Paso, Texas, as the most important city along the U.S.-Mexican border, the Queen City of the Southwest, like a New York City for European immigrant groups.[30] El Paso, or "the pass" in English, was centrally located along an important trade route that historically connected the movement of people and goods from Mexico to the interior of the Southwest. After the Treaty of Guadalupe Hidalgo, the central trading port with Mexico shifted from Santa Fe, New Mexico, to El Paso.[31] During the Spanish occupation (1659–1821) and Mexican independence (1821–1846), the Camino Real (Royal Road) was used to transport goods and laborers.[32] In the early days, settlers used wagons to transport goods and caravans accompanied by military guides helped to ensure safe passage. Mules carried loads of up to 400 pounds and traveled 12–15 miles per day, but they were more susceptible to Indian attacks.

By 1850 El Paso's population was small, with perhaps as few as 300 residents, most of whom were Mexican.[33] Similar to New Mexico, Anglo residents married Mexican women and accommodated to the Mexican majority. Mexicans held political positions and made up 95 percent of voters.[34] Adjacent to El Paso was Ciudad Juárez in Chihuahua Mexico, and Anglos sought to reduce racial friction. Nevertheless, with the coming of the railroad, Mexicans in El Paso were segregated by occupation by primarily working blue-collar occupations, whereas Anglos worked white-collar jobs.[35] Historian Monica Perales stated that the railroad ensured that "El Paso became the nerve center of the flow of capital—in the form of money, resources, and labor—throughout the region."[36] Mineral resources were brought to the American Smelting and Refining Company (ASARCO) in El Paso from locations throughout the United States and

FIGURE 1.3 Historical Trade Route Map.

Mexico as a site that was unique because of its border location and its abundant supply of cheap labor. Mexicans were residentially segregated into the poorest housing areas with unpaved roads and lack of sanitation. They worked primarily in mining, ranching, and agriculture as unskilled workers. Historian David Romo stated:

> Until the arrival of the railroads in the 1880s, the strategy adopted by El Paso's first Anglo settlers was one of accommodation. Because Mexicans were the overwhelming majority in an area isolated from other white population centers, those settlers had little choice.[37]

However, Anglo presence began to exert changes as reflected in the San Elizario Salt War of 1877, where conflict emerged due to new notions of private versus communal property.[38] The Texas Rangers and Mexican residents on both sides of the border engaged in skirmishes. Romo continued, "After 1883, Mexican Americans were almost completely disenfranchised from city and county politics."[39] The Anglo commercial elite regarded the Mexican American population with contempt, ". . . as a mixed breed, an inferior whose principal traits were ignorance, indolence, and backwardness. By nature he was lazy, irresponsible, untrustworthy, and dirty—in a word, he was labeled 'a greaser.'"[40] Nevertheless, the labor continued to consist of Mexicans: "From the beginning of the twentieth century, El Paso was built upon cheap labor from Mexico."[41]

Between 1880 and 1917, the border was open and there was a constant flow of people and goods. The growing population resulted in an increasing level of attention devoted to vice and gambling, as many individuals entering El Paso were miners, cattlemen, soldiers, or railroad workers.[42] Thus, the entertainment industry became big business. Prostitution in El Paso was largely concentrated in several sections of the city, beginning as early as the first railroad in 1882 and continuing as a regulated occupation at least until the 1940s.[43] The *El Paso Times* quoted Detective Juan Franco, who described how cattle rustlers and smugglers of "Chinamen" were a problem in 1895 as there were almost nightly gunfights.[44] He stated that El Paso was considered one of the toughest cities in the Southwest, with killings and shooting scrapes as common as automobile collisions.[45] A historian concurred that El Paso became known as the six-shooter capital.[46] In another newspaper report, Juan Franco, who was one of the twelve members on the police force back in 1897, reported a somewhat more relaxed situation: "Our greatest trouble in those days . . . was the keeping down fights in saloons and preventing mischievous boys from stealing watermelons and fruit."[47] Unfortunately, no homicide or crime data exist from this time period to compare these numbers with the present. Nationwide, the collection of crime data did not begin until 1930 under the Uniform Crime Reports.[48]

New Mexicans Gain Federal Political Rights—1912

Nativist fears of Mexican inferiority prevented the state of New Mexico from joining the union as a state until 1912. Many Anglos feared nonwhites would dominate the state numerically and culturally.[49] They disapproved of what they described as the mixing of Native Americans and Spanish. Senator Daniel Webster of Massachusetts argued against allowing non-Anglo-Americans as citizens. Historian David Holtby captured Webster's sentiment, "[Nuevomexicanos] are as deficient in energy of character and physical courage as they are in all the moral and intellectual qualities. In their social state, but one degree removed from the veriest savages. . . ."[50] Holtby argued how the U.S. Congress remained opposed to granting Nuevomexicanos full voting privileges while they accepted fifteen other states into the Union between 1850 and 1900. Government fears consisted of whether Nuevomexicanos could assimilate in language, religion, and in the institutions of court, school, and public office. New Mexico residents were considered violent and lawless. Since 1900, most authors argued that Anglos were in control of the state of New Mexico despite being a numerical minority.[51] At least three fourths of residents lived on farms or ranches. Despite Anglos never succeeding in completely removing Hispanos from political control, as was accomplished in California and Texas, the Hispano loss of political power was exacerbated by Euroamerican men taking control after statehood.[52]

The Mexican Revolution and Prohibition

Events developing in Mexico and in El Paso continued to shape an oppositional context against Mexican Americans and Mexicans in the early twentieth century. The three primary reasons were the Mexican Revolution, increased social control of immigration, and the passage of the Eighteenth Amendment (i.e., the prohibition of manufacturing, selling, or transporting of alcohol). The beginning of conflict in 1910 contributed to fears of spillover violence and resentment on both sides for Americans and Mexicans.[53] The Mexican Revolution led to a million deaths, the redistribution of millions of acres of land, and major changes to the political order.[54] Peasants and workers began striving for change and challenging the ruling elite. The battles themselves became spectacles of violence as residents on El Paso's side watched the fighting from rooftops and purchased photographs of the dead. Rather than simply a story of negativity, historian David Romo argued that the Mexican Revolution produced a cultural renaissance in El Paso.[55] Revolutionary activities inspired new forms of leaders, newspapers, music, and film. In 1911, Ciudad Juárez also established gambling to generate revenue despite the period of political instability.[56]

Fort Bliss, a United States Army post located in El Paso, was established in 1848 to defend the international border and to protect settlers from Apache Indians.[57] However, after the start of the Mexican Revolution, Fort Bliss transitioned from a small and isolated infantry post to reach national and international significance. An early task was the control of arms as the Francis Bannerman and Sons surplus arms company of New York became major suppliers of arms and ammunition into Mexico through the Shelton Payne Arms Company.[58] There were large numbers of rich and poor Mexicans moving to El Paso at the same time the number of Fort Bliss troops began to surge. Romo stated that, in 1916, there were 6,500 Mexican refugees in El Paso who had fled from the revolution, and by 1927 there were 72,000.[59] The number of Fort Bliss troops were estimated to be anywhere between 70,000 and 100,000. An October 24, 1931, *El Paso Herald* article included an interview with the city's chief detective, who claimed that 1916 was the worst in the city's history. The population boomed with 100,000 "undisciplined" Fort Bliss troops along with tensions developing from the Mexican Revolution. The chief detective reported countless murders and assaults occurring at the time, and the city's hospital was extremely busy. Battles between the Villistas and Carrancistas turned El Paso into a garrison town: "Pistol toting, considered by pioneers to be the outstanding menace to life and a peaceful existence in early days, broke out with new popularity in 1916, with popular enthusiasm manifesting itself in countless murders and assaults."

The increase in Fort Bliss soldiers during the Revolution also brought African Americans. Historian Gerald Horne stated that the border had been problematic for Southern states because Mexico did not practice slavery and there were constant efforts to keep slaves from escaping prior to the Civil War.[60] Nevertheless, thousands of enslaved Africans escaped into Mexico, which was often seen as a better alternative than the United States. With time, the increased numerical presence led to conceptions of Mexico as a revolutionary haven. Along the border region in the early 1900s, U.S. anti-miscegenation laws were disregarded as many black men married Mexican wives and spoke Spanish. Horne cited the work of Linda Gordon, who reported, "In some places in the Southwest, blacks were white [sic] and Mexicans were not."[61] In the West, "white" meant American. Horne reported how many blacks described increased opportunities as negative actions were often directed at Japanese, Chinese, or Mexican residents. With the fluidity of race came situations in which

Mexicano, Tejano, or Native American rebellions were brought down by black soldiers, particularly the Buffalo Soldiers, who were African American soldiers from 1866 to 1917 who, despite segregation, fought fiercely in every major war against Native Americans on the western frontier in addition to the Philippines, the Spanish–American War, and in Pershing's efforts to kill Pancho Villa.[62] Despite the admiration from the African American community, such instances brought to light the political critique of using the military as an avenue for racial inclusion. Many have argued racial and ethnic minorities were more likely to be placed in direct combat and to suffer higher fatality rates than white soldiers. Upon returning home, these soldiers often continued to experience second-class treatment. In the border region, the Buffalo Soldiers, some Native American scouts who were used against other tribes, and members of the Mexican elite reinforced a symbolism that skin pigmentation was not necessarily a marker for marginalized group kinship.[63]

A larger segment of residents moving to El Paso were white southerners. They brought cultural biases and Protestant religious beliefs that looked disfavorably upon Catholicism and nonwhites. These new residents kept to themselves and remained separate and isolated. They launched moral entrepreneurial campaigns as early as 1904, such as the Citizens Reform League, which organized and pressured "Blue Laws" to ensure anti-gambling laws were enforced. The city council pushed for the closing of saloons and businesses on Sundays along with enacting ordinances that prohibited the gathering of groups on city streets and sidewalks. They developed legislation for the closing of dance halls and the prevention of carrying a pistol without a special permit.[64] Latin American historian Nicole Mottier reported how national legislation banned opium imports in 1906, followed by the Harrison Narcotics Act in 1914 and the outlaw of the sale of marijuana in 1920.[65] Scholars noted that such actions received community opposition while simultaneously moving a large portion of vice underground. During this time, the police were looked upon less favorably because they were used by politicians to gain votes. Professionalization efforts continued as law enforcement officers began wearing uniforms in 1909, but they were still considered corrupt until at least the 1930s.[66] El Paso police officers were also allegedly employed by Mexican officials to lure revolutionaries into Juárez, where they could be killed.[67]

Historian Miguel Antonio Levario reported, "By the mid-1910s, social relations in West Texas had become thoroughly racialized."[68]

To provide support, Levario outlined a series of major incidents that began in 1916, including the El Paso Race Riot, martial law, the El Paso Jailhouse Holocaust, Bath Riots, Villa's raid of the New Mexico border town of Columbus, and General Pershing's incursion into Mexico along with border posts established by the home guard and the National Guard. Historian Shawn Lay also found that, between 1910 and 1920, racial tensions undermined the city's previous approach of cultivating racial accommodation.[69]

Tensions with Mexico's revolutionary leader Pancho Villa began when President Woodrow Wilson offered his support to Villa's political rival Venustiano Carranza. After this slight, Pancho Villa told Americans to leave Mexico as he and his soldiers would no longer allow safe passage. Attacks against U.S. citizens were rare at that time, and some business foreigners did not heed this threat. A train leaving one of the mines was attacked, and seventeen U.S. citizens were killed. When the bodies were returned to El Paso, Anglo residents began advocating an attack on Mexicans both in Mexico and in El Paso. Crowds of Anglos grew to almost 1,500 as residents selected Mexican residents for punishment. Mexican residents from El Segundo Barrio rose up to defend themselves. General Pershing, stationed at Fort Bliss, stepped in and issued martial law, under which he created "dead lines." Mexican residents were forced to stay in the Chihuahuita neighborhood, and it did not matter whether they were U.S. citizens. The border with Mexico was also closed off. Thus, according to Levario, the social positions of Anglos received affirmation as superior. This affirmation continued when the El Paso Health Department claimed typhus fever could enter through Mexico and thus began requiring Mexicans to take a bath involving kerosene, vinegar, and gasoline to enter the country. The city hospital and jail also required Mexicans to take such a bath when admitted.[70]

Immigration acts of 1917 and 1921 continued to make it difficult for Mexicans to cross the border.[71] Romo reported "It [the Immigration Law of 1917] required that immigrants at all points of entry have a passport, take a literacy test, and pay an $8 head tax."[72] According to the Population Reference Bureau, three of the four immigration waves occurred during this time period.[73] Wave One occurred prior to 1820 and included Europeans from England, France, Netherlands, and Spain, who combined to represent 60 percent of the population. African slaves and indentured servants were transported during this time. Wave Two consisted of the years from 1820 to 1860, and immigrants, primarily

German, British, and Irish, were used to help the United States with frontier expansion. Wave Three was during the period of 1880–1914, when immigrants from southern and eastern Europe moved primarily to Eastern and Midwestern states. In 1910, the foreign-born proportion reached 15 percent of the population, which was considered the greatest presence since the founding of the United States. During the third wave, several forms of legislation were passed targeting immigrants from China, Japan, and southern and eastern Europe. The years between 1915 and 1964 have been described as an immigration pause because numerical limits were placed on immigration. At this time, the national origins formula gave preference to northern and western Europe, and 80 percent of immigrant visas went to people from this region. Capturing the exclusionary legislation of waves one to three, critical race theorist Haney-Lopéz (2006) argued that from 1790 until 1952, being a "white person" was a condition of citizenship. By 1880, in addition to nonwhites, the United States prevented prostitutes, low-skilled workers, Chinese, and individuals considered "mental defectives" from becoming citizens. Haney-Lopéz emphasized the ambiguous and shifting rationale used by the courts to legally rationalize the racial category of whiteness.

Another key form of geographical separation resulted from Texas's anti-alcohol legislation in 1918 and then the U.S. Constitution's Eighteenth Amendment, which was signed into law in 1919 and prohibited the manufacture, transportation, and sale of alcoholic beverages. Historian Shawn Lay reported,

> If national probation had had an exceptionally disturbing impact on the city of El Paso, this impact paled in comparison with what the 18th Amendment had effected across the Rio Grande. As a result of American prohibition, Ciudad Juárez underwent an incredible transformation, from a relatively quiet Mexican town into a gaudy, sinful tourist mecca, a bustling city of over 20,000 residents dedicated to providing thirsty and lustful Americans with whatever they wanted.[74]

Such actions led to increased tourism into Ciudad Juárez to visit its red-light districts, bars, carnivals, casinos, and an emerging jazz scene.[75] It created a context for increased profits for the smuggling of liquor and narcotics into the United States. Border officials increasingly came into conflict with Mexicans, and U.S. officials began incorporating incarceration as punishment. In Ciudad Juárez, these actions developed the roots for organized crime. Taking liquor into the United States was not illegal in Mexico.[76] Whiskey and spirts were in large supply at the time because Ciudad Juárez became one of the depositories for liquor that had to be removed from the United States.[77] In addition, Mexican residents started their own distilling businesses.

In this climate, the U.S. government continued to fear that Mexican leaders or residents would attack. Certain events were used as justification for such fear, including Pancho Villa's raid on Columbus, New Mexico, in March of 1916, and the "Plan de San Diego," which was reportedly a threat near the end of World War I that Mexicans, with the help of Japan, Germany, and blacks, would take back the land stolen during the U.S.-Mexico War.[78] In response to these perceived threats, the U.S. government sent General Pershing of the U.S. Army and his soldiers into Mexico. Unable to capture Pancho Villa and encountering public pressure to leave, the United States withdrew these soldiers in 1917.[79]

Whereas New Mexico remained isolated, El Paso became a busy place of commerce. In historian Wilbert H. Timmons's overview of El Paso, he found five distinguishing characteristics that made El Paso unique: El Paso is historic (four centuries); El Paso is multi-cultural but primarily bicultural; El Paso has a long military tradition; El Paso is in Texas, but it should be in New Mexico; and El Paso is an international community.[80] Based on this history, which community (Southern New Mexico or El Paso) would be the first to have groups defined as gangs?

The revisionist history outlined in this chapter highlights several key themes that created the context in which gangs would emerge. First, marginality in terms of class, citizenship, generational status, race, and ethnicity due to double colonization and urbanization. New Mexico and the border region developed a tri-cultural relationship. When powerful groups imposed colonization upon a population, the residents were segregated into different sections of the community and were characterized as different based on culture, unfamiliarity, possession of something desired, and ethnicity or race, all of which intertwined with heightened levels of social control. Second, policies deprived Mexican Americans and Mexicans from equal protection and gave privilege to Anglo Americans. Mexican Americans continued to be treated as second-class citizens or foreigners. Local leaders ensured a forced separation between residents who lived on both sides of the border. A racialized hierarchy was imposed that emphasized pure-blood Anglos, a reluctance to accept pure-blood Spaniards who had maintained dominance during the colonial control of Spain and Mexico, and the wholesale demotion of individuals considered mestizos and Native Americans. Third, violence was a tool used by the Anglo colonizers to control colonial subjects, but this did not entail acceptance, nor did it change the perceptions of who was considered violent: Mexicans. Such a context upheld white social control to advocate for federal government acceptance and local dominance over residents. Native and mestizo women continued to experience heightened levels of gendered oppression. In essence, the border region developed a different conception of race where skin color was somewhat ambiguous and so nationality became an additional indicator of who belonged. Ancestry determined who was white and who was not. Spanish ancestry was not entirely accepted as being white. Whiteness provided a privileged status that did not require connection to the land (ancestors) but rather a perceived entitlement to the land. Fourth, Mexicans and Mexican Americans were constantly presumed to be a threat to successful colonization efforts, thus attempts were made to erase history, property holdings, and previous forms of political power. However, these factors encountered a numerical minority majority population that could problematize such efforts of social control. It is in this context that the first gangs of Mexican descent formed.

CHAPTER TWO

The Formation of Gangs in El Chuco

After studying the topic of gangs in this region for nine years, I was grateful to have the opportunity to do an ethnographic update after putting together a historical puzzle that comprises this chapter.[1] *Gangs of Mexican descent did not just emerge from El Paso—they created a style of resistance during a timeframe of exclusionary policies and an obsession with using this population for its labor. It was the first and a half to second generation of youth who joined together to fit in. Walking the neighborhoods in Chihuahuita and El Segundo Barrio one hundred years after revolutionary tactics were first inspired offers a first-hand observation of a particular place and how it has changed over time.*[2] *Along El Paso Street, the small shops are filled with pedestrians moving from store to store, browsing and purchasing items. The street continues to the international bridge known as Paso del Norte that was built in the 1800s to connect the United States with Mexico. The Spanish language is present everywhere, from the music playing in the background to the conversations occurring around me. There is no tension in the air. There are no fights or gun shootouts. This is El Paso, one of the safest large cities in the United States, situated adjacent to Ciudad Juárez, Mexico, which has recently moved past one of the most violent periods in its history.*

As I walk further into the neighborhood, away from the international shopping strip, the heat keeps most residents who are home inside. The light sound of music emanates from windows covered with bars. Occasionally older men or women sit on the front stoops of their homes or apartment doors. Four housing projects are scattered throughout these two neighborhoods. Many of the buildings possess some amazing murals, many of which have been chronicled and featured as one the key sights to see in El Paso.[3] *I walk into the library to cool off from the heat, where a free lunch program offers food to children and their families. I venture back outside and observe three Latino police officers talking to an older man who appears to be of Mexican descent. They arrest the man and place him in the back of the police van. I think about how in the 1950s each block was controlled by a gang, but as I walk block after block I do not encounter one group of youths or adults who confronts me. I am aware that if I were to be bothered or attacked, it would defy current data trends. I continue to move through the neighborhood, taking pictures, writing notes, and observing residents interact.*

Gang scholar James Diego Vigil's concept of multiple marginality is one of the central frameworks for explaining the development of gangs.[4] Vigil states, "Multiple marginality encompasses the consequences of barrio life, low socioeconomic status, street socialization and enculturation, and problematic development of self-identity. These gang features arise in a web of ecological, socioeconomic, cultural, and psychological factors."[5] Gangs exist on the margins of society in terms of class, education, politics, and social constructions of race. For Mexican Americans, gangs first emerged among the second generation, who were struggling to assimilate into U.S. culture. The groups identifying as gangs lack political power and domestic control, and they offer youth protection, identity, and opportunities for resistance, yet the behaviors highlight a generational and societal disconnect from mainstream officials and institutions. Agents of the state do not classify groups with social power as gangs. In the border region, there have been strategies to resist marginalization. Understanding the process of resistance to marginalization requires a revisionist analysis of history that continues from chapter 1.

The Creation of Pachuquismo and the Rise of the Ku Klux Klan

Researchers have acknowledged that the geographic region of El Paso possesses a style of culture known as pachuquismo as early as the middle of the Mexican Revolution, which later influenced residents in Los Angeles, California, and other locations in the Southwest. Frederic Thrasher, considered the first gang researcher, reported how a man named Roy Dickerson gave him the following account in 1924:

> In the Mexican section of El Paso is a group of three or four hundred Mexican boys composed of from twenty to twenty-five gangs, each

with its separate leaders. These gangs have been growing steadily for eight or nine years and now embrace a rather seasoned and experienced leadership in all sorts of crime. Eighty per cent of their members are probably under fifteen years of age; most of the older boys are under eighteen. Stealing, destroying property, and all kinds of malicious mischief are their chief activities. In fact, these groups are almost literally training schools of crime and they seem to be related to each other in a sort of loose federation. For the most part, the boys do not go to school or do not work unless it be for an occasional day. Fifty of them have been sent to the State Industrial school, eight are in jail, twenty-five or thirty are being specially investigated, and about two hundred are under surveillance. These boys may be observed in their characteristic groups every evening on street corners and in vacant lots and alleys. The park, which is their favorite meeting place, with its double rows of tall hedges, its trees and shrubbery, affords them a good place to hide and to conceal their delinquencies.[6]

Based upon Thrasher's footnotes, it was unclear who Roy Dickerson was or how he gathered information on El Paso gangs. He claimed gangs had existed since 1915 or 1916, which is difficult to verify based on the historical records. Raúl Tovares, a communications professor and author of *Manufacturing the Gang: Mexican American Youth Gangs on Local Television*, critiqued Dickerson's claims on three points: 1) gangs were seen as a problem in the Mexican section of town [implying a lack of concern with white gangs]; 2) the groups were described as well organized, hierarchical, and having a criminal intent [not supported by data]; and 3) the argument may have been fabricated not just by the media [the theme of Tovares's book] but by changing political, economic, and cultural values.[7] Roy E. Dickerson comes up in a couple of other searches for the timeframe. In 1919, Dickerson was listed as the General Secretary of the Young Men's Christian Association in Tucson, Arizona, for which he wrote an article titled "Some Suggestive Problems in the Americanization of Mexicans," where he provided information on Tucson and El Paso. Dickerson stated Mexicans were an undercounted population largely concentrated in the Southwest with low levels of education (fifth grade), high dropout rates, little knowledge of the English language, poor pay, and living in homes often lacking a father or mother. Dickerson advocated ". . . the best efforts of our best citizenship must be given to these problems in a much more vigorous and effective way than has hithertofore been manifested."[8] Thus Dickerson's article and comments to Thrasher may have reflected his method of advocacy or enhancing social control upon Mexican residents.

Possibly a more accurate description of gangs of the time was provided by El Paso historian Mario T. García, who mentioned a lack of organized crime in El Paso except for an occasional gang in 1919 and on rare occasions some residents participating in "dope rings."[9] One of these individuals, Manual Morales, reportedly participated in a dope ring that distributed drugs on both sides of the border from the Chihuahuita neighborhood. He was arrested for the illegal sale of opium. García found disproportionate police concentration, raids, and curfews in the Mexican neighborhoods as the police chief attempted to remove undesirables from the city. Such actions continued the ongoing discrimination against Mexicans, particularly in South El Paso, as reported by historian Miguel Antonio Levario.[10] Moreover, Dickerson's concerns about youth of Mexican descent not attending school or working does not reflect García's findings regarding school segregation and reports of youth not being encouraged to attend school beyond the fifth or sixth grade.[11] The schools primarily emphasized a curriculum geared towards teaching U.S. patriotism and preparation for manual labor.[12]

Similar to a lack of media panic suggested by Raúl Tovares, it was difficult to find any mention of gangs in the local newspapers from 1915 to 1924.[13] Contrary to Dickerson's statement to Thrasher, a 1919 *El Paso Herald* article titled "Oh Skinnay! The Gangs All Up in Court!" described a knife fight between regular boys, one of whom was described as "the red headed, freckled faced, titled nose boy" and another a tall and skinny boy, and they went by names such as "Fat" and "Peewee."[14] The judge placed the boys on probation for their behavior. Other newspaper articles from 1919 describe the country after World War I, the conflicts in Mexico, an editorial dislike toward Pancho Villa, local violence, and claims regarding El Paso becoming a center of lawlessness due to being adjacent to Juárez.[15] According to Gaspar Cordero's oral history interview from 1975, Gaspar was born in South El Paso in 1908 and reported that gangs in the 1970s were different from the 1920s because it was more ". . . like kids getting together, and one guy going up against another, but really nothing vicious. Maybe rock throwing and things like that—nobody ever got hit."[16] Such accounts merge with those of other gang scholars, who found that gangs often began as neighborhood groups and families simply providing protection for one another.[17]

Gang scholar James Diego Vigil reported that "the rise and formation of the gang subculture, to reiterate, revolves around the broader backdrop of culture conflict and choloization [i.e., the idea that gang members encounter greater difficulty acculturating than non–gang members] of much of the second-generation Mexican American population."[18] Vigil continued, "It was in El Paso, Texas, that the pachuco style originated, although it might be traced to Pachuca, Mexico, where baggy pants were common among males." The word pachuco was considered by many to have been created to refer to individuals from El Paso, Texas, and it originated around the time of the Mexican Revolution.[19] Thus, although the term gang has become politicized, the language, style, and mannerism of pachuquismo is well established as emerging from this geographic area. David Barker, who wrote one of the earliest articles on pachucos in 1950, received information from two of his interviewees who suggested the caló or Spanglish language originated among marijuana smokers and dope peddlers in the El Paso underworld and possibly by members of the 7-X gang. According to the timeline of El Paso gangs in appendix 2, the 7-X gang was one of the earliest groups, but it is unclear whether this organization could date back decades prior.

The caló language intertwined with a unique clothing style and demeanor. Many of the youth had a tattoo of a cross on the hand. In some of the earliest accounts of pachucos and pachucas, scholars argued how the mixing of cultures (American, Mexican, and Native American) and not belonging precisely to either culture resulted in the creation of pachuquismo, which is a hybridization of cultures.[20] However, only a small number of Mexican American boys and girls participated in the pachuco style of language and dress. The entire Mexican culture was impacted by discrimination, but they did not passively accept second-class status. Anthropologist Laura L. Cummings emphasized that although pachucos have been analyzed primarily through a deviance lens, most of the youth were not gang members or criminals.[21] It was a broader style and culture found within the working class, and it included females. They too had their own style of dress and participation in the use of caló.[22]

While marginalized Mexican American youth were creating a culture to resist colonization, El Paso's elite Anglo residents were seeking to solidify control of formal institutions and social life. The Ku Klux Klan emerged during the early 1920s to capitalize on foreigner fears of

Mexicans and Catholics. They encouraged a greater emphasis on Protestant morals. The Frontier Klan No. 100 Knights of the Ku Klux Klan was established in El Paso in 1921, and it began its recruitment efforts with prominent individuals in the community.[23] Similar Klan developments were occurring across the nation, including Denver, Colorado.[24] Klan membership experienced a "rebirth," growing from 85,000 members nationwide in 1921 to somewhere between three and five million by 1925.[25] By 1922, the electorate in El Paso had become primarily Anglo, consisting of many residents from the South and overwhelmingly middle class. Klan rallies were held on Mount Franklin, where ceremonial fires were lit. Klan membership in El Paso was estimated to include as many as 3,500 members, and it influenced all sections of the city.[26] According to the *Frontier Klansman*, segregation between blacks and whites was enforced in El Paso, whereas in Juárez whites were reportedly bullied by blacks and the Mexican policeman did not care.[27] The *Frontier Klansman* described a wedding ceremony in Deming, New Mexico, involving hundreds of Klansmen from El Paso and southern New Mexico. They received an unwelcome reception from the Mayor of Deming, for which the Klan threatened its growing presence in the southern New Mexico area and how it was targeting bootleggers and crooked politicians.

In addition to attempting to gain political control, the *Frontier Klansman* encouraged closing off the bridge that allowed residents to pass back and forth between Ciudad Juárez and El Paso. The author stated the following,

> Is there a bridge closing issue in this town? No. There is an issue between cleanliness and immorality. Count your men, citizens. Make no mistakes. Juarez is a hell hole. It is all that is evil. Excuses don't go. It is a nest of houses of prostitution. It is a street of low saloons. It is an open market for narcotics. It is unsanitary. It is a disease menace. The world knows it.[28]

The author continued to argue how U.S. citizens continued to be ruined by visiting this location across the border. However, tourism into Juárez was one of El Paso's biggest sources of hotel income, thus continuing a sibling type of relationship between both cities.[29] An estimated 419,000 tourists visited from El Paso to Juárez during the first year of prohibition, and a wide range of entertainment existed, both those of vice and mainstream family events. Increasing public pressure resulted in the closing of the border in 1923, and ongoing federal concerns led to the creation of the U.S. Border Patrol in 1924.[30] Historian Kelly Hernández stated that Anglo American nativists played a crucial role in designing the National Origins Act of 1924, which introduced a nationality-based quota system that limited the number of immigrants allowed to enter the United States each year.[31] The Act prioritized Europeans and excluded Asians. Agribusiness prevented nativists from putting Mexicans on the excluded list, but this was primarily because Mexicans were considered to be a temporary and marginal population that was needed for labor purposes. Nevertheless, the Border Patrol's focus became the policing of Mexicans. Edwin M. Reeves's oral history in 1974 described working as Border Patrol Officer in the 1920s and 1930s. He stated that any offense (e.g., liquor violation, narcotic violation, property crime, or illegal entry) required notifying different agencies from U.S. Customs, the narcotics division, or the local sheriff.[32] A first offense for illegally looking for work resulted in a voluntary return, whereas individuals who had been apprehended two or three times were charged with a Section 1 offense, which resulted in the individual being sent to La Tuna Federal prison in Anthony, Texas, or to Leavenworth in Kansas.

In the early nineteenth century, border enforcement was primarily focused on Asians, but the influence of the Ku Klux Klan and prohibition ensured the focus remained on individuals of Mexican descent. Miguel Antonio Levario situates such acts of militarized segregation along the border as continually defining ethnic Mexicans as an enemy of the state that ". . . must be subdued lest their presence undermine the social, political, and cultural fabric of white America."[33] Conflict over smuggling and determining who was engaging in illegal activity was an early problem between the Border Patrol and Mexicans entering the United States. A colonel of the Border Patrol estimated that about eight officers and a hundred liquor smugglers were killed during the prohibition years.[34] Another estimate during prohibition was 19 border patrol officers killed and 50 smugglers.[35] Finally, a Border Patrol agent claimed in his autobiography that, between 1924 and 1934, agents killed 500 smugglers and lost 23 officers.[36] Edward Langston's dissertation described a number of gunfights resulting in death and the difficulty to quickly determine whether someone was crossing into the United States for work or for some illegal activity like smuggling drugs or alcohol.[37] Most Border Patrol agents at the time were Anglo males between the ages of 20 to 40. Historian Kelly Hernández stated that the primarily white Border Patrol officers took vengeance upon the wider Mexican population if any of their agents were killed. She emphasized how the white Border Patrol men primarily enforced immigration laws upon poor, brown-skinned Mexican males.[38]

Although media reports were claiming that the Klan was decreasing in numbers, the Klan argued an increase in membership up to 3,000,000 "native-born, white, Protestant American citizens" nationwide.[39] Eventually the Klan in El Paso encountered increased opposition from Catholics and Juárez politicians, and it struggled to maintain a secret society as one of the local El Paso newspapers threatened to publish a membership roster.[40] By 1924, the Klan reportedly ceased to be a significant influence, and membership in Texas declined from 12,000 active members in 1927 to less than 2,500 a year later.[41] It is unclear how the Klan's membership patterns were affected in New Mexico during this time period.

Despite a nationwide decrease in Klan membership, racist portrayals continued against the region's residents, as did patterns of keeping Mexicans as manual laborers. In July 1925, *Harper's Monthly Magazine*, out of New York, described as "the oldest general interest monthly in America," published an article titled "New Mexico and the Backwash of Spain." In this article, the author Katharine Fullerton Gerould criticized residents by stating, "New Mexico is, all in all, a wild and uncivilized state. Life is cheap, ignorant Mexican juries are easily packed, and if a sheriff grows (which seldom happens) too zealous on behalf of law and order, it is pretty difficult, in the end, to find out who killed him."[42] New Mexico was described as corrupt and un-American for allowing the Spanish language to continue. Fullerton Gerould confusingly wondered why the dominant white race had failed in this area compared to other parts of the Southwest. The Mexican sheep-herder received an even more negative depiction from Fullerton Gerould: "But he is too ignorant, too mongrel, too indolent a creature to win any long-drawn-out contest, or even to express in his own person the perpetual question, 'What are you going to do about *me*?' We are not going to do anything about him except wait for the generations slowly to oust him."[43] Fullerton Gerould described pueblo Indians more positively compared to Mexicans, despite the fact that this racial group continually being denied federal and state citizenship.[44]

Several authors have reported better race relations in New Mexico and El Paso compared to other sections of the country and Texas overall, but this does not mean problems were non-existent.[45] Mexicans continued to be marginalized, and blacks were a numerically small population. For example, a police officer in El Paso reported to the *El Paso Herald* in 1929 how lynchings were a problem in other parts of the South but there were no issues in El Paso, "a good-sized country town," because, Sergeant Mathews reported, "The negroes here attend strictly to their own business."[46] The Sergeant Mathews did recall an incident where a black man asked a young white woman on a date, which resulted in him receiving a 60-day sentence on a chain gang for disturbing the peace. Mathews said that, about a month later, the man was found dead on the other side of the river. Despite the infrequent lynching of African Americans, new research on mob violence against Mexicans in the Southwest by historians William Carrigan and Clive Webb in their book *Forgotten Dead* highlights a significant number of deaths that occurred from 1848 to 1928, which conservative estimates place in the thousands.[47] Many of these occurred in New Mexico and particularly in Texas. Thus, racial contestation was not enough to alter whites becoming the elite, Mexicans being pushed to the bottom, Asians being excluded, Native Americans being isolated, and blacks being kept numerically less prevalent.

The Rise of Organized Crime in Ciudad Juárez and the United States

Prohibition in the United States created the perfect environment to supply the needs of U.S. residents with goods emerging from the Mexican side of the border. From 1920 to 1934, legalized gambling in the Mexican state of Chihuahua kept tourism the center of politics in Mexico.[48] Nevertheless, federal officials often opposed such practices, which led to divisions between Chihuahua and the capital in Mexico City, resulting in the international bridges between El Paso and Ciudad Juárez occasionally being closed to regulate businesses. Federal immigration and customs officials controlled the bridge and, due to conflicts, Juárez municipal leaders created their own police to protect their interests. In addition to federal officials, conflicts also emerged with Mexican military soldiers, many of whom took advantage of their positions to reap some of the gambling proceeds.[49] Much of the city's vice had been pushed to Ciudad Juárez with at least 40 percent of businesses operated by individuals with non-Spanish surnames.[50] Robin Robinson, in her dissertation at Arizona State University, stated:

> While the elites competed over gambling, everyone else struggled for the remaining vice. No matter who ruled Juarez, violence and corruption plagued the city. As a border town, Juarez possessed all the predictable vices. The prohibition era increased demand for already practiced public gambling and bootlegging. The existence of these enterprises required official sanction, legal or otherwise. At the top, politicians and generals took advantage of their positions to enrich themselves through kickbacks, partnerships, and "fees." In the middle, local businessmen produced and distributed the liquor smuggled across the border. At the bottom, low-level police and border agents practiced extortion, bribery, and shake-downs.[51]

Nicole Mottier, a Latin American historian, estimated that by 1926, two thirds of all business in Ciudad Juárez catered to tourism and employed a large proportion of the workforce.[52] She argued that from 1928 through 1934, Enrique Fernández and La Nacha led the first organized crime organization to influence local and state politics. Anthropologist Howard Campbell concurred, saying that La Nacha, or the "Dope Queen," was first employed by Enrique Fernández and her real name was Ignacia Jasso González.[53] According to Mottier, in 1930, members of the Quevado family ran drugs and received protection because they also held positions of political power. The influence of the drug market occurred at a time of economic instability and political fluctuation. Mottier outlined four types of gangs based on degrees of responsibility, authority, power, and income: 1) the politically and economically connected; 2) those in charge of dealing large-scale shipments, many of whom were local officials; 3) the owners of opium dens with less protection; 4) pistoleros who killed rival gang members and the Juárez madams who were bold drug traffickers. She argued that the pistoleros were the majority of gang members and the most frequently caught. Mottier's conception of gangs more frequently overlaps with the organized crime literature rather than that of U.S. gangs.[54] However, even Campbell argues drug trafficking organizations should be conceptualized as more shifting, contingent, and temporal in that alliances, conflicts, imprisonment, and death continued to keep these organizations in flux. Thus, rather than a pyramidal structure, cartels should be conceived more as rectangular.

In the United States, sociologist Howard Abadinsky reported that, prior to prohibition, organized crime primarily consisted of corrupt city officials or police officers, whereas afterward it led to a new form of criminal organization.

> In order to be profitable, the liquor business, licit or illicit, demands large-scale organization. Raw material must be purchased and shipped to manufacturing sites. This requires trucks, drivers, mechanics, warehouses, and laborers. Manufacturing efficiency and profit are maximized by economies of scale. This requires large buildings where the whiskey, beer, or wine can be manufactured, bottled, and placed in cartons for storage and distribution to wholesale outlets or saloons and speakeasies. If the substances are to be smuggled, ships, boats, and their crews are required . . . and there is obvious need to physically protect shipments through the employment of armed guards.[55]

Such ventures required association and connections with legal institutions. It was during prohibition that several crime syndicates became organized in Chicago, Detroit, and New York City. Street gangs on the other hand were often conceived as poorly organized youth groups living in poverty and existing in several cities such as Boston, Cleveland, Denver, El Paso, Los Angeles, Minneapolis, and St. Louis.[56] Along the U.S.-Mexico border, during prohibition, liquor traffic remained in local hands, and it was not taken over by U.S. crime syndicates.[57] Such a finding is supported by a different culture and language that was required along the U.S.-Mexico border region, which the primarily European organized crime syndicates did not possess. This does not mean, however, that U.S.-based companies with pre-existing financial and corporate ties did not play a role in distribution; rather, it simply was not controlled by U.S.-based organized crime families.

From 1929 to 1939, the United States fell into the Great Depression, and Juárez politicians and business leaders pushed to capitalize on this market potential. Robinson stated:

> The U.S. public and less informed government officials of the 1920s placed much of the blame for border vice problems on Mexico and its citizens. Americans believed Mexicans, and border Mexicans in

particular, to be morally deficient, receptive to and encouraging of vice, and possessing a government without concern for the health and morality of its citizens. Another general misconception is that prohibition created a liquor smuggling problem of overwhelming proportion.[58]

During this time, the Quevado family's struggle for leadership resulted in a number of deaths of people working for Fernández in 1933 and 1934, and eventually Fernández's own death that same year. Alcohol sales were made legal again in El Paso in 1933, and the U.S. prohibition ended in 1934, ending much of Juárez's tourism.[59] The Commissioner of Prohibition estimated that possibly only one twentieth of smuggled liquor was seized.[60] The administration of Mexico's President Lázaro Cárdenas (1934–1940) focused on eliminating gambling and prostitution. After the death of Fernández, Campbell reported that La Nacha developed her enterprise to last for the next 50 years by shifting from the sale of alcohol to the distribution of marijuana and heroin. Her ability to maintain stability may have been influenced by her philanthropy in helping the poor and disenfranchised by financing an orphanage, offering a free breakfast program, and never becoming over-zealous.[61] By 1936, the drug trade was reportedly led by members of the Quevedo family. This family too lost political power as an individual named Talamantes took over in 1937 and then targeted Quevedo's gambling empire.[62] Throughout this period there were back and forth stances on gambling, in which it was occasionally stopped for moral reasons and then renewed due to financial needs.[63]

Poor Living and Working Conditions Coincides with Increased Attention on Gangs

In 1930, the sociologically trained Emory Bogardus outlined the context for differential outcomes resulting from Mexican and Mexican American populations being segregated to live on the other side town across the railroad tracks. Bogardus stated the reasons for segregation, included Latinos not wanting to become citizens, reaping the benefits of the United States without citizenship, loyalty to their native country, and continuing to be treated as greasers and seen more as laborers than as "full-fledged human beings" when attempting to fit in.[64] Neighborhood segregation resulted in schools that were primarily Mexican and did not receive the same resources and opportunities. Anthropologist James Diego Vigil elaborated on how Mexican immigration in the 1920s consisted of 1.5 million to 2 million residents who were being utilized for cheap labor along the southwestern railways and farms.[65] The railroad brought the pachuco culture westward in the 1930s and 1940s. There were several notable Chicano leaders from the Ciudad Juárez–El Paso area who had since moved to Los Angeles, including Oscar Acosta, Bert Corona, Ruben Salazar, and Luis Rodriguez. Bert Corona, the influential labor and community activist, observed that many individuals from El Paso moved to Los Angeles during the Great Depression because there were more jobs in California.[66] Thus, individuals along the line from Ciudad Juárez and El Paso to Tucson and on to Los Angeles shared cultural influences.[67]

The zoot suit generation, along with its music and style, were captured perfectly in Anthony Macías's book *Mexican American Mojo: Popular Music, Dance, and Urban Culture in Los Angeles, 1935–1968*.[68] Similar to others, Macías described how the style in Los Angeles emerged from El Paso. Don Tosti, an artists who had become successful in Los Angeles, was born and raised in the Segundo Barrio of El Paso. His hit "Pachuco Boogie" later went on to influence the work of another famous musician of the time, Lalo Guerrero. Musicians during this period created a blended style from jazz, blues, doowop, Motown, and Afro-Latin music. Public officials often looked upon the excitement and style of this culture with disdain. Early pachuco writer David Barker even suggested that the El Paso Police Department may have threatened prison sentences on some youth unless they left town.[69] The State Juvenile Training School, located 582 miles away in Gatesville, Texas, housed at least sixty boys from El Paso each year.[70]

In New Mexico, racialized histories existed in a state that avoided at all costs any discussion of racial inequality. Political leaders continued to fear that the majority population (mestizos and Native Americans) would eventually no longer tolerate white Anglo domination.[71] As tourism became identified as New Mexico's industry of the future, the title of "Land of Enchantment" was adopted in 1937.[72] Illusions of inclusiveness hid the power of wealth and social standing that dictated the creation of a Spanish American culture. From the point of time of pursuing statehood, to adopting a tourist slogan, the term Mexican began to be used by state officials as a derogatory term. Even in El Paso, Texas, when officials desired to give the population a positive connotation, they used the term Spanish or Latin.[73]

The news reporting of gangs began to increase in frequency after 1936 as captured by this article in *El Paso Herald-Post* report, titled "South El Paso Gang Scored."[74] The article's author reported how the secretary of the Sacred Heart Church believed gangs were endangering the lives of residents near their church. The gang had destroyed a $300 fence, and drug addicts had gathered near the church and planned robberies. Historian Mario T. García describes how the Sacred Heart Church was located centrally in the segregated Chihuahuita neighborhood where Mexicans had lived in slum-like conditions.[75] In response to the problematic conditions, a tenement ordinance was put into effect in 1930 and housing projects were initiated in 1933.[76] On March 12, 1940, a "gang clean-up" was issued, and twelve "Mexican speaking youths" between the ages of 16 and 22 were arrested. The youth were described as not attending school, playing dice, hanging out on street corners, and being a nuisance.[77] In 1941, raids continued as thirty-two men were jailed during additional "clean-up campaigns" in South El Paso.[78] Pedestrians and automobile drivers reported feeling unsafe and filed complaints with the police department. Police officers confiscated brass "knucks," butcher knives, pocket knives, and clubs. Police charged the youth with vagrancy. The Captain of the Sheriff Department believed most of the petty thefts, breaking into parked vehicles, and simple assault cases were a result of these gangs. Arrests continued during the spring and throughout the summer; on August 14, 1942, the *El Paso Herald-Post* described a "War on Gangs," during which thirteen young men between the ages of 17 and 23 were arrested.[79] Despite law enforcement efforts, the Captain believed gangs would be an ongoing problem.

Regardless of an increase in media attention, the overall proportion of youth who were involved in groups identified as gangs appears to be minimal. Jamie F. Torres's personal narrative about growing up in El Segundo Barrio from 1925 until 1943, prior to being drafted into the Navy to fight in World War II, only included one paragraph about gangs in a book 514 pages long.[80] He notes, "We did have our share of young punks that can be found in all dense neighborhoods," but he had no personal recollection of gangs and he didn't recall any mention of them in the newspapers. Although he agreed the term pachuco was coined to reflect residents from El Paso, the zoot suit presence appeared to become more of a fad in the early 1940s. His own life reflects doing well in segregated schools and later attending college. After leaving the military, Torres attended college through the GI Bill and had a successful engineering career. Although the historical record for gangs in El Paso between 1916 and 1936 was sparse, the same cannot be said about the timeframe afterward, when the discussion of gangs became a prominent issue. A noted change occurred among these groups during this time frame: organizing for defense in the early days shifted into rivalries among neighbors who lived in different neighborhoods.

Enhanced punishment designed to target gangs increased in Los Angeles, California, after the June 1943 Zoot Suit Riots. This event also intensified tensions between U.S. soldiers and individuals of Mexican descent in other cities such as Denver, Colorado.[81] The Zoot Suit Riots brought pachucos nationwide attention.[82] Sociologist Emory Bogardus argued that most Zoot Suiters and Mexican American youth were not gang members, and U.S. society needed to demonstrate greater racial tolerance and understanding.[83] He chastised U.S. sailors involved in the riots for taking the law into their own hands and police officers for creating a feeling of injustice. Carey McWilliams participated in a legal case preceding the riots (Sleepy Lagoon case) and served on a committee to study the reasons for why the riot occurred.[84] He emphasized the discriminatory actions of law enforcement officials, military officers, and the general public in their response to Mexican Americans during the Zoot Suit Riots. He challenged the inflammatory news articles of the *Los Angeles Times*. McWilliams stated, "The riots were not an unexpected rupture in Anglo-Hispano relations but the logical end-product of a hundred years of neglect and discrimination."[85]

By World War II and after the Zoot Suit Riots, Macías referred to Los Angeles as the nation's pachuco capital, and the early notoriety of El Paso seemed to be forgotten.[86] During World War II, officials in El Paso began developing its closest relationships in history with Ciudad Juárez.[87] Mexico joined the United States as an ally and provided a steady flow of war materials. Fort Bliss grew from 3,000 soldiers in 1939 to 40,000 by 1944 and was considered the third largest military base in the country. Although no clear accurate numbers were available due to being categorized as white instead of black, it was estimated that more Mexican Americans served in the military during World War II and received medals of valor and other accomplishments than any other racial or ethnic group.[88]

In July 1942, the Bracero Program began, which allowed U.S. farm owners to hire Mexican agricultural workers.[89] The numbers grew annually from 4,200 in 1942 to 238,500 by 1945, including 121,350 Mexican workers repairing railroad tracks. As a state, Texas was not allowed to have Braceros until 1947 due to the Mexican government condemning this state for its unfair treatment of Mexicans. Despite this ruling, El Paso businesses constantly negotiated opportunities to utilize undocumented labor. Wartime efforts began to improve health standards, although the overall health status of most residents living along both sides of the border was very poor.[90] There were higher rates of sexually transmitted diseases, tuberculosis, typhus, typhoid fever, whooping cough, and infant and maternal mortality. Winifred Dowling, in his dissertation at the University of Texas at El Paso, stated:

> Venereal disease was one of the greatest health concerns along the U.S.-Mexico border. It was exacerbated by the growing number of U.S. military men stationed near the border. With so many young men there came young women. Leaders on both sides of the border took a number of steps, including the Pan American Sanitary Bureau's emphasis on venereal disease.[91]

Juárez closed its legal zone of prostitution in 1942, and El Paso did the same in 1941, yet much of the activity continued underground. The source of much of the poor health was attributed to poverty and horrible conditions in South El Paso. Once the war ended, relations between the two countries became strained once again. In addition, returning Mexican American veterans began to realize that their fight for U.S. freedoms did not ensure this treatment was provided once they returned home. Still often treated like second-class citizens, Mexican American servicemen started a reform-focused group called the American G.I. Forum, which was focused on obtaining equal citizenship rights.[92]

Gangs of the 1950s—El Paso's Peak Period and the Arrival of the Bicycle Priest

The summer of 1950 began with a series of investigations into gangs. An *El Paso Herald-Post* reporter stated that a grand jury had begun investigating juvenile gangs.[93] The grand jury noted that while gangs had been primarily confined to South El Paso, these groups were appearing in the northern section of the city and many of the members came from prominent families. Most of the members knew each other through nicknames, and the gangs emphasized the importance of secrecy. Informants encountered vengeance, often in the form of the mark of a large cross scratched onto informers' foreheads. The newspaper reporter stated that several residents told him they were living in terror of these organizations and the police offered little protection. Gang activities ranged from destroying lawns, vandalism, throwing rocks, molesting girls, and racing down streets. Similar to most news stories, there was very little or no data presented as to rates, total numbers, or comparisons among various years or groups. Nevertheless, sensational stories continued. A grocery store display window had a large rock thrown threw it with a note written from the "Dukes."[94] Duke members denied involvement. Police broke up potential rumbles between the X-2 gang and the 7–11 gang and arrested several youths for vagrancy and loitering, booking them into the county jail.

A probation officer called for a meeting between county and city law enforcement agencies in an attempt to create a plan to combat gangs and "rat packs."[95] Parents were urged to supervise their children, and efforts were focused on gathering intelligence on gang-involved youth and publicizing their names through the radio and newspaper when taken into custody. The El Paso County Grand Jury felt they had conducted an exhaustive survey of the juvenile situation and believed that, unless officials corrected the existing conditions, there would be cause for alarm. Another story the same day reported that several members of the Dukes who attended El Paso High School were arrested for carrying rifles, zip guns, and an assortment of knives and home-made blackjacks. Fights centered between members of the X-2 gang and the 7–11 gang of East El Paso. During the summer of 1950, a news story reported a bigger boy beating a smaller boy to be initiated into the group in front of a crowd of older youth.[96] They all wore white shirts. In another section of town, police found a sign that read "7–11 has been here." The police and city leaders were looking into how to break up groups they called "rat packs." The next day, a judge told parents to take charge of their kids to prevent fights and mischief.[97] The gangs of the time were considered to be in open warfare, and they included several Southside gangs (7-X gang, OK-9s, Old Fort Bliss gang, and Lucky 13s), whereas East El Paso was "terrorized" by the 7–11 gang.[98] On the Northeast it was the Dukes and the female auxiliary group known as the Duchesses. Such feuds between gangs led to a 15-year-old boy being shot, stabbed, and dying from these injuries in December 1951.[99]

Such a context shaped the entrance of white Jesuit priest named Father Harold J. Rahm, S.J., who arrived in El Paso, Texas. on July 12, 1952; he brought with him little insight into the area but spiritual faith.[100] He had spent the previous summer working in Cuba. Not entirely fluent in Spanish, he was given the task of serving as the assistant pastor for the Sacred Heart Church. In the early 1950s, Father Rahm reached out to youth and attempted to create a safe place where they could play sports and participate in church activities.[101] He noticed that El Paso was separated into five areas (East, North, Northeast, South, and Sunset Heights), and he was assigned to work in South El Paso, the most deprived section of the city.[102] At the time, the city had a population of around 250,000 residents, and Juárez had 150,000. South El Paso consisted of 30,000 residents: one or two of them were Anglo, and there were twenty black families, and the rest were Latin American. Father Rahm purchased a bicycle and rode around the neighborhoods and was invited into homes. He observed and was told about a wide variety of problems in the community involving issues such as domestic violence, health complications, interpersonal violence, officer-involved shootings, poverty, teenage pregnancy, unemployment, unsanitary housing, and many more difficulties. At first he was unsure how to be of best use, but he understood that the service organizations that existed were understaffed and underfinanced.

Father Rahm described how the community's Latin Americans were divided into three groups: 1) American, 2) Chicano, and 3) Juareno. Americans were the most assimilated and smallest in number in South El Paso because they primarily lived in middle-class areas. Chicanos were the largest in number and many had one or both parents born in Mexico. Juareno's had greater difficulty with the English language and were from Mexico. Within the city there was conflict between Anglos and Latins, but not between "Negroes" and Latins. Gang scholar James Diego Vigil reached a similar conclusion that gang culture emerged out of the Chicano culture's opposition to the dominant culture.[103] In El Paso as in Los Angeles, the largest number of gang-involved youth came from high-poverty neighborhoods, and many had disrupted families. Father Rahm first reached out to the fathers of the households. The kids played sports in the street and had nowhere to go for activities. During his bicycle travels, Father Rahm, found a deserted building and obtained the rights to purchase it. He and others cleaned up the building, and soon it opened as the Our Lady's Youth Center. It averaged around 250 teenagers and children every day.[104] Father Rahm utilized his previous experience visiting Boys Town, which was an internationally recognized boys' home in Nebraska that began in 1917 to provide services to disadvantaged youth.

As the Our Lady's Youth Center continued operations, Father Rahm realized that for the center to survive he would need to focus on gangs. The gangs consisted a variety of groups, the largest being the 4-Fs (Mesa Street), Little 9ers (Frontera Park), Lucky 13s (5th and Oregon), 14s (4th and St. Vrain), and 7Xs (Durango Street). South El Paso was divided into two with the 14-7X allies and the Lucky 13–9 allies (See Figure 4). Our Lady's Youth Center existed in 13–9 territory. Throughout these neighborhoods there were small pockets of other gangs, such as the Charms, X9s, LMs, Terrengers, DDT's, TPM, and Rebels. The names of the gangs largely emerged from the street where they existed and were primarily in English. One previous gang that was known as notorious was the K9s, whose members departed due to adulthood or prison incarceration. The neighborhoods and housing projects shaped which groups the youth joined. Residents at the Alamito Housing project became a 14. The youth who didn't join were known as squares or independents.[105] The smuggling of narcotics rarely influenced the youth, who were themselves loosely organized. Based on the notes and reports of the participant observers working with the gangs, Father Rahm described gang activities as follows: "Mostly gangs don't do anything. They just sit around talking, arguing, bragging, telling stories. They make elaborate plans, which are mainly group phantasies that never happen. They drink, they take pills, they have parties, they talk about girls, and occasionally they fight."[106] The social worker assigned to each gang attempted to reduce conflict between the groups and help members to attain summer employment. The main conflict in the neighborhood continued to be between the 4-Fs and Lucky 13s. Father Rahm believed the Center had a positive impact with the 4-Fs, but little impact on the Lucky 13s or the Lucky 9s. He hoped the overall efforts of Our Lady's Youth Center would help shine light on the needs of South El Paso.

By 1954, efforts to focus on gangs continued as detectives and probation officers visited Austin High School to talk with boys regarding a teenage theft ring involved in looting and stripping parked cars.[107] The district attorney reported how the parents of these teenage boys might

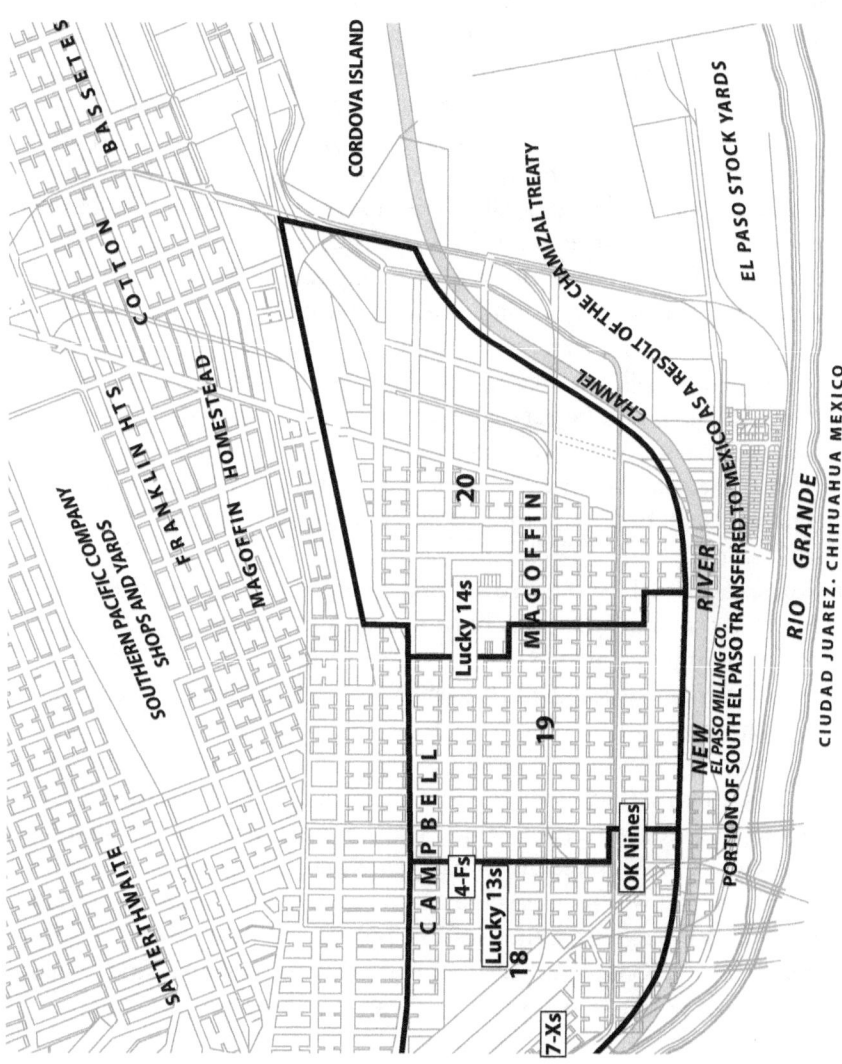

FIGURE 2.1 El Paso Gangs in the 1950s.

be called before a County Grand Jury. By 1956, an *El Paso Herald-Post* reporter stated that there was a presence of fifty organized gangs of teenagers, and that some of these groups had fifty to seventy-five members "roaming" the streets of El Paso.[108] Their activities included beatings, stabbings, zip-gun shootings, thefts, burglaries, vandalism, auto-thefts, and drinking. During the year, one person had been shot with a zip gun, several individuals were beaten or stabbed with at least eight requiring a visit to the hospital. It was reported that such levels of violence had only been present in 1950–1951. However, no data were provided to compare the time period changes. All of the high schools reportedly had the presence of a gang. Throughout the 1900s to 1950s, the public schools were segregated, and it was unclear from any data I could obtain what changes may have been occurring in each school.

Politically, El Paso accomplished one of its greatest feats in the election of Raymond Telles as mayor in 1957, the first Mexican American mayor of El Paso, and he served as mayor until 1961. Jaime Torres, a neighbor and friend who supported Telles's political campaign, emphasized how Mexican Americans were the numerical majority, yet they had no representation in the local or regional government.[109] According to historian Mario T. García, between 1900 and 1950 no Mexican American had been elected as mayor or as a member of the city council.[110] Raymond Telles was born in South El Paso in 1915. He had served in the military and worked as a county clerk before launching a peoples' campaign designed to gather Mexican American and Anglo votes, because votes from both racial and ethnic groups were needed to secure a victory. After his election, he increased the number of Mexican Americans attaining city jobs. García described Telles's political strategy as the "politics of status," which was not geared toward combating the root causes of Mexican-American underdevelopment but was more reformist in that it was focused on ensuring treatment of his ethnic group as full-fledged U.S. citizens. In assessing Telles's role as the first Mexican American mayor, García stated, "Conservative in personal and social outlook, Telles in retrospect was a moderate reformer but one liberal for his own historical period."[111]

Despite such a political accomplishment, the conditions in the community repeated previous historical patterns. The El Paso Police Chief ordered a crackdown on youth gangs after two Southside families were assaulted.[112] The families planned to move out of the neighborhood, and residents reported living in fear. Officials believed the gang responsible included twenty members of the 7-X gang, which had been in the area for fifteen or twenty years.[113] The city enacted a 10:00 P.M. curfew. Less than a month later, the Lucky 13s were believed to be involved in the beating and kicking of a 35-year-old man after he refused to give them a nickel.[114] Similar to previous efforts, Mayor Telles appealed to parents to increase their level of surveillance on their children. Shortly after, the community mourned the death of a 19-year-old man who was fatally stabbed at the Our Lady's Youth Center.[115] The young man was a 4-F and was killed by a Little 9er. Father Rahm began having the youth hold a night court where they could settle their differences one on one.[116] Mayor Telles thanked Father Rahm for his increased efforts to reduce violence. A city council member stated that new laws were needed to curb gangs and encouraged support for a law that would try youth who were 17 years of age as adults instead of juveniles because they could only be held until the age of 21 at the State Reformatory.[117] The police were giving close crew cuts for "sanitary reasons" to youth detained in the city jail, which they hoped would serve as a deterrent for resuming gang activities. Despite increased public punishment, a 14-year-old boy was shot in the back with a .22 caliber rifle and died, reportedly due to gang warfare between the X-14s and the Cypress Kids.[118] Residents stated that a member of the Scorpions had been knifed by an X-14 member, and the Cypress Kids went to avenge that attack by firing zip guns at rival members. During the same day, a 17-year-old was beaten to death with a steel bar.[119] A Captain of El Paso County's Detention Home stated that a year before there had been fifty-two gangs. The problem of gangs was described as increasing since 1951, brought down in 1953 due to police efforts, but it re-emerged in full force in 1957 with three youths dying from stab wounds and the comeback of members of the 7-X gang.

By the end of the 1950s, gangs were reported to have gone underground.[120] The areas that were once hotbeds for gang activity had since gone quiet. There were no more reports of stealing hubcaps, crashing parties, drinking, arrests for vagrancy, drunkenness, traffic violations, burglary, theft, or possession of dangerous weapons such as knives or zip guns. The churches and schools were given credit for providing alternatives to gangs and violence through athletic recreational programs. A newspaper article written twenty years later reported that if you were to walk in the Southside during the 1950s you risked getting beat up.[121] It was described as a time when the 7-X gang was on a crime spree and in open warfare with its rivals. The police department and city hall responded with "an all-out attack," and a grand jury in 1951 investigated the problem. Bill Rodriguez's oral history captures many of these themes.[122] Mr. Rodriguez, who was born 1936 to a Mexican father and an Anglo mother and eventually became the chief of police in El Paso, stated that in the mid-1950s he did not care for the police. At that time the police were physically aggressive with the Mexicans and the gangs, yet no one ever filed a complaint because it wasn't considered macho. Once he became a police officer, he began to realize that, to advance in the police department, you had to be selected by the Anglo leadership, and that despite doing well on tests he continued to be overlooked. In response he went to college and earned a degree. He then went on to become a police sergeant and worked in community relations to help improve the police image among minority groups. By 1977 he was Chief of Police and served in this role until 1986. He continued working in law enforcement and various community positions for the city.[123]

Gangs of the 1960s–1970s

Compared to the 1950s, the 1960s was a quiet period of gang activity despite the departure of Father Rahm, who was sent to continue his religious efforts in Brazil in 1964.[124] The decade began with an act of violence that made it appear gang activity may re-emerge. A 15-year-old boy was beaten and stabbed to death in South El Paso.[125] He had previously been in a fight with members of the Lucky 14s, but several of his friends reported they did not believe the recent killing was from members of the Lucky 14s or the 7-Xs. Contrary to persistent negative media coverage of gangs, the *El Paso Times* wrote a four-part series devoted to the Charms and how several of its members had gone on to become heroes in the marines and athletics and it all began through youth athletic programming.[126] The Charms was formed in 1956 by members of the 4-Fs, Lucky 13s, and Little 9s who were 14 years old and wanted to have fun. At the time, gang problems and rivalries were high and almost led to the closing of Bowie High School.[127] Fred Morales, born in 1954 and raised in South El Paso, reported in a 1975 interview that gangs were very active during his years in grammar school and junior high.[128] He thought the pachuco influence, machismo, and being el más chingón influenced youth to fight among each other and with Juárez gangs across the river. He mentioned several gangs, including the

7-11s, Eagles, Trampas, Alley Cats, Crusaders, Cougars, Jokers, Lucky Charms, and Shamrocks.

William E. Wood, who provided an oral history in 1994, stated he was a former government real estate appraiser during the Chamizal settlement. He reported that South El Paso had a lot of gangs, but in the early 1960s it was safe to walk the streets and the residents were hard working.[129] A 1962 city ordinance outlawed discrimination in El Paso two years prior to the Civil Rights Act of 1964.[130] In 1963, the Chamizal dispute was settled between United States and Mexico, and the agreement provided an additional 193 acres of land to the United States. Bowie High school was later relocated to this area, and more residents were relocated to the Tays Housing Projects.[131] Residents were displaced by Southside housing projects and brought to new places.[132] According to the Population Reference Bureau, the fourth wave of immigration occurred from 1965 to the present.[133] One law scholar argued that the Immigration Act of 1965 was historic in its elimination of discriminatory national origin quotas. However, despite massive reforms compared to the previous waves, naturalization laws still imposed tighter entry requirements and increased enforcement.[134] By 1965, the country shifted its policy from national origin to people who had relatives in the United States. The Civil Rights Movement argued on behalf of removing racial and ethnic discrimination in immigration law. The United States allowed access to previously excluded or underrepresented groups from Asia and Latin America.

Although gang activity dissipated in the 1960s, the root causes for gang formation were never resolved. A probation officer interviewed in a 1976 news article stated that he had been part of gang in the 1960s.[135] At that time, a gang member had been killed and several of the gangs decided things were getting out of control, so they formed a Mexican American Youth Association (MAYA) to fight the system, but it failed to sustain leadership. According to the probation officer, many in the barrio were now junkies getting high, from spray paint to heroin. In 1971, several researchers from the University of Colorado's Mexican-American Studies Program published a report titled "South El Paso: El Segundo Barrio."[136] In this report, the authors provided a historical overview of the neighborhood and current conditions by providing census data along with poetry and pictures. One of the poets who contributed to this work, Abelardo Delgado, described how South El Paso gave its residents a strong foundation educationally, recreationally, spiritually, and at home, yet it also served as a geographic prison. Paisano Drive, also called the Tortilla Curtain, was the main street separating Chihuahuita and Segundo Barrio from the rest of the El Paso. The report went on to describe the population, manufacturing jobs, and Anglo domination that persisted in the city of El Paso. Close examination was given to the Chihuahuita neighborhood, and census tracts 18, 19, 20 in particular (See Figure 4). The authors looked optimistically to the El Paso Boy's Club and the opening of the Marcos B. Armijo Community Center in 1968. They criticized the city for failing to act on numerous reports of the need to "clean up" South El Paso since 1901.

The Marcos B. Armijo Community Center was a central place of activity for a sports club known as the Thunderbirds. Due to the location of the Center, the facility encountered challenges similar to those experienced by Father Rahm at the Our Lady's Youth Center. In early April 1972, a conflict emerged between the Thunderbirds and group of individuals called the Tecatos, of whom most were described as heroin addicts and former convicts from the state penitentiary. Several Thunderbirds allegedly told Tecato members to inject their heroin somewhere else and that they could no longer use the handball court.[137] After some time, the dispute increased to the point where several Tecatos drove up in a vehicle and fired upon Arturo Corrales, the leader of the Thunderbirds, killing him and wounding four others. Arturo Corrales was a Vietnam veteran who had previously attended Bowie High School.[138] Members of the Thunderbirds reiterated to the news media how they were a sports organization in South El Paso and had been active for the past two years.[139] The Thunderbirds had formed with the purpose to help the poor and keep kids out of trouble. They sponsored picnics for fatherless children and provided help to needy families. They worked to keep the area clean and keep trouble out of the neighborhood. The police said the "T-Birds" were a gang, and the *El Paso Times* ran a headline "Clubs or Gangs" with a news story acknowledging the difference between the groups of the time and the gangs existing fifteen years before, such as 7-X, Little 9s, and 7–11, but nonetheless concluded that the "T-Birds" were a gang.[140] An El Paso policeman concurred that the evidence suggested the Tecatos were using drugs in the back of the Armijo Center, but the facility or the police should have been notified rather than the "T-Birds" assuming responsibility.[141] These news articles also laid out the description of where each group existed (See Figure 5).[142]

By 1976, gang issues and juvenile delinquency continued to be a source of concern. The police department expanded its force by twenty

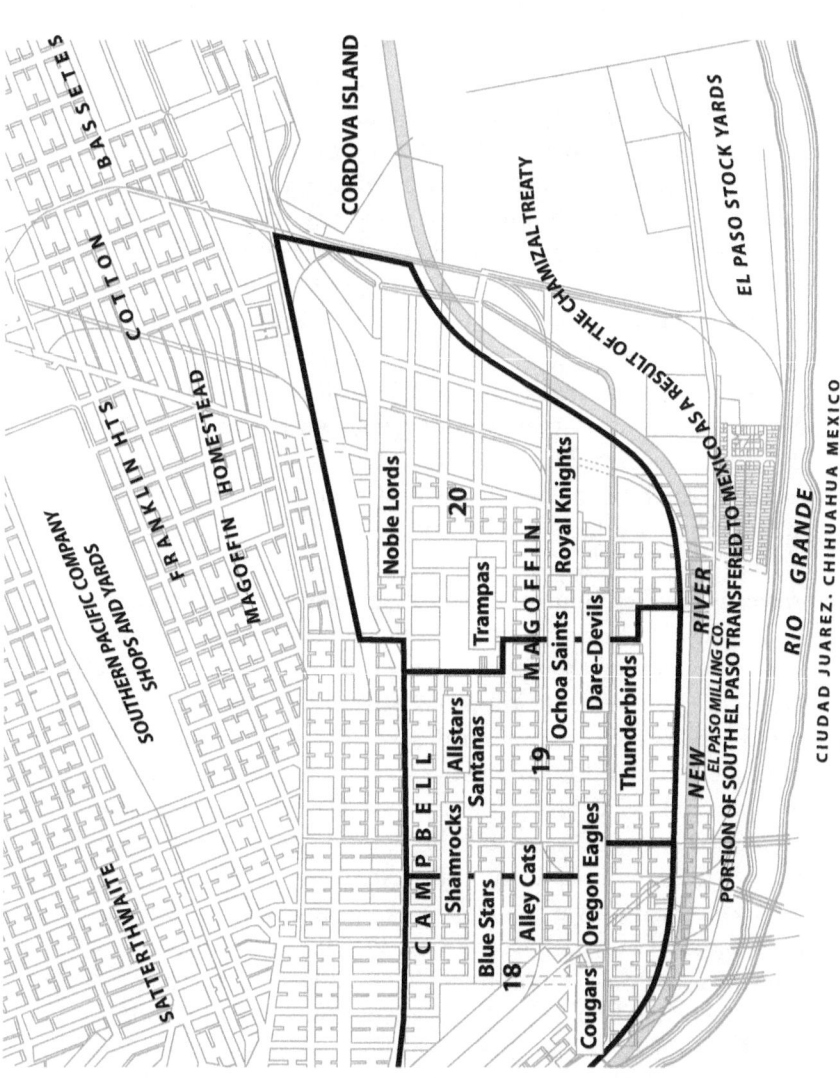

FIGURE 2.2 El Paso Gangs in the 1970s.

men to help with case overloads, and they created a new youth-service division.[143] Officials also became concerned with a young man given the nickname "El Raton" or "The Rat" because he snuck back and forth across the border committing property crimes and harassing elderly residents with his gang.[144] One of the housing projects in Segundo Barrio, the Ruben Salazar housing complex, was described as being controlled by four gangs: Flaming Angels, Fonzies, La Sana, and Chicanos In Action (CIA).[145] Residents stated that the gangs didn't bother anyone if they were left alone. However, in September an 18-year-old man who lived in the projects was shot to death while talking with friends when a car of several individuals drove by and fired shots at him.[146] The Flaming Angels sent flowers to his grave. The City of El Paso created a diversion unit.[147] In September 1976, 583 juveniles received a referral, of whom 216 (37 percent) were Anglo, 336 (58 percent) were Mexican American, thirty (5 percent) were black, and one (less than 1 percent) was Asian. The newspaper reported that various gangs existed in the city, including Chicanos in Action, Blue Stars, Los Demonios, Flaming Angels, and Southside.[148] Much of the gang activity was described as resulting from inadequate schools, a lack of jobs, and illegal "aliens."

The following month, a 16-year-old boy who lived in the Ruben Salazar project was killed and was allegedly a member of a gang from San Antonio, Texas.[149] The police said that the housing complex included the Thunderbirds gang, whereas the Metizos [sic] and La Sana were Central El Paso gangs. Another gang known as the Lords was present on the east side of El Paso. As the year continued, several South El Paso gangs continued shooting at each other despite the creation of a youth assistance program the previous year.[150] Nevertheless, most agencies were not focused on youth gangs. Due to the repeated killings, residents in the Salazar housing projects asked for more security.[151] Reportedly, several youths who were causing problems at Bowie and Douglas Elementary were from one of the housing projects. Two youth were arrested for the murder of a 23-year-old man who was shot off his motorcycle in South El Paso.[152] The newspaper stated that there had been at least four killings since 1972 in feuds between gangs in South El Paso, but gathering information was difficult because gang members did not talk with authorities. Some residents blamed the police, whereas the police blamed parents. There was an overall distrust of Anglos. The Executive Director of the El Paso Boys Club, William H. Brown, called the organizations groups instead of gangs because the members didn't have jobs and started as clubs or social groups.

Pete Jurado wrote his master's thesis on a gang he gave the pseudonym the Chicano Aggregation (CA, which appears to be Chicanos In Action [CIA]) by covertly interviewing some of their members through his history of growing up in the neighborhood and working at the El Paso Job Corp Center.[153] The gang existed in the Second Ward, which continued to have the highest concentration of Chicanos, deteriorated housing, and poverty. The members were between the ages of 14 to 33 years of age, and they all grew up near Our Lady's Youth Center. Jurado described the conflict between the Saints (a pseudonym for the Thunderbirds) and the Tecatos. He stated that the Saints began around 1964 when a youth worker from Our Lady's Youth Center organized the youth into a club for recreational and social activities, and they rarely were involved in delinquency. After 1969, several members had returned home from Vietnam and they began to re-establish old friendships, but they had become more interested in using marijuana or alcohol. They continued to hang out at the Our Lady's Youth Center. Some members got married, whereas others continued to participate in athletic tournaments. In 1971, they began to get harassed more by the police and were having problems with the law and with the most powerful gang in the Second Ward, the Los Machos. After the shooting of Marales (pseudonym for Corrales), Jurado reported that the Saints didn't hang around the Our Lady's Youth Center for a period of time, and in their place emerged a group of youth named CA. They even challenged members of the newer Los Machos, now called Latin Lords (the pseudonym appears to be the Noble Lords), to a fight. Several Latin Lords were stabbed, and the CA became the toughest gang in the Second Ward. They continued to battle the Latin Lords and Tecatos, even killing one in 1975 at the Tays housing project. Jurado stated that the CA sold marijuana to make money. At the time, several members were in jail for this activity, and the gang had participated in at least two murders. Over time they stopped fighting with many other groups because at the time only two others existed (the Santana Revivals and the Alley Cats). Members of the CA received respect and were not bothered.

El Paso has a long history of gangs. The earliest accounts of these organizations range from 1915 to 1919. However, most this activity seems to be in the form of a wider style of cultural resistance to colonization in the form of pachuquismo. Mexicans were largely segregated at the time and were concentrated in the poorest housing conditions of the city in South El Paso. The Ku Klux Klan, which emerged among Anglos in the early 1920s, did not influence the area for long, but the overall sentiment of anti-Mexican and anti-Catholic sentiments had persisted since colonization. As these communities continued to be neglected, the 1940s brought neighborhood groups into conflict with one another. By the 1950s it became dangerous to walk into other territories. Father Rahm, in conjunction with the churches and community centers, stepped in to help gangs evolve into athletic clubs, and the violence decreased. The Chicano Movement helped displace some gang activity in the late 1960s, but the lack of sustained leadership did not allow the city's activism to reach levels such as that seen in Denver, Colorado, or in Crystal City and San Antonio, Texas.[154] The 1970s reflected these shifts as the groups focused on giving back to the community, but members of these organizations faced addiction and other issues after Vietnam as well as conflicts with individuals who had been incarcerated or addicted to heroin. It is this context that shaped the conditions prior to my arrival in the border region.

CHAPTER THREE

Moral Panic Under a Research Microscope
The Organizational Scene Prior to Arrival

Which stories do we believe? What type of evidence do we require for someone to convince us that something is occurring? Social sciences have developed over the years by increasing its methodological training, by standardizing expectations for data requirements to make certain statements, and by questioning value claims. Still, which voices matter and which accounts are accepted continue to be shaped by ideologies or common ways of thinking. We maintain beliefs about what is wrong and what is right, and despite the privilege given to research in universities, the general public often isn't convinced. One of the biggest changes that occurs with college students is getting them to think about the social world after they have taken two key courses for any discipline: theory and methods. One is based on more abstract ideas and linking larger patterns, whereas the other is focused on concrete tools for structuring inquiry and determining the best modes of observation to answer the research question.[1] To attain a Ph.D., students are pushed to master these skills and to demonstrate them through their own individual research project, known as a dissertation. All knowledge claims are open to scrutiny through peer review. Professors who continue in research learn new ways of building these skills by asking better questions and improving how they collect data, yet there are always strengths and limitations.

The challenge in this chapter highlights the role of law enforcement agencies participating in data collection while not necessarily being trained in research, analysis, or theory. Law enforcement agencies make certain claims. Researchers often use these data and utilize law enforcement as a source to learn more about crime and social problems in the community. The data that law enforcement collects are known as official data, and researchers can use this information to support, counter, or *question patterns in society. For example, how many gang members live in my community? How many gangs exist? What types of crimes are they involved in? Who joins these groups? How long do they remain members?* Answers to these questions hint at the shift from the revisionist history in part one toward the perspective of part two, which is focused on an ethnographic foundation. One of the challenges I regularly encountered in chapters 1 and 2 was the difficulty of finding an origination story for gangs and whether the events unfolding were worse than other periods of time.[2] In the 1980s, not only did law enforcement officers respond to crime occurring in the community but they also began to discover and report on the type of gang situation they perceived to exist. While the purpose for their data collection has traditionally been in the name of suppressing crime, another growing reason was to acquire increased funding and inter-agency cooperation. By themselves, increased funding and inter-agency cooperation appears to be a legitimate rationale that is not usually thought to include a conflict of interest. The problem occurs when those who require funding develop the definition of gangs and apply that label themselves. This is where independent research studies must examine some of these claims. Most of the general public is not trained in data collection, analysis, or theory, and so they may be less likely to question official institutions or the media, which often develop their stories with the help of these law enforcement agencies. The key is to introduce independent data collection and analysis.

This chapter highlights competing claims about gangs. On one hand, official institutions will provide a view, and then research studies offer contrary findings. Thus, the organizational scene prior to my arrival highlights the complex political context of the communities and the larger narratives about threat that shapes—and always has shaped—learning about gangs in a context structured by efforts to control, eliminate, or oppress marginalized groups in the United States.

The #1 City for Gangs in Texas: El Paso?

The gang scene in El Paso during the 1980s carried forward structural difficulties from previous decades involving a lack of sustained funding for community programs and a fear about re-emerging violence. On February 16, 1981, two news articles were featured on the front page of *El Paso Times's* B section. One story focused on providing a current assessment of the gang problem, and the second account examined the issues that were occurring in the 1950s when gang activity was at a high point.³ A youth services division officer stated that there were more gangs in existence in 1981, but they weren't discussed in the same way as in the 1950s due to a fear that media reporting could inspire the gangs to engage in more violence. Most members were described as joining for self-protection. For example, the officer said a 15-year-old girl had told him that other kids won't mess with a chola because it meant they would have to fight all the cholas. Nevertheless, violence still occurred as it was revealed that a young man was shot and killed the previous summer in the Salazar Housing Projects and six gang-related shootings had occurred in the past six months.⁴ Toward the end of 1981, the T-birds reiterated the continued harassment by the police.⁵ Several members who were in their 20s and even in their 40s explained how they were an athletic club seeking to improve the community by sponsoring activities for young people. A police lieutenant stated there was a wide variety of members in gangs and they joined for different reasons. Another officer agreed that some officers used harassment tactics, but most were simply doing their job. The decade concluded with a call for the new mayor to provide more funding for gang-intervention programs as violence between gangs was at a high in 1985 with nine deaths, as well as a shooting death in 1988 at the Fiesta de las Flores annual Hispanic celebration.⁶

If there had been a lack of media attention focused on gangs in the 1980s, this quickly changed in the 1990s. A Texas Attorney General Report released in 1992 stated that El Paso had the worst gang problem in Texas based on surveys conducted with metropolitan police specialists in cities with populations greater than 250,000.⁷ First, law enforcement officials reported a higher number of gangs and gang members in El Paso compared to other large size cities in Texas (e.g., Dallas, Houston, and San Antonio). Most of El Paso's gangs were considered turf-based (41 percent), followed by delinquent (29 percent), gain-oriented (25 percent), or violent/hate-related (4 percent). Second, El Paso was found to have a higher number of gang-related homicides, with thirteen gang-on-gang murders and nine murders involving a gang member killing someone who was not in a gang.⁸ In conclusion, the Texas Attorney General Report stated that Texas had an "emerging" gang problem as opposed to a "chronic" gang problem. Nevertheless, the report characterized El Paso as standing out as a center of relatively intense gang activity.⁹

The initial response by the media to this report involved an interview with a gang task force sergeant, who explained the findings.[10] The sergeant estimated that the city had 290 gangs with 15–30 members, but seven gangs had 150 members or more, for a total number of gang members of 4,908, with 924 juveniles (19 percent) and 342 females (7 percent). Gangs were spread throughout the city, but only 3 percent of gang members committed hard-core crimes like murder. The problem had been traditionally in South and Central El Paso but had since moved to the Lower Valley, Northeast, and Westside. As much as 75 percent of the members belonged to trend or fad gangs, whereas established gangs included the T-Birds, Diablos, Fatherless, Chicos Tres, Sunset Heights, Los Vatos de la Sana, and Mestizos. One gang task force officer stated that gangs were more mobile, with El Paso gang members committing crimes and then fleeing to California.[11] The Texas Attorney General Report supported a belief that Los Angeles gang members were migrating to El Paso. Another officer contradicted this point, saying that he hadn't seen any Los Angeles gangs in El Paso. A magistrate judge concurred that Crips and Bloods were not a local problem and that such allegations were simply rumors.

Not entirely convinced with the accuracy of the Texas Attorney General's findings, a reporter with the *El Paso Herald-Post*, Raul Hernandez, wrote an article critiquing the El Paso Police Department's Gang Task Force's roster of gang members.[12] The newspaper reporter inquired how a high school cheerleader with a 4.0 GPA, an 8-year-old child, and a 43-year-old hard-core man could all be on the same gang list. The article summarized how El Paso was placed in the limelight after being listed as the state's Gang Capital in April. The *El Paso Herald-Post* obtained a copy of the long alphabetical list of members in June and reported that much of the information was incomplete, inflated, or contained bogus information. The 5,000 gang members and 270 gangs included information interpreted from graffiti, children under the age of 10, and groups not typically considered gangs, such as car clubs and dance groups. The mother of the 8-year-old child was upset after learning that her son was listed as a gang member. She said her son was a good boy and showed his third grade report card, which showed A's and B's. The El Paso National Association for the Advancement of Colored People (NAACP), along with the American Civil Liberties Union (ACLU), were going to look further into the list for bias because such secret lists could be used for, or based on, harassment. After the *El Paso Herald-Post* scrutinized the list, a sergeant conceded that the police department would re-evaluate the gang list by having a criminal analysis detective and city auditor re-check the information. One task force member reported that the cheerleader was an informant, and another officer described her as an associate of a California-based gang, but she had been removed from the list because she no longer met the criteria for inclusion. At the same time that the task force numbers were being scrutinized, several students at Hanks High School filed accusations against the specialized unit for brutality. Four task-force officers were reassigned to other units, and a lawsuit filed against the officers was unsuccessful. As discovered in *Gang Life in Two Cities*, Denver also had a problematic gang list that, when compared to the population by age and race, resulted in two out three black males in the city being considered gang members by law enforcement officials. Contrary to El Paso, Denver advocacy groups never attained a copy of the secret gang list, but their story of racial profiling did achieve national news attention.

Four years later it appeared that the internal audit in El Paso didn't affect the numbers. In August 1996, the police department stated there were 5,000 gang members in 471 gangs.[13] This news report was accompanied by information provided by the El Paso County Juvenile Probation Department, which found an increase in the number of referrals from 2,042 in 1991 to 3,117 in 1995.[14] Violent referrals also increased from 258 in 1991 to 375 in 1995, although 40 percent of this increase was attributed to the number of referrals for "engaging in organized criminal activity (mostly gang activity)." It was not clear from the news report what this behavior consisted of and why it had increased so much in its occurrence in 1994 and 1995. On March 2, 1996, the *El Paso Herald-Post* reported a gang shooting that resulted in the death of three El Paso teenagers. Several additional gang-related killings occurred in 1996 and 1997.[15]

As noted throughout several chapters, most news articles were not attached with research studies. Thus, many allegations captured the perceptions of individual actors, but rarely could we explain beyond the incident why these events were occurring or the context that was the most problematic. Criminologist Ramiro Martinez studied six cities that had high proportions of Latino residents and found that, despite having social and economic conditions like blacks, these communities had lower homicide rates.[16] He argued that this pattern could largely be attributed to the importance of the neighborhood, immigration, and higher social integration into the labor market. Thus, contrary to the violent gang-member stereotype often given to Latinos, the outcome was more of a paradox. First, he analyzed the annual homicide averages from 1985 to 1995. Of the six cities analyzed (Chicago, El Paso, Houston, Miami, San Antonio, and San Diego), El Paso had the lowest citywide homicide rate of .067 per 1,000 residents, whereas Miami had the highest at .378. When Martinez examined El Paso neighborhoods, South Central El Paso had the highest rate at .18, whereas Northeast El Paso had the lowest rate at .058. Based on listed motives in 1990, police department reports listed 2 percent of the motives citywide were attributed to drugs, 14 percent attributed to gangs, and 28 percent attributed to escalation (arguments that escalated from a non-lethal event to death). Of the six cities, El Paso ranked fourth in motives attributed to gangs. Interestingly, the homicide rate from 1980 to 1995 by race and ethnicity was only slightly higher for Latinos than for whites, and much lower than that for blacks. Hence, based on research data during this time frame, gang violence wasn't higher nor was homicide violence. Since Martinez included two additional cities in Texas (Houston and San Antonio), his findings found more gang-motivated homicides citywide in San Antonio (25 percent) compared to El Paso (14 percent) and Houston (2 percent).

Mike Tapia studied the evolution of gangs in San Antonio, Texas, and noted higher levels of gang activity after the 1950s.[17] Based on his analysis of San Antonio Police Department homicide data from 1993 to 2003, he found that 1993 was a particularly violent year with slightly less than 240 homicides, of which a little more than fifty were considered gang homicides. Although the number of homicides decreased substantially to a low of around seventy-five in 2003, gang homicides continued to be about 15.7 percent, which he stated was comparable to the national rate. Based on the data analyzed by Martinez and Tapia, it appears that San Antonio had a higher rate of gang homicides, but these numbers may have been reduced after 1996. Not having the number of homicides that were listed as gang homicides in El Paso after 1996 leaves me to question whether San Antonio remained higher or became equal with El Paso. Either outcome may be possible, but clearly San Antonio had a much higher overall homicide rate, a topic I will revisit in chapter 7.

Looking back at what was reported in the media, there were certain events involving the El Paso Police Department that stood out. The El Paso Police Department Tactical Team Gang Intervention, founded in the late 1970s as an anti-robbery squad and composed of thirty-nine officers, shifted its focus in the late 1980s to gangs. In the early 1990s the gang unit began documenting the number of members and gangs, but it came with a wide variety of complaints. In 1992 the El Paso Police Department's Youth Service Division began devoting time at middle schools in El Paso and Ysleta school districts as part of Operation Community Action to Control Hoodlums (CATCH).[18] The focus of the CATCH program was to make arrests and collect information for criminal investigations.[19] Determined to establish a presence and justify the value of the gang unit, a police officer named Mary Lou Carrillo reported in her six years of experience working with gangs that parents continued to believe their kids were not involved; therefore the gang unit also sought to educate the community on how children could join these groups as early as third or fourth grade. Consequently, the gang unit continued its assertion of how youth 10 years of age or younger could be gang members. Mary Lou Carrillo reported how the police chief created a Drive-by Shooting Response Team in 1995, which investigated shootings until an arrest was completed. The unit was reported to be successful in ensuring an increased arrest rate, but these results were not independently verified. Nevertheless, the El Paso Police Department continued to face challenges beyond the lawsuit filed in the early 1990s against the gang unit. In December 1998, a 15-year-old boy was shot and killed by an undercover officer and another uniformed law enforcement policeman while they were working in specialized units for the El Paso Police Department.[20] Both officers were eventually fired for violating the department's use-of-force policy despite being cleared twice of criminal liability by a grand jury.[21] The officers stated they were doing their job, whereas the mother, who witnessed the shooting, said her son did nothing wrong when he was shot in the head and then shot several more times.[22] The autopsy determined Nicholas was shot once in the head, once in the chest, once in the right arm, once in the right thigh, and grazed in the left arm. The officers attempted to appeal their dismissal by stating some of their justification for the shooting was because the young man was a known member of a South El Paso gang and involved in an auto-theft ring. However, the defense argued that while the teen had traffic tickets, he had no history of violence. A forensic scientist contradicted the officers' claims as to whether one of the officers could have been injured by a moving car.[23] The police chief, Carlos Leon, testified in the decision to fire the two police officers. The chief advocated a new philosophy of discipline in the police department.[24] In May 2000, an independent arbitrator for the police department ruled the punishment was too severe, and both officers were placed back in uniform.[25] The outcome of the mother's wrongful-death civil lawsuit against the city is unclear. Based on the data available, a significant portion of homicides occurring in 1998 occurred at the hands of law enforcement officers.[26] Thus, removing officer-involved shootings could make the city of El Paso safer, and the rate of these shootings may actually surpass those labeled as gang-motivated.

From 1999 to 2005, the news stories ranged from the central regional command and the police department's gang unit initiating a two-day operation to arrest ninety alleged gang members.[27] An officer stated that this was the first time they had focused on arresting alleged gang members. The roundup was a spinoff of a previous police department operation used in 1998 called JAWS, or Jail All Wanted Subjects. It was reported there were 278 active gangs with 6,973 active members. Despite the gang unit in El Paso having a questionable beginning and being modeled after a disbanded task force in Los Angeles, it appeared that the decision to disband the Community Response Against Street Hoodlums (CRASH) program met resistance.[28] The unit was credited with decreasing the number of drive-bys, and it had received support from individuals writing letters to the editor reporting a fear that gang crime would increase without its presence, and so the unit was allowed to continue operating.[29] There was a gang-related homicide in the shooting death of a 15-year-old, and the offender was sentenced to thirty years in prison.[30] The young man was the tenth homicide of the year in 1999. El Paso law enforcement received $200,000 in federal funds to reduce gun crimes.[31] They were also receiving money to combat gangs, and the El Paso Police Department utilized its funding from the Edward Byrne Grant to buy new AR-15 rifles. In addition, El Paso was awarded money to hire a part-time anti-gang prosecutor as part of Project Safe Neighborhoods.[32]

The 1980s and 1990s institutionalized gang enforcement by identifying gang members and gangs without having to defend the accuracy of such claims. Data were being used by these agencies as a means to demonstrate a need for resources on the basis of a claim of an existing problem. Research studies have contradicted the Texas Attorney General's ranking of El Paso as the number one city for gangs in Texas, indicating the fluctuating nature of these events and how violent crime rates have continued to decrease nationally since the early 1990s.[33]

Do Gangs and Gang Members Exist in New Mexico?

For a state that had been stigmatized and unaccepted, New Mexico's overall isolation seemed to provide a buffer to similar challenges that other states such as California, Illinois, New York, and Texas were experiencing. Chronologically, most of the attention regarding gangs in this region was focused on El Paso, Texas, but in the late 1980s New Mexico officials joined in the process of institutionalizing gangs. The population of Las Cruces had been growing; in 1960 there were 30,000 residents, and by 1990 there were 62,000 residents. The Governor's Organized Crime Prevention Commission (GOPC) published a report in 1991 focusing on New Mexico's street gangs. The Executive Summary outlined how the focus on street gangs began in 1987 after consultation with Oregon and California law enforcement officials, who believed that such gangs could ". . . become extremely burdensome to New Mexico society and law enforcement."[34] Law enforcement gang experts from these states assessed the nature of gangs in Albuquerque and diagnosed the city as having an emerging gang problem. It is ironic that the gang assessment came from California and Oregon, whereas gangs had reportedly been a persistent issue in El Paso from an earlier point in time and shared more regional similarities with New Mexico. These outside law enforcement experts recommended that local officials form a multi-jurisdictional task force comprised of state, local, and private entities to combat gangs. Subsequently, Albuquerque, New Mexico's largest city, formed a police gang unit in 1988. The GOPC formed the New Mexico Street Gang Task force in January 1990. In July 1990, the Commission contacted thirty local law enforcement agencies in jurisdictions throughout New Mexico where an estimated 127 gangs with between 4,200 and 5,800 members; the majority of these gangs were in Albuquerque, and 80 percent of them were involved in drug trafficking. It was alleged that gangs such as the California-based Bloods and Crips had migrated into New Mexico to sell drugs. However, most of the local gang members were Latino. Gangs were described as an organized crime problem. The survey results from Doña Ana County, with Las Cruces as its largest urban center, reported the presence of ten street gangs with about 400 members who were Latino and black, including members of the Bloods and the Crips, which allegedly controlled the trafficking of crack cocaine. State officials began working on gang legislation to suppress gang-related violence, and the Las Cruces Police Department became one of the participating organizations. The 1993 and 1994 Street Gang Updates provided by the Department of Public Safety continued this "danger, danger" estimation by arguing that gangs were only getting worse and growing in membership. Special attention was devoted to a reported increase in girl gang members, People and Folk Nations (i.e., Chicago-based gangs), gangs in prisons, and gangs on Indian reservations.[35]

Criminologists Charles Katz and Vincent Webb conducted research on several gang units.[36] They found that neighborhood groups had existed in Albuquerque for a long time, but it was only in the mid-1970s that public official started identifying them as a problem. The Albuquerque Police Department received consultation from the Los Angeles Police and Sheriff Departments in the 1960s on how to begin identifying gang members. Police officers in Albuquerque believed that California-based gangs had migrated to the city during the 1980s. They considered black street gang members belonging to the Bloods and Crips to be involved in the distribution of drugs. Katz and Webb received information that the specialized gang unit in Albuquerque was created in 1989 and included five officers. By 1993 the gang unit had documented 3,253 gang members in 155 gangs, but they believed the number of individuals involved in gangs was between 6,000 and 7,000. The overall purpose of Katz and Webb's study was to understand how police gang units respond to community gang problems. They did this by doing ridealongs with police officers, interviewing gang unit officers, reviewing official documents, and conducting interviews with non-gang unit personnel and stakeholders. Their book, *Policing Gangs in America*, provides some important critiques about the rationale regarding gang units and whether they are effective in reducing gang membership or gang crime.

Throughout this time period of numerical growth in Albuquerque, the border region counties in Southern New Mexico remained small and isolated. They also lacked attention focused on gangs. The city of Las Cruces in Doña Ana County became the exception as it grew to become New Mexico's second largest city by 1980. Despite being only forty-five miles away from El Paso, the development of gangs in Southern New Mexico was distinct because it was not entirely clear whether it was produced by actual gang problems, or rather by state initiatives focused on gang enforcement and public officials who wanted to appear diligent in addressing these fears. With increasing initiatives statewide, the Las Cruces Police Department formed a gang suppression unit in 1989. In April 1990, there were seventeen gangs identified with an estimated 650 members. According to the City of Las Cruces Gang Task Force (Task Force) Work Session Report, the Task Force was established on October 15, 1990, with its first meeting of seven members occurring in February 1991.[37] They focused on four areas: a law ordinance review, needs assessment, community awareness, and community resources. In October 1991, the Task Force was expanded to eleven members. One of the eleven members, criminal justice professor Larry Mays from New Mexico State University, conducted a survey of 164 institutions for which the majority (61 percent) reported not encountering gang victimization. In a community survey of 492 respondents, 89.3 percent of the respondents had not been threatened or bothered by a gang member, and 96 percent of individuals completing the survey along with their family members had never been hurt or victimized by a gang member. However, a little more than half of the respondents reported thinking gangs were a fairly serious or very serious problem. Additional surveys of school administrators and at community forums were conducted. In the final report produced in February 1993, the Task Force provided the following as the official version regarding how these efforts were initiated:

> In the summer of 1990, gang-related problems within the City of Las Cruces escalated to the point where the community became concerned about the seriousness of the level of gang activity. No longer were gang-related activities resolved by fist fights or dialogue; the use of weapons and evidence of gang activity throughout the community were on the rise.

The data to provide support for such conclusions may not have existed, as was noted when the research on this geographic area began to be published. However, based on the Las Cruces Gang Task Force survey's internal research, 77 percent of the fifty-six respondents believed the gang problem was serious, and these fears were supported by an annual increase in the number of juvenile referrals from 765 in 1987 to a high of 2,417 in 1992. In the school section, it was reported that in the spring of 1992 a middle school student was shot on the school grounds, and 67 percent of middle school students and 50 percent of high school students reported occurrences of gang intimidation. In July 1991, the Las Cruces

Public School Board of Education adopted a policy on gangs.[38] After providing information from law enforcement, schools, community reports, and an inter-agency team, these stakeholders offered the following advice: "It will take an effort by the entire community to implement the recommendations submitted in this report in order to have a positive impact on gang-related problems and activities." From 1992 to 2001, the number of gangs fluctuated between eight to eighteen gangs, and membership ranged from 250 to 800 members.[39]

In one of the earliest published research studies on gangs in Las Cruces, criminologists Larry Mays and Thomas Winfree, along with their graduate student Stacey Jackson, outlined how the initial response to gangs in the area started with denial, but then some graffiti and drive-bys in the late 1980s in conjunction with media reports led to overreaction.[40] A series of town meetings were held by the newly created Task Force. There was a wide variety of opinions regarding whether Las Cruces had a gang problem, but overall it was not perceived to be as bad as other cities. The researchers believed most members were joining gangs due to friendship or family. The gangs appeared to meet the needs of some youth. To investigate further, these researchers joined with colleagues to administer a questionnaire to randomly selected ninth- and eleventh-grade students in March 1991. They found difficulty with how gangs were defined, ranging from self-identification to more restrictive definitions requiring an initiation process, and this was reflected in the number of youth who self-reported gang involvement.[41] They found 45 percent of the sample to have some interest in gangs. Of those expressing interest, only 33 percent were active gang members under the looser definition, and with the restrictive definition only 18 percent were active members. Thus, most of the youth were primarily wannabees (interested in gangs but not joining) or former members (least common). In another publication using the same data, Mays and Winfree, along with a graduate student, outlined how this geographic area possessed a 170-mile border with Mexico and some of the nations' oldest gangs existed in El Paso.[42] In 1990, the Las Cruces population was listed at 62,000 residents, whereas El Paso was a city of 581,000. The county (Doña Ana) was reported to have high levels of immigration, both legal and illegal, during the past decade, which made it one of the ten fastest-growing areas in the nation. The authors wrote, "It is an area of cultural blending and culture clashes, an area with some degree of affluence and abject poverty."[43] In this rather unique setting, they found self-reported gang members claiming to be involved in higher rates of offending than non-gang youth and wannabes.

Another opportunity for social scientists to conduct research in the mid-1990s came through the National Evaluation of the Gang Resistance Education and Training (GREAT) program.[44] Criminologist Tom Winfree, who was a key researcher conducting these studies, compared Las Cruces students with other areas including Phoenix, Arizona, and examined different criminological theories. Police officers who ran the GREAT program received training in Phoenix, and the program was implemented with seventh-grade students in three middle schools in Las Cruces that were targeted due to reported gang problems.[45] Las Cruces was described as primarily Caucasian but with a large Latino minority that exceeded 35 percent. The per-capita crime rate in Las Cruces was lower than national averages except for rape. It was estimated there were 350 gang members in twenty-three different gangs; in comparison, Phoenix had 3,800 confirmed active members in 140 street gangs. In other words, Phoenix had ten times the number of gang members compared to Las Cruces, and Las Cruces was described as more pro-police and less delinquent. This rate, however, was not compared to the population; even if the 350 gang members were used as a base, there would be a higher rate of gang involvement in Las Cruces (5.5) compared to Phoenix (3.83), thus begging the question of whether the number of gang members or the level of activity was the problem. The researchers themselves, based on the data they reviewed, did not consider gangs in Las Cruces to be more serious than in Phoenix. They stated:

> Phoenix is clearly a city with much more crime than Las Cruces, both in terms of the volume of crime and the per-capita rates. From a self-report perspective, however, the Phoenix students may not have been more gang-involved than their peers in Las Cruces *once we account for the attitudes and orientations of the students.* We suspect that youth gang members in the two cities appear to be at different stages in gang development.[46]

The authors considered the city of Phoenix to provide earlier exposure to both gang and drug behavior, and thus more further along the highly differential "deviantizing process."[47]

Criminologists Winfree and Mays continued to serve as advisors to students who completed their master's theses by studying gangs through the criminological theory of social learning and by evaluating the GREAT program.[48] Three theses during this time are worth highlighting. First, Jackson collected 202 questionnaires at community meetings around Las Cruces regarding gang activity and then conducted a content analysis of local newspapers from October 1, 1990, through October 1, 1991, in her master's thesis.[49] Ninety-one respondents offered support for more employment opportunities for youth, community centers, and counseling services; 88 percent of respondents supported increased recreational activities, and 63 percent thought more police officers were needed to control gang activity. Most respondents considered drugs and gangs to be synonymous (60 percent), and perceived the court system to be ineffective in stopping or curtailing gang activity (81 percent). Regarding the content analysis, the overall message presented in the media involving 167 news articles over a period of one year was the emphasis on increased crime control with law enforcement primarily used as the authoritative source. Despite a punishment message designed by law enforcement and the media, Jackson was impressed to see that the community did not fall for the media hype regarding gangs and instead favored primarily social services to alleviate gang activity. A thesis written by Delgado included interviews with several members of the largest gang in Las Cruces, which went by the name East Side.[50] Delgado wrote that the LCPD Gang Task Force reported in 1996 that schools were the primary recruiting area for gangs, particularly the middle schools. The largest gangs were reported to be East Side, with other gangs consisting of street gangs, drug/turf gangs, taggers, and stoners. Delgado explained why it was difficult to obtain accurate numbers regarding the current gang situation. Third, Arevalo Becerril's master's thesis focused on three young Latino gang members and five factors (marginalized environments, pervasive violence, disrupted family systems, underground market economies, and psycho-social stressors) that contributed to gang involvement.[51] Arevalo Becerril argued that the criminological literature tended to pathologize gang members and legitimize power structures. He emphasized understanding the difficult situations that many of these young people encounter and remembering that they are human beings when designing policies to address these issues. These three theses were unique because they acquired information from the community and from gang members, and they evaluated the legitimacy of the concerns that were presented to support increased punishment.

Some of the gang activity reported in the newspapers from 1999 to 2005 included an ongoing conflict between the Dukes gang and Mesquite Locos at Gadsden High School, which included threats of drive-by shootings.[52] Three students wearing black ski masks burst into a classroom at Mayfield High School searching for rival gang members.[53] From 2004 to 2006, the Latino Governor of New Mexico sought legislation to increase punishment for those participating in gangs.[54] Each year these bills failed to make it out of the Judiciary Commission due to fear of encountering constitutional scrutiny in the court system.[55] Another Gang Task Force initiative was launched after school officials reported a dozen gang-related fights at the beginning of the school year. School officials continued to take a zero-tolerance approach. The Las Cruces Police Department estimated that there were 250 to 350 members with eight active gangs; the statewide estimate was 300 gangs and 6,500 members. Most crime in Las Cruces did not stand out when compared to nationwide trends except for rape, which was higher than the national average and had been for a long period of time.[56] Murders were infrequent. One exception was a 14-year-old boy who was shot and killed by two young men in 2004.[57] One of the individuals admitted to being in a gang, but the incident was not considered gang-related. The city had three homicides in 2004, one in 2003, and three in 2002.[58] Prevention efforts were increased as the county received a $475,000 state grant to continue its Gang Resistance Education and Training (GREAT) programming at four middle schools.[59] Doña Ana County was awarded $240,000 in federal money to end gun violence and crimes related to drug trafficking and gangs.[60]

The Challenge of Defining a Gang and a Gang Member

Assessing the nature and extent of gangs and the number of gang members in the areas of El Paso and New Mexico presented a challenge. Law enforcement agencies were using a broad definition to identify the number of gang members. Classifying an individual as a member of a group was different from making an arrest in that, for an arrest, there should be alleged probable cause that a crime had been committed and that this was the person who had committed the act. As the literature has shown, individuals can often join or leave gangs with little acknowledgement, whereas in the law enforcement framework they remain in the system for a period of five years.[61] Gang labeling is not included in constitutional protections or under any form of judicial scrutiny. Individuals were not advised of their Miranda rights before being asked about gang involvement, which has many forms of consequences later in life in the form of injunctions, enhancements, vertical prosecution, and housing restrictions if incarcerated. In the late 1980s and early 1990s, gang intelligence became more formalized with gang lists, which allowed law enforcement agencies to provide the size and scope of the problem.

Several current research studies have attempted to determine the size and scope of gang membership. Criminologists David Pyrooz and Gary Sweeten analyzed the National Longitudinal Survey of Youth from 1997, which included eight subsequent interviews for youth born between 1980 and 1984.[62] They found the prevalence of youth gang membership between the ages of 5 and 17 to be 2 percent, with the age of 14 being the year with the highest membership (5 percent). They noted higher levels of gang membership for males and for blacks and Hispanics. Estimates for a specific city received additional scrutiny as criminologist Mike Tapia utilized various sources of official data and compiled information to compare these numbers with the population.[63] For San Antonio, Texas, he estimated 8.5 percent of Chicano youth were involved in gangs in the 1950s, and slightly less than 10 percent in 2007, thus reinforcing the finding that most youth, and even most youth of color, do not join gangs.

TABLE 3.1
Official Reports of Number of Gangs and Gang Members Compared to the Population

City	No. of Gangs	No. of Gang Members	Population	Rate of Gang Members per 1,000 Residents
El Paso, TX (1992)	290	4,908	546,444	8.98
Las Cruces, NM (1990)	17	650	63,124	10.30
Albuquerque, NM (1993)	155	3,253	406,440	8.00
Phoenix, AZ (1990)	140	3,800	992,511	3.83
Denver, CO (1993)		6,567	508,388	12.92
Ogden, UT (1994)		598	67,557	8.85

Based on the information obtained through this research, El Paso would be considered a chronic gang city and Las Cruces an emergent gang city.[64] Although public officials used these results to justify the existence of a gang problem, they rarely compared the findings with other locations or with the racial and ethnic demographics from which these data were primarily drawn. Different from most places, most residents in the border region were of Mexican descent, but the proportions still underrepresented the number of white youth who belonged to groups considered to be gangs. The numbers continued to fluctuate, but providing data as to lower numbers of gangs or gang members as a benchmark of success was never a requirement. There was some emphasis on decreasing the number of crimes, as seen with El Paso advocating for the importance of the injunction or keeping the CRASH unit, but more so in the effort of maintaining these additional forms of social control. The gang literature has traditionally argued that gang involvement increases delinquent and criminal involvement, but based on these historical observations, such a relationship does not necessarily exist. Although the data may be consistent in individual, anonymous, self-reporting, which makes up a large portion of gang research, it does not necessarily exist on a wider community scale and thus should be evaluated with caution. These numbers continue to perpetuate enhanced social control and differential targeting of blacks, Latinos, and other marginalized racial or ethnic groups in society and follows my argument of a war on gangs outlined in *Gang Life in Two Cities*.

Based on the data analyzed, gangs were not necessarily a problem in Las Cruces and had decreased influence in El Paso since the 1950s. However, money and institutional resources were available for those who could document the presence of gangs and gang members, and both El Paso and Las Cruces created units to put together a list of gang members that was never transparent or independently analyzed. The ways in which law enforcement framed the gang problem coincided with media attention and helped push for institutionalizing gang enforcement due to perceptions that, without such a focus, gangs would continue to grow, become more organized, and increase their involvement in violence and drug trafficking. Independently verifying this information on the other hand did not make exciting news or capture institutional interest.

Exceptions to Gangs: Motorcycle Clubs, Familial Drug Networks, and Prison Gangs

Conceptually, the study of gangs has been kept separate from research on other organizations such as hate groups, motorcycle clubs, drug networks, and prison gangs.[65] However, for setting the geographic context, I will outline several other organizations that were operating in Ciudad Juárez and in Southern New Mexico and El Paso, Texas prior to my arrival in 2006. This will help distinguish the difference between gangs and other types of organizations.

Groups involved in organized crime possess more political and labor networks for the participation in large-scale illegal activities. In 1973, an El Paso District Attorney told the *El Paso Times* that while there may not be mafia in El Paso, there still was organized crime.[66] The Organized Crime Control Unit focused on learning more about criminal organizations, including the possibility of "local hoodlum" connections with La Cosa Nostra and the Dixie Mafia, which was presumed to be in New Orleans. "La Nacha" was described as the most sophisticated organization operating in Juárez, but no such organizations were reported to be operating in El Paso. The Organized Crime Control Unit, which began in 1971 through funding from the State Criminal Justice Council, was terminated by the El Paso Board of Governors in 1974 due to unclear success and accomplishments beyond money for new patrol cars.[67] When the Texas Organized Crime Prevention Council published its report on organized crime in Texas in 1978, many of themes from the Crime Control Unit were found in this document, including the trafficking of drugs through Texas, the role of organized crime, and specific illegal activities such as gambling, stolen property, prostitution, pornography, vehicle thefts, and white-collar crime. They also devoted attention to motorcycle clubs, La Cosa Nostra, and the Dixie Mafia, along with the influence of business professionals and leaders in the community participating in drug trafficking. O. Leon Dobbs, the head of the FBI office in El Paso, stated that four or five prominent El Paso residents invested money in crime, mostly in the drug trade, and then acted like they don't know anything.[68] He offered El Paso residents six weeks to come into his office and tell him what they knew. He didn't work in El Paso long and retired four months later.

A *Chicago Tribune* report continued provoking nationwide fear with the headline titled "Tunnels Carry Mexican Bandits into Border City."[69]

Although the Organized Crime Control Unit was dismantled, this did not mean the federal focus on drugs waned. The El Paso Intelligence Center (EPIC) began operations in August 1974 due to a recommendation to have a regional intelligence center to collect and disseminate information as captured in a report titled "A Secure Border: An Analysis of Issues Affecting the U.S. Department of Justice." Media headlines continued to portray a dangerous image of the border. In 1977, the *Los Angeles Times* wrote a news story with the following headline "A New, Ruthless Breed: Mexican Gangs Pouring Narcotics Across the Border." In this news story, the journalist stated that the Mexican Mafia were moving huge quantities of drugs into the United States.[70] To counter such efforts, the Mexican government began running a program named Operation Condor to target narcotics trafficking, for which one of the three primary routes listed was El Paso.[71]

One of the first major trafficking cases involved Joe Renteria, an El Paso actor and singer, who was sentenced to thirty years after being found guilty of smuggling nine tons of marijuana and cocaine into the United States from Colombia.[72] He was in the 1973 movie *Toke*, which was filmed in El Paso.[73] Also charged were Renteria's press agent, Bill Garcia, and Rick de la Torre, the vice president of First State Bank.[74] Renteria (Bowie High School) and Garcia (Jefferson High School) were both honors graduates in the 1960s. Renteria was held in solitary confinement at La Tuna Federal Correctional Institute. The Drug Enforcement Administration believed they dealt the smuggling ring a major blow with these arrests and convictions, along with the 1976 seizure of 17,000 lbs. of marijuana in Oklahoma and a 1977 plane crash in Colombia that killed one of group's members.[75] The first trial of the "El Paso Ten," so dubbed by the media, only included five individuals from El Paso and resulted in a hung jury. Lee Chagra, the defense attorney who created doubt for the jury, was a successful lawyer who had defended several trafficking cases along with providing defense to Donald Chambers of the Bandidos.[76] Not long after, the FBI was investigating the December 23, 1978, murder of Lee Chagra, who was found shot to death in his law office.[77] His death received national media attention and it allowed justification for El Paso to be labeled "a major new hub of drug traffic."[78] When Mr. Chagra was murdered, there were large amounts of money missing from his office. He had allegedly bet $15,000 on the Sun Bowl football game earlier in the day, but a larger sum of several hundreds of thousands of dollars was stolen. Three men were charged in his death, including the organizer (Louis Esper) and two suspected shooters, David Leon Wallace and Don White, both of whom were Fort Bliss military soldiers. Wallace, originally perceived as the primary assailant, was found guilty and sentenced to the death penalty.[79] He was 20 years old when he was arrested by FBI agents in mother's home in Compton, California. He was the first man to be given the death penalty in El Paso since February 1967.[80] On appeal, Wallace was determined to not be the shooter and was instead given life in prison. After Lee's death, the Chagra family continued to face legal troubles. The murder of U.S. District Judge John H. Wood, Jr., was attributed to Jimmy Chagra, Lee's younger brother, and Charles V. Harrelson.[81]

Research on participants in upper-level drug dealing and drug smuggling often highlight middle- to upper-class backgrounds, often individuals who embraced self-indulgence but did not stand out in a way that made them targets by authority figures.[82] They maintained legitimate occupations and political connections, and they could use their social standing, money, and political connections to bribe and influence public officials. These connections were not available to most lower-level street dealers and drug mules, especially those who were more likely to be targeted and arrested.[83] Social work professors Avelardo Valdez and Charles Kaplan's research on South Texas drug markets found that Mexican Americans and Mexicans had an invitational edge because they had greater levels of association with both legal and illegal markets in the United States and Mexico, which increased the ability to make quick money. This exposed law enforcement personnel and ". . . small and large business owners, civil service workers, government employees (at all branches), retirees, students, and many other individuals . . ." to a level of influence that could sway them to corruption by participating somehow in the drug trafficking business.[84] Valdez and Kaplan found a complex hierarchy that involved the mixing of professionals, criminals, and immigrants, which allowed individuals to blend into the everyday life of these communities. This research study found that the drug market was decentralized and diverse, with individual entrepreneurs operating independently. Anthropologist Howard Campbell's book *Drug War Zone: Frontline Dispatches from the Streets of El Paso and Juárez* portrays a similar picture as Valdez through his ethnographic observations and interviews of community members and practitioners.[85] Campbell emphasized how the U.S. demand for illegal drugs continued to maintain a Drug War Zone between El Paso and Juárez.

Another group receiving a lot of media attention and federal prosecution efforts in the early and late 1970s was the Bandidos Motorcycle Club. In 1972, the founder of the Bandidos, Donald E. Chambers, was arrested along with eleven other individuals for the shotgun deaths of two men found in a shallow desert grave three miles outside of the El Paso city limits.[86] According to a news article in *Texas Monthly*, Chambers started the Bandidos in March 1966 at the age of 36 while working in the shipping docks in Houston, Texas.[87] He was a Vietnam veteran feeling restless and enjoying Harley-Davidsons motorcycles when he began a club of outlaws, most of whom were white males, but Chambers was also open to accepting Latinos. Chambers was sentenced to two consecutive life terms in prison for his part in the murder of two individuals in a drug deal gone bad.[88] An *El Paso Herald-Post* news article in 1976 featured one of the member's funerals (El Chico), who died in a motorcycle accident in Corpus Christi, Texas.[89] More than 300 "brothers" and "sisters" assembled at St. Ignatius Catholic Church in South El Paso to honor the 30-year-old man. The following year, several Bandidos were convicted of murder and sentenced to life in prison for killing three individuals whose bodies were found in Doña Ana, New Mexico.[90] The wife of one of the victims told authorities that her husband went to tell the gang he wanted to quit, but he never returned. By 1979, it was alleged that several Bandidos played a role in the shooting attack of an Assistant U.S. Attorney in San Antonio, Texas, which resulted in police raids in El Paso, Corpus Christi, and San Antonio. In the El Paso raid, they arrested Rudolph James "Shakey" Maio, 31, president of the Bandidos' El Paso chapter and national vice president, along with Ronald Paul "Frankenstein" Drummond, 35, chapter treasurer and two women in their early 20s. The police confiscated several firearms and one pound of marijuana.[91] Federal grand juries were held with secret testimony provided that implicated Bandidos members in allegations involving racketeering, international drug smuggling, gambling, and prostitution.[92] The club was alleged to be operating 40 to 50 prostitutes in bars throughout the city. A federal court jury in Austin, Texas, found El Paso Bandidos leader Rudolph James "Shakey" Maio guilty of felony assault on federal officer and misdemeanor possession of marijuana.[93] Maio and his defense attorney claimed continued harassment from the FBI. A former civilian employee with the El Paso County Sheriff's Department was tried on perjury charges for lying to a federal grand jury in San Antonio earlier in the year. The man had begun working for the El Paso Sheriff's office back in 1973 to gather "intelligence" on the Bandidos, but due to reported threats on his life, he lied to a grand jury and was found guilty of perjury.[94]

Mainstream business officials and motorcycle clubs were different from a third type of organization that primarily involved street youth who organized themselves while incarcerated. Gang scholar Joan Moore's collaborative research in East Los Angeles during two different decades found a significant number of residents who were going to prison in the 1970s primarily due to the use and distribution of narcotics, primarily heroin.[95] Youth gangs had existed in these Los Angeles neighborhoods since the late 1930s and early 1940s. The conditions in the barrios produced a tripartite economy involving legitimate, welfare, and illegal markets. Gangs were territorial and involved in fighting amongst each other. Prison norms were based on socialization in the barrios and conflict existed between different neighborhoods. State-raised youth began to form prison gangs to respond to the challenges they were encountering during incarceration. Moore emphasized how the primarily Mexican and Mexican American residents of East Los Angeles were socially marginalized, effectively a class of people left out of society.[96]

Four years after the movie *American Me* was released in 1992, which focused on the Mexican Mafia based in California, an *El Paso Times* article reported that prison gangs were real and El Paso was home to sixty parolees who belonged to such groups.[97] The *El Paso Times* listed the strongest local prison gang as the Barrio Aztecas with 500 members. Prison officials reported this gang had been trying to run the jail and had engaged in violence with staff, other inmates, and their own members. Seven inmates died in county jails between March 1994 and March 1995, including three homicides and three suicides. In 1997, an alleged member of the Mexican Mafia was killed in the El Paso County Jail.[98] One of the defendants, Richard Morales Castillo, had previously been found guilty of two other murders.[99] Castillo was first arrested for murder in 1980 at the age of 15. He was later arrested in 1993 for the death of a 20-year old woman and sentenced to prison. The final charge over the death of Richard Bracknell ended in a hung jury, Castillo was found guilty in the retrial and was sentenced to life in prison.[100] In another case, federal and local authorities launched an eight-month investigation into an additional killing inside El Paso County Jail, which resulted in the arrest of fifty-nine men and three women who were all alleged members of Barrio Azteca under Operation Carnalitos.[101] Authorities stated that although the individuals were involved in the smuggling of heroin from Mexico, the gang members did not have close ties to the Juárez drug cartel. The incident that sparked the investigation was the 1994 murder of a Texas Syndicate member, a 1995 beating, and a 1997 killing. The Texas Syndicate is considered one of the earliest prison gangs to form in Texas in 1975.[102] This prison gang has also received more research attention regarding how it formed.[103] Officials have said Barrio Azteca was created in the late 1980s by inmates from West Texas who banded together to protect themselves from other prison gangs.[104] Several of the members were being charged under the Federal Racketeer Influenced and Corrupt Organizations Act (RICO). There were reported conflicts between the Aztecas and the Mexican Mafia.[105] They were also reported to charge taxes to drug dealers.[106] Although La Tuna was considered a lower-level federal prison, one of the oral history respondents stated that this prison was extremely dangerous because of the Barrio Aztecas.

The City of El Paso used a civil gang injunction against thirty-nine alleged members of Barrio Azteca in Segundo Barrio back in 2003, and it lasted for two years.[107] These individuals were not allowed to associate with one another, had a 10:00 P.M. curfew, couldn't use cellphones or pagers in public, and certain locations were off-limits. Violating the injunction resulted in a Class A misdemeanor punishable by up to one year in jail and a $4,000 fine. At the time the injunction was passed, El Paso estimated it had 486 gangs with 5,445 members. Officials stated that Barrio Azteca was targeted because it was considered the "most violent" gang in El Paso. The *El Paso Times* was so in favor of the injunction that they wrote several editorials praising its success and claimed that it was a successful model from Chicago.[108] The editors must have overlooked how the Chicago injunction was ruled unconstitutional by the U.S. Supreme Court in 1999.[109] Despite the heavy attention given locally to the Barrio Aztecas, this group was not included in any of the prison gang research that focused on Texas.[110]

Deportations ensured that Barrio Aztecas existed on both sides of the border. Several news articles featured how members of this group were deported.[111] Federal efforts through the U.S. Immigration and Customs Enforcement (ICE) focused on deportation and incarceration, including "Operation Community Shield," "Operation Predator," and "Operation Return to Sender." From 2005 to 2008, federal agents arrested a total of 11,106 alleged street gang members and associates nationwide.[112] Immigration officials worked closely with local law enforcement to target undocumented individuals in cities across the nation. The individuals arrested were deported, held in immigration detention centers, or sentenced to federal prison. Law Professor Jennifer M. Chacón critiqued how the gang label established broad parameters that allowed marginal and even non-gang members to be caught in a net for deportation.[113] For example, none of these individuals received a court hearing to prove beyond a reasonable doubt whether they were in fact gang members; instead their immigration status prevented access to the U.S. judicial system. In addition, many of these individuals may have never committed a crime. Law Professor David Cole described how immigration laws were powerful tools to prevent individuals from having access to criminal courts where constitutional rights and safeguards apply.[114] In addition, these laws allowed individuals to be deported for a wide range of technical infractions. Cole argued that after the terrorist attacks on September 11, 2001, the United States continued its long historical practice of ethnic profiling with the social constructions of "enemy aliens" and "enemy races," which only served to undermine the country's legitimacy by creating double standards. According to Cole, immigration policies continued to have numerous problems, including the expansion of the federal government practices of deporting, detaining, and denying human rights for undocumented immigrants.

In 2004, conflicts with the Aztecas and its rival the Mexicas were occurring in Cereso prison in Juárez.[115] Riots and deaths at Cereso prison had occurred in December and March, and several Azteca members were sent to other prisons to reduce the conflicts.[116] Officials continued to describe the violence as being linked to the Juárez cartel.[117] There were fears from affluent businessmen regarding kidnappings in Juárez, and FBI officials held workshops for some of these families in El Paso on how to protect themselves.[118] Juárez officials reported 122 homicides as of October 1999, with 80 percent of the incidents estimated to involve youths between the ages of 13 and 17.[119] A sociology professor from the University of Texas at El Paso stated that cartels were using young people as both drug dealers and as executioners. In the late 1990s, national attention shifted toward Ciudad Juárez for a large number of feminicides.[120] Amnesty International counted 370 female murders from 1993 to 2003, and most of these incidents did not result in an arrest or conviction. Allegations as to who could be committing these murders ranged from a maquiladora bus driver, to an Egyptian chemist, to drug cartels, to public officials. Maquiladoras, officially known as the Border Industrialization Program (BIP), were established in 1965.[121] It was estimated that by 1974 there were sixty-two plants employing 10,000 workers, and by the 1980s there were 180 plants employing more than 100,000 workers. The majority of the workers were female (85 percent), and this system offered low pay, long hours, and disrupting patriarchy. In 2004, a newspaper reported information regarding the Carrillo Fuentes drug cartel and how eleven bodies found in Juárez were suspected to be from a rival drug cartel.[122] Cartel killings began to increase, and they were believed to be due to drug seizures around 2004 and 2005, but the homicide rate at the time was considered to be lower than that of Chicago.[123]

In 2002, an incident on the U.S. portion of the border occurred between Anapra in New Mexico and Anapra, Mexico, when two El Paso FBI agents were beaten by eight alleged members of a Mexican gang based in Anapra known as "Siete Dos" ("Seven Two").[124] The agents had staked out the railroad in Sunland Park to stop train robberies. Residents began throwing rocks at the agents, and when they crossed into Mexico they were beaten with sticks and pipes. One of the agents had severe injuries and went into a coma. She was able to return to work six weeks later, and she began speaking about the incident. She described attempting to stop a man who was fleeing across the border. She (five feet and four inches tall and weighing 130 pounds) jumped on the back of a man who was six feet tall and weighing 200 pounds. As he fled under the fence, she was carried along and that's when rocks began to be thrown. There appeared to be some confusion as to whether Mexican and or U.S. authorities were at fault for some of these actions or the subsequent arrests.[125] Burglars from Anapra continued to be seen as a problem.[126] The number of crimes reportedly declined after the U.S. government built a twelve-foot fence in 1996.[127]

The organizational scene prior to my arrival included a lot of reporting that the number of gang members in El Paso, along the U.S.-Mexico Border, and in New Mexico were greater in number than most areas in the country. Despite the estimates, the data was not consistent as toward the accuracy of these claims or how they were produced. Research findings challenged most of these assertions since El Paso had one of the lowest homicide rates among large sized U.S. cities and how the creation of gangs in southern New Mexico was more of a moral panic rather than a real gang problem. Data gathering on behalf of law enforcement officials who were not trained in research experienced difficulties in that they simply needed to exhibit there was a presence so that they could apply for federal funding and create joint task forces between multiple jurisdictions. The focus on street gangs appeared overstated as several other organizations such as organized crime, motorcycle clubs, and prison gangs maintained a stronger invitational edge on illicit activities occurring in the community. Social networks beyond the barrio were needed to change a social group to become something bigger and many of these manifestations were introduced by the state through prison incarceration and deportation. However, the individuals who were perceived as mainstream had the potential to have the strongest financial support whereas those with prison and gang ties were targeted for more punitive policies. Other acts of violence, such as those occurring against women went underreported, unsolved, and largely ignored.

PART TWO
An Ethnographic Foundation

Part Two will highlight my field observations and interviews conducted during this seven-year period living along the U.S.-Mexico border. Moving toward an ethnographic analysis will also incorporate other sources of data collection to supplement the qualitative findings. In the beginning, a lot of my work required establishing the existence of an issue quantitatively before I could use immersion to answer the questions that resulted from these research studies. Contrary to other methodologies, ethnography places the researcher in direct contact with the individuals and social issues of interest in the actual geographic context. The researchers' background along with various forms of intersectionality, including class, ethnicity, gender, language, race, citizenship, and level of street versus academic smarts, influences the levels of rapport and commitment to understanding whether such forms of adversity are perceived as a mutual problem.[1] My shared ancestral background with New Mexico's residents along with the investment of seeing my children successfully grow up in the area shaped my community interests. Based on this foundation, my research was designed to address various forms of racialized inequalities that had been institutionalized historically.

CHAPTER FOUR

How Youth of Mexican Descent Encounter Criminalization

When my family and I moved from Denver to Las Cruces in 2006, we enrolled our oldest daughter in sixth grade at the middle school and our two other children at the elementary school. My oldest daughter had the hardest transition and began encountering problems. It began with a lack of response from administrators regarding her schoolwork, and then came problems as she got into trouble with her friends, and then boys starting to come into the picture. She came home from school and told me about fights after school where the students would shake hands and then slug it out in the desert. To help provide an outlet for her, we signed her up for volleyball. Sports were probably the most frequently used activity to keep youth and their families busy with games and practices. It was around this time that I joined several colleagues to evaluate Disproportionate Minority Contact (DMC) for the State of New Mexico. In addition, I joined a colleague to study DMC for the judicial district where I was living, Doña Ana. For the first time in my academic career, I had professional credentials and a tenure track position at New Mexico State University.

Opportunities in my department allowed me to begin working in an official research capacity where I was given access to judges, prosecutors, members of law enforcement, school officials, and various community practitioners working to reduce juvenile delinquency and status offenses. Based upon media coverage of my previous work and background, I was regularly invited to speak to schools, at-risk youth, and parents. I began to realize the struggle of raising children in an area without many resources beyond sports. Although my interest from the beginning was gangs, the process for learning about these groups began indirectly through learning about juvenile delinquency, juvenile justice, and the larger community. Beginning this work indirectly allowed me to analyze gangs and gang activity in a broader context of community issues. Because I already had established an inside and ex-gang member viewpoint on gangs through my previous research, this roundabout approach was helpful for ensuring I understood the context before exploring how these groups compared elsewhere.[1]

In this chapter, I will incorporate official DMC data as well as school and juvenile probation records with interviews of community members and local practitioners. Integrating DMC data to understand gangs is important for several reasons. First, it allows researchers to compare differences by race and ethnicity, a central starting point for examining racial oppression as outlined in *Gang Life in Two Cities*. Second, youth of color were more likely to create groups that identified themselves as gangs or were labeled as gangs based upon living in divergent social worlds.[2] Third, youth of Mexican descent were more likely to have their behavior and the groups to which they belonged evaluated negatively: from school discipline, to delinquency, to criminalization.[3] An analysis of DMC data explores patterns of differential contact between whites and youth of color in the juvenile justice system, patterns that exacerbate societal structural inequalities. The DMC effort began to demonstrate quantitatively the existence of disparity and then moved toward ethnographic data to provide additional insight into the reasons for these differences.

Disproportionate Minority Contact as an Analytical Tool to Examine Differential Outcomes by Race and Ethnicity

Although the study of gangs dates back to a publication by Frederic Thrasher in 1927, the study of Disproportionate Minority Confinement (DMC) did not begin until 1988, when it was brought to the attention of Congress in an annual report by the Coalition for Juvenile Justice.[4] These studies focused on whether youth of color were overrepresented in the juvenile justice system and, if so, how to implement best practices to reduce this overrepresentation. Congress made an amendment to the Juvenile Justice and Delinquency Prevention (JJDP) Act of 1974, thus requiring states to address DMC. In 1991, five states (Arizona, Florida, Iowa, North Carolina, and Oregon) initiated studies. In 2002, DMC was conceptually broadened beyond "confinement" to include an expansive discussion of "contact" that included nine decision points (arrest, referral, diversion, detention, petition, delinquency findings, probation, confinement, and transfer to adult court). To reduce DMC at each level, the Office of Juvenile Justice and Delinquency Prevention (OJJDP) began providing research funding, training, technical assistance, support catalogues, and a website to share data for all states willing to participate. Funded grants required researchers to follow the DMC reduction cycle, which involved five phases: 1) Identification; 2) Assessment and Diagnosis; 3) Intervention; 4) Evaluation; and 5) Monitoring.

The scholarly literature on whether youth of color were overrepresented in the juvenile justice system and the reasons have been extensively covered by the work of criminologist Carl E. Pope and several of his colleagues.[5] In a review of forty-six research articles from January 1969 to February of 1989, Pope and Feyerherm found that two thirds of these studies indicated that youth racial status made a difference in treatment beyond legal characteristics. In a second literature review, Pope and several colleagues analyzed thirty-four research articles from 1989 through 2001 and found empirical support for either direct or indirect race effects, and most often the effects were mixed.[6] The reasons for racial disparities were considered to result from one of two mechanisms: 1) differential treatment/processing/discrimination, or 2) differential offending. In addition to these summaries, the National Council on Crime and Delinquency found that youth of color were disproportionately found at every stage of the juvenile justice system, from arrest to sentencing, with black youth being especially overrepresented.[7] Criminologist Kimberly Kempf-Leonard emphasized the cumulative effect that begins during the early stages of decision-making and then continues to build like a snowball rolling downhill toward later decision points.[8]

New Mexico and Texas began their interest in DMC studies in the 1990s. Officials in New Mexico began expressing interest in DMC in 1994 when a report from New Mexico Highlands University was submitted to the Governor's Office Commission on Civil Rights. There were several concerns of overrepresentation in confinement at the time. In 1998 there was encouragement to create a uniform data collection protocol or a structured decision tool. The data revealing disparity in New Mexico led to the creation of the Blue-Ribbon Panel, which had its first meeting in November of 2001. The panel met and began working on a statewide plan to eliminate the problem within the next five years.

According to the Public Policy Research Institute at Texas A&M University, Texas began examining DMC in 1996, and by 2002 they had developed a Risk Assessment Instrument to monitor the use of detention.[9] In one of the earliest studies conducted on DMC, they found offense-related factors and not race determined juvenile processing decisions, with the exception of detention.[10] A later analysis found that Latino youth appeared in referrals at rates similar to their population, Anglo youth were underrepresented, and African American youth were overrepresented at nearly twice the rate of the general population.[11] After analyzing the data with multivariate statistics, the researchers determined that being Latino increased the probability for a referral more than being African American. They found that Latinos were more likely to face prosecutorial action than Anglos or African Americans, but Hispanic males were more likely to have their cases resolved in deferred adjudication or dismissal. The largest risk factor for African American youth was disciplinary history in school. The researchers concluded, "Although Hispanic youth are not disproportionately represented in the juvenile justice system, there is in fact greater evidence of potential system bias against this group than any other."[12] Thus, proportionate representation did not itself mean system fairness.

Several of my colleagues and I were hired in 2008 to create a Technical Assistance and Resource Center (TARC) for the State of New Mexico.[13] We began our efforts with the identification phase to determine whether racial and ethnic disparities existed in New Mexico. According to the OJJDP DMC training manual (1–1), there were three reasons for focusing on identification: 1) to describe the extent to which minority youth were overrepresented; 2) to begin to describe the nature of that overrepresentation by evaluating decision points; and 3) to create a foundation for ongoing measurement of DMC. The method used for the identification phase was the Relative Rate Index (RRI), which compares the relative volume activity at each stage and compares it to white youth.[14] With this background, our research team began by asking "Does Disproportionate Minority Contact exist in New Mexico, and, if so, how does it vary for Mexican Americans, Native Americans, and blacks compared to whites?" A total of 509,574 incidents were separated into nine decision points over a period of seven years. Arrests accounted for the greatest seven-year average of 26,087 per year, whereas cases transferred to adult court had the lowest mean (average of 22 incidents per year). The RRI remained relatively consistent except for cases resulting in secure confinement and cases transferred to adult court, which were more affected by smaller numbers of youths who received that sanction. The thirty-three counties in New Mexico varied in terms of demographics, density, history, and population, and most counties in New Mexico were rural.

Statewide Patterns of White Diversion versus Minority Delinquentization

For the seven years of data analyzed (2002–2008), white youth in New Mexico were underrepresented in all areas of the juvenile justice system compared to their proportion of the population within the state. During this period, 34 percent of the population between the ages of 10 to 17 included whites, yet only 23 percent of all cases involved whites as the offender ($n = 118,854$). On average, white youth were less likely to be arrested (24 percent), referred to juvenile court (22 percent), have cases involving secure detention (20 percent), have charges filed (22 percent), receive delinquent findings (21 percent), receive probation (22 percent), encounter secure confinement (17 percent), or have their cases transferred to adult court (18 percent), which included 28 cases over the seven-year period. White youth were consistently underrepresented in all points except for overrepresentation in diversion, which is a decision point that keeps youth from entering further into the system.

Over the same time period, Mexican American youth averaged 50 percent of the population, but they made up 63 percent of all incidents handled within the juvenile justice system ($n = 321,284$ cases). According to the census data, only 10 percent of New Mexico residents were foreign-born, of which 78 percent were from Latin America. The Children, Youth and Families Department's data do not provide detail on the proportion of youth who enter the juvenile justice system who were Mexican nationals or from other Latin American countries. Mexican American youth, on average, were arrested at a 77 percent greater rate than white youth (1.77).[15] They were less likely than white youth to have their cases diverted, which ensured greater sanctions and further advancement into the system. Decision points nine and ten demonstrated higher rates of secure confinement (69 percent of all cases) and cases transferred to adult court at higher rates (72 percent of all cases).[16]

TABLE 4.1
7-Year Averages (2002–2008) for the State of New Mexico by Race and Ethnicity

Decision Points	White	Hispanic	Native American	Black	All Minority
Population at risk (age 10–17)	80,319	117,165	29,000	4,860	154,799
Juvenile arrests	6,300	16,301	1,799	791	19,402
Referred to juvenile court	2,522	7,483	648	446	8,827
Cases diverted	3,768	8,796	1158	346	10,543
Cases involving secure detention	807	2,309	446	182	3,044
Cases petitioned	1,585	4,829	413	297	5,675
Cases resulting in delinquent findings	1,017	3,160	305	172	3,727
Cases resulting in probation	922	2,781	257	145	3,263
Cases resulting in confinement	54	224	21.86	15.43	267
Cases transferred to adult court	4	15.86	.43	1.29	17.71

Rates	White	Hispanic	Relative Rate Index		
Juvenile arrests per 1,000 persons in population	78.44	139.13	1.77		
Cases referred per 100 arrests	40.03	45.91	1.15		
Cases diverted per 100 referrals	149.41	117.55	.79		
Cases involving detention per 100 referrals	32.00	30.86	.96		
Cases petitioned per 100 referrals	62.85	64.53	1.03		
Cases resulting in delinquency per 100 petitions	64.16	65.44	1.02		
Cases in probation per 100 delinquency findings	90.66	88.01	.97		
Cases resulting in confinement per 100 delinquency findings	5.31	7.09	1.34		
Cases transferred to adult court per 100 petitions	.25	.33	1.32		

Rates	White	Native American	Relative Rate Index
Juvenile arrests per 1,000 persons in population	78.44	62.04	.79
Cases referred per 100 arrests	40.03	36.02	.90
Cases diverted per 100 referrals	149.41	178.70	1.20
Cases involving detention per 100 referrals	32.00	68.83	2.15
Cases petitioned per 100 referrals	62.85	63.74	1.01
Cases resulting in delinquency per 100 petitions	64.16	73.85	1.15
Cases in probation per 100 delinquency findings	90.66	84.26	.93
Cases resulting in confinement per 100 delinquency findings	5.31	7.17	1.35
Cases transferred to adult court per 100 petitions	.25	.10	.40

Rates	White	Black	Relative Rate Index
Juvenile arrests per 1,000 persons in population	78.44	162.76	2.08
Cases referred per 100 arrests	40.03	56.38	1.41
Cases diverted per 100 referrals	149.41	77.58	.52
Cases involving detention per 100 referrals	32.00	40.81	1.28
Cases petitioned per 100 referrals	62.85	66.59	1.04
Cases resulting in delinquency per 100 petitions	64.16	57.91	.90
Cases in probation per 100 delinquency findings	90.66	84.30	.93
Cases resulting in confinement per 100 delinquency findings	5.31	8.97	1.69
Cases transferred to adult court per 100 petitions	.25	.31	1.24

Source: Family Automated Client Tracking System.

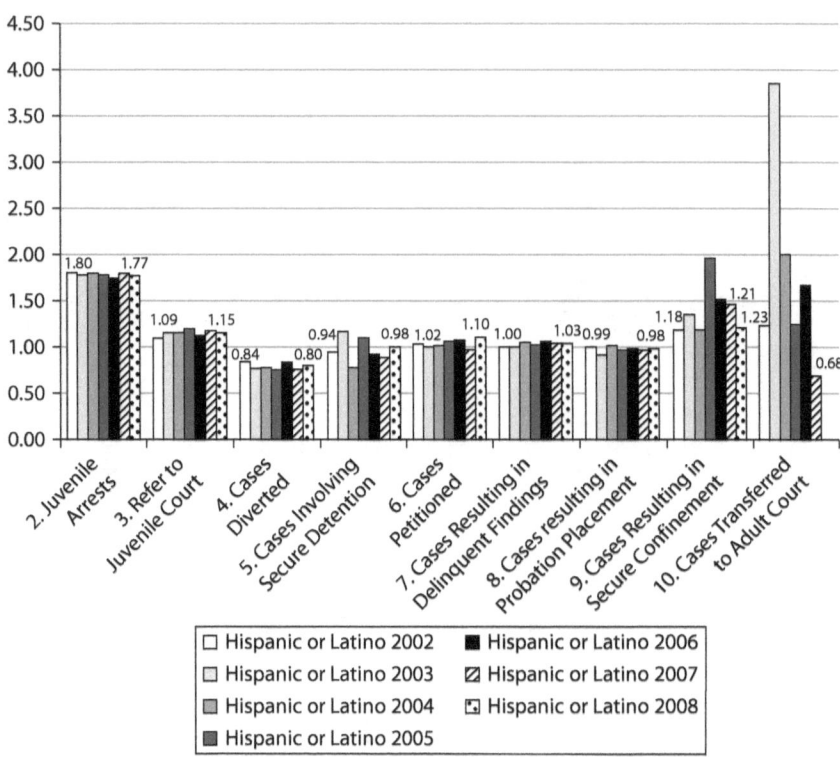

FIGURE 4.1 Hispanic or Latino Relative Rate Index (RRI) Compared to Whites.
Source: Family Automated Client Tracking System.

In summary, whites were underrepresented in each decision point in New Mexico, with the exception of the most beneficial stage, diversion. For this reason, social justice researcher Carlos Posadas and I emphasized the structural outcome of white diversion and minority group delinquentization.[17] The RRI data did not reveal whether the reasons for these racial and ethnic disparities were due to differential treatment/processing/discrimination or to differential offending.[18] Thus, in an effort to develop greater clarity about why youth of Mexican descent experienced greater contact with the juvenile justice system, I set out to answer this question using qualitative data. I reached out to schools, law enforcement agencies, detention centers, non-profit organizations, college students from or working in the area, and community members. The data show overrepresentation, but understanding how and why required an investigation that examined specific neighborhoods, schools, and the records of young people who were on juvenile probation. Rather than moving toward a multivariate analysis as done in Texas, we were curious about how the structure of these interactions shaped race relations in a setting where great efforts had been exerted historically to make the discussion of race non-existent.

The Neighborhood Context along the U.S.-Mexico Border

According to an analysis of the Neighborhood Change Database 1970–2010 Tract Data, most neighborhoods in southern New Mexico and El Paso, Texas, had higher concentrations of whites or Mexican Americans beyond county averages. Census tract data and field observations showed a higher level of income, wealth, resources, and education levels in white neighborhoods compared to Mexican American neighborhoods.[19] These concentrated neighborhoods have remained that way for the past thirty to fifty years. The four counties in southern New Mexico, with a population of 273,000, averaged a mean of 62 percent Hispanic, 35 percent white, and 1 percent black. In addition, 11 percent of neighborhoods were 89–99 percent Hispanic.[20] El Paso, Texas, had a much larger population than all of the New Mexico counties combined. According to the census in 2010, the county was listed as having a population of 800,000, of which 82 percent were Hispanic, 13 percent white, and 3 percent black. Based on census tract data, 10 percent of neighborhoods in 1970 were 89–99 percent Hispanic, whereas by 2010 46 percent of neighborhoods met these criteria.

White neighborhoods provided a geographic separation from the socioeconomic and educational difficulties faced by other residents, particularly the highly concentrated Mexican American census tracts. Of the two judicial districts in New Mexico, Doña Ana County had higher levels of white segregation (1.8 times greater than proportion of population) from 1980 to 2010, which may have been related to the presence of a national university and its primarily white-collar workforce (i.e., most administrators and faculty were white). For example, one census tract was reported as being 72 percent white despite being in a county where less than 30 percent of residents were white. While many residents did not report thinking along the lines of race or ethnicity, it was apparent that the ideology of colorblindness was not supported by census tract or observational data.[21]

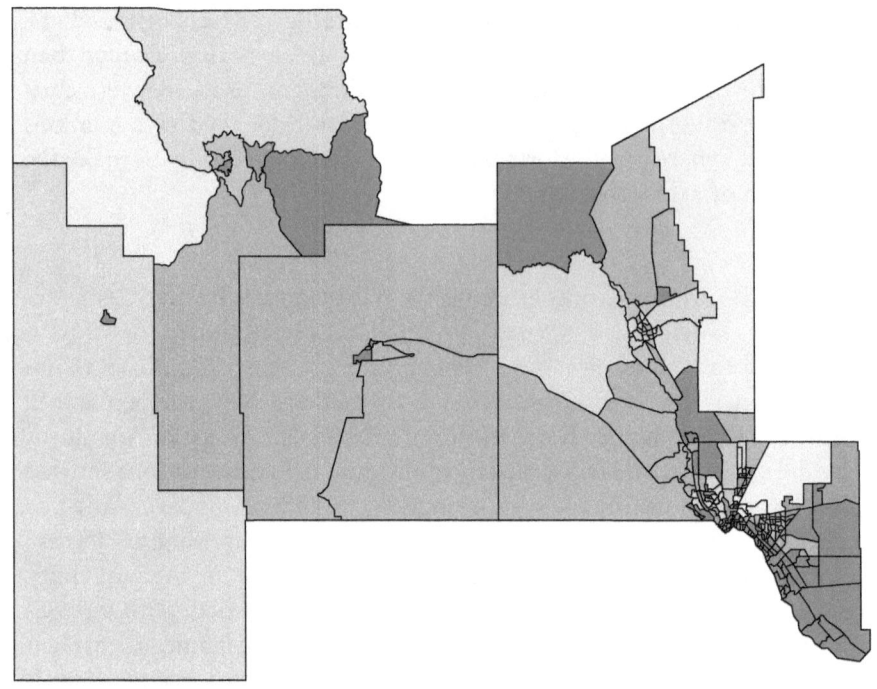

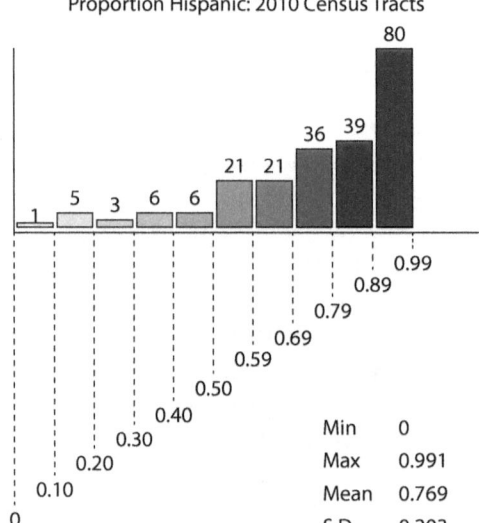

FIGURE 4.2 Levels of Concentration of Latinos in Southern New Mexico and El Paso.

In southern New Mexico, Doña Ana County contained the most highly concentrated Mexican American neighborhoods, noted in several census tracts as having an average of 91 percent Latino between 1980 and 2010. These areas were primarily concentrated along the U.S.-Mexico border. Poverty rates were nearly 36 percent, which was very close to a categorization of "ghetto poverty" given by urban sociologists to describe the most economically depressed neighborhoods in the nation.[22] Practitioners explained how economic divisions led to a higher proportion of Mexican American youth having greater contact with the juvenile justice system than white youth. In addition, large sections of the U.S.-Mexico border were rural. Social justice researchers Lisa Bond-Maupin and James Maupin's study of a rural setting in northern New Mexico found that, contrary to many positive perceptions about rural communities, the primarily Mexican American youth in this region encountered considerable police surveillance and received a high number of referrals compared to white youth.[23] Another study in the rural setting of southern New Mexico found that youth felt a sense of boredom that led to increased troublemaking and drug use.[24] These researchers found that Latino males were more likely to feel trapped and unable to escape negative labeling, while adult figures transmitted similar reputations to siblings.

Overall, New Mexico had a low proportion of foreign-born residents (10 percent) compared to the United States overall (13 percent); however, residents along the border region had a much higher proportion (28 percent). In El Paso, the average foreign-born proportion was 12 percent in 1970 and 27 percent in 2010. According to several researchers, higher levels of immigrants are often correlated with lower levels of violence.[25] A United States Government Accountability Office study confirmed that border counties in New Mexico had lower levels of violence and property crimes than non-border counties for the years analyzed (2005–2011).[26] Such a geographic and social boundary had the power to shape youth experiences, as noted by Bejarano:

> Border narratives demonstrate young people's vulnerable and complex lives as well as the turmoil they confront. . . . One might say that these concerns are no different than what other youths confront, but I argue that Latina/o youths face more difficulties as youths securing "rights" claims because of their undesirable ethnic status in the United States and their secondary knowledge of the English language.[27]

Several researchers have emphasized the nuances of the immigrant experience, which varies according to the region of the United States and the country of origin. Border scholars Cecilia Menjívar and Cynthia Bejarano, for instance, conducted interviews with immigrants from Cuba, El Salvador, Guatemala, and Mexico in Phoenix, Arizona, and concluded that "not all immigrants, not even all Latinos, share the same experiences."[28] However, in New Mexico and El Paso, Texas, most immigrants were from Mexico.

Because most youth of Mexican descent had been born in the United States, each community was somewhat different based on the primary types of economy. Some of the small New Mexico counties depended on the stability of area mines or farming, whereas the larger cities of Las Cruces and El Paso provided more occupational options. Mining communities described high levels of unemployment, many retirees, and transient populations. All of these places described the communities as great places to live, but if you were a young adult looking for opportunities, there were more options available in large cities. Small communities thrived on social networks, such as who you knew or whom you were related to by blood, when it came to how you would be treated by authority figures. Many of these attributes and perceptions about families had been shaped by two or three generations of family members. Drugs and alcohol continued to be problems, primarily smoking marijuana, drinking alcohol, or taking meth and heroin. Community members and practitioners acknowledged that, with nothing else to do, some people turned to alcohol and drugs. Family isolation and disruption could result in higher rates of domestic violence and child abuse. Chris, a county city manager who grew up in the community as a young child before attaining his current position, reported the following:

> The community has changed. Not really the city limits, but more so from the challenges of the past where every three or four years there was a strike and people would move. It was sometimes seven or eight years between layoffs. Now with the university and hospital we have more stable employment than in the past. While the economy has been struggling, we have increased crime and kids are affected by domestic violence. Some businesses went bankrupt, but the economy is coming back slowly.

Thus, several patterns reflect the neighborhood experience along the U.S.-Mexico border. First, because these were majority minority counties, areas with a higher proportion of whites tended to have higher levels of segregation and forms of social control designed around the perspective of help. Second, networks often existed with relatives and family members on both sides of the border, and being bilingual was more normative. The fact that New Mexico had a higher proportion of residents who were Mexican prior to the area becoming a part of the United States led most residents to possess Mexican, Native American, or Spanish ancestry while being U.S. citizens. Third, the primarily rural landscape of New Mexico differed greatly from the urban centers of El Paso, Las Cruces, and Ciudad Juárez, and the level of community resources was shaped by where you lived. Poverty and lack of resources shaped the entire region, but urban areas were often able to provide a greater number of institutions such as hospitals, schools, and social activities. Neighborhood dynamics played an important role in schools, juvenile probation, detention, and policing as well (discussed in chapter 5).

This is the starting point for youth, and when it comes to the issue of gangs, these neighborhood dynamics intersect to influence the formation and institutionalization of gangs. Communities that had higher levels of gang activity shared a similar pattern of low-income, segregation, and lack of activities for young people, as well as a toughness and willingness to defend family or friends due to wider levels of societal prejudice or aggression. A poor neighborhood alone was not enough to lead to the formation or institutionalization of a gang. To examine the influence of neighborhoods and its relation to gangs, criminologists Charles Katz and Stephen Schnebly analyzed ninety-three census tracts in Mesa, Arizona, and found that neighborhoods characterized by high levels of economic deprivation or social/familial disadvantage had higher concentrations of gang members.[29] Interestingly, they also found that, at certain levels of disadvantage, the level of social networks become so sparse that they no longer possess the social structures to form gangs. Based on my data, New Mexico communities such as Chaparral, Columbus, Hatch, Lordsburg, and even Deming experienced such high levels of economic inequality and transition on a townwide level that the function for creating and maintaining a gang served less of a purpose than the larger cities of El Paso and Las Cruces. Another feature that seemed to maintain gangs were communities along the linear path between El Paso and Las Cruces, such as Anthony, Doña Ana, and Sunland Park. Because El Paso is only a forty-five-minute drive from Las Cruces, many of these small and extremely impoverished communities, similar to what were described by Katz and Schnebly, have still maintained such groups.[30]

Based on the data I collected by walking neighborhoods, talking to residents, and analyzing census tract data, conflict was the primary purpose for the creation of gangs and for their ongoing institutionalization. Most of this conflict was grew out of white segregation and differential treatment, but over time this isolation led to conflict between other Latino neighborhoods.

Schools as a Context for Heightening DMC

Schools played a prominent role in the lives of children, teaching various forms of educational and socialization knowledge in addition to being one of the earliest forms of social control. Criminologist Aaron Kupchik outlines the problems with school discipline in his book *Homeroom Security*, which examined zero-tolerance policies in several schools.[31] He cited the research of David Tyack when he outlined how schools began to act as socializing agents to create better workers, thus enforcing habits such as punctuality, silence, and precision, so that factory workers could "toe the line." Despite being majority minority communities, the national push for English-only instruction in schools was pushed by Anglo administrators and teachers in the early twentieth century, as the Spanish language was prohibited on school grounds. These forms of segregation coincided with race. Black students were segregated from Latino and Anglo students. Mexicans were segregated from American students. The schools in Doña Ana County remained formally segregated until 1954 when the U.S. Supreme Court ruled in Brown v. Board of Education that such segregation was unconstitutional.

According to the U.S. Department of Education, New Mexico ranked second lowest in terms of on-time graduation rates, and the Annie E. Casey Foundation continually ranked the state in the bottom ten.[32] In 2016, Texas was ranked thirty-second in education. However, El Paso, Texas, continued to share more similarities with New Mexico, with a higher number of non-English-speaking households and lower levels of educational attainment. As of 2010, District Three (Doña Ana County) contained three school districts of 39,367 students enrolled in K–12, District Six (Grant, Hidalgo, and Luna Counties) contained five school districts for 10,571 students, and El Paso Public Schools had 63,000 students.[33] These schools varied in terms of the rate of arrests by grade level, school, and geographic area. For example, for 2005–2008 in District

Three, middle schools had the highest referral rates (average of 47 per 1,000) compared to high schools (average 40 per 1,000) and elementary schools (two per 1,000). Police Officer Steve reported the schools started using School Resource Officers in 1996 when the community began having block parties at the parks with the National Guard. He stated:

> However, over time we have noticed that it is important for school administration to allow SROs [School Resource Officers] the ability to do their jobs as [police] officers and not be influenced by principals to make unnecessary referrals. The SROs already have one boss and they do not need two, and this has often been difficult for schools to realize that SROs are autonomous from the school.

Some of this conflict may have been why some schools wavered between having their own private security officers or whether to incorporate officers from the police or sheriff's department. Private security firms offered increased supervision beyond law enforcement officers, who were often short-staffed, rotated occasionally between several schools, and more independent.

According to the data analyzed in Doña Ana, one third to one half of all juvenile arrests were occurring in K–12 educational institutions. One school official reported that if only 35 percent of all arrests were occurring in the public schools, it should be considered an accomplishment. He calculated that, with 24,000 students, to only have 613 arrests per year was very small compared to the number of youth with whom they interacted with five days a week. This would indicate that less than 3 percent of youth received a referral. He believed that most youth spend the majority of their day at school and that the schools were providing a structured setting where kids were less likely to get into trouble. They pointed out that for a student to be allowed to leave campus they needed to be a sophomore and have a good grade point average. They mentioned a Center for Disease Control report that found 60 percent of youth did not feel safe at school, and so the school system was working to create programs to make youth feel safer. They thought most fights were occurring at lunchtime when kids bumped into each other in the narrow hallways. A counselor conveyed that one of the biggest indicators of student success was whether students felt safe or connected; to assess this, the counselor asked students, "If you missed school, would anyone care or notice?" Half of the students reported not having anyone to make them feel connected. School officials described the importance of providing more things for kids to do. They were appreciative of the Weed and Seed Safe Haven, Boys and Girl Clubs, recreation centers, and sport teams, but they still felt that there were not enough things for youth to do, particularly those from low-income families. There were youth who could not afford sports fees, uniforms, and registration requirements. They noted that parental involvement was lacking and that some families needed intervention.

As a parent, I observed an encounter in which a school principal received a tip that several middle school girls on a sports team, including my daughter, were smoking marijuana near the school. The next day, the principal brought each student into her office with the SRO and began an interrogation. The officer did not conduct the questioning—it was the principal. It was determined that some of the girls had smoked marijuana while some of the girls were merely present at the time of the offense. The principal wanted all of the girls involved to be cited with a delinquency referral and to be removed from the sports team. However, parental advocacy ensured that those who were not smoking did not receive a delinquency referral or school suspension, although they were still removed from the team. The SRO agreed with the parents, which placed the SRO in a strange situation because the principal wanted referrals for everyone. This example demonstrates how school discipline, including the possibility of a delinquency referral, operated without any form of legal protection on behalf of the youth. There were no lawyers, and parents were kept at a distance under the idea that the school acted as the legal guardian while the students were at school. Criminologist Aaron Kupchik, in his second book *The Real School Safety Problem*, outlined how schools have gone too far in the promotion of school security and punishment by creating a series of practices that harm students, schools, families, and communities.[34] In this analysis, a bully does not have to be a fellow student but could be a teacher or an administrator enforcing unfair rules and punishment.[35] Sociologist Victor Rios's research on youth interactions with teachers and school security were strained by numerous interactions based on incorrect cultural interpretations of the behavior of Latino youth.[36] The authority figure interactions often began as well-intentioned but quickly turned more punitive when the desired outcomes were not obtained.

An interview with an SRO summarized the challenges for enforcing laws alongside school discipline. Lisa, a five-year veteran as a school resource officer, reported how she tries to be proactive and to mediate problems before they get out of hand:

> I go around to help. I'm a friend to the students, but if you break the line, you have to pay the price. The most important goal is kid safety. I don't always file a referral. If the law is broken, then yes, or if it is criminal damage to the school or taking an iPod or cell phone. Some parents want charges filed. The schools utilize the counselors to try and mediate conflicts, mediate girl bullying, and they keep a harassment log. Some of these youth have special education needs or ADHD. Most of the time I stop and talk to the youth. "What do you like doing?" Try and work things out and get to solutions. I learn the kids' names and I take their safety personally. . . . The schools operate by a point system. They could get in-school suspensions (ISS) or a Category A, B, C, and D, and these are categorized by severity and can result in a letter sent home to short- and long-term suspensions.

As one of the small number of female police officers, it appeared Lisa had a good rapport with the students and administration. Although delinquency referrals were issued from law enforcement, there were a wide range of consequences that school officials initiated for student misbehavior. Based on internal records provided by one of the school districts, most school violations from 2006 to 2008 were given to young males (83 percent) and to Latinos (86 percent), primarily for violating a JICF-RA (Violent, Gang and/or Gang-Like Activities; 49 percent). These could range in seriousness from wearing gang-like clothing to engaging in a physical confrontation. The second most frequent violation was JICH-RA (Alcohol, Tobacco, and Other Drugs) at 29 percent of the total violations.

Sociologist Anthony Peguero and his colleagues have been analyzing data obtained from the Educational Longitudinal Study, a nationally representative longitudinal study of tenth graders in 2002 and twelfth graders in 2004. These researchers' analyses found school discipline was affected by race, ethnicity, gender, and immigration generational status.[37] Latino youth who had been in the United States longer (i.e., generationally) received more discipline from the school than white youth. In addition, Latino males and females had lower levels of academic-self-efficacy, which increased their risk of dropping out of school.[38] The context for such marginalization was highlighted by a study by Portillos, González, and Peguero, who found that the high school attended by Chicana/o and

Mexicana/o youth made them feel inadequate, both directly and indirectly.[39] Moreover, the educational operation of the institution did not integrate or respect their cultural heritage. In this setting, school surveillance and security in the name of safety only produced greater levels of criminalization despite not being intentional.

Professors in the College of Education at my home institution of New Mexico State University continued to emphasize the importance of bilingual education and more opportunities to learn about the students' cultural history.[40] Despite this encouragement, most schools in the area continued to operate in a color-blind manner, thus ignoring the role of colonization as well as the richness of the local Indio, Hispano, Native American, Spanish, and Mexican cultures. A letter to the editor in the *Las Cruces Sun News* by a retired individual with a Ph.D. in English criticized the public education in Las Cruces as the "worst of times."[41] He questioned whether the all-white school board was meeting the needs of its Hispanic student body, and why the district was operating without parent or community support. He argued that excluding parents and public participation only resulted in continued poor educational performance. My wife and I had moved from Denver, where parental participation was encouraged and even required at one school, it was a surprise to us that we needed to complete and pay for a state and federal background check when we desired to volunteer, along with completing a nine-page application involving signatures and notaries.

Despite schools appearing to take an aggressive stance based on internal records, field experience, and the number of delinquency referrals, some law enforcement officers still perceived schools as being too lenient. For example, Officer Mark, a white officer with the police department, while emphasizing that this was just his opinion, expressed frustration with trying to get schools to take behavior problems more seriously:

> I think that they take too much of a 'let's hold your hand' approach to the problem. When you got 2,500 students at [high school name omitted], I don't think there is any room for putting up with problem behavior. I mean, he should not be allowed back into the [school district name omitted]. It then becomes the parents' problem. They can take them to a private tutor or send them to private schools, but that is just my opinion. And again they [the schools] think we are a little bit too aggressive. When we go to identify these kids, the ones who are on intensive juvenile probation, the ones that are on contract, the ones that are on bracelets. We'll just walk up and start talking to them.

"Hey," you know, "where were you last night? We checked with your JPPO and they said you were out until four in the morning. Are you still hanging out with those gang members, which is a violation of your probation?" And they [the schools] are like, "Whoa, whoa, whoa, he doesn't need that now, he is at school." "Well, okay." It's just something we're working on and again we've been into several meetings and we've done gang presentations and helped them out because they [schools] truly don't know.

Officer Mark reported how many of these children have family members who were part of gangs or organized crime groups. He believed local gangs were huge problem, but the schools considered them only a moderate problem. He wanted his children to be safe. In two of these counties, officials concluded that gangs were the primary reason for increasing the rate of referrals for Latino youth compared to white youth. They described local gangs as multi-generational with involvement beginning as early as third grade. At the elementary school my children attended, I did not observe any gang members nor did I at any of the elementary schools I visited throughout my research sites.

District attorney offices in these geographic areas established truancy programs to monitor and issue citations to juveniles and their parents for excessive school absences. This effort not only tried to hold juveniles accountable but also parents whom the district attorney could cite for their child's truancy. Quentin, a middle-aged, white, community police officer who had worked to address some of the issues involving youth in the community, encouraged a more active stance against truancy and problematic families:

We have to respond to issues such as weapons on campus. We need to be proactive. Schools aren't proactive enough. We deal with truancy issues. Some youth don't want to be back at school. We try to educate those who want to learn, but what about those who feel left out? We have to have the proper services to deal with incorrigible students and dysfunctional families. What happens when we don't find an alternative? The kids don't want to be in school. Some of them have nothing that shows them the value of education. The parent collects welfare. They only know family history. They live for the moment. They know about food stamps and how to get them. Alternative schools are great but what about when the kid gets suspended? If there is nobody at home, then it leaves the youth vulnerable to other types of crimes.

> They are hanging out at [fast food restaurant]. Going to the beer parties. We can tell them state law requires them to be in school but it's often not enforceable. Some kids are out of school for a whole month. We can't address the issue if they have ADHD. We don't want to suspend. We don't want to get the parents in trouble. But often the root of the problem is the family. We don't have a problem with the higher economic and educated communities, who are giving direction and providing role models. We have issues with lower economic areas where their only issue is survival every day. You can't make enough to get welfare and afford to live in a high rise. Look at the high school. We have different juvenile backgrounds who are causing havoc. There are tons of runaways. At lunch time, you see the youth hanging out at the [fast food restaurant] for Las Cruces, the [fast food restaurant] for Oñate, or the pizza place for Mayfield. The best thing would be to make schools a closed campus.

Despite a general feeling from law enforcement and even school officials assigning fault to the parents for youth misbehavior or lack of educational success, I consistently remember that for every school function that invited parents to attend (e.g., awards, singing, magnet programs, etc.), the gymnasium was completely filled with parents and family members. Thus, while a higher proportion of family members continued to struggle in a structural environment with many odds against the residents, families continued to persist and to offer encouragement and guidance for their children. Criminologist Aaron Kupchik's research emphasized how school discipline and punishment not only hurts the students but also their families.[42] The youth themselves struggled in a social environment that did not necessarily value their language, culture, or families' ability to share in their broader educational support. Schools seemed to fault the parents for the lack of resources they received to provide a supportive atmosphere for educational success. However, the parents were living in neighborhoods that were far from fair in ensuring economic and social equality. Thus, rather than collectively organizing on a broader scale to challenge the regional inequalities that existed, it was much easier to fault the parents, and if the majority of students could graduate, then the smaller number who dropped out or were kicked out became the responsibility of other institutions. Based on the data available, while there were some students in the schools who belonged to gangs in middle school and high school, most students did not.

Juvenile Probation Contributing to the Snowball Effect of DMC

If youth behavior was considered more serious than could be corrected by school discipline, Juvenile Probation and Parole Officers (JPPOs) were the institution to review all status and delinquent referrals and determine the consequence. Law enforcement issued the referral, but they were not the agency given the authority to implement punishment. JPPOs responded to referrals in several ways, from handling the situation informally (the majority) to petitioning the case to go before a district court judge. According to the Children's Code in New Mexico (32A-2-7), the JPPO office has the power to informally dispose of up to three misdemeanor charges brought against a juvenile within two years. A felony charge or four misdemeanors automatically brought the juvenile before the Children's Court Attorney. Once a youth received a referral, 60 percent of these individuals received a subsequent referral; overall, 96 percent of these juveniles had obtained one to three referrals by the age of 18. A small proportion of juveniles, 5 percent, had four or more referrals per year.[43] The TARC database allowed us to track specific youth cases over the years of 2002 to 2008.

According to New Mexico's Family Automated Client Tracking System data and DMC web-based data entry system, District Three (Doña Ana County) and District Six (Grant, Hidalgo, and Luna Counties) averaged 3,392 arrests per year from 2005 to 2016, with 79 percent of these cases occurring in District Three. The high point for the number of arrests during these eleven years was 2009 with 4,355 arrests, and the low point was 1,492 arrests in 2014. The data for El Paso were more problematic for analysis. Despite being a large city, the data were reported to be in progress, unavailable, or inconsistent. Some years reported an RRI rate equal to whites, whereas other years were skewed so as to be extremely divergent.

Another way to research youth referrals was to review a random sample of juvenile probation files. My colleague Carlos Posadas and I each reviewed eighty-two juvenile probation cases separately and then discussed the findings for coder reliability. Of these cases, 81 percent consisted of Latinos, 10 percent whites, 7 percent mixed race and ethnicity, and less than 2 percent involved a black or Asian youth. In addition, 77 percent of the cases were male and 23 percent female.

The first trend to emerge from reviewing the probation case files were the small number of families with both biological parents residing in the same home. Only 21 percent of juveniles fit this pattern. It was more common for juveniles on probation to live with their mother (48 percent) or for the primary caregivers to be grandparents or other family members (21 percent), leaving 31 percent of mothers who were listed as uninvolved in the child's life due to prison, deportation, death, alcohol and drug abuse, or living away from the child. Half of the fathers were listed as absent or not having any contact with the juvenile who was on probation (13 percent were in prison, 11 percent deported, and 5 percent deceased). Thus, 30 percent of fathers were removed from the home due to criminal justice, deportation, or a life-altering event; 9 percent of fathers were listed as the primary caregiver because mothers also faced difficulties in their lives, although at a lower rate compared to fathers. At least 13 percent of the juveniles were in the primary care of transitional family care, group home, or adopted family. There were a variety of reasons given for the difficulty in maintaining families for the juveniles on probation, such as a problematic relationship between parents, alcohol and drugs, incarceration, deportation, or simply being uninvolved in the child's life. Social justice researcher Vera Lopez conducted a study on system-involved girls in her book *Complicated Lives*.[44] She found that a large proportion of the girls she interviewed had grown up with absent fathers and with greater exposure to parental drug use, incarceration, and violence. These difficult experiences led to adultification, a concept in which children assume adult responsibilities.

Many arrest and referral descriptions capture difficulties with maintaining a nurturing social environment for these children. Even the task of making sure a child gets to school could result in a call to law enforcement and a subsequent referral. In addition, referral charges of incorrigible behavior, running away, truancy, domestic disputes, and/or drug and alcohol abuse highlight possible challenges occurring within these households. Some of these behaviors often carried over to the school, where teachers and administrators reported difficulty in handling disruptive students. Nearly one in four juveniles in the sample received their first referral at the age of 11 or younger. These juveniles went on to receive 39 percent of the total referrals. The average time between when a juvenile received a referral and a subsequent or second referral was 342 days. We found that early involvement (10–14 years old) with the juvenile justice system coincided with chronic status and petty crime offenders, whereas later involvement (15–17 years old) resulted in more serious offenses.[45]

Juveniles with higher rates of referrals were not necessarily engaging in more serious offenses, but they were frequently referred for status and probation violations or defiance to authority.

Based on this random sample of 82 juvenile probation cases in 2008, 32 percent of juveniles who had contact with the juvenile justice system were identified by decision-makers in the system as being involved with gangs. This is comparable to the finding of 33 percent by Winfree in 1992 when a loose definition of gang involvement was used, but more than the 18 percent when a more restrictive definition is used. Based on the data collected, the youth on juvenile probation had more problematic lives than the general population. Gang-labeled juveniles in this sample accounted for nearly 54 percent of total referrals, indicating frequent levels of interaction with the court and the JPPO office. However, despite the image of gang-involved juveniles committing a larger number of serious crimes, only 8 percent of total felonies were committed by gang-labeled youth as compared to 14 percent committed by non-gang-involved juveniles. Probation officers may devote greater surveillance and negative perceptions of rampant delinquency to gang-involved, or perceived gang-involved, juveniles than non-gang-involved juveniles.

Interviews with JPPO officers captured the context for many of the themes laid out in the juvenile probation files. Raquel, a senior Latina juvenile probation officer, stated:

> The biggest challenge for youth is the easy availability of drugs in the area and fitting in. Girls doing meth because they need to lose weight. Youth want immediate gratification. It's scary when you have a star quarterback testing positive for meth because he needed more energy. Everyone wants everything immediately. Society is moving fast but at what cost? And their perception is it would be a great benefit if they could run faster, work harder, or be thinner. We have grandparents raising children because the parents are incarcerated or lost to drugs or suicide or abandonment issues and drugs and alcohol. How do we provide help to a 16-year-old mother, whose own mother is in prison for heroin, and the baby's father doesn't claim the child? A lot of times I disagree with releasing the kids back to their parents because the parents are using drugs, too. It is often generational and hard to break the cycle. There are a lot of dysfunctional homes that enable youth to misbehave and make wrong choices.

Another senior Latina juvenile probation officer, Diana, expressed the increased difficulty of working in the border region:

> We face border issues and more so in Luna County compared to the other two counties. We have around 400 to 600 kids bussed to school every day. In the past, the cartels used kids to cross the border and bring drugs into the schools. We have about eight busses that pick up kids near Palomas, Mexico. The busses arrive between 6:00 and 7:00 and there are one to two INS agents testing requirements otherwise the kids get left behind. Kids will get left even if they are standing in line. Angela Kocherga of KVIA News has covered stories regarding people losing a parent to violence or having a parent deported. Truancy is an issue here and missing the bus is often unexcused because the parent can't communicate with school. We [the JPPO office] receive truancy referrals. There are meth problems in Mexico. I remember for a period of time the violence was so high in Mexico that JPPO officers felt they needed to wear bulletproof vests. We have had ugly things happen in Palomas and we have to send kids back home. This one time we had a pregnant girl who was committed for being caught with fifteen pounds of marijuana, and we knew she could be killed when she had to go back home because she had lost the drugs to seizure. The cartel had threatened to kill the girl and her baby. All of the students who come here are citizens, but we also have some youth who are arrested who are undocumented. We were finally able to get one of the shelters to house her.

Melissa, a senior Latina juvenile probation officer, also described challenges with the communities and providing the needed services:

> We had a big problem with gangs in 1997. There were shootings and stabbings at school. A lot of people were sent to prison but around 2007 many of the prison gang members began returning to the community. They seem to be recruiting younger kids. Instead of 14 or 15 we get 8, 9, or 10 [years old]. We often have youth committing property offenses. The mines shut down but have now re-opened. When they shut down it reduced enrollment in the Cobre and Silver school districts. We deal with drugs, weapons, and bullying. We do our best to stop fights. Sometimes it is the grandparents who are raising these kids.

In summary, juvenile probation and parole officers in southern New Mexico saw themselves as working toward youth rehabilitation. Much of this perspective was most likely shaped by this institution being housed under the New Mexico Children, Youth and Families Department, which had a mission statement that emphasized being kind, respectful, and responsive along with working to build a culture of accountability and support. Most cases that came before juvenile probation could be deferred successfully through a variety of local community programs, including a citation program, a teen court, restorative justice circles, or community service. Many of the youths who later went on to be placed on juvenile probation successfully completed their requirements, while a small number continued to receive multiple referrals, which resulted in juvenile probation officers filing probation violation orders that were more likely to result in the youth being brought in front of a judge or spending time in detention.

Statewide Changes in the Use of Detention

In 2008, the State of New Mexico entered a new sentencing scheme that required officers to call a JPPO (on-call) regarding whether to detain a youth for an offense. The JPPO was then required to call Santa Fe (state headquarters) to verify whether the offense met a criterion for detention. Officers reported that a youth "practically had to kill someone" to be detained. In one county, according to a detention center administrator, judges maintained greater latitude as some youth detentions resulted from failing to pay traffic tickets, traffic violations, and or having various status offenses. In counties without a detention center (Grant and Hidalgo counties), many law enforcement officers did not want to expend the time and energy required to transport juveniles to detention centers that were one or two hours away.

Brian, a senior administrator at the jail/detention center, stated the following:

> The housing here is one side for adults and another side for youth. We can house up to fifteen youths. We have room for five females. It's a very small area. We are the only county in the district that houses youths, but we also get some from Carlsbad and Otero Counties. There are stricter requirements to run a juvenile facility and tighter regulations to

run as dual [adult and youth]. Most youths are from Luna and Grant County. The length of stay is generally short term, less than seventeen days, and midterm for heavy drug trafficking cases where the youth might have five to six federal charges sometimes. We also house immigrants. Their offenses range from truancy to murder. No judge leaves a child here very long, but I do feel we are over-utilized, especially during the weekend. Every Thursday there is a weekend lockdown. Youth are told to follow the rules or get locked down. Luna County is a little county with fewer resources. Police bring the youth in and they over-utilize these four-day holds for truancy and curfew violations. JPPOs incarcerate as punishment. They can offer more services in the community. Most of the youths do nothing in here but try and sleep all day. Since March, 75 percent of the youths are here between one and fifteen days, 1 percent over 90 days. The average stay is fifteen days, but we have two youths who are here long term. It is like a rotating door. [Is it doing any good?] We still have recidivism. Me and the Chief JPPO talk all time. Me and her are getting more settled. Detention is not a resource for rehabilitation. There is minimal programming, and we are not equipped for a school. We don't have social workers or counseling. No family reintegration. Are jails a resource? To be correct, it is a big baby-sitter service. The kids are here, and they are safe and secure. They are clean, fed, but then comes education. How do we get resources? There are more resources in Doña Ana County.

A female correctional officer who worked in the detention facility and the jail for eleven years reiterated many of the comments of this administrator. She said the youth can play basketball or handball. She reported how the kids were not bad, but they often had bad home environments and often kept coming back. She emphasized the importance of treating people with respect and that you often receive it in return, and that is the philosophy she follows with the detained individuals.

Diana, a senior juvenile probation officer, concurred with many of the changes involving detention:

In the past, JPPOs used to be able to make the decision to detain a youth for having a runaway status offense by using exceptions to the children's code. For example, a municipal court detaining for a traffic warrant or traffic offenses penalty such as not having a driver's license or failure to appear. We get a roster for every single day. A daily roster for who is in there. Some district judges use the detention center by signing a warrant. In another district the [district attorney's] office stopped the practice right away. Now we call in for a Risk Assessment. Any time a youth is detained, it becomes a district-wide email. The Governor came on board to create more transparency. Most of the time it requires a felony to be detained.

Because the State of New Mexico had provided the detention data from 2004 to 2008, I briefly looked into the use of detention prior to the new sentencing scheme in the district that had decreased its use of detention. Based on the data, Latino youth were overrepresented in being detained compared to white youth. Even when the system recommended not to detain, this was often overridden by the JPPO and the youth was kept in custody.[46] For the years analyzed, at least one fourth of all detentions were for probation violations. Therefore, the statewide change in policy had significantly limited the ability of law enforcement officers and probation officers to detain and removed their ability to override the system. This change was not viewed positively by law enforcement officers.

The Law Enforcement Critique of the Juvenile Justice Approach

Overwhelmingly, the view from the law enforcement officers interviewed was that there was too much leniency. The State of New Mexico was perceived as not holding youth accountable for violating the law. In addition to a perceived lack of detention, police officers argued that, in most instances, it took three to four months before the youth appeared before a JPPO. Once seen, the JPPO often handled the case informally. As a whole, law enforcement appeared frustrated with this informal handling, and there was a perception that the system would finally become more punitive only when a youth turned 18. JPPO officers reported statewide efforts to improve the timeframe between when law enforcement filed a referral and when a juvenile probation officer held an initial preliminary inquiry. Both law enforcement and the juvenile probation officers reported being understaffed and overwhelmed with a caseload that required greater resources.

A white sheriff's officer named Jesse expressed his frustration with the juvenile justice system:

> They are charged but many keep reoffending. As an officer, you send a kid to the JPPO office and they won't issue a warrant for the kid's arrest. The kid bumps into court by mistake and they plead guilty. The judge will say, "Don't do it again." If you cut back on arrests, it won't do anything anyway. The entire state of New Mexico is worthless, and probation isn't going to change the hardcore youth who are unsupervised. No one is reporting if they are breaking probation.

Officer Juan, a top law enforcement official, reiterated a similar sentiment with the juvenile justice system:

> The only consequence for youth now is to extend probation or [go to] the detention center. The district judge has relayed his frustration to us regarding juveniles, but his hands are tied. They no longer want to continue four- or five-day holds. The point system where JPPO has to call up and see whether a youth can be detained is a huge failure. The kids who commit burglaries laugh. Now I advocate most youth don't belong in jail, but when you put in there they need sanctions and they need rehabilitation. Incarceration by itself is not the answer. I've been in policing for 38 years. I've seen my share of discriminatory practices, but they are not as prevalent here. I would like to see JPPO have two parts: a resource part and an enforcement side. Often there is no time to do both. A sanction side and resource side. Need two divisions because one can't do both. I like graduated sanctions. Children can be charged but it takes a lot of people. School we can change. Not all families give a shit. [What about good families?] With good families, there is an outside influence. An underlying problem is you have to earn kids' trust, which takes a long time. I'm passionate that things can be fixed. It's frustrating so many victims lose out. We don't need more laws. Quit breaking the laws we have and establish clear boundaries.

Quentin, the white law enforcement officer, continued to express his frustration with the juvenile justice system:

> It's repetitive to arrest X for so many numerous times. It takes up to one hour per arrest with the paperwork. It costs citizens up to $30

for that hour but runaways continue reoccurring. Two days later we are making the same report. Nothing is really in place to educate the parents about the consequences. It doesn't happen. There is no hammer in place unless the youth commits a crime, and then you can start to monitor. It takes six to eight cases of running away before a consequence puts someone on probation. If it continues to occur, then it becomes a higher priority. I don't mind dealing with these cases, but the laws have no bite, no strength. It all falls back on parents. Even if arrested at the pizza place for starting fires. The fire marshal calls parent the first time, but it's not important. The parent has no time. So, then we have a 14-year-old parent who needs money for food and laundry. Most of them are busy and can't pay rent. They have two or three jobs. Others have substance-abuse problems. No wonder why [they're] in survival mode. They get all their help from the state. Can't or won't on their own. Don't create another generation. We have five generations of single-parent families. How to combat? It's a social issue. Some care. We need more families like that, whereas we have other families we continue to see like a revolving cycle.

Law enforcement officer frustrations were regularly expressed to me with a desire to help change youth behaviors, but the process outlined required more punishment. The root cause of many of these issues were a result of historical and structural inequalities that the institutions of school and juvenile justice continued to enhance through their benevolent practices. This was a slow and methodical process of enhancing DMC, although it appeared that many of the law enforcement officers whom I interviewed desired a more abrupt life-changing sequence, similar to what I observed in Colorado and Utah, states that had greater resources but were also majority white.

Comparing DMC Patterns to Gangs

Based on an analysis of neighborhoods, schools, juvenile probation, and detention, the thesis I am proposing is that the geographic areas with greater racial and ethnic disparity, including greater levels of overrepresentation for youth of color, will result in more gang involvement and activity that coincides with increased levels of punitive responses. For example, for the seven-year period of 2006 to 2012, the arrest RRI for

Latinos in El Paso was .84, in Doña Ana 1.36, in Denver, Colorado 1.6, and in Ogden, Utah 2.05. The seven-year RRI arrest rate for blacks in Doña Ana was 1.07, in El Paso 1.26, in Ogden, Utah 3.21, and in Denver, Colorado 3.39. Thus, El Paso would have a lower rate of perceived gang problems of Latinos compared to blacks and whites, whereas the other communities would experience higher fear of Latino gangs but even higher fear of black gang members. One may inquire whether whites could have a higher gang population in El Paso based on my thesis. It would be possible, but because whites are not structurally disadvantaged in U.S. society or in segregated communities, such an outcome is not expected. In Peterson and Krivo's *Divergent Social Worlds*, they found whites living in communities with lower disadvantage. This matches my ethnographic observations of neighborhoods. Although there were whites who lived in some of the more concentrated Latino neighborhoods and shared common living conditions, they still experienced larger group advantage. Groups of white youth in these communities did not form on the basis of protection and survival due to discrimination. Most, if not all, white ethnic groups of the past have largely assimilated into the mainstream. This does not mean white youth can't join Latino- or black-dominated gangs, or that they can't belong to primarily all-white groups involved in delinquency or criminality—they just aren't called gangs. Based on the data I have collected, it appears that during adulthood whites can become part of groups that were stigmatized as seen with the Bandidos, but this was largely a stereotype based on group membership rather than the ecological contamination encountered by black and Latino segregation.

This indirect form of evaluating whether a community has a gang problem overlaps with my ethnographic observations of racial and ethnic inequality playing a key role in the creation and involvement of the response to gangs. These patterns can change with time, as it was the early days of discrimination and revolution that created gangs in El Paso; however, it is clear that racism does not always stay overt. I observed more individuals identifying as gang members and participating in gang-related activities in Denver and Ogden than I did along the U.S.-Mexico border region, and I saw more targeting of people of color and group behavior in these other communities. Yes, there are many structural problems in the border region, but this does not necessarily coincide with heightened gang involvement or violence. It is my hypothesis that the recommended increase in punishment would result in an increase in gang involvement and delinquent and criminal activities. A greater political emphasis on border walls and an increased number of U.S. Border Patrol agents will add to the isolation and separation of families and friendship networks that have existed when this region of the country was part of Mexico, Spanish territory, or indigenous lands. This does not appear capable of altering the long-standing trade route, but it may alter who is in control of that trade—which may in fact be the primary point.

The data provided in this chapter highlights the challenges encountered by youth living along the U.S.-Mexico border in southern New Mexico and west Texas. They live in social environments that are not conducive to economic or educational opportunities. Nevertheless, most youth stay the course by playing sports, socializing, and growing up in preparation to create families and attain jobs. The structural problems, however, highlight that numerical majority minority population areas by themselves do not uproot racism. Despite most residents following a color-blind ideology where race supposedly does not matter, the primary beneficiaries in New Mexico's juvenile justice system are white youth as they maintained the lowest rates for all racial and ethnic groups.[47] Nearly two centuries have passed since the region was brought into the United States, which removes the ability to pinpoint that advantage without recognizing the data from previous chapters. This structural advantage plays a role in all the institutions that could influence youth criminalization. Schools are an active participant in not only issuing referrals to youth but also utilizing school district policies to provide additional consequences for youth misbehavior. The fact that one third to one half of all juvenile arrests occur in schools, in addition to various internal disciplinary consequences, brings attention to the critical overlap of educational consequences (drop-outs and push-outs) that interact to increase DMC rates.[48] Juvenile Probation and Parole Officers describe the challenges they encounter in an attempt to be more rehabilitative and the resources they have to work with in creating solutions, whereas members of law enforcement desire greater punishment. Nevertheless, all the data I reviewed from the schools and the juvenile probation offices indicate that youth do encounter discipline, and, based on my research in Colorado and Utah, many of the consequences in place or under consideration only serve to enhance current levels of inequality. So where do we go from here? There are high levels of external criticism of youth and the institutions where they reside, as punishment is perceived as not existing until adulthood. I have outlined the challenging conditions that exist in this region of the country produced through colonization. Rather than increasing punishment, greater attention should be focused on alleviating and correcting these structural problems.

CHAPTER FIVE

Contradictions in Law Enforcement

In *Gang Life in Two Cities,* I *primarily presented a view of Latino and black community members, some of whom were gang members, and the negative interactions they had with the police. Law enforcement, in general, appeared united in their harassment of minority youth, but the border region demonstrated internal contradictions. Rather than a united war on gangs, it appeared there were more pressing issues related to the geographic area that took precedence. Comprehending life on the border region requires an awareness of how the U.S.-Mexico border has increasingly become a militarized zone that stretches 100 miles northward, with most of the focus concentrated on the geographic line that divides the two countries. In El Paso, the high fences, river, cameras, and Border Patrol vehicles were stationed every 100 yards to maintain a physical obstruction. In southern New Mexico, the desolate area was divided by vehicle barrier fencing and Border Patrol officers in the vicinity in case anyone attempted to get close to the border. Border enforcement prevented people from entering the country if anyone attempted to gain access without going through the ports of entry maintained by U.S. customs agents.*

To learn more about border enforcement in the remote and isolated regions of southern New Mexico, where populated communities do not share a border, I drive along isolated roads and visit ports of entry. The terrain in southern New Mexico is a barren desert with cactus, shrubs, and lava rock. The wind blows steadily. I do not observe anyone walking around, and no humans were in sight for as far as the eye can see. There aren't any homes. On the highway I primarily pass Border Patrol trucks; not many other vehicles travel on this road, which connects El Paso with the small town of Columbus, New Mexico. Everywhere I stop near the border fences, a Border Patrol officer pulls up near my vehicle while I take pictures and begins to inquire about my actions. Most were friendly, but still highly suspicious of my intentions. When I drive into Columbus, a town of 1,600 residents, I see small apartment complexes and homes, and I am followed by Border Patrol vehicles. At the border checkpoint, I park my vehicle and walk around. A school bus pulls up and drops off about thirty high school students, who walk across the border and into the town of Puerto Palomas, Mexico.[1] The Border Patrol officers sit in their vehicles and watch all the activity.

    I drive further and come across a remote road that takes maybe an hour to drive from the deserted town of Hachita, New Mexico, south on Highway 81 to Antelope Wells. I bring my 13-year-old son as my research assistant. Along this road, as with many of the rural areas near the border, there is often no cell phone service. We travel south and see a lot of things that look like wires in the road, but I later realize they were snakes. The border crossing at this location is not open around the clock. After reaching the border station, I turn around before crossing into Mexico and begin driving back. Ours is the only vehicle traveling north. A few semi-trucks pass me going south. As I pass the Border Patrol vehicles this time, they act as though they hadn't seen me driving south, and immediately one of their trucks begins following me north. I try to guess the speed limit on this open road to avoid getting pulled over. Eventually another Border Patrol SUV comes up behind the one following me, and their overhead lights begin spinning. I pull over to the shoulder, and I sit in the car with my hands on the steering wheel so that my hands were visible. The officers walk to my car door and ask me to exit the vehicle. They question me about what I'm doing and ask for my ID. I tell them I'm researching juvenile justice programs for the Sixth Judicial District and am interested to learn what impact the border had on Hidalgo County residents. They ask to search my vehicle and have me open my trunk. While waiting, I absentmindedly put my hands in my pockets, and they remind me to keep my hands where they could see them. They run my name and license through their system and continue questioning my activities. I comply with all of their requests, but they appear to have never heard the type of story that I had given. They inquire whether I am catching snakes. They ask whether I have any drugs in my vehicle. They ask whether my son's mother gave permission for him to be with me. I am released after a twenty-minute investigation.

    Despite humans living in this region of the country for a thousand years, the political designation of this geographic area as two separate countries is less than two centuries old and the enforcement of socially controlling residents and materials is less than a hundred years old. During the past two centuries, humans have crossed the imaginary and later the physical border to work or obtain higher standards of living. Historian Wilbert H. Timmons stated:

> Nowhere, it has been noted, does a political barrier separate two nations with a greater economic disparity. Even though some border sections in the United States are the poorest in the country, and some border sections in Mexico are relatively well off compared to the rest of the republic, the imbalance of the economies which meet at the border is enormous. As one specialist has noted, "neither the per capita gross national product nor the per capita income of any country in the world even comes near the *amount of difference* in per capita between the United States and Mexico."[2]

The transportation of materials, both legal and illegal, has been long standing. However, while the border itself is the most intensely observed area, Border Patrol jurisdiction extends 100 miles north of the border,

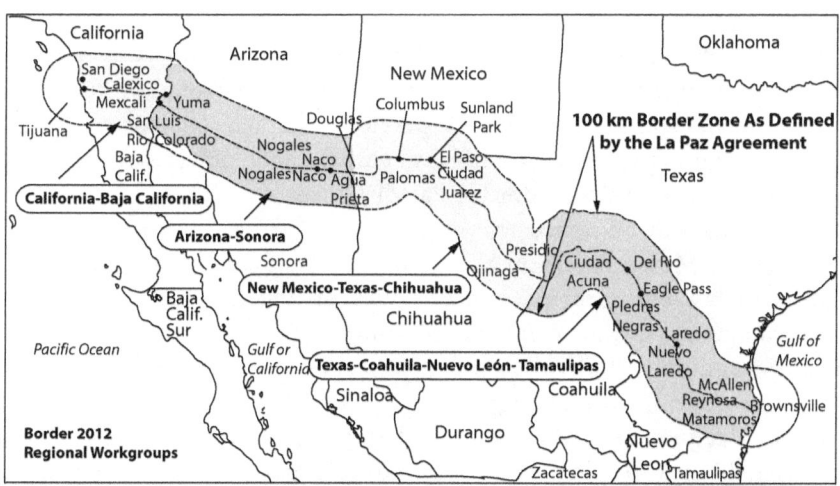

FIGURE 5.1 Border Region: Border Enforcement Enhanced 100 Miles North of the Border.
Source: http://www.theglobalarc.org/index.php/about/regions/u.s.-mexico_border.

thus their presence is felt in a wide variety of communities such as Lordsburg and Las Cruces, and along several major highways and Border Patrol check points.

Along the border, law enforcement has shaped the human experience in a way that is different than many urban communities nationwide because of the broader array of law enforcement agencies and the legal breadth to investigate both criminal and civil violations. The Disproportionate Minority Contact (DMC) Technical Assistance Manual categorizes an arrest as the first of nine decision points involving the juvenile justice system.[3] As DMC studies expanded from the original focus of confinement (one decision point) to contact in 2002 (nine decision points), scholars began to question why the study of policing remained the most important yet understudied topic in the juvenile justice system.[4] Criminologists Pope and Feyerherm stated, "Police are the gatekeepers controlling who is funneled into the juvenile courts. If such decisions are in any way racially biased, minority youth may be more at risk later during the correctional processing stage."[5] Some researchers have attributed the lack of progress in reducing DMC to the lack of focus on the front end of the system.[6] I began with the following research question: "Why are youth of Mexican descent who live along the U.S.-Mexico border overrepresented at the point of arrest compared to white youth?" Figuring out whether and how youth encountered law enforcement began by exploring neighborhood census tracts, observing neighborhoods and schools, and reviewing juvenile probation files and detention data as outlined in the previous chapter. The focus of this chapter involves interviews with law enforcement officers, ride-alongs with sheriffs, a six-week Border Patrol Citizen's Academy, and public listening sessions on police activities.

Youth of Mexican descent had higher levels of contact with the institution of law enforcement, and this was enhanced by differential living conditions, group membership, and a lack of resources available in the community. Individual police officers possessed the authority to initiate a referral for a delinquent act or status offense, to give a warning, or to request federal authorities determine citizenship status. Along the U.S.-Mexico border, there were multiple law enforcement agencies operating in largely rural and poor geographic settings. New Mexico communities that were incorporated into a city had their own police departments, which ranged in size from three officers to 161 officers, whereas the local sheriff's department monitored the overall county.

The El Paso Police Department consisted of 1,005 sworn officers, and the El Paso County Sheriff's Office had 260 sworn personnel.[7] State (New Mexico State Police and New Mexico Motor Transportation Police) and federal agencies (Border Patrol, Federal Bureau of Investigations, and U.S. Customs) supplemented local law enforcement. In addition, the U.S. National Guard often helped Border Patrol with surveillance. Other forms of social control were present on the military bases (e.g., Fort Bliss and White Sands), private property (e.g., schools and stores—from Wal-Mart to local malls), and universities (e.g., university police officers).

Contrary to many law enforcement agencies across the nation, which are lacking in racial and ethnic diversity, the agencies in this region had a sizeable—in some communities along the U.S.-Mexico border, equitable—representation of the communities they serve.[8] For example, 50–57 percent of the Sheriff's Office in District Three (Doña Ana County) and the Las Cruces City Police Department were Latino, which was only slightly lower than the county (64 percent).[9] The El Paso Police Department was 79 percent Latino and 12 percent female. Latino and white officers were also more likely to be bilingual. Law enforcement agencies in this area that appeared to have equitable representation in terms of race and ethnicity appeared to have better rapport with the residents and countered overt claims of racial or ethnic bias.[10] It also created interest in youth for pursuing careers in law enforcement. Criminal Justice was the most popular major at the local university, and students, primarily between the ages of 18 and 24, often brought with them socialized conservative feelings for legitimate behaviors and the punishments required to change these actions. Many of the students reported a desire to fight and solve crime. Anthropologist Josiah Heyman found that, despite many similarities between Latino officers and the populations they policed along the U.S.-Mexico border, these officers generally held a moral distance from recent immigrants, identified themselves with the institution of Immigration and Naturalization Service (INS), and emphasized personal accomplishments that entailed a separate identity and an overall restrictive viewpoint on immigration.[11]

As I set out to do my interviews, I was curious about officers of Mexican descent and what role they played in perpetuating or challenging levels of inequality. In criminologist Nicole Gonzalez Van Cleve's book *Crook County*, she outlined how a primarily "all-white cast" of prosecutors, judges, and defense attorneys perpetuated a system of inequality for which primarily black and brown defendants were seen as criminals.[12] Everyone in the courtroom workgroup maintained the structure of color-blind racism. My data allowed me to focus not only on practitioners who were white but also those who were Latino, and I wondered whether they too maintained these racial hierarchies, intentionally or unwittingly.

Border Enforcement

The national borders of oceans and land combine for a total of 7,500 miles that surround the mainland of the United States. Politicians described the security challenges involved with the 2,600 miles of coastal borders with the Atlantic and Pacific Oceans, the 5,500 miles of shared border with Canada, and the 2,000 miles shared with Mexico. In 1978 the Border Patrol was listed as having 2,580 agents, which was much smaller in comparison to the fiscal year of 2009, which disclosed more than 20,000 agents, most of whom were stationed along the border with Mexico. U.S. Border Patrol apprehensions have grown from 200,000 in 1970 to 1.7 million in 1986, then decreasing and rising again.[13] From 2005 to 2010, fewer than 1,100 Canadians were apprehended by the U.S. Border Patrol, whereas there were 404,365 apprehensions of Mexicans in 2010 and more than a million in 2005.[14] Of these apprehensions, 97 percent have occurred at the Southwest border, of which 86 percent were male and 39 percent were 24 years of age or younger. Mexican nationals made up the greatest proportion of apprehensions (87 percent), followed by people from Guatemala (4 percent), El Salvador (3 percent), and Honduras (3 percent).[15] Border militarization has consisted of increased numbers of Border Patrol agents, fences, cameras, unmanned airplanes, and other types of technology that have pushed migrants desiring entry into the United States to pursue more dangerous routes, including deserts, canals, and places where vigilante groups regularly prey on the undocumented immigrants.[16] Anthropologist Josiah Heyman argued that this separation had even become a virtual wall because of advanced surveillance using computer technologies along with the massing of police forces.[17]

Several researchers have analyzed the substantial increase of federal enforcement along the border and its impact on border communities.[18] Sociologist Timothy Dunn outlined how the border region has grown over time into a militarized zone of low-intensity conflict.[19] The 2008 economic crisis only strengthened the rhetoric of saving jobs for U.S.

citizens and encouraged the deportation and incarceration of undocumented populations. Political scientists Jacob Hacker and Paul Pierson reported divergent experiences as the rich continued to see record-breaking profits and billion-dollar federal payouts, whereas most Americans experienced a loss of jobs, housing, and security.[20] The focus of punishment continued to be the poor immigrant. According to U.S. Immigration and Customs Enforcement, during the 2012 fiscal year, the Obama administration recorded a record-setting year with nearly 410,000 deportations.[21] Immigrants from Latin America proportionately represent 38–51 percent of all immigrants from 1960 to 1999, with the majority coming from Mexico.

Officer Juan, a top law enforcement official working in one of the border counties, reported his top two priorities:

> Our number one issue is kids coming from Mexico transporting narcotics. Something we have discovered when we have searches is kids bringing drugs into schools. Second, the U.S. Attorney's Office and the Feds won't process juvenile cases unless it's a huge amount of drugs. They won't prosecute for carrying dope into the communities. The cartels know the interstates and the flood systems. If law enforcement officers arrest a juvenile, the parents can't come across and intervene, even if it is a juvenile. The youth will get a narcotics violation and more than likely get probation, but if you live in Mexico, there is no enforcement. There is a four-day hold by the system and then they are deported. The four-day holds are not made to handle these types of cases. Nowadays there are more narcotics used by kids and they are involved in selling and distribution. They live in a poorer economy and have chaotic family situations. The government can do repossessions and families lose vehicles, but a lot of parents have substance abuse problems. And they lose everything. What is going on in Mexico is brutal and often the kids are told they have no choice. Before they would often come in vehicles but with Border Patrol now there will be a high-speed chase.

During the time of this study, Ciudad Juárez in Mexico became one of the most violent cities in the world as conflict between drug cartels escalated. Juvenile Probation and Parole Officers and teachers reported the challenges for many of their students and staff who lost family members in Mexico due to violence. Although there were allegations of some high school students living along the border and carrying fifty-pound backpacks of drugs, having bundles of money, or participating in assassinations, empirical evidence of these claims was less available. Based on New Mexico's statewide Children, Youth and Families Department (CYFD) data, law enforcement officers made anywhere between two to eight arrests per year for a juvenile possessing 100 pounds or more of marijuana, and these primarily occurred in the border counties of Doña Ana, Grant, and Luna. The numbers for possessing eight ounces or more of marijuana were equally small in number, but these occurred in other regions of the state. The CYFD data was of U.S. citizens only, so we don't know how many non-citizen arrests occurred. One reporter found that U.S.-born youth were pressured to smuggle drugs into the country.[22] For the year she reviewed, she found four incidents where Customs and Border Protection Officers had apprehended juveniles for attempting to bring marijuana into the country. School officials were quick to emphasize that some of the top students, even some valedictorians, were from Mexico, and thus criminal or drug-trafficking stereotypes should not override the good and long historical relationship between both countries. Countering negative stereotypes was a constant challenge because the involvement of one minority individual was transmitted to the entire minority group, despite the fact that the greater rates of involvement of white males in school shootings, mass shootings, and domestic terrorism are never transferred to all white males in the United States.[23] In a society based on colonialism, images of violence and rampant drug trafficking became commercialized portrayals that affected the broader population and region.

Border Patrol officials and Customs agents were often on the news highlighting drug seizures from vehicles attempting to gain legal entry. Occasionally stash houses or tunnels were found. For example, in 2018, Border Patrol officials discovered 2,003 pounds of marijuana hidden near a road in Lordsburg, New Mexico.[24] In 2008, I attended a six-week Border Patrol Citizens Academy, where 22 citizens could learn the official version of border enforcement. Each week was organized into themes such as border observations, immigration detention centers, bike and dog patrols, SWAT, technology, immigration and custom inspection laws, and finally a graduation ceremony at the Border Patrol Museum.[25] The Latino and white Border Patrol officials took us along the border. One personable agent of Mexican descent described how he too had family on both sides of the border, but his job was not personal. Whatever the law said, he followed. One day at the Border Patrol Museum, a team of Border Patrol officials entered and I inquired what was required to be one of them. A young blond man responded, "As long as you can keep your mouth shut and head down, then you will be good."

In these two districts, children who were undocumented were often unable to receive governmental resources because most programs for social services required a Social Security number. Mexican youth picked up by the Border Patrol were detained for a short period and then brought back across the border; in some cases, they were detained longer, until several individuals from their country of birth were arrested. During my visits to these facilities, I noticed how they looked like correctional facilities, with women housed in one section and men in another, although in the temporary holding facilities there was also a room for women and their children. Deputy Jeremy, a younger member of the Sheriff's Department, outlined his responsibility when encountering someone he perceived as being in the country without legal documentation:

> If someone is illegal, I can only stop and call Border Patrol to come pick them up, but it cannot be for a long period of time or it becomes a violation. And so usually an officer can spend time to run the vehicle registration and identification but not any longer. The second time someone is caught without papers it is a felony. We have assisted federal police with Operation Stonegarden.

Local police and sheriff departments working with federal law enforcement were not regularly aligned here as they were in Arizona, but there were moments when they joined forces. In 2017, the county commission in Doña Ana agreed to accept $700,000 in funding from the ongoing Operation Stonegarden to fight border-related crime, but they assured civilian groups they would not participate in federal immigration enforcement (i.e., the raids that were protested in the introduction).[26] County policy was to not inquire about legal status during vehicle and pedestrian stops.

Policing of Border Communities

Law enforcement officers acknowledged how the neighborhood influenced their policing style. Based on field observations, highly concentrated white neighborhoods received lower levels of law enforcement patrol than did highly concentrated Mexican American neighborhoods. However, the more densely populated cities of Las Cruces and El Paso received more police attention than the more rural geographic areas. Geographically there was a wide variance in how officers responded to youth misbehavior. Officer Steve, who was Latino and a twenty-year veteran of the police department, believed certain areas of the city provided more economic buffers for youth from getting in trouble. He reported:

> Poverty does not make bad people, but having money provides buffers. For example, Sonoma Ranch [high concentrated white neighborhood], there are all kinds of buffers from the diagnosis of mental illness to households that have money to put their kids in programs. They can afford to have their kids play sports or put their son or daughter in basketball camp and pay the $500 fee. In lower-income areas, having both parents is unusual. Some of these youth live with grandma or change households every six months, and that creates a chaotic environment.

Having knowledge of a lack of services in the community pushed certain law enforcement leaders to become more proactive by working with city, county, district, and state officials to search for grants and partner with other agencies. Several federal grants, such as the High Intensity Drug Trafficking Areas (HIDTA) Program, the Edward Byrne Memorial Justice Assistance Grant, and the Weed and Seed program offered funding geared toward increasing law enforcement resources. Officer Steve elaborated on how he, along with several other officers, helped establish a Weed and Seed Safe Haven center in one of the poorest and highest concentrated communities of Mexican descent in the city. He reported:

> One of the primary findings from these early studies was that the youth needed a safe haven within the community where they could go after school and have community support. A house was chosen in the Mesquite neighborhood for such a location, and the house was stripped and rebuilt with the help of officers and community leaders to transform the house into a service-oriented building. . . . At first the community was resistant to the idea of law enforcement officers stationed in the community, but later they began to give their

support. Officers learned that when they dressed in plainclothes the community would be more interactive and engaging than when they wore their police uniform, even when they already knew they were law enforcement.

Officers reported that the Chief of Police was crucial for efforts to develop community policing and partnerships with residents. As the chief position rotated, it often moved back and forth from administrators supporting community policing to some not wanting any "headaches" and scaling back autonomous flexibility. Officer Steve shared the top three reasons the police department has contact with juveniles: 1) driving, 2) incorrigible at home or school; and 3) runaways.

As I rode with the Deputy Jeremy, he showed me his routine areas of patrol. First, we established that the patrolling of Chaparral was much quieter compared to Anthony and Las Cruces due to the lower call volume. There was a lot of graffiti on signs, abandoned buildings, and occupied trailer homes. The most common graffiti appeared to be SUR X3 and East Side.

> It is pretty hard to stop the graffiti out in this community, and there are no codes for removing the spray paint and so it usually stays on the wall. There are not as many reported gangs in this community compared to Anthony, which includes Teners, Dukes, and East Side. There are occasionally some major crashes on a few sections of these roads where young people have lost their lives. We often have runaways or supervise on-scene medical requests, which the Sheriffs provide assistance with until they receive support from EMT personnel. Sheriffs are on the scene for all emergencies to make sure everything is safe. . . . There isn't much for youth to do in the community. [We observed a few young children playing soccer in the dirt.] When fights occur, most of the time they do not get reported. The parents often call, but the kids do not. We respond to harassment phone calls due to jealousy between girls over boys or vice versa. Some of the commonly used drugs in the area are marijuana, cocaine, and meth. [We then discussed the substandard housing that was evaluated as colonias or near-colonias, which are rural communities in close proximity to the U.S-Mexico border and lack access to basic services such as water, sewer, or housing. He mentioned a lot of contractors don't want to build in this area]. They have had U.S. Congressman come to the area and talk about how the

area has no running water or connection to a septic system, but how these improvements are expensive. You can't force people to take care of the property, and many residents aren't fond of the county. Sunland Park is incorporated. Hatch is the same. Anthony has a development plan. The problem with being unincorporated is that there is no property tax money. Few businesses receive grants. We have a First Bank here, a couple pizza places, but they have to compete with El Paso and Las Cruces. There are extreme differences between the counties. Hatch is an old farming town and a transient community with people moving in and moving out. In Anthony you have the Teners, which threaten others to fight, but it's more talk than action. Youth egg cars and engage in vandalism. They scratch cars. Sometimes there are felony offenses. Some of the youth don't have a driver's license. You can have 13- or 14-year-olds driving nice cars. There isn't much for kids to do around here [Chaparral]. There is a skate park, but not a regular park. A baseball field. A community center, but not a lot to do. That's probably why kids get in trouble. They don't play around at the high school. They suspend youth for nine days and then have a meeting to see if they will let you back in. It's a closed campus. Of the seven [policing] districts, Anthony has the most activity.

Just as Deputy Jeremey stated, my ride-along in Anthony was busier in terms of activity, people, and a greater amount of interaction between other deputies. The shift began with a briefing by the sergeant, and then the group went to a Mexican restaurant to discuss recent events. They reported how a local bar was recently raided because drugs were being run within the business. The deputies discussed the patrol strategy for the night, finished their meal, and then walked out to their patrol cars. The meal was on the house. I rode out with Deputy Jesse.

In Anthony, 80 percent of the people are illegal with a different mindset. They are used to dealing with police where they have no human rights. Same thing with the gangs. In Anthony, they have more of the hardcore gangs like the Aztecas, where it is professional business. It is a job. They carry business cards. They fight back and run. They have a Mexican mentality, which gives them a different outlook on things. You need to be wearing your vest. The law is often gray and subject to interpretation. You have to go to a scene and know the law or at least the elements of the law to make arrests and to serve the community.

Out of academy you learn when the law is broken and to act accordingly. In Berino there was an 18-year-old who was shot. The gangs out here include the Berino gang, Sur Trece, East Side, West Side, Dukes, tons of gangs. The substation is right in the heart of this territory. In Las Cruces, it's territorial because a lot of gangs are close. When they call the news out here, you can't talk, only the Public Information Officer. Anthony is a hub for drug distribution here and elsewhere. There is one gang that takes over and claims its own territory. We had some hardcore members move here. I used to be assigned to the Berino community, and I would knock on doors and I was used to being ignored. Before we used to patrol all over Doña Ana County. This is our first year to have regions. The goal is to help know people and their background before you give a ticket. The more you know the more helpful. Everyone lies to the cops. You stop someone for speeding. They lie. You have to try and find truth. We have difficulty combing through the evidence at the scene because you know everyone is going to lie. In basic training and on the job, you spend years studying body language. Sometimes people want to fight you, and you can get your ass turned, so you have to be one step ahead of these people. Make sure their hands are out of their pocket. I don't know you and so you have to ask the right questions and look at the whole picture. You review the statements, the evidence, and the scene. You have to be good at reading people. People are going to lie, run, avoid, or try and change the subject. You can't hesitate. Maybe not, but also maybe a criminal hiding something. Sinner bullshitting is not as easy as people think. Sometimes we respond to calls such as runaway, truant, suicidal kids, children as young as 12, 13, and 14 who run away. They don't want to stay at home. We have runaway juveniles who are 15, 16, 17 and some are more into gangs, and we are called in to be the parent. You concentrate on the speeding, but you learn to look beyond the stop. Now look over everything. They might say they left their license at the house. You get a lot of white lies, but you have to know how to ask the right questions and not get distracted. The worst calls are domestics as they can turn bad so fast. Rather go and separate the man and woman. Police officers have discretion. Usually as long as the parent has the necessities such as running water and air we don't remove the child, but we look for paraphernalia. If you have nothing to hide, then why are you afraid? If you did nothing wrong, then why are you afraid? So why block me from entering your home or car?

Jesse was personable, and I even learned he was a family member of a friend. He knew his job. In *Gang Life in Two Cities* I had learned how marginalized community members did not trust the police and considered everything the police said to be a lie. Thus, in these encounters, Deputy Jesse had the power instead of the person undergoing questioning. Societal and cultural stigmas placed certain individuals at a greater risk for perceived illegality. Several organizations from the American Civil Liberties Union to the Border Network for Human Rights have been documenting abuses of the law and pursuing legal and public policy-oriented efforts to create change.

Domestic Family Issues

Victoria, a senior law enforcement official, described the challenges she has observed in the community:

> Weak parenting is prevalent here. A lot of one-parent families because the other family member is in prison, Mexico, or gone. Everything is focused on the now and getting things easy. In the last fifteen years there has greater pressure to not spank and child abuse is properly called bad. It's not okay to throw things and so if you do something wrong you get sent to your room. But children need to be spanked if necessary. Kids live with their mom who doesn't answer her phone because she's at her boyfriend's house. There is a lack of discipline and it's not the job of [police department name omitted] to enforce the rules. Some of these families want law enforcement to be the parent and it goes overboard. We get calls from parents who won't bother to call the police and report my kid won't get up for school and it's a parenting issue. Then you say, "That's why the kids aren't listening."

Officer Quentin concurred with Victoria and continued:

> A lot of what we see is generational. Third and fourth generation. In the poverty bracket. Both parents aren't together. No one is in charge. Number one problem we encounter is ignored kids. I mentor two now. We have numerous kids with men not involved. The families fall into a socioeconomic group that expects money and doesn't see a way to get out of that lifestyle. It's the same dynamic. The kids continue that path

with drug use, alcohol use, and they commit a crime. They don't get enough attention. Most kids have one or both parents in jail and it's the path they are destined to go. Take family members where everyone ended up in jail and you are seen as a little bitch if you haven't been to jail. There is a gang mentality and it's the path you're expected to fit. Their reality and it's not right. The parents are either working or divorced. We don't see a lot of families with two parents and there is no one who stays at the home. There are a lot of younger ladies who didn't get love or attention in their home and they have babies not knowing. We have a 14-year-old with a 6-month-old kid they have no idea how to raise. There is no food for the baby and the baby becomes malnourished. There is no program in society that teaches how to be a parent. How to teach kids what's wrong. Kids think it's okay to steal if you don't have the money. It's not seen as bad, but rather just don't get caught. If you are seen as weak you get taken advantage of. There is an economic dynamic where a large portion of single-parent families are trying to work. The parent holds a job for week or two and then loses their job. The parents can't be absent at work but there is no one to deal with the kids. We have to hit parents in the pocket, but if they are on welfare things won't change. We are fighting a losing battle, but it begins with educating the parents.

Officer Jack, a white, fourteen-year veteran of the police department, described how the state needed more options for removing children from problem homes:

Most of the time, youth are returned immediately back to their parents after receiving a Class Three [delinquent] referral and thus face little to no consequence. One time we removed a child for using meth at a drug house. The same drug house where her mother had overdosed three times and her aunt. We had to return her back home, and thirty minutes later, we received another call that she was at home using meth again. The judge detained her due to being a harm and danger to herself. She was sent to Ruidoso Treatment, but still has the potential to go back and use with such a family environment. There have been a few high-profile cases. One of our first accomplishments was shutting down a heroin drug house that had been in operation for a long period of time. There were mostly retirees living there and we were like, why tolerate this house in the neighborhood? So, we met with landlords and leasing companies.

For reasons such as these, most practitioners, including law enforcement officers, believed the family unit was a major source of the problem.[27] These practitioners identified the problem as generational and nothing was in place to break the cycle. Officer Jack mentioned how men were often the head of household in traditional Mexican families, and in single-parent families, young boys often took on an authority role. Parents were perceived as no longer disciplining their children, and officers felt overburdened when calls to the police requested help in getting children to go to sleep, to make them go to school, or to do simple household chores. One law enforcement officer stated there was a difference between discipline and child abuse and stated that as long as parents didn't strike their children in the face, he wasn't going to give a ticket or a warning.

Using Referrals to Create Change

Law enforcement is clearly not the institution to resolve family problems, and several officers reported a belief that giving juveniles a referral was a strategy to get young people the services they needed, both in the community and from the juvenile justice system. Officer Steve reported:

> I strongly believe in immediate assessment. My view is that it is better to report than to ignore misbehavior. For example, take the un-reporting of domestic violence in the past and how ignoring or dismissing a problem did not make it go away. Therefore, when we created the Safe Haven there became an increase in delinquency and crime because before a lot had gone unreported, but that began to change. The East Mesa area of Las Cruces has a lot of activity, but in terms of resources, the officers do not have the number of officers to go out there regularly and patrol delinquent activity. My goal is to prevent youth from falling through the cracks, and it is important to make an impact and provide resources for kids.

Las Cruces had established an immediate assessment and reporting center but encountered difficulties in its staffing because it was not run by juvenile probation. The practitioners did not have access to any internal information regarding the background of youth, if they had received prior juvenile or state care, or if they had received referrals in the past. Beyond an immediate assessment and reporting center, many officers and city officials had an interest in maintaining the Police Athletic Leagues and other partnerships with the community. However, these programs were difficult to maintain without federal or statewide grants to provide staff members or to pay law enforcement officers who received greater compensation for working additional shifts.

Gang Enforcement

The 2011 National Drug Threat Assessment reported how law enforcement officials considered New Mexico as one of five states in the country with the highest per-capita number of gang members. In addition, law enforcement officials considered the southwest border region to be a continuous criminal threat to the United States, an area where gang activity had increased in seriousness. With the long history of law enforcement involvement with gangs in El Paso and the increased focus in southern New Mexico since the 1990s, I devoted a lot of attention to learning more about how the gang units were operating. Part of my regular activities included attending presentations by gang units and even inviting officers to speak to my classes to learn their perspective. Most of my students desired careers in law enforcement. In 2008, a member of the gang unit told my class that the city had 417 members with most activity involving graffiti.[28] They noted how one gang was primarily feared because it linked the streets and prison. The city was described as not having a specific gang prevention or intervention program. In a follow-up interview, Officer Mark elaborated on the gang issues that he saw in the community:

> When you go down there [Anthony] and start talking to some of the Sheriff's investigators, you're going to be very surprised of how ingrained the gang lifestyle is down there. We've gone down there for gang operations and it was absolutely amazing the per-capita of number of gang members in the southern part of the county. It's just immense. And being so close to the border, I mean on the border, Anthony has good ties to criminal organizations, cartel organizations, and the prison gangs. We work with a coalition of various agencies to share information. Federal, county, local, etc. Our goal is to manage. We can't stop. We can't arrest our way out of it. So, we work with various agencies. In [agency name omitted] we have a five-person

gang unit. It seems like our Sureños and our East Side gangs all have some kind of formation back to the prison-level gangs, whether it's the Mexican Mafia out of California, which is made up of a huge influx of California Sureños. They are coming to New Mexico through Arizona and Colorado; we've seen a huge influx of that. And some of our East Siders are from third- and fourth-generation gangs, so they have family members who have ties to SNM [Syndicato de Nuevo Mexico], Los Carnales, and the penitentiary system, federal and state. [I asked Officer Mark if he had any numbers regarding gangs.] We've gone in there [the Crime Statistics Analysis Office of the police department] and tried to show them, "Look this is how we correlate our stats." And we tell them, "Statistics can be swung in any way, and any direction," but including outcomes is especially important for what we do. We are on this side of the fence. Our view is over here. So, I kind of wish we had stats that we could just give to somebody to give them a fresh view. Because when I, at the end of the year, correlate my stats I'm doing it as a [position omitted] who has gone to the drive-bys, who has gone to the hospital to see who got shot at. I'm one of the guys who has searched the cars and pulled the guns and the dope out. So, my view is over here, whereas an assistant at the university might be right down the center of the road. But we are starting to collect. We do have stats, a full-time stats person at the police department who does take care of that for us. So, we are trying to bridge those gaps. We can get better and put together more up to date information. [I inquired how they determine whether someone is really a gang member.] If there is such a thing as gang wannabes, why am I picking up shell cases every day? Why am I going to the hospital for stabbings and shootings? I understand the term, but I don't think we're interested in what's a wannabe and what's a true gang member. And anybody that says that I will tell them, you know what, it would be a great benefit for your students to see this aspect of where it all comes from. I would take them out to the security housing units at Southern New Mexico Penitentiary. It's a level-six maximum security penitentiary and you let them hang out with some of these Mexican Mafia members. Well, don't let them hang out, but you get them to see how they work and how they live, and you're going to be like, "Oh, wow." It's a very eye-opening experience. The first couple of times we went out there it was quite eye-opening. You'll see. This is some serious crap out here, and then they'll believe.

My student networks provided me with the opportunity to tour one of the prisons, a jail, and an immigration detention center. The prison and jail both had Security Threat Group Units that housed inmates who were considered members of gangs. Since 2015, one of the prison gangs, Syndicato de Nuevo Mexico, continued to face numerous criminal prosecution cases.[29]

My conversation with Officer Mark continued:

The *Sun News* wanted to do a thing on it [story on gangs], they have been wanting to do one for a number of years, but they haven't quite found a formula. You know what we go through and you guys report, because they send someone to [the police department], you know it's all public information, you know they sit there and start going through all the reports. "God, you guys have a lot of drive-by shootings. There's a lot of stabbings," and stuff like that. I'm like, "Yeah, we kind of do." They start reading some of the information on the reports and it's like, "You guys have a gang problem here." "Yeah, we do." And so they wanted to cover the story. They sent a reporter out to do a ride-along for about a week with the gang unit. And they were like, "Wow, I didn't know this was happening all over the city." You know some of the places down in Anthony, around California, and other places its neighborhood-specific. In Las Cruces it's not, I mean you'll have a Sureño gang member who lives right next to an East Sider. Well, there's always going to be a higher concentration [of gangs] in the lower-income neighborhoods, I think that's pretty much anywhere you go. What we've seen is a rather large influx of them, we have our hot spots, we've seen a lot of them on the East Mesa. Back in 1998, 1999, we had a huge issue with our East Side Locos gang with the FBI, with the Las Cruces Police Department, Doña Ana Sheriff's Department, and State Police. There was a multi-jurisdictional task force that went and did an investigation (it was about a year and a half long) and they did everything, wire taps, the whole nine yards. And they got a ton of information and everybody went to prison for a very long time, and they worked it under the RICO statute. Hit them federally and pretty much shut the organization down for about a month. And then the vacuum was filled and it's back to what they were doing. They are big time into cocaine, trafficking weapons, and human trafficking. When we first started, we borrowed a lot from Albuquerque. . . . They have a great gang unit. They have what's called a Repeat Offender

Program, which is very aggressive, you know, because they understand their recidivism rate of certain offenders. This guy gets out and he is on probationary status; they know within three or four days this guy is going to be back doing what he was doing and so they follow him around do surveillance twenty-four hours a day, and they catch him in the act. So, this guy is doing a murder in the background, but these guys are sitting there saying, "Let's go, you're going back." We're are not at that level yet. We went to training—oh, God, we've been all over the country for training. We've been all over, man, you name it, we've been there. Everybody in the unit is certified as a gang specialist through this training program so now they can testify in court. They have testified in court. You know I won't use the word expert, there are very few experts on what goes on. So, they can testify as to the trends, the colors, and the aspects of what's going on. A lot of stuff is going on the Internet, computer-based gang names that we are seeing now. YouTube, Myspace, Facebook, that kind of stuff, these guys are all very up to date on. So, they've been used numerous times if they need them for a search warrant or anything else.

The courts in New Mexico are very weak. I'm not saying the judges are weak, it's that this system is not conducive to aggressive law enforcement at all. People want an aggressive strategy when it comes to dealing with the gang-level violence. This summer we are going to see drive-bys, we are going to see stabbings, and people are going to get frustrated. They are going to be calling their counselors. They are going to be calling the newspapers asking for a response, and the response is I pick the kid up. The kid does a drive-by shooting, I call JPO [Juvenile Probation Office], and they say you don't have to detain him, and I turn him over to mom. I mean, I've done that several times, but they are getting better. I catch a kid who is doing a burglary who cut off his ankle bracelet because he did a drive-by a week before. I called JPO and they say we don't have to detain him. Kick him back loose, he's back on the streets in twenty minutes. So, it's kind of weakening when you're talking to people, especially these California-based Sureños that are coming right out of L.A. [Los Angeles]. These are the guys who are working in 18th Street Gang. The Sureños is just a brand name. It's not like anyone says "I'm a Sureño" and then "What set or clique are you from?" So, it's just a name brand, but these guys are coming from California, they are coming from Phoenix, they are coming from Colorado. We sat and debriefed some of them and said,

"Why are you guys coming to New Mexico?" I mean there are a ton of them coming here, here and Albuquerque. They said, "Your state is wide open. You guys have lax lax drug laws. You guys don't have any gang injunctions. You don't have a three strikes rule." Hell, we just signed away the death penalty. "We can do whatever we want out here and we know it." That's why they say they are coming here. My personal opinion is that's why you are seeing an influx of gang violence throughout New Mexico. A lot of these guys are pushing in from these different areas because they are getting pushed out. I remember when I first started, I started asking questions. "What if we really don't have a gang problem?" That's funny, I responded to the call. You know, I'm stopping these kids every single night and taking guns from them. Tell me, why are we not saying this is a gang problem? The information I was given back from them is we don't want to scare the community because this is a retirement community. A lot of people are moving in here and we don't want to scare them. Oh, ok, I don't know if that was true or not, but like I said last year when we did the [statistics], I had to go through it and it took me about a week just going through some stats, reading reports, and getting everything collected and gathered. And again, it wasn't a hundred percent correct, but from what we know we had twenty-five drive-bys just last year—that's just drive-by shootings. Twenty-five drive-bys and that's just in the city, not the county, not for State Police. On top of that we had fifty shootings or stabbings, whether it was at a party or park or something like that, and these were all gang-related. This isn't a domestic-related shooting, and everybody is like, "Wow," in the community and I'm like, ok. So now I've got twenty-five drive-bys, fifty shootings or stabbings that would fall into a felony category, which would be close to death or great bodily harm. And I got four guys to handle it. And it's like, "Wow, now you're starting to see what we are in for." Oh, then we'll start talking about the level of graffiti we are seeing, and then we start talking about how many times we have to go out and gather some intelligence. So, we realized what we needed to do. Resource allocation, we had to get everybody involved, everybody from the shift levels, the school resource officers, administrators, supervisors, we had to get everybody involved. Then we had to, I mean this, last year the guys have done a tremendous job of going out there trying to educate members of the community, the schools, they've done presentations for CYFD, they've done them for the private sector, they've done them for if somebody calls and says, "Hey, can you guys do a presentation or demonstration and presentation for us on gangs?" What we are seeing here in Las Cruces, you got. Of course, we always get my cousin in from L.A. Ok, I've sat down with investigators from L.A. I sat down with investigators from Chicago, Dallas, Phoenix, and they have a lot of great information. And I understand the political overtones. Obviously, being a [position name omitted], I have to protect my organization with the best interest of my organization at heart. But then again, I can't sit there and tell people that what they are seeing isn't what they are seeing. That's part of our presentation. We go out there and say you know what, and we try to tell them.

There was no doubt that Officer Mark was passionate about his job and his perception of gangs, crime, and the various networks between street gangs, prison gangs, and cartels. As he says, "I am the one making the stops, taking the guns, and doing the debriefings." In *Gang Life in Two Cities*, community activists who had been involved with gangs in their past along with those who were attempting to improve relations between the community and the police rightfully challenged many of the claims made by the gang unit and other members of law enforcement. Similar to their role of community advocacy, it was clear that Officer Mark felt he was in a similar role of advocacy for this gang unit and the larger police department. The dilemma becomes clear when one analyzes the law enforcement data and sees how it often contradicts most law enforcement claims that had been provided to the media and distributed to the public. Institutions of law enforcement, from police officers to district attorneys, have based their punishment practices on the legitimacy of these claims, and they have often been reluctant to share such information with researchers because of these potential difficulties. This is not to dismiss Officer Mark's claims but rather to place them in their proper context. Malcolm Klein's book *Gang Cop* highlights the contradictions between gang enforcement and gang research, as does *Policing Gangs in America* by Katz and Webb.[30]

Officer Juan described some of the changes he noticed with gangs:

Back in 1995 we had gangs as an issue here, and we created the Gang Unit because we were not prepared for when they were shooting each other. Back then the discussion was do we treat them as adults. The Sheriff said we had no gangs, but that was political talk. Now the trend is still gangs but they are more into the money now. We have a little bit of tagging. Sporadic, not like it used to be. Now it's about money. Not tattoos. So, we gather intelligence. In the past they were proud to say they were in gang and we would use it against them. The local gangs today are scaled-down versions of the past. Prison gangs are influential, and we know there are connections with SNM.

According to the National Institute of Corrections, in 2015 New Mexico had a lower rate of incarceration (335 per 100,000) than the national average (458 per 100,000).[31] Texas had the seventh highest rate of incarceration (568 per 100,000). Officer Steve elaborated on how most of the gangs have a community base and how incarceration has affected some of these members in Las Cruces:

> I see a lot of this emulation for youth wanting to become involved in gang behavior. Gangs have been active in this neighborhood for at least the last twenty-five years, and it started with the 45ers at Colin Park [This would be around 1987, but I think he mentioned somewhere about the 1970s in the interview.] This later developed into the East Side gang. [M]ost gangs are reflective of the community demographics, and in a lot of these poor communities that is more likely to include Hispanics. Some of the old-day gangs include the 45ers and Donañeros. Las Cruces membership is throughout the community and not specific to any neighborhood. There are no white gangs. A lot of members have been in gangs for multiple generations. East Side then changed to a prison gang but then both.

The mining community of Silver City was also perceived to have several gangs, including East Side Folk and a smaller gang known as Brown Pride. They also had a group called China Town Locos, which included several members who had gone to prison and were recruited into SNM. The police officer I interviewed said drugs and gangs were two of their biggest problems.

Internal Frustrations and External Criticism

Every law enforcement officer interviewed reported frustration with juveniles from a lack of parental discipline, school discipline, and the Juvenile

Probation and Parole Officer's inability to be more punishment-oriented. Individually, law enforcement officers seemed to feel an overwhelming burden of being unable to change the conditions they were witnessing. They could not change youth misbehavior, family home environments, schools, or the juvenile justice system, and the reasons for such obstacles were broad in a geographic area with a lack of resources. These overall frustrations seemed to make law enforcement officers somewhat reluctant to work with other institutions. However, rather than presenting a blue wall of loyalty, several officers criticized their agency's policies, practices, and different types of law enforcement officers as part of the problem. Disagreements arose regarding leadership styles, the age of officers, strategies for the use of force, and whether to initiate or ignore referrals. Younger officers attempted to take a more aggressive approach. Officer Steve, who seemed very grounded and respected in the community, reported the following:

> A lot of difficulty with community perceptions of the police are often influenced by rookie officers who are more aggressive. . . . A lot of crime in the community was going unreported because residents did not trust the police. In terms of officer behavior, it is important for officers to recognize that they are given authority, but they *are not the authority*. Officers must be willing to serve the community. [He reported that there are a lot of good officers in the department who are more dedicated to service, but there is also group of officers who perceive themselves as the authority.] It may be a 50/50 split. A lot of times, this is the younger officer. Currently, the police department is short-handed in terms of law enforcement personnel.

Officer Steve was not alone in seeing challenges within the department. Some officers described a discrepancy between the counties with regard to how much training was required to be a law enforcement officer. They stated in some of the communities in New Mexico an individual could be certified as a law enforcement officer and begin working without even being required to have training because there was leeway of one or two years. Officers thought this presented a safety issue for the community and was a possibly a reason why some agencies encountered public scandals. However, even with training there were some practices that seemed inappropriate. Officer Juan critiqued the use of force training when he stated, "I tell my rookies not everyone is a scumbag, and they go to training in

Santa Fe and get some incorrect training. There are other ways to resolve problems than by using your gun." Thus, when 5–40 percent of deaths in El Paso and Las Cruces, depending on the year, occurred at the hands of law enforcement, it creates a need to take another look at where the violence originates. As mentioned by criminologist Ramiro Martinez in chapter 4, an average of 14 percent of homicides were gang-motivated. Thus, depending on the year, law enforcement could be killing more residents than people involved in gang-related activities. The use of deadly force on the border was also a source of contention as the killing of a 15-year-old boy named Sergio Adrián Hernández Güereca, who was shot and killed by a Border Patrol agent, drew criticism.[32] On June 7, 2010, Sergio and his friends were playing near the international port of entry between Ciudad Juárez and El Paso. Their game involved touching the fence and then running back. A U.S. Border Patrol agent detained one of Sergio's friends on the U.S. side, and allegedly the youths began throwing rocks. Sergio ran away from the agent, who shot and killed Sergio on the Mexico side of the border. Video footage demonstrated that Sergio was not one of the youths throwing rocks. The case was under review by the U.S. Supreme Court to determine whether the family could sue the Border Patrol agent, but it was sent back to the appeals court.[33]

Several additional officers talked disparagingly about officers convicted of misconduct or corruption.[34] The court found one detective guilty for sexually assaulting a 17-year-old girl serving as a police intern, and officials later discovered he had been sexually abusing a child relative. Another police officer ordered a pizza naked while he was off duty, and in a subsequent case he extorted a woman to obtain sex. District attorneys tried and convicted a mayor and a police chief for running guns to a Mexican drug cartel.[35] A former chief of the FBI in El Paso was indicted and convicted for lying to investigators about his relationship with a Mexican racetrack owner who trafficked drugs and laundered money.[36] The Border Patrol was sued by a woman subjected to a body cavity search that did not result in finding any drugs.[37] A Border Patrol agent was arrested and later pled guilty to criminal charges of accepting bribes to allow the safe passage of drugs into the United States.[38] Charges of driving under the influence of alcohol or drugs brought down several law enforcement, school, and juvenile probation officials. Instances of corruption, unethical behavior, and criminal misconduct expanded criticism beyond juveniles to law enforcement officials. It even carried over into the prisons. One of the correctional institutions that I visited had a wall of pictures that included officers who were charged for smuggling contraband items into the secure facility or engaging in illegal activities with inmates. They called it the wall of shame and used it as example of how to be a better employee.

A public official criticized some of the law enforcement decision-making, describing an incident in which a foster dad brought several kids to a skate park. The police cited everyone for not having helmets and handcuffed the children to a bench. The official criticized this zero-tolerance approach as being ridiculous. The official desired to improve relationships with law enforcement and other institutions, but occasionally law enforcement officers were told by the chief of police not to attend these meetings. The official criticized the police for not knowing the law, in some of these cases preventing the district attorney from filing criminal charges. Law enforcement officers reported how one district attorney ran her political campaign on a 90 percent conviction rate and wouldn't pick up a lot of cases that were more questionable. The officers stated they would have to try these cases themselves, but they had little experience in selecting a jury or prosecuting a case.

Another official criticized the police practices as being old-fashioned and focused more on a desire for punishment and stricter sanctions instead of being focused on rehabilitative juvenile justice:

> The police department caught a kid with weed, a half a joint, and wanted him put into detention. So I called it in and he only received a score of one on a scale of one to ten. So they told us to release him back to the parents, but because he was talking back to the officer they wanted him detained.

A juvenile public defender named Amber summarized some of the difficulties with local conditions:

> Law enforcement is a mixed bag. Some officers are lazy and could care less. It's almost a sense of the Wild, Wild, West. Officers in New Mexico don't seem to think the fourth amendment applies. They are used to autonomy with little oversight. They know how to keep people in check, and the cops use these tactics to their advantage. I don't like to see how many young kids are treated. I want to see respect, but XYZ happened. There is a massive disillusionment. The police departments around here have serious issues and are underpaid and overwhelmed.

We all know who killed so and so. Everyone knows who killed this kid, but the police won't investigate. . . . Everything here is hearsay. The judge rules it doesn't matter. What you need here is a genealogy chart rather than rules of evidence.

To help ease some concerns, one of the city councils hired an independent agency to review its police department's handling of civilian complaints and use of force. I attended several of these public events and listened to community concerns.

Law enforcement officers, for the most part, seemed to work toward creating a positive community image. They mentioned the difficulties of being understaffed and lacking resources. Although the expectations of the job were overwhelming, the officers I interviewed reported a desire to help the community. In my position as a criminal justice professor, most of the encounters I had with law enforcement officers in the community were professional, which was a significant difference from my experiences in Colorado and Utah. However, not everyone in the community agreed that law enforcement was accomplishing these goals, as indicated by the number of complaints, lawsuits, and criminal charges against the police. Most residents were not deterred by the structural problems, as there remained a long line of recruits ready to replace any officers who lost their position due to disciplinary issues.

Along the U.S.-Mexico border region of southern New Mexico, law enforcement officers arrested Latino youth at higher rates than white youth. In El Paso, the numbers appeared less disparate, but as highlighted by the research conducted on Disproportionate Minority Contact in this state, proportional arrest rates could disguise other forms of bias. Because arrests were the first critical decision-making point in the juvenile justice system, analyzing the explanations provided by members of law enforcement provided additional insight into understanding disproportionate minority contact and how it was enhanced through border and gang enforcement.[39] Similar to the work of criminologists Vera Sanchez and Rosenbaum, law enforcement did not describe the policing of white and Latino neighborhoods as involving race or ethnicity, but they gave alternative explanations.[40] In this study, police officers described the issue as economic in nature and involving problem families. Latino and white officers reported issuing referrals primarily as a way to get poor youth from troubled families and home settings to receive additional resources from the juvenile justice system and the various community partners who responded to informally handled cases. This study found that greater resources were in fact devoted toward these youths due to referrals, but this support came primarily from institutionalizing agencies that, while designed for rehabilitation, often relied upon punishment to correct problematic living conditions and home environments. Thus, differential living conditions involving racial, ethnic, and economic segregation shaped youth experiences and the way they encountered the police. Identifying a moral high ground in terms of which groups or individuals were bad and which ones were good was impossible in a world made up of shades of gray.

CHAPTER SIX

Participatory Action Research Teams at a Minority-Serving Institution

It is January 2008, and I am 31-year-old assistant professor at New Mexico State University (NMSU). When I began teaching at NMSU, I had to challenge stereotypes because I did not look like a typical professor. I still looked young, wore baggy clothes, and had tattoos. Students continued to remark how they thought they were being pranked that I was their professor. NMSU is a Hispanic-serving institution and a minority-serving institution, but most professors do not match the backgrounds of their students. I have been teaching three courses per semester, but to teach a class I am interested in teaching, a course on gangs, I accept a fourth class. Teaching universities require faculty to teach four courses a semester, whereas research universities require two courses. NMSU took the middle approach. However, accepting a fourth course was my chance to share my knowledge regarding gangs, introduce students to the fun of data gathering, and outline how research can inform and shape policy. Moreover, I wanted to continue my interest in collaboration by drawing upon the skills and insights of my students.

From 2008 to 2012, I had a total of 111 students, including both undergraduate and graduate classes, who participated in data-collection efforts. Throughout these five courses, we set out to learn more about the level of impact gangs had in the surrounding communities. Supportive course technology allowed an online data-entry page for each group and for each individual so that I could provide feedback and guidance to field notes. Contrary to Utah and Colorado, New Mexico had a lottery scholarship that provided youth who graduated from high school the opportunity to attend college.[1] Such a program helped diversify the university racially, ethnically, and economically. I had research teams composed of many students from the general area, and they were diverse *in terms of backgrounds, gender, and race or ethnicity. Collaborating in this research gave all of us the opportunity to expand networks.*

My beginnings in research were intended to build upon the emphasis that Joan Moore, my dissertation committee member and esteemed gang scholar, placed on collaboration by incorporating academics, convict-addicts, the Chicano square community, and the organized outside Chicano groups.[2] Her work had a significant impact because learning required the inclusion of insiders who could provide access and support. In Denver and in Ogden, I had friends who guided my data gathering, and I describe them as key partners. In the U.S.-Mexico border region, I had my students and colleagues, along with access provided by a wide range of official institutions. The foundation of such a strategy began with concepts such as the "right to research," "research as praxis," and "students of color as holders and creators of knowledge." Some researchers in the discipline of psychology have incorporated collaborative research under the name of participatory action research (PAR).[3] The work of psychologist Michelle Fine, along with several colleagues, have contributed greatly to paving new paths for sharing the experiences of oppressed populations through PAR.[4] According to Fine, PAR insists that the most structurally disenfranchised have a right to engage in research and develop solutions. Taking this one step further, social psychologist Yasser Payne developed an approach he called Street PAR, which involves street-identified researchers.[5] In addition to work by Joan Moore, previous gang studies by David Brotherton, Luis Barrios, and John Hagedorn have incorporated gang members as part of their research teams.[6] These researchers have utilized their working-class backgrounds and involvement in social activism to scrutinize societal power structures. Involving members of the community has the potential to provide additional individuals to serve in crosschecking information and expanding networks.

At the beginning of each semester I asked my students to select a geographic area they were interested in learning more about in the area surrounding NMSU. Within each geographic area, participants were encouraged to focus on a theme such as schools, law enforcement, graffiti, etc. Before getting started, I always gave my students an analogy: Collecting data is like filling an empty swimming pool with water. The students were anxious about how to do such a thing, but I always told them that even no data is data, thus efforts to pursue information that resulted in a lack of support was also worthwhile information. For example, if an effort to contact a certain agency was made and the request was met with either a yes or a no, both answers offered an opportunity to inquire why. Although a yes was the most desired outcome, a no could spark interest as to why this institution was not receptive to sharing information on this issue. Ethnographers have often emphasized the role of gatekeepers as providing access to institutions as information.[7]

Inclusion of Underrepresented Groups

Although sharing a similar race and ethnicity, gender, or background has never been a research requirement, the lack becomes glaring when one sees that most of the studies of marginalized communities are rarely conducted by people of color. Academia's minimal inclusion of marginalized groups has resulted in only a small number of researchers who come from communities similar to those where they conduct research.[8] Bonilla-Silva and Herring wrote, "The percentage of top-ranked sociology departments without a single African American or Latino faculty member, or with only token representation, is simply shameful."[9] De la Luz Reyes and Halcón outlined an ironic yet paradoxical situation in which a greater number of Hispanic Ph.D.'s exist in academia compared to the past, but they encounter difficulty attaining academic positions at institutions of higher education.[10] As large numbers of minorities struggle to graduate from high school, the small proportions who attain educational success continue to encounter various forms of racism when it comes to finding employment in these fields. Maintaining historically white colleges and universities in academia has co-existed with critiques against other forms of knowledge such as lived experience and qualitative research.[11] Historically, the social sciences have given privilege to heterosexual, middle to upper class, white males and increasingly white females, and in many cases these are the people who have come to dominate the accounts of marginalized groups in society.[12] Such an epistemological supremacy to an "outsider" in oppressed communities, who methodologically could be either qualitatively or quantitatively inclined, pushes scholar activists to question ignored calls for decolonizing research.[13] Thus my students, who were overwhelmingly of Mexican descent with smaller numbers who were of Native American, African American, or white backgrounds, allowed for another angle of observation. My challenge was guiding them to learn research methods and to develop a sociological imagination so that they could learn, reflect, and account for what they discovered.

In this chapter, I provide thirty-five different narratives written by students who were part of the undergraduate classes.[14] Twenty-eight of the students were Hispanic (eleven female, seventeen male), and seven students were white (five female, two male). These narratives are first organized by location and then by thematic focus. One of the central tasks was to assess what level of threat the gangs they came across posed to the community. Depending on their source of information, the threat level could range from 1 to 10, but the overall average for these communities was 5 or 6. Some communities had somewhat lower or higher levels, which also varied somewhat by year. During the time frame in which students conducted their research, my sense of the general perception in the media, law enforcement, and by community members was that the level of gang threat was possibly as high 8 or 9, although some of these perceptions had been shaped by propaganda about the region and increasing levels of violence in Ciudad Juárez and Mexico in general. The students didn't have access to previous reports, so seeing the repetition in some of the findings was noteworthy. The student accounts vary somewhat in their level of analysis and data available to analyze. They had three months to understand an issue, and if they had continued in these efforts, their analysis and findings would become more developed. Nevertheless, I continued to be impressed by what they could find during these short periods of time. I do not agree with all the accounts or the information provided but, in an effort to share their voices, this was what they found.

Larger Communities of El Paso and Las Cruces

El Paso, Texas

Diana, a Hispanic female in the class of 2010, provided the first analysis in trying to determine the level of gang influence in El Paso:[15]

> I have heard some estimates of over 500 known gangs in the city of El Paso, but I don't know exactly where they are located. I would have never imagined that there were so many gangs in El Paso because I haven't been involved with or victimized by gang members. I wish

I could find out more information at the various high schools that I went to, but unfortunately, they weren't as cooperative as I would have hoped. From the schools I visited, I learned that the northeast part of El Paso was where there was more violence. There wasn't as much violence at the schools compared to the neighborhoods located around the high schools.

Two years later, Jose, a Hispanic male in the class of 2012, followed up on this number of 500 gangs:

> From the research we conducted for this course, we found out that there are over 200 gangs that are recognized by the El Paso Police Department. Unfortunately, these numbers may not be considered reliable because in the year 2009 there were over 500 gangs that were identified. The problem here is that in the span of three years, over 300 gangs apparently vanished. As an explanation for this phenomenon, we discovered that the media plays an important role. During this research, I discovered that many of the gangs in the area can be considered a threat, because many of them are very organized and have branches from other gangs spread throughout the country. El Paso is considered one of the safest cities in the nation, therefore many residents and even tourists might think that El Paso does not have a gang problem. This might be the case, considering that there does not seem to be much violence in the area. We discovered that many of the gangs in El Paso are sometimes divided by the area in which they operate. I personally visited the west side, northeast, and south side of El Paso and could find tagging that pertained to gangs in the area.

Mario, a Hispanic male in the class of 2012, attempted to answer this question by also looking at the number of listed gang members:

> The irony is that El Paso is known to be amongst the safest cities in the United States, yet they are home to one of the most notorious and dangerous gangs in the United States, the Barrio Azteca. Based on the data collected by our team, I was asked to rank the El Paso area threat level, with 10 being the highest and 1 being the least serious. There are many gangs in El Paso, Texas. However, difficulties arise when someone is asked to prove the relationship between the crimes committed in the area in relation to gangs. In 2009, El Paso Police reported

539 active gangs; this year there are only 246. So, what happened to other 293 gangs? El Paso's gang population has dropped by nearly 2,000 members in the past two years, according to police statistics, which raised questions about how gang members are documented. The police department this week released statistics showing El Paso has 3,677 documented gang members this year compared with 3,653 gang members in 2010 and 5,665 in 2009. "So, 2,000 gang members just disappeared from one year to the next?" asked Rob Gallardo, director of Operation No Gangs, a local gang-intervention program (Borunda, 2011)." His opinion was, "Should we give the El Paso Police Department the benefit of the doubt? . . . I doubt it!"

Determining the number of gangs and membership has historically been a struggle, but such notable deviations from one year to the next raised questions. In addition, why did the reported number of gangs, whether larger or smaller, not influence levels of violence?

Jacob, a white male from the class of 2008, provided a potential source of gang membership that I had not considered:

> I can honestly say that what I have learned about gangs in El Paso is exactly what I expected. I knew there would be a high amount of drug problems and a lower amount of other crimes. But I guess the one thing that did surprise me a little is that there is, supposedly, a low amount of gang-related homicides. The most surprising thing was learning about the worry about the return of some of the troops to Fort Bliss among law enforcement. There are tens of thousands of troops returning and many of which are believed to be involved in gangs. Law enforcement fears these members will train others in the combat that they have learned, have access to weapons, and increase gang crime in El Paso. There will always be gangs in El Paso and there will always be some level of a problem.

Zamara, a Hispanic female from the class of 2010, was the most determined to use her Fort Bliss sources to see if the military had any impact on the local gang scene:

> At the start of this project, I immediately wanted to focus on an area that would not be thought of as having a problem with gang activity. I chose to focus on the military because I had heard how several gang

members joined the Armed Forces to either get out of gang life or to hone combative techniques and gain tactical knowledge of weapons. I learned that the problem is far larger than the audience knows . . . I would describe gangs in this area of El Paso, TX, as present, but kept under wraps to protect the view we hold of our military. . . . It seems that if you don't mess with gangs, they tend to be more involved in tagging, small fights, and misdemeanors. In terms of my perceived level of threat and what we have found regarding gangs, I would say I was shocked by the information we found about gang life on military bases. You tend to think that the military is solely made up of good and honest citizens defending you and the country. The thought that there are some who are just in it to learn how to be the perfect criminal is quite frightening. As far as solutions for gangs in this area, I think that in terms of the military aspect of gangs, tougher screening could be performed. After all, weapon trafficking is one of the biggest problems with military gang members, so the proper knowledge of these members' status within their supposed gang is key to preventing weapons and information from landing in the wrong hands.

Various presentations I had attended on border violence emphasized the estimate that 90 percent of the guns smuggled into Mexico came from the United States. Marco, a Hispanic male from the class of 2010, followed this line of inquiry regarding the military and questioned whether soldiers had been participating in some of the violence occurring across the border:

There is a big difference between my perceived level of threat and the people I talked to regarding gangs. Mostly white communities are not aware of the level of gang activity in their city. They are just happy there is enough marihuana to go around. A solution to the problem is what everyone is looking for, but the amount of money involved is just too high. Another serious problem that has not yet affected El Paso is gang members receiving military training at Fort Bliss. My dad's theory is that the U.S. people are the ones killing for hire in Juárez, so maybe gangs are already taking advantage of their training. I saw a video with a gang member saying that it could not be more perfect, they are getting what they want by getting taught how to properly use weapons, plus they are getting paid for it. They say, "We would have done it for free."

These three students brought up good points about the vagueness of information pertaining to the role of soldiers at Fort Bliss in gang-related activities. Historically, they had been associated with the bar scene, being overrepresented as customers in the red-light districts, and having the one incident with the 1978 robbery and murder of Lee Chagra. Overall, the military appeared to be very well respected and thus less susceptible to criminal accusations.[16]

Robert, a Hispanic male from the class of 2008, focused on graffiti and one gang:

> Here in El Paso we do have these problems, but with less frequency. In addition, most gang activity seems to be highly concentrated in one area of the city as opposed to Albuquerque, where it was all over. Most graffiti I found was south of I-10, from both taggers and street gangs in parts such as downtown, Socorro, and Segundo Barrio. Not to say there is none north of I-10, but over there the graffiti is more scattered, with no areas dominated by it. Another important note on El Paso gangs is that most are petty criminals, and a meager portion are small-time drug dealers. The only real legitimate criminal empire in El Paso is the Barrio Azteca gang. This gang has been the only one to make the *El Paso Times* and in recent months there has been a federal and local crackdown on them, which has resulted in the arrest of more than a dozen members. The charges have ranged from possession with intent to distribute all the way to murder. It's extremely rare to see gang articles in the newspaper, which may come from the city not wanting to receive negative perception or simply because there is a very low level of gang crime in El Paso. The Barrio Azteca gang has been the only one to receive media attention in recent years and appears to be the only gang whose organizational style resembles that of gangs found in Los Angeles and Chicago. However, for the most part the rest of El Paso gangs appear to be low-key and more like "social groups" than the stereotypical street gangs we see in larger cities. Gang homicides are a rare occurrence in the city, and if I'm not mistaken El Paso hasn't had one this year and had less than five last year. Most criminal activities committed by El Paso gangs, if any, are simple petty offenses such as vandalism and larceny. In addition, out of all the "declared" gang members I've seen, none have distinguishing tattoos or "brands," something that is a norm for the traditional street gangs found all over the country. The only gang whom I noticed to have gang-affiliated

markings was the Barrio Aztecas, bearing the number 21 (B is the second letter in alphabet, and A is first letter, Barrio Azteca) in addition to the Aztec calendar. The only distinguishing traits El Paso gangs seem to use are the clothing they wear (Dickies, Low Rider Sunglasses, Nike Cortez, Red/ Blue colored clothing).

Joshua, a white male from the class of 2010, inquired at the jail about gang activity, and the Barrio Azteca gang was also featured in the information he received:

I spoke with my friend, who works as a corrections officer in the El Paso County Detention Center downtown. He provided me with a great deal of information that I did not know about gangs. He told me that the biggest gang right now inside the jail is the Barrio Aztecas, and they are the ones who cause the most problems inside the jail. Since they are so large in number and cause so many problems, all confirmed Azteca members are placed on lockdown and kept separate from the rest of the population. In addition, ex Barrio Azteca members are placed on lockdown because of the threat they pose. He stated that the Aztecas are always fighting with another gang known as the Paisanos, or Paisas. They are the Aztecas' biggest rival inside the jail, and they were formed just to fight with the Aztecas. The Paisanos are tougher to identify because they do not have as many tattoos as the Aztecas, but they are still just as ruthless.

Although most of the focus was on Barrio Aztecas, Sophia, a Hispanic female from the class of 2008, described several additional types of groups that could be categorized as gangs:

How would I describe the gangs in this area? Well to begin with I would say some are very organized and the others are just little street gangs made up of teenagers who are bored. We have gangs like the Aztecas and the Mexican Mafia that are well organized and are also in the prison systems, and you have little gangs that are run from projects and neighborhoods. There is also a wider area and they call themselves "crews," you have party crews, you have tagging crews, you have biker crews, and you have racing crews. These can be considered gangs, but they call themselves crews. I have also found out that once a teenager is seventeen years old, they are considered an adult in the [criminal justice] system of Texas. So, all these crews and gangs (prison and street), if caught in crime, they are no longer a juvenile but an adult.

According to the media and the Department of Justice, several members of the Barrio Aztecas continued to receive indictments for drug offenses, money laundering, murder, obstruction of justice, and racketeering.[17]

Las Cruces, New Mexico

Sarah, a Hispanic female from the class of 2008, obtained Las Cruces Police Department (LCPD) crime data for a period of time to assess the level of threat gangs exhibited in Las Cruces:

> I think some of the biggest problems Las Cruces faces are misdemeanor offenses that end up classifying an individual as a gang member. From statistics that were pulled by the LCPD Crime Analyst, ninety-five of the incidents reported from January 2008 to April 2008 were for calls regarding harassment, loud parties, vandalism, affray, and phone threats. Many of the reports taken did not lead to arrest. I do not doubt that Las Cruces has a gang problem, I do however doubt the threat it plays on the city. Many of the incidents were juveniles younger than 17. . . . Before I began this process I was skeptical that I would find anything less than what we are programmed to believe. "Gangs are bad, dangerous, and full of criminal involvement." During this research, we have obtained information that does seem to discredit the stereotype local law enforcement has given gangs. Talking with schools, none of them have suggested heavy gang presence or problems on their campus. Maybe this is incorrect, and school administration is protecting the credibility and reputation of their school and does not want to be branded as a school with a gang problem. If that is the case and the people that we have talked to are not forthcoming with information, how are we to accurately measure the threat of gangs? If administrative entities would rather save face than admit to potential problems that could be dealt with proactively, then the information we uncover will come across as reactive measures to a dangerous problem that was something that could have been dealt with using prevention and intervention techniques. Until the data we have obtained can be

reevaluated, then there is no benchmark to measure how accurate our data is. I have to measure my findings not on personal opinion, prejudice, or stereotypes but on a true analysis of research evaluation. Our job as a researcher needs to be unbiased and conclusions made on the evidence compiled in front of him. With the evidence our team has obtained, I have to say the gang problem is present but not threatening.

The difficulty of finding instances of serious crime reminded me of the gang-unit data analyzed in Utah, but this did not prevent law enforcement officials and some of the media from contributing to a moral panic that resulted in a gang injunction, which as practiced was later ruled unconstitutional.

Matt, a Hispanic male from the class of 2010, continued this line of inquiry by trying to determine what types of gang members exist in the community:

Based on my group's research, I have to say that the level of gang activity is at a 4 or 5. The reason for this is because I do not think that the gang members who live in our community are what most people think of as a gang member. The members that we have here in Las Cruces are wannabes and are all talk and no show. These people are not in the gang to hurt, kill, or harass anyone, they just want to belong. I think that it is safe to say that if we lived in a larger city where gangs are prominent, the [threat] level would be much higher. If you do not go looking for the gangs, you will not find them. This is the attitude that I have from living here in Las Cruces. I have never thought of Las Cruces as having a high gang rate. I have lived here all my life and have never had a run in with a member. Is there a difference between current and previous threat levels here? I would have to say no; the level has not changed from my point of view in the last fifteen years. On the other hand, the officer that I spoke to said yes, things have changed dramatically in the last fifteen years. Gangs have evolved and are more self-oriented instead of group-oriented.

Felix, a Hispanic male from the class of 2010, compared crime data in Las Cruces to other cities:

The involvement of local gangs in committing crime is on the lower end of the spectrum such as tagging, burglary, larceny, drug dealing, and drive-by shootings. Relatively speaking, the crime rate in Las Cruces is lower than most metropolitan cities. They are not as organized, but with time and lack of resources there may be an uproar in the crime rate. Gangs use their names to intimidate others in their schools and neighborhoods. Most of the members are young kids looking up to the older kids or young adults coming out of prison.

Stevie, a white female from the class of 2012, drew upon reports from her entire group to provide her account of the level of gang activity:

> This semester I was a member of the group that was researching gangs in Las Cruces. I have lived in Las Cruces all my life, so I thought this would be a good way to gain insight into a possible gang problem in the city that I may have overlooked. Based upon my research, I have concluded that gangs and gang activity are not a common problem in Las Cruces. I thought that the gang problem would be much worse than it is. I was expecting to find that I had been overlooking a gang problem in this city because I have lived here my whole life. While conducting the field research for this project, I learned that Las Cruces does not have a major gang problem. The gangs are present, but I would not consider them a problem. I would describe gangs in this area as very subtle, as they are not seen very often and are not known well. They make their presence known by doing things such as tagging or an occasional act of violence. We learned that these acts of violence very rarely have any impact on the average citizen in our community. I heard this from known gang members, who to want to remain anonymous. They said that they are not trying to cause a problem in the community; they just want to continue doing what they are doing, and if they have an issue with anyone, it is usually some rival gang member or an ex-gang member. They mentioned that law enforcement also sees them as a bigger threat than they are and they do not think the community feels they are a big threat. The opinion of law enforcement thinking that gangs are a bigger threat than they are was proven to be true from the research done by the team. We learned that law enforcement is very worried about gang activity in Las Cruces, even though there is very little gang activity there. I think this level of concern comes from the media presentation of gangs in Las Cruces. When we researched the media coverage of gangs, we did not find many stories on gangs or gang activity, but the ones we did find were made to seem

very serious. I think this shows how the media is the biggest informer on gangs and the impact they are having on Las Cruces. From talking to people in the community who wish to remain anonymous, I learned that community members do not see gangs as a threat, but more of a nuisance. People are not afraid of gangs, but know they exist. I also talked to a public school teacher in the Las Cruces area who wishes to remain anonymous, and got her opinion on the issue of gangs in schools. From my discussion with this teacher, she admitted that she does not think there is a gang problem in schools but more of a bullying problem. She believes that this makes the children form a gang-like group to bully another child or group of children. She thinks more needs to be done about bullying and therefore, less focus would have to be put on gangs. The teacher also told me that she thinks parents generally need to be more involved in their children's lives. She thinks this would help to stop gang involvement when the child got older if they knew that their parents would find out and be upset with them.

Stevie points to the media as the culprit for heightening gang tensions, but my interviews with law enforcement suggested they were often the source from which these stories were written.

Carlos, a Hispanic male from the class of 2012, also drew upon his group's knowledge and the challenges of attempting to assess the impact gangs had on the community:

It was a very interesting assignment to look at a particular area and assess from different resources what kind of gang problem that area is dealing with. Tackling an assignment like this was somewhat of a challenge at first, because you simply do not know where to start. However, once we began our research, information started coming from every direction. Before I started my research on Las Cruces, I had no idea the amount of resources and attention the city devotes to the control on gangs. Our first goal as a group was to simply drive around and see what we could see. To our surprise, we found a lot of covered up tagging, but like Professor Duran mentioned in class, no information can be information within itself. Everywhere we turned, we saw blotches of paint that resembled cover-ups, so our next goal was to find out who was doing this. Later, we found that a program called "Keep Las Cruces Beautiful" was the one responsible for many of the cover-ups. It was interesting to discover such programs that were good for the community, especially for the amount of work they do and the fact that many of the Las Cruces citizens have no idea that these programs exist. Once we had a better view of the city and we were at least somewhat aware of what was going on there, we split up assignments so that we could begin our research from different perspectives. We split up the group so that we could focus on different areas such as media, community, policing, and schools to get different angles on gangs in Las Cruces. My task focused on policing, so I was hoping to find someone to interview, so I could ask questions such as "What are you all doing as a department to combat gang problems in Las Cruces?" and "Do you feel threatened as a police officer due to gang activity in town?" Based upon the data collected by our team, I would rate Las Cruces as a 2 due to its low involvement in gangs. As discussed earlier, we found definite activity in the city, but when compared to surrounding cities like El Paso, I feel much safer living in Las Cruces. Adding to that, my experience living in Riverside, California, also helps me judge Las Cruces, because my everyday life here is much safer. I remember living in Riverside and being somewhat afraid to walk to the local liquor store or even to look at someone the wrong way. Here in Las Cruces, I feel very safe day or night, and hardly see any gang activity other than in the media. In our research, we found that gangs in Las Cruces don't tend to involve the community in their problems with each other.

Randy, a Hispanic male from the class of 2012, was skeptical about the information he obtained from news sources and felt relieved that his group accumulated data to counter this image:

We also observed the tendencies of the media and how they viewed, reported, and interacted with gangs in the area. We read and reviewed article after article that had content linked to gangs. We realized that most articles focused on reporting the most interesting and emotionally provoking stories. Usually these stories included statistics on how volatile gangs are, along with stories on violent crimes, murders, and large-scale drug-smuggling operations. However, our group seriously doubted these media sources as credible, as they mainly seek out and report information from old sources and from the local police. These statistics can be somewhat misleading, because old data is almost never a true representation of the current problem, and police resources will almost always report to the public what is in the best interest of their department. Therefore, we were quite skeptical of their stories and how they tried to escalate the gang problem to a level that we felt was inaccurate. Overall, after all our research was conducted, assessed, and rated according to the threat level, I was surprised to see that we all agreed Las Cruces does not have a very serious gang problem. All our data showed that the entire community felt no real threat of gang activity. We believe this is due to ways in which the community and schools have complemented one another by enacting prevention programs that help to suppress gang activity with step-by-step procedures to identify and treat at-risk youth.

Ubaldo, a Hispanic male from the class of 2012, wrote:

From all the data that we collected as a field research team, I believe that the gang problem here in Las Cruces would be rated at about a 3. The reason for this rating is because although gangs are present here in Las Cruces, there is little violence. As stated earlier, crimes committed are against other gangs rather than against the public. Therefore, they are not a problem to the public, but a problem with each other. Additionally, some of the gangs that we found are comprised of juvenile members and as they grow out of the gang, they don't last very long together. This rating surprised me, because going into this research I thought that it was going to be much higher. Since this is a city with a growing population, I would have thought that various gangs may be moving in from other cities and bringing their affiliations to Las Cruces, but from my research I only saw this at Southern Correctional Facility.

Samantha, a white female from the class of 2008, developed a new line of inquiry as she noticed graffiti was more concentrated in certain sections of the city:

Before I started this project, I hardly noticed the graffiti in the Las Cruces area. Now I can't go two blocks without spotting some graffiti. When Anna took me to the Butterfield park area, I was in shock at how much graffiti is all over the place. In my neighborhood, there is virtually no graffiti; in the Butterfield Park area, the streets are covered by paint. I was told by many officers that it is important to remove the graffiti quickly, so you don't get a name war going on.

Joseph, a Hispanic male from the class of 2010, assessed the gang issue in Las Cruces based on a local and federal level:

> Since the commencement of my research in January of 2010, I have gained a wealth of knowledge about the gangs in and around the surrounding areas of Las Cruces. I analyzed two types of gangs for this research. The first type is gangs on a local level. The second is gangs on a federal level. On the local level, I found that a larger gang presence is found outside of the city limits. Early in the year, I went out and took photographs of graffiti that was visible in the community. I noticed that graffiti inside the city limits of Las Cruces was rare. I would attribute this to the work of the Codes Enforcement Department. They do an outstanding job of removing graffiti quickly, making it hard to obtain gang graffiti photographs. However, out in the county area, it is a different story. The places where I observed most gang graffiti was in the following areas: Mesa Grande, Butterfield, Weisner, Holman, and Moongate; just east of Las Cruces City limits on Highway 70. The two predominant gangs that I detected in the graffiti photographs where SUR 13 and E.S.L. (or East Side Locos). These tags appeared as if they had been there for quite some time, something rare inside the city limits. The SUR 13 tags were tagged in blue spray paint and usually crossed out by a big "X", with ESL written over the original SUR 13 tagging. On one picture, the number 1-8-7 was written next to a nickname of what I assume was a rival gang member. However, in making my observations, I spoke with some of the Spanish-speaking residents of the area. My overall understanding of their point of view of the gangs in the area was that these gangs are not extremely violent. One older gentleman stated that these tags were nothing new, and it was the local kids who had nothing better else to do, "It's just a way for them to act out." He went on to state that, since the area is extremely rural, these kids walk around on adventures, tagging anything and everything that crosses their path. Another resident did express concern, stating that she has heard of gun shots being fired late at night in the area. I was unable to confirm any shootings that may have occurred recently, or any calls for shots fired that law enforcement may have received. Overall, I did not perceive extreme danger to the community from these two (local) gangs. I would describe these gangs as more like social groups, who make threats for fun, because it's easier for them to try to intimidate one another via graffiti rather

than carrying out "hits" as the media may sometimes portray. The issue of gangs on a federal level is a different one. I discovered that on a federal level, gangs are a serious concern to local and federal law enforcement agencies. According to the United States Probation Office, District of New Mexico, some of the gangs that they mainly supervise are Aztecas, Sureños, New Mexico Syndicate or Syndicato Nuevo Mexico (prison gang), and Mexican Mafia. It should be noted that all the gangs mentioned above, except for the New Mexico Syndicate, are gangs that have a presence not only in Las Cruces, but also in parts of Texas, such as El Paso, and many Texas correctional facilities. In doing research on the Aztecas, I found that there seems to be disagreement about the structure of the gang. I first believed that the Aztecas and Barrio Azteca (or B.A.) were two very different and separate entities with close ties to each other, but with different leadership governing them. The reasoning behind this was that most literature states that Barrio Azteca was founded in the Texas prison system. However, during a presentation in class, we had a guest speaker who was familiar with the Juárez conflict. From his presentation, he gave me the impression that these two gangs are one and the same, both receiving orders from bosses in the Juárez area. The only difference is that one resides on the U.S. side, and the other the Mexican side. I suspect law enforcement and the media are just as perplexed by the different names, as both the media and law enforcement use Barrio Azteca and the Aztecas interchangeably.

Small Rural Communities: Anthony, Chaparral, Doña Ana, Horizon City, Sunland Park

Anthony, New Mexico

Probably one of the biggest markers of a gang presence in rural communities is graffiti. As mentioned earlier, some of these communities were unincorporated and were considered colonias and thus lacked city services to clean up the markings put on walls, buildings, and signs. Murals were used as a better alternative to protecting walls in El Paso and some sections of Las Cruces, but open spaces in these rural communities were often prime targets to let others know which group identities were being adopted. Laura, a Hispanic female from the class of 2008, provided this analysis for Anthony:

> Based upon my own field research, I learned quite a few things about gangs in Anthony, NM. First, personally I don't think there's a visible problem within the community itself. What I mean by visible is that there aren't any gangs that are walking around or causing problems in the community. Although it is important to mention that Anthony does have a huge graffiti problem. Unfortunately, it is very difficult to see a wall in the community that has no graffiti of some sort on it. It is with the graffiti itself that we then can see that the gang problem becomes more and more visible. It is through these means that rival gangs get at each other by crossing out rival graffiti.

Guadalupe, a Hispanic female from the class of 2010, continued this finding two years later:

> Many people in the community agree that the lack of resources plays an important role in the development of gangs. They believe change will occur now that Anthony is a city, at least with the law enforcement more present in the city. Gangs in Anthony, NM, in the past four years have had a big increase in their graffiti and tagging, not so much in their structure and organization, just in causing problems or making the community upset. People who live in Anthony say that the gangs there are not a serious threat, they are just a bunch of bored kids with a lot of spare time on their hands. According to law enforcement, there have been fourteen drive-bys in Anthony in the past four months (January–April). It is also important to mention that a young man was killed in Anthony while he was traveling from San Antonio. It has been said that the three people who killed him were associated with some type of gang.

The 2010 story of a young 20-year-old man killed at a rest stop along the freeway while traveling from San Antonio, Texas, to California shocked the local community. The three youth involved in the robbery were sentenced to prison: one for life, another for thirty-eight years, and the third for eighteen years.[18]

Robert, a Hispanic male from the class of 2012, drew upon his experience attending schools in Anthony to assess the influence of gangs:

The gangs in Anthony are not new to me. I grew up near Anthony and I attended Gadsden Middle, Gadsden High, and Desert Pride Academy. Throughout the years, I saw the gang lifestyle first-hand. Whether it was seeing gangs, or me participating in gang activities, it was always there. I am not going to say that I am surprised about the gangs being there or doing what they do, but at the same time, I did learn a fair amount of how the gangs are nowadays. . . . I would describe the gangs in Anthony as kids or young adults committing delinquent crimes because they do not have anything else to do. The community of Anthony does not offer any recreational activities so that children can keep themselves occupied. In my opinion, the gangs in Anthony are not like some of the gangs that we have read about in our book. There are some similarities, like gangs being affiliated by neighborhood. Many children come from a working-class family, so there may not be much attention coming from home. If there is no authority at home and the children can run free, they will more than likely turn to gangs for excitement or even love. Granted, there are adults who are in gangs as well, but they seem to age out of the lifestyle, find a job, or start a family. When these situations occur, gang members don't pay attention to the gang as much because they have priorities to occupy their time. I see no threat right now from the existing gangs, but I do see potential for the gang violence to escalate.

Michelle, a Hispanic female from the class of 2008, had an aunt who worked at an alternative school in the area, and she used this connection to bring her research group to the area:

The kids are at this alternative school because they couldn't or didn't like high school. So, college is not even in any of these kids' future goals. It's almost as if no one knows that the little town of Anthony exists. Everyone always passes along that area and smells the cows and never thinks twice about stopping. The government or community sure doesn't care to do anything about the tagging, low graduation rates, pregnancy rate, or low income. So, a lot of these kids don't care either, they group up with some friends, claim they're gang, and cause trouble. As they're doing all this, they run into drugs and most of them will try it out because all their friends are doing it. I have learned a lot of the same gang traits from L.A. and the bigger cities, but this doesn't even come close. I feel that there is still hope for rehabilitation for this town to see improvement in these kids, so they know what is available out there as far as college and work. They see the same thing day in and day out, so they don't know any better because they're bored, uneducated, and lonely. My aunt got me involved at this school because she is a teacher there. She always comes home to tell me these sad stories of these kids. They're good kids, but have bad parents, or need to be pushed in the right direction, or don't know any better. I give her credit for working with these students to help them out and tell them that a gang, violence, and drugs are not the answer.

Michelle's comments regarding how many of the schools and teachers were trying to help was reflected in a middle school in Anthony where I served as a volunteer. Many of the administrators, teachers, social workers, and school nurses whom I observed and interacted with constantly tried to stay creative in their ideas of being student oriented. Several teachers also mirrored similar backgrounds as the youth, which helped in their ability to develop rapport. Not all schools or teachers, as reported in chapter 4, could make this claim.

Danielle, a white female from the class of 2012, elaborated on the problematic conditions in which many of these young kids grow up:

When this project first started, I thought that there was a serious gang problem in Anthony because of all the shootings and violence that is shown on the news. I learned that the gangs are not as bad as the media would like us to think. The gangs only interact with each other and tend to leave non-members alone. Much of the gang activity in Anthony is because there is nothing for kids to do. For example, there are no recreational places or entertainment for kids, so they turn to gangs because they are bored. I also learned that Anthony is a poor community. The median household income for Anthony is only $25,129, which is almost impossible to live on these days if there is more than one person in the home. Anthony is also a very uneducated town: 54 percent of the population did not finish high school, 20 percent finished high school, 15 percent have some college education, 4 percent have an associate degree, 5 percent have a bachelor's degree, and 2 percent have a graduate degree. The local school system also has a zero-tolerance policy for gangs. I think this is because they do not want to deal with the problem, so they just get rid of the kid instead of trying to help them. As mentioned above, I would describe gangs as kids trying to find something to do. Nothing good ever comes out of bored kids, no matter what city they are in. The gang's main criminal activities are graffiti, property offenses, and drug offenses. Many of the kids who join these gangs are lonely. They look to the gang to fill an empty hole in their life whether it is family, friends, loyalty, or protection. Many of these kids have family problems at home, and the gang seems like a good escape.

Chaparral, New Mexico

Chaparral, the community where I did my ride-along with the sheriff deputy, the community where I participated in a protest and first heard the so-called gang expert David speak, received this evaluation from Gabriel, a Hispanic male from the class of 2012:

> Gangs in Chaparral are, in most ways, basically the same as gangs from anywhere else. On my first visit to Chaparral, I immediately noticed the economic condition of the town; this was a poverty-stricken area where there were very few middle-class homes. Also, while cruising through the town, there was lots of graffiti. Almost everywhere you looked there was tagging; you name it and it was tagged. However, what caught my attention was the location of these gang tags and how they were going about their tagging. Though there was tagging everywhere, it was very difficult to be able to distinguish "whose part of town" you were in from the graffiti. This was a clue to me that there were gangs in Chaparral, but the organization and threat level of these gangs was not very serious. As our team conducted interviews and research, we gathered that there wasn't too much of a gang problem; this information was based on our own field research, interviews with law enforcement, interviews with school administration, as well as a community perspective. Looking back on the town and the gang problem there, I think it will be very hard to develop a solution. This is mainly because the composition of the town will make it hard to help fix the gang problem.

Maria, a Hispanic female from the class of 2012, also discussed the level of poverty in the area:

> While doing field research in Chaparral, NM, I realized that it is a very poor town. Most of the houses are mobile homes, others are abandoned or vandalized, and many areas are tagged by several gangs or "crews." I also learned that the racial/ethnic composition of gangs in Chaparral is mainly young, Hispanic males, and that there is almost no female involvement. Females that are involved are usually the gang members' girlfriends, who they call "rucas." The main reasons why the youth in Chaparral join gangs are because they lack parental supervision, because of drugs, and because they have been victims of bullying. She also added that there is no danger to wear certain colors in the wrong neighborhood unless you are a known gang member and you are deliberately flashing the colors. A deputy said that the portion of serious crime attributable to gangs is mostly graffiti.

Before Chaparral High School was built, the high school students were bussed to Anthony, which contributed to some of the turf-oriented conflicts that appear to have since faded away.

Doña Ana, New Mexico

Doña Ana is a small community north of Las Cruces that doesn't have many public services. Haydee, a Hispanic female from the class of 2010, grew up in this community and noticed some of the changes occurring in the area:

> Based on my research, I learned that gangs in Doña Ana are not very big or dangerous. However, even though Doña Ana is a very small town, gangs are still present. For example, the NSDA, Eastsiders, and Sureños seem to control this town. Gangs in Doña Ana could be described as non-threatening to the community or to the town of Doña Ana. At this time, it's known that the gang activity located in Doña Ana has decreased. From the data collected with my team, I would rate the gangs of Doña Ana to be a 1 based on a scale of 1–10, with 1 being non-threatening to the community of Doña Ana. I have lived in Las Cruces all my life. I have known that gangs in Doña Ana have

slowly decreased in their gang activity and in any threat to the community. About three or four years ago, if I would have been asked how threatening the gangs in Doña Ana were, I would have answered a 5. The media presented gang activity as frequent within this town. The gang activities that were present at the time included drive-by shootings, attempted murder, stabbing, fights, robbery, and a lot of graffiti. As time has passed the gang activity has decreased.

Victor, a Hispanic male from the class of 2010, assessed the gangs in Doña Ana to be a minimal threat:

> I would describe gangs in this area as non-violent youths who are just out there trying to make a reputation for themselves as being tough. I discovered that gangs in Doña Ana are not as dangerous as they are perceived to be. The graffiti in the community is what makes others think that there is a gang problem; however, my research demonstrates that it's just teens who would rather write on walls and buildings instead of paper.

One of my students was a former gang member from Doña Ana. He mentioned that the U.S. Border Patrol had really increased their presence in the area. For fun, many of the youth have parties in the desert because there aren't any clubs, bars, or entertainment businesses in the area.

Horizon City, Texas

Jesus, a Hispanic male from the class of 2012, provided an account that is very different from most of the student reports given. Although the group itself placed Horizon City around a level of threat of 6, Jesus maintained a different perspective. When Jesus and his group selected Horizon City, I didn't know anything about this small community of 17,000 residents, but after traveling out there I found it was much longer drive than I imagined. Jesus stated:

> I have lived in Horizon City for many years, and it has never been a violent area, until what started as a kidnapping and later became a murder in Ciudad Juarez. A man was kidnapped, then taken to Juarez and murdered by Barrio Azteca members. The deceased was also a

Barrio Azteca member. It is hard to believe that about ten years ago Horizon had no serious crimes, and now Horizon has its own hit-men "sicarios," who could be living right next door to a school teacher. Although as we first visited Horizon most of my teammates' perceptions of the area were that Horizon was small and that there was no activity going on. Horizon even seems like an abandoned town at night! These were just perceptions to our naked eye, but when we had legitimate information we found Horizon a little more prone to gang activity than most places around the city of El Paso.

My own drive through the community did not produce any fear or concern for my safety. Based on community statistics, this area seems to have lower levels of crime than Texas overall. His group reported that the police had told them that stickers on the back of car windows signified associations with different cartels. In 2017, I came across a news article that reported the conviction of a Sinaloa drug cartel member who was convicted of abducting a Horizon City Man back in 2009, taking him to Ciudad Juárez, and killing him for allegedly being responsible for the loss of 670 pounds of marijuana at a Border Patrol checkpoint.[19] Public officials however, emphasized how this one incident did not change the overall data collection efforts that have found this city safer than even El Paso.

Sunland Park, New Mexico

Sunland Park shares a physical border with Mexico. During my tour with Border Patrol, there were areas where we could see the homes of people who lived in Mexico through the barricade. When we were with the Border Patrol, our tour group and the residents of Mexico stopped for a moment to chat. There was no conflict between the groups and everyone chatted like friends, but it symbolized to me how politics divide humans. Mercedes, a white female from the class of 2012, discussed some of the patterns she noticed:

> I learned that there are three major gangs in the area that are considered a threat, which are the Barrio Aztecas, Meadow Trece, and Anapra. The police officer that I interviewed told me that there are other smaller gangs that exist, but they are not relevant because they pose very little threat and are not as active as these other three main gangs. The Barrio

Aztecas are involved with the drug cartel from Juarez and, because of this, they are the biggest threat to society. They have been getting into a lot of trouble recently though, so now they are in hiding because the cops have been keeping such a close eye on them. As a result of this heightened scrutiny, if you drive around the streets of Sunland Park it is rare that you will find any tagging from them. Anapra is not being seen as much either but it is still very active. Meadow Trece's tagging can be found pretty much all over the place. You can basically go down any random street and you are more than likely to find something tagged up by them. I would say that the gangs in this area are very active, but I honestly do not worry too much about it. As an El Paso resident, you learn how to avoid certain circumstances and because of that you can live a drama-free life for the most part. One thing that I learned about that I had no idea even existed before was this underground tunnel. It is used by gangs to smuggle their drugs across the border. The officers told us that bundles have been found in this tunnel and that people set bonfires in there as well. We investigated it and there was evidence of people still going down there often. This goes to show just how much is going on in the world, in our own cities, or even in our neighbor's yards that we don't know anything about. I would have never even known that this tunnel existed had the officers not taken me to it, because from the roadside it cannot be seen whatsoever. Not only that, but it is off to the side on a road that usually only Border Patrol and maybe police officers take. I could tell that it was a well thought out location, so that it would be as unnoticeable as possible.

My colleague and friend Carlos Posadas and I walked this neighborhood and took pictures of different points of interest. It looked like a typical working-class area where residents worked hard to maintain their property, although some houses were not able to keep up because of the economic pressures. Samantha, a white female from the class of 2012, showed a level of unfamiliarity with the area, but a nearby gated community gave her a different angle to look at how economics shaped graffiti patterns:

When I first encountered the places with graffiti, I was taken aback to see so much of it and that people didn't seem to care to cover it or that resources weren't in place for the community to cover it. In places where graffiti is present, there is usually lots of litter and no sign of care for the community appearance. Sometimes graffiti was on houses, inside schools, on fences, or on mailboxes, street signs and pretty much anywhere else the gangs feel like tagging. It was sad to see the community defaced by the gangs and their presence. The tagging made the neighborhoods appear scarier and made it obvious that gangs are there. I think that even though it does not seem harmful, the tagging has some influence on the gangs and their power. I also had the opportunity to get a different look at Sunland Park where no tagging exists, no cops are present, and the people seem unaware as to what is happening on the more impoverished side of town. In conducting my ride-along adventure with the police, I was also taken to a gated community in Sunland Park and was surprised at the difference that I saw. These houses were so extravagant and huge. Some had acres and acres of land and were so beautiful. It was funny because I asked a sergeant how often the cops come here, and he replied that he could not even recall the last time he had been there prior to that night . . ., it appears my opinion of the potential threat, compared to the people that live there, is different. Even after interviewing the principal of a local middle school, it seemed that she did not see much of a threat from gang members. She saw kids as being "wannabes" rather than something dangerous.

Martin, a Hispanic male from the class of 2012, lived in Sunland Park and he noticed some changes over the years:

What I've learned about the gangs in the area I researched was that they are currently active, though I assumed the gangs in Sunland Park had faded away. Currently I reside in the area and it feels like there is no potential danger from gangs. Residents don't know if there is a problem, because much gang activity is not immediately apparent. Some residents know that there are gangs in the area and can also name the gangs, such as Mero and Anapra. These two predominant gangs have the same initiation ritual, which is getting "jumped in" by current gang members or performing criminal activity that would benefit the gang. About five to six years ago, gangs were more active. I know this because one of my friends was in the Anapra gang and he used to tell me that it was getting hot because some members of their gang had to jump a gang member from Mero and got badly hurt. Consequently, a form of retaliation arose in which both gangs were fighting each other, tagging on opposite gang turf, and damaging property. To date, my friend still has problems with Mero. Currently, I hadn't heard of any violence between Anapra and Mero, so I thought that gang problems had faded away, but I was wrong. When our team investigated more on the matter, we obtained information from an Azteca gang member, which have been invading Sunland Park. He told us that the Aztecas are trying to make the other gangs work together for the distribution of drugs and other delinquent activity.

Hector, a Hispanic male from the class of 2012, was also from Sunland Park and provided the following account:

I have lived in Sunland Park for about thirteen years now, and all I can say is that times have changed. From when I first moved into Sunland Park, gangs were the least of my problems. It would not be until the end of my sixth-grade year that I noticed friends becoming gang members. As the years have gone by, I began to make friends with a few of the Meadow 13 and the Anapra gang members. Meadow 13 and Anapra are rival gangs. The few friends I knew who became members began their journey in elementary school. All they did was drink, tag, and have the occasional fight here and there. In high school, they began to get a bit more serious with the gang. Drug dealing was, and still is, the number one thing going on with gangs in Sunland Park. From knowing several members, or known associates, I have learned that everything they do at a serious level is kept on the down low. The most common thing that all gangsters do is binge drink, and every weekend you have the notorious house party. Upon conducting my research, it became clear to me that these two rival gangs no longer run the show in Sunland Park. The Barrio Aztecas are the ones who control most, if not all, of the turf in Sunland Park. The reason that I had not known this, even though I live in Sunland Park, is because the Barrio Aztecas have been very discrete. Although various other gangs are formed, the Aztecas are the ones that make most of the drug-dealing shot calls. During my research, I found out that there have been three arrests of known Barrio Aztecas in Sunland Park. . . . I had always known that there were gangs in Sunland Park, but if I had not known about the Barrio Aztecas and their connection with the drug cartels, I would have given Sunland Park a 2 or 3 simply because Meadow 13 and Anapra are not much of a threat. As I had mentioned above, I currently live in Sunland Park and have lived there for thirteen years. Local police have been doing a great job in maintaining the peace, with the help of Border Patrol and various other law enforcement and federal agents.

My efforts to interview officers from the police department in Sunland Park were unsuccessful. The city experienced several challenges due to local politics.

Ciudad Juárez, Mexico

In 2010, when I inquired which groups students wanted to study, one group came together who wanted to study Ciudad Juárez. My initial response was no, as I imagined the university would not allow students to cross the border to conduct this informal study. However, my concerns were alleviated as the students who were part of this group traveled back and forth on a regular basis. Thus, they were simply doing what they normally did: cross the border. Bernice, a Hispanic female from the class of 2010, described what she saw occurring:

> Another thing that I saw in the research was that we did not have gangs, but we have cartels. Even though they think that Barrio Azteca is a gang, they act more as a cartel than a gang. In my opinion, I will say that any gang that can get too much power is turning into cartels. Going back to Ciudad Juárez, they have the two most powerful cartels in all the Mexico Republic: El Cartel de Juárez, better known as La Linea, and El Cartel de Sinaloa. In addition to all of this, what is happening in Ciudad Juárez right now is they are fighting to gain power as one of the biggest "fronteras," because it is an easy way to pass drugs to the United States, and it is one of the biggest populations because Ciudad Juárez and El Paso look like one big city.

Diana, a Hispanic female from the class of 2010, continued the discussion regarding which groups operate:

> Now street gangs are behind most murders in Juárez these days. Law enforcement efforts have made it more difficult for drug cartels to transport cocaine into the United States. For this reason, the increased patrols forced the cartels to find alternate routes. That created a separate battle between Juárez gangs that are now hunting for additional

income. The Aztecas and their rivals, the Mexicles and Artistas Asesinos (Artists Assassins), are now fighting for control of the retail distribution of drugs in Juárez. The Aztecas are linked to the Juárez Cartel, and the Mexicles and Artistas Asesinos are linked to the Sinaloa Cartel. Nearly 5,000 people have been killed in Juárez since 2008. The killings were initially part of a dispute between the Juárez and Sinaloa Cartels over who would control the drug-trafficking routes through the border city. Ravelo is a capo, or the leader, of the Barrio Azteca gang's operations in Ciudad Juárez, just across the Rio Grande from El Paso. Barrio Azteca started as a Texas prison gang and has expanded to carry out crimes in West Texas and Juárez. The gang has also formed a strong alliance as hit men with the volatile Vicente Carrillo Fuentes drug cartel in Juárez. Gangs in this area are very violent and well organized. This leads the criminal justice system to experience more problems in its attempts to find and capture gangs. However, the criminal justice system in Juárez is very corrupt. The corruption leads to the problems and makes them worse than they are already. The drug cartels are violently taking control of the entire country of Mexico and using the border (Ciudad Juárez) into one of the most powerful countries in the world as an entrance. What is happening now is that each gang, Barrio Azteca, La Linea, Artistas Asecinos, are being divided by each different drug gang cartel, the Sinaloa Cartel and La Linea, which are rivals. The most recent news was that the Sinaloa Cartel already took control of Juárez, taking La Linea out of the "drug business," and also leading Barrio Azteca and Artistas Asecinos to being at the service of Sinaloa Cartel. So, basically, a true war between gangs is a reality of life in Juárez.

On January 19, 2017, Joaquín "El Chapo" Guzmán was extradited to the United States to face criminal charges. An associate director for the Center for Law and Human Behavior at the University of Texas at El Paso reported that he thought the absence of this Sinaloa cartel boss was the reason for escalating violence, which reached 772 homicides in 2017.[20]

Michael, a Hispanic male from the class of 2010, described the issue of corruption and how being a law enforcement officer in Juárez presented itself to have a lot more challenges:

From my research, I learned that the police in Juárez are controlled by the cartels through bribes handed down through the ranks. No officer can refuse to accept the bribe because if they do they are murdered.

It is not like here in the U.S. where someone can choose to be crooked. In Mexico, you have no choice but to cooperate with the cartels. Officers must live by a saying, "Plato o plomo," which means "Eat or die." You take the money from your superior officer and you go on your way. Now, I don't want you to get the wrong idea by me saying that all officers in Juárez must take bribes, because this is not necessarily a decision made of their own free will. If they don't, they will be killed. There is no way to be a 100 percent legitimate cop in Juárez. Even though they can't be 100 percent legitimate, it doesn't mean that they are not still trying to make a difference, it just means that they have to do it in a different way. A good officer in Juárez keeps contacts between the police and the cartels to make sure that everything is operating smoothly on both sides whenever anyone is arrested, or a bust is about to occur. Every decision made by the officer must go through both the cartels and the police to make sure everyone is on the same page. Not only do the cartels control the police, they also control the economy. Recently, over 10,000 businesses have closed due to extortion or death threats. The problem is that the extortion business in Juárez has been getting out of hand. There is no one to control the market of what a fair price for protection is, so what you have is a bunch of small time thugs extorting ridiculous amounts of money from businesses. Extortion in Mexico is not something that just suddenly occurred. It has been a part of life in Mexico for years, but recently the extortionists are asking for too much, which is putting these people out of business. When the small thugs are not controlled, they are free to suck the city dry of everything. When small businesses are closed because of excessive extortion, thousands of jobs are lost in the rubble. The unemployment in Juárez is the biggest problem the city faces. Without legitimate jobs for people to pursue the only thing left is a job running drugs. The lure of the lavish drug lifestyle can get to anyone in a country where a decent income is hard to find. People in Mexico want to work, which is why there are so many illegal immigrants living in the United States. The problem is that the country of Mexico provides few opportunities for its people; so, working for the cartels is sometimes the only option. The terror these people must live with is unquestionable, and until this conflict is resolved the people of Ciudad Juárez will continue to feel its effects. The reason there is no control in Juárez is because of the massive drug war that has plagued the city for the past few years. You have the Sinaloa Cartel trying to take over the

Juárez Cartel, causing a bloodbath in the streets of Juárez. When there is war in the drug world, there is little control over the soldiers. This is why there are people being murdered in public streets instead of the desert like before. There is no respect during war and it has shown its mark over the past few years. When you ask me how big of an effect the cartels have on Ciudad Juárez, the only response I can give is that they have instilled fear in the community by killing people in gruesome manners. The people of Juárez can't even call the police to report a crime for fear of losing their own lives.

As a professor, I have learned a lot from my students during the eight years that I taught at New Mexico State University. Another class project required students to research and write about their family history and the neighborhood where they grew up. Despite my pride in their educational success, a challenge these students encountered upon graduation was securing employment, especially with the degree they had worked so hard to attain. There were more low-end service jobs available than professional occupations. Everywhere I went in the community, I came across former students. Some students went on to graduate school, and some went into criminal justice fields, whereas others obtained occupations very different from the degrees they earned.

This chapter highlights how the inclusion of students through participatory action research can broaden the focus of that research. It demonstrates how lived experience can be an asset, and how conducting research requires gathering various sources of data to make a convincing argument. There was a lot of variation between gangs by community. The large cities of El Paso and Las Cruces had the longer histories of different types of street organizations, but it was the smaller communities of Anthony and Sunland Park that appeared to have the higher number of gang conflicts. These images often came with negative stereotypes. All the communities existed with a lack of services, but some towns were more isolated such as Chaparral and Doña Ana. Ciudad Juárez was on a scale different from the U.S.-based border communities. Students set out to answer questions about crime and the number of gangs and gang members. There was primarily one gang that was found in multiple geographic communities and institutions, whereas the others were localized to each community.

CHAPTER SEVEN

Empirical Miracles and Where Do We Go from Here?

In my first book, Gang Life in Two Cities, *organizing for political power was perceived as central for fulfilling Chicana/o self-empowerment and addressing the root causes of gang membership. This was my recommended solution for areas where Chicanas/os were a numerical minority, but would such a solution be effective along the borderlands where this population was the numerical majority? On August 30, 2012, a Thursday, Ernesto Vigil and I drive from Las Cruces, New Mexico, south forty-five minutes to El Paso, Texas, to attend the fortieth anniversary commemoration of La Raza Unida Party's 1972 National Convention.*[1] *In 1970, Mexican Americans formed their own political party seeing how Democrats and Republicans were not meeting the needs of Chicanos.*[2] *The original convention in 1972 brought over 3,000 participants from seventeen states and the District of Columbia. The commemorative event included many of the original speakers and some developing leaders.*

The original speakers represented different aspects of the Chicano struggle, including farmworkers, urban activists, political representatives, and land grants. It had been a long forty years since these issues and these individuals of Mexican and indigenous ancestry were presented at the forefront of the nation. The monumental event presented a viewpoint of how there was a lack of progress and many things may have become worse. Several panels offered a new vision that moved beyond previous barriers, and one key difference was the greater inclusion of women leaders. After listening to the organizers, I felt more energized re-entering the community, but I was cognizant that the Chicano Movement was no longer an active presence. The border was not an ongoing place of political activism; instead it was an area of hybridization, militarization, and a struggle to stop various forms of oppression. El Paso was an urban mix of residents coming and going, whereas Southern New Mexico included primarily isolated rural communities. In both areas, residents were working to fit in, raise their families, and overcome generations of exclusion.[3] *Such a context created a complicated paradox in which all of the social conditions existed to make gangs and violence worse, but it wasn't.*

Toward the end of my time in New Mexico, I had become complacent. Most residents were not caught up with challenging colonization or debating racial and ethnic inequality. They recognized that immigration status allowed people to be treated differently, but beyond that many residents perceived everyone in the same way, whether white or of Mexican descent. In my eyes, it appeared that the propaganda of settler colonialism had been successful. White professionals continued to reap the benefits, while individuals with brown skin or Mexican (or Spanish or indigenous) heritage debated among themselves about how they simply needed to work harder and not blame society. Honestly, I never wanted to leave, whereas my wife never wanted to move back to the state where she was born and had lived until the age of 12. She had been teased as a child for looking more Native American than Hispanic. If we had received better institutional support from our home institution (New Mexico State University), we probably would never have left. I served as a researcher for the communities of Anthony, Chaparral, Columbus, Deming, Hatch, El Paso, Las Cruces, Lordsburg, Silver City, and Sunland Park. My colleagues and I were not begging for anyone to save us. We diligently persisted in our evaluation of institutions and worked to create change in small steps. It was a big difference from our experiences in Denver and Ogden, but at least here we were at the local decision-making table.

Many researchers and journalists emphasize crime and illegal trade along the U.S.-Mexico border or in Mexico specifically.[4] *During the rise of violence in Ciudad Juárez from 2007 to 2012, such characterizations appeared generalizable to everyone in southern New Mexico and El Paso. Such claims, as has been outlined historically, supported allegations of spillover violence along with policies and legislation advocating increased walls, Border Patrol, National Guard, federal law enforcement, and power in the hands of local police. However, such a sweeping portrayal of the actual level of threat would be inaccurate if we did not cover the entire story. There were structural problems in that residents often internalized their pain or boredom in the form of alcohol and drug abuse, teenage pregnancy, graffiti tagging, and occasionally suicide, but not necessarily engaging in higher rates of violence or joining gangs despite conditions that should increase these numbers for both types of activities.[5] The border region and New Mexico were unique for providing a couple opportunities different from other locations. One positive outlet was college, which increased the level of education and the types of jobs residents could obtain. Another opportunity was increased access to work in a variety of types of employment from blue collar to white collar. Individuals of Mexican descent were also involved in local politics. The utopia of the masses, however, was probably athletics, as youth could compete, achieve local stardom, and stay mentally and physically fit. The purpose of this chapter is to highlight the empirical miracles and to outline recommendations that could address some of the problems in the communities.*

It was a unique situation to study a regional location where some of the most powerful responses to colonial control have occurred in such disparate forms as revolution, opposition, and increased efforts toward assimilation. In my eyes, Denver was more actively involved in protest, but that was in response to a contextual framework of ongoing opposition and marginalization, as well as a smaller numerical presence. Las Cruces and El Paso had majority minority control in terms of population and social influence, but not in terms of economic or political power. If necessary, the residents could mobilize, as seen in Chaparral, and for this reason leaders may have sought strategies that appeared to not push too hard.

The concept of moral panic captures many of the patterns found when analyzing the border region and how different groups have been targeted, such as gangs, drug smuggling, or "illegal aliens." Each negative characterization attempts to legitimize mistreatment. Moral panic is a disjuncture between a real threat and a perceived threat.[6] We have seen how these themes have been enhanced by propaganda in the border region. Throughout this book, I have sought to challenge these claims and will finish by revisiting three miracles. First, the border region has demonstrated lower rates of gang involvement. Second, the border region has exhibited lower rates of violence. Finally, there is a significant number of success stories of individuals who overcame adversity. This section emphasizes such empirical miracles.

Lower Rates of Gang Involvement in Southern New Mexico and El Paso, Texas

The first empirical miracle I observed, that this region of the United States has demonstrated lower rates of gang involvement compared to other communities that I have studied, was not expected before moving to Las Cruces and devoting ten years to data gathering and analysis. These findings contradicted reports by the National Gang Intelligence Center (NGIC) and the National Drug Intelligence Center (NDIC). These federal agencies claimed that New Mexico had one of the highest per-capita number of gang members in the country and that the border region with Mexico continued to be a "continuing criminal threat to the United States."[7] These claims were based on law enforcement agency surveys, but official accounts of data provided in the past do not entirely support the assertion made by federal officials. Nevertheless, based on the data collected in southern New Mexico and El Paso, Texas, along with several other communities, law enforcement officials' ability to identify the number of gang members was highly problematic. Law enforcement officers were not trained as researchers, as noted in the interview with Officer Mark. Gathering information was coercive and definitions were very broad, and the forms of verification resulted in large numbers of individuals labeled as gang members. Law enforcement data continued to indicate that most gang members were black or Latino, but when the numbers were compared to the population, they ran counter to common sense.[8] Another important point with gang membership was that most youth transitioned into other groups with age, and thus these neighborhood connections do not always last for the five years that is part of the law enforcement designation for gang membership in their data.

Based on my observations, most youth and adults in the border region do not join or belong to gangs. The number of gang members and gangs varied by each community and by the definition of gang used. This vagueness about who and what was a gang or a gang member led me to study the community context rather than the stereotypical notions of individuals being in a fixed category. Gang scholars have often classified gang definitions as process-based or delinquency-based.[9] Process-based definitions emphasize the characteristics that lead to the formation of gangs. The delinquency-based definitions emphasize how crime is the distinguishing point that separates gangs from other social groups. Sociologist Victor Rios used the term "gang-associated" to refer to youth who were "perceived as, self-reported as, or informally or formally labeled" as an actual gang member.[10] Thus, his definition may present a third approach to the process of labeling of individuals rather than how a gang member differs from a non-gang member.

This difficulty in defining gangs has not prevented researchers from attempting to determine the number of youth who join. Nationwide, researchers Pyrooz and Sweeten estimated the prevalence of gang membership, based on the National Longitudinal Survey of Youth involving 7,335 youth, to be 2 percent, and peaking at 5 percent at age 14.[11] Geographically, we know certain cities have a longer history with gang activity and involvement than others, which has led to the labels of traditional and emergent gang cities. However, even in Los Angeles, California, a traditional gang city that has often been described as one of the gang capitals of the United States, gang researcher James Diego Vigil estimated through ethnography that only 4–10 percent of individuals joined a gang.[12] As discussed in chapter 3, Mike Tapia estimated through ethnography and comparisons between law enforcement numbers and census data that slightly less than 10 percent of individuals in San Antonio, Texas, join a gang.[13] Using the self-nomination technique, researchers found the prevalence of gang membership to be 14 percent for eighth-grade students in eleven cities.[14] Criminologist Tom Winfree and colleagues provided an estimate of 18 percent gang involvement in Las Cruces in the early 1990s but noted that self-reports of eighth-grade students did not equate with higher levels of drug or criminal involvement compared to Phoenix, Arizona. My random sample of juvenile probation files found that 32 percent of individuals were considered by law enforcement to be gang involved, but they did not have more serious offenses than non–gang labeled youth. Moreover, this higher number does not necessarily represent the same general population of middle school or high school students, because the juveniles on probation experienced a more strained family background.

The resident culture in New Mexico includes individuals with variations of brown skin, short-cropped hair styles for males, tattoos, and friendships, but none of these indicators equate to gang membership. Such patterns are also found with military veterans, law enforcement officers, and college students. The endeavor to gather accurate numbers can be important, but the ability to accomplish this task without using stereotypes or biased definitions of gangs and gang members currently makes this practice unrealistic. Although my argument that there was a lower rate of gang involvement than other communities where I've conducted gang research (Denver, CO, and Ogden, UT), this was not based on a quantitative survey of residents, but on original data collection and analyzing various official data sources. If an accurate data-gathering tool existed, I'd question whether group identities were the real problem. There were a wide variety of groups observed in the community, but only a small proportion met the definition of a gang, and membership was often a short-lived identity. The first amendment to the U.S. Constitution maintains the right of association. Current gang legislation, however, argues that "gangs" are not regular groups but those designed for committing crime. The second empirical miracle will highlight the flaw in this way of thinking.

Lower Rates of Gang Violence and Homicide

The official assertion of a higher number of gang members was used to obtain more institutional resources for law enforcement agencies and to contribute to the image of the border region as dangerous, but the second empirical miracle of lower rates of violence offers another empirical quandary. If there were more gang members, as law enforcement officials asserted, why were there lower levels of homicide? Was gang involvement decreasing violence? As noted earlier, I disagree with the first assertion that there were more gang members, but why would an area with high rates of poverty and a lack of resources have lower rates of homicide than other areas in the United States with similar economic and structural problems? Nationwide, Latino neighborhoods often met the criteria of above-average disadvantage as outlined by sociologists Peterson and Krivo, who studied 87 cities. The conditions in the border region would be expected to heighten the level of disadvantage, so these patterns of lower rates of violence and homicide were most unexpected.

Many researchers have equated gangs with violence, so much so that this is considered one of the established facts about gangs.[15] This has not always been the case. According to gang scholar Joan Moore, Latino gangs have changed a great deal over the years.[16] The perception of gangs in Los Angeles in the 1940s and 1950s was largely sensationalized and led by moral panics, which drove a punishment-oriented response to gangs. The gangs of the 1970s and 1980s had become more involved in violence, and this was attributed to greater access to deadly firearms, trying to outdo previous cohorts, and increased job instability, which kept members in gangs longer. Over time, gangs had become more deviant and institutionalized, but they weren't economic organizations as reported by some researchers regarding gangs in other cities, such as Chicago and Detroit. Based on the data collected for this book, general violence and gang violence appears to have been heightened during the Mexican Revolution and the 1950s in El Paso. However, without accurate numbers to provide a comparison, it may have been an unsupported assertion made from newspaper articles and technical reports emphasizing these time periods.

Although I question the ability to measure the rate of gang membership or the number of gangs, homicides can be measured more accurately. However, I did not have the data to determine the proportion of total homicides that were gang-related versus non-gang-related.[17] Researchers have stated that gang and nongang homicides differ both quantitively and qualitatively.[18] However, criminologist Ramiro Martinez's earlier work in El Paso found that 14 percent of motives for homicide, on an annual basis, were due to gangs, and I will use this number to generalize for the other years. In contrast to El Paso, criminologists George Tita and Allan Abrahamse studied Latino and African American gang killings in Los Angeles from 1981 to 2001 for youth between the ages of 10 and 24 and found that gangs played a significant role in the rates of homicide.[19] In fact, 30–40 percent of all homicides were attributed to gang killings since 1989. Much of this difference was attributed to less lethal tools existing before the 1970s, e.g., zip guns compared to semi-automatic pistols.[20] They found a sharp increase in homicides among Latinos from 1989 to 1996, which slowly decreased but never reached pre-1989 numbers. Tita and Abrahamse found that the rate of homicides for African Americans was two and a half to three times higher than Latinos. Another study in the city of Chicago found that gang-related homicides were reported to be 35 percent of all homicides.[21]

The overall homicide data that exists for El Paso from 1960 to 2016 shows that the years of 1979, 1980, and 1993 were some of the highest in the city, but in comparison to most large cities in the United States, these numbers were still very low. In comparison to several U.S. cities of comparable size, the city of El Paso continued to have a lower number of homicides in 2017 with 19 killings, which would be a rate of .03 per 1,000 with 683,080 residents. This differs greatly from cities such as Baltimore with 343 killings (a rate of .56 per 1,000 residents with 615,000 residents total), Detroit with 267 killings (a rate of .40 per 1,000 with 672,795 residents total); Washington, D.C., with 259 killings (a rate of .38 per 1,000 with 681,170 residents total); Memphis with 200 killings (a rate of .31 per 1,000 residents with 652,717 residents total), and Milwaukee with 118 killings (a rate of .20 per 1,000 residents with 595,047 residents total). Comparatively, across the border in Ciudad Juárez, Mexico, the residents continued to encounter a

TABLE 7.1
Number of Homicides per Year in the City of El Paso and Rate per 1,000

Year	Number	Rate	Year	Number	Rate	Year	Number	Rate
1960	11	.040	1980	54	.127*	2000	20	.035
1961	11	.040	1981	35	.082	2001	20	.035
1962	11	.040	1982	41	.096	2002	14	.025
1963	10	.036	1983	33	.078	2003	21	.037*
1964	5	.018**	1984	24	.056	2004	11	.020**
1965	9	.033	1985	22	.052**	2005	14	.025
1966	16	.058	1986	45	.106	2006	15	.027
1967	13	.047	1987	30	.071	2007	17	.030
1968	18	.065*	1988	33	.078	2008	18	.032
1969	15	.054	1989	41	.096	2009	13	.023
1970	13	.040	1990	35	.068	2010	5	.007**
1971	16	.050	1991	52	.101	2011	16	.025
1972	11	.034**	1992	50	.097	2012	23	.035*
1973	18	.056	1993	56	.109*	2013	10	.015
1974	19	.059	1994	43	.083	2014	21	.032
1975	21	.065	1995	38	.074	2015	17	.026
1976	25	.078	1996	30	.058	2016	18	.027
1977	31	.096	1997	25	.049	2017	19	.028
1978	21	.065	1998	18	.035	2018		
1979	33	.102*	1999	14	.027**	2019		
Average	16.35	.06		35.95	.05		16.22	.027

*Highest rate for the decade. **Lowest rate for the decade.

TABLE 7.2
Number of Homicides per Year in Las Cruces and Rate per 1,000

Year	Number	Rate	Year	Number	Rate	Year	Number	Rate
2002	3	.040	2008	4	.044	2014	7	.069
2003	1	.013	2009	4	.043	2015	3	.030
2004	3	.037	2010	6	.059	2016	5	.049
2005	6	.072	2011	3	.030	2017	5	.049
2006	4	.046	2012	6	.059	2018		
2007	6	.067	2013	7	.069	2019		
Average	3.8	.046		5	.049		5	.049

TABLE 7.3
Estimated Number of Homicides per Year in Ciudad Juárez, Mexico, and Rate per 1,000

Year	Number	Rate	Year	Number	Rate	Year	Number	Rate
2002	371	.290	2008	1607	1.24	2014	438	.310
2003	315	.240	2009	2601	2.00	2015	312	.220
2004	338	.260	2010	3116	2.40	2016	545	.390
2005	320	.250	2011	1933	1.49	2017	773	.552
2006	315	.230	2012	790	.610	2018		
2007	301	.230	2013	530	.410	2019		
Average	327	.250		1763	1.36		517	.368

Data obtained from numerous news agencies including *Southern Pulse*, CNN, *El Paso Times*, and governmental agencies such as U.S. Department of State. These numbers vary slightly across news agencies. Several journalists have reported these high number of deaths have been difficulty to tabulate accurately.

level of threat that was on a different scale from most cities in the world. In 2010, CNN reported that the city reached 3,000 homicides (a rate of 2.14 per 1,000 with population at 1.4 million), whereas in 2007 the number was around 300 (a rate of .21 per 1,000 residents).[22]

El Paso was one of the safest large cities in the United States, if not the safest. If we include southern New Mexico, realizing that immigration plays a role in reducing homicide rates, there were clearly other factors involved because most residents of Mexican descent have been born in the United States and have lived in these geographic areas prior to colonization. Not once in fifty-seven years did El Paso even come close to the number of killings in other cities, as the average number was 23 killings per year (a rate of .05 per 1,000 people). The highest recorded year for homicides was 1980, with 54 killings for a rate of .13, and the lowest number of murders was 5 killings in 2010 for a rate of .01. Thus, if the border were truly a threat and gang membership increased the homicide rate, these patterns should not be occurring in El Paso and in the border region of southern New Mexico. Based on my interviews with practitioners, it was difficult to imagine many officials willingly embracing these empirical miracles because the need for resources and the issues that youth encountered continued to be important. Comparatively speaking, however, some social issues, such as lower levels of gang membership, lower levels of violence, and higher levels of Hispanic representation, were better here than in other places.

One important omission in the discussion of violent deaths in southern New Mexico and El Paso were homicides that occurred due to law enforcement actions. Sociologist Alfredo Mirandé described how the public and media were more interested in Chicano gang violence and criminality rather than reports of police abuse or denial of equal protection under the law.[23] Based on the numbers, El Paso averaged 2.2 law enforcement shooting deaths per year, whereas Las Cruces averaged 1.2 shooting deaths per year. When using Martinez's number of 14 percent for the years of 2000 to 2017, gang homicides would average 2.3 deaths per year in El Paso, only slightly higher than law enforcement shootings.

Higher Rates of Higher Education and Labor Inclusion

From my first days at New Mexico State University, some of my greatest influences have been faculty members who have grown up in the area. They were members of the Departments of Biology, Chemistry, Criminal Justice, Education, Government, Language and Linguistics, and Social Work. Where I was from in Utah, individuals of indigenous and Latin American descent did not regularly attend college, and despite several student activists whom I described in *Gang Life in Two Cities*, none of them went on to attain a Ph.D. At my undergraduate institution, there were probably only two Latina/o professors in a city that was 30 percent Latino. Moreover, the student body population at Weber State University for Latinos was only 5 percent. The numbers were more comparable at New Mexico State University and the University of Texas at El Paso. I felt very welcome in the border region, particularly in New Mexico, and my friendships were broad. I felt proud as I observed these Latina/o professors and administrators in an area where our students were also numerically represented.

One of the central themes I learned from my first book was that the success of any people has always revolved around the leadership and appreciation of our women. Many indigenous communities were built and maintained through matrilineal societies, and thus the European patriarchal social structure adopted by Spain was not always the rule in the Americas. In this section, the experiences of two women in navigating their lives on the border will be highlighted. One Latina transitioned back and forth between two countries, whereas the second Chicana encountered physical threats for being born in a contested border area. Both are success stories in that they have achieved educational success along with offering a style of leadership that continues to help guide future generations. Their voices highlight how empirical miracles can be hard to attain among such high levels of adversity.

In my interview with Daniella, we drove around the town of Anthony, which straddles the border between Texas and New Mexico, as she showed me where she grew up and described her experiences as a child. In 2010, this community was considered to have 9,000 residents. It was located between Las Cruces and El Paso, about twenty-four miles to either city. I first asked Daniella to describe this place and how it compared with other places around the country:

> Well, it's an interesting question because I always tell students like I grew up here and our students are from this area. For the most part you don't realize that you grew up in poverty or you grew up different from other people until I was getting educated and started leaving the area. Then you realize it's not just poverty, but its abject poverty for U.S. standards. Sadly, it was only four years ago that I learned Anthony is a colonia, so I had no idea it was meeting the federal designation of a shanty town basically that lacked infrastructure, running water, electricity in some parts of town, and for me growing up it was very normal to have graffiti everywhere. The graffiti, the gangs, I was affiliated generationally and didn't bat an eye at it. We had a pretty normal existence as a kid. We would normalize the violence. We would

learn it isn't customary to walk certain routes to school or have your parents worry about you or have friends who affiliated themselves with different cliques.

She continued to describe how Anthony, New Mexico, was much poorer than Anthony, Texas, and thus a state line separated the resources available in the community. Because Anthony, New Mexico, was unincorporated until 2010, the community lacked street lighting, trash pick-up, city athletic leagues, and local services such as a Boys and Girls Club. It was reported by the U.S. Department and Housing Development that there were a number of colonias in the New Mexico counties of Doña Ana (37), Grant (27), Hidalgo (8), Luna (8), and in El Paso County, Texas (200). Thus, most of the communities studied met this designation of lacking adequate infrastructure and other basic services. According to geographers Christopher Davies and Robert Holz, racial discrimination was the foundation for border inequities as the minority Anglo population became the majority land holders, whereas the dominant Hispanic population claimed little or no land.[24] Daniella continued:

> When you think about rural poverty or semi-rural poverty, there is absolutely no resources in the town that's not incorporated. . . . So there really wasn't anything. . . . There wasn't after-school activities. There wasn't libraries. There wasn't really anything, nothing, nothing, nothing, to rely on or outdoor activities. Nothing to keep kids busy.

She described how most of the time she did not leave her town, even though there were the larger cities of Las Cruces and El Paso not very far away from where she lived. I inquired about how this geographic setting shaped territories between youth groups and how I had heard several practitioners tell me that gangs here were not territorial.

> I'd say things are very territorial. . . . I grew up in Anthony, New Mexico, and then there is Anthony, Texas, just down the way, which is equivalent of maybe three large city blocks distance between them, and you knew not to go into Anthony, Texas. Like specifically the rivalry for us as young girls had to do with sports and that's like the only time we came together. It wasn't gang or turf war, but [it was] very clear everyone had a space and knew where their place was and where you were safe.

The local high school even had a reputation as being rougher, and people were always surprised that she had graduated from this school. Two towns in New Mexico, Anthony and Sunland Park, also had their rivalries.

> So, all these kids from all these little towns went to their respective elementary schools, but when you hit junior high everyone came together and that's when everyone would go to Anthony because that's where the school was located, at least when I was coming up. All the kids from all these little villages came together and there you started to see the rivalries. You knew where people were from and there never seemed to be problems between certain towns, but the kids from Sunland Park and Anthony, that's where the rivalry was.

Recently, many of these smaller communities obtained their own junior high and high schools. She named a number of the gangs that existed in the 1980s: Corner Pockets, Papas, and Varrio Anthony Locos (VALS). She believed the VALS had been around for at least three generations, and probably the Teners as well. In Sunland Park, Meadow Trece had also been around for that long. We drove by some of the housing projects and schools during our conversation. She said that no one was really forced to join these groups, but where you were from often was the key to how you related with other kids. Most of the time when she was growing up, the police didn't patrol the area because it was far from the sheriff's station. Residents weren't known for calling the cops. The arroyo was where a lot of people shot up heroin, and people stayed away from that area unless you were dumping trash or wanted to use drugs. We talked about how she thought she would have faced more pressure to join these groups if she had been a boy, but that sports, school, and her parents helped her stay out of trouble. There were female members in some of these gangs. During our drive we came across some graffiti that read "Queens." We discussed how this may possibly be a new female group. Our final interview exchange summarized some of the key points.

> I think going through a community like Anthony and El Paso, you see what families are confronting. It goes back to these issues of structural violence and how do families cope with these levels of poverty or lack of structure. Are gangs the first and foremost concern, or is it putting food on the table for your family, and there is nothing for

kids, absolutely nothing for kids. It's very easy to be enticed by gangs when you don't have other resources available to you. A lot of it is generational. . . .

We concluded our conversation by speculating on the role that Mexican drug cartels may have in attempting to smuggle drugs into the United States. In a geographic area impacted by structural violence, the shared border between one of the wealthiest countries and poorest countries had been shaped by centuries of colonization and global resource extraction.

My 2011 conversation with Jennifer attempted to understand more of the issues between the United States and Mexico. She was born in El Paso but grew up in Ciudad Juárez, Mexico.

It was hard for me because of the language. Most of my friends spoke Spanish, and going back and forth it was hard. Friends would be like "you're a little gringa" because friends think you are upper than them, and then I didn't have as many friends in Mexico because I didn't talk to them like I used to. Back then, if you looked at me wrong I'd say something. I was kind of like a gang girl, I guess you could say. Over there they would call me chola because I was a little preppie. Kinda of how I would dress. I'd wear skirts and dresses, and I didn't wear colors or say bad words. People assumed I was innocent.

Her mother had obtained a college degree in New Mexico. Both her parents thought it was important for Jennifer to learn English.

I think they wanted me to learn English and they thought it would be a better life over here. I think they saw it as a better life and more safe than over there. To be honest, I like living over there, it was more fun. Here they protect you more. You have be at home at certain time or have to be at school. Over there if you wanted to ditch, no one is going to stop you. So, living in Las Cruces, it was nice for my parents. It was calm, and nothing got stolen, but for me more boring because I couldn't hang out. Then I was able to start getting involved in sports in high school. [I inquired about knowledge of gangs or cartels in Juárez]. I knew about gangs, but not cartels. Back then the gangs were kind of friendly. They weren't supposed to have guns or knives. It was more one on one. If you see my grandma or another grandma walking with bag from store they would help them, it was kind of protective of them. They used to fight and people would watch. In El Paso, I didn't see any gangs. I'd see a lot of graffiti, but I didn't have time to hang out. In Las Cruces, I didn't see anything in middle school until I hit high school. I remember my second day, there was a big ol' fight and there were a lot of people fighting and it was exciting. Everyone was running to see who was fighting. [I inquired whether she felt pressure to associate with these groups.]. No, they were afraid of me. I'd say I was from Juárez and they were like "oh." They think Mexican gangs are more hard than here.

We talked about the difference between being a girl compared to a boy and how it shaped her experiences.

Well, I did have a lot of pressure, but from other girls and not the guys. They [the girls] would be like, "Oh, I want that guy." But to the guys, we were like their sisters to them and some were brothers or cousins. In high school it was more like, "Oh, you look nice," but not when I was little. When we were kids it was more about playing but it changed as we started growing up. Guys wanted to touch us, but when we were kids it was more about having fun. I was always seen as the innocent one. The shy girl. The one who would never do nothing. I'd be like "I go to school and had, like, straight A's." I was in honors class and everything.

She talked about the dangers of being a girl in Mexico and how she was afraid of vehicles with campers because they would kidnap people. Even the police were seen as a threat, and they often had to be paid off with bribes. They were seen as corrupt. She stated that most of the problems started with the election of the new president, Felipe Calderón, who was the leader of Mexico from 2006 to 2012.

It is scary because you could be out at the wrong time and get shot. They are killing each other because they want the power. It's all about who has the power. They have to pay the border patrol here and they won't stop you. Nowadays about 8:30 or 9:00 you don't see people outside walking around. You turn on the news and you see the Aztecas, La Linea, Sinaloa, and people getting killed. You can get money over there as sicarios (assassins).

We discussed how the limited number of jobs made getting money from the cartels more attractive. She even mentioned how criminal justice was a dangerous major because it was seen as threatening and could get people killed.

> I don't feel like we are the same anymore [her old friends]. The way they act. They have guns. I don't want to ruin my career. . . . So I'd rather not be around. I would say hi but not talk to them. I'd say hi and bye. They [rival groups] could be like, "Oh, she talked to them and so she must be in this." I'm afraid to be seen with them.

We discussed how, through a family relative, she knew someone who was a member of one of the main cartels. This individual placed the responsibility of for the violence on the government and said that it involved way more players than Mexicans. She had dreams of becoming a detective to stop people from doing bad things. She wanted to protect little girls like herself when she was younger.

> It's just sad to see Juárez like that. It's sad even for my parents. There has to be a revolution. The government can do whatever it wants. It takes the people to change it. . . . If Colombia did it, we can do it.

Jennifer was optimistic that things could go back to how they used to be when she was growing up. As the earlier sections have indicated, Ciudad Juárez reached its peak in murders during the Calderón presidency. Both Daniella and Jennifer thought this research project was very important, but they cautioned me to be wary of whom I interviewed or asked questions. This was a strange aspect of the border: while for the most part everything was safer, there was also an understanding that if you crossed the wrong individual you could wind up missing.

Where Do We Go from Here?[25]

It has not been mainstream for researchers who were outsiders to the social environment and groups they studied to express an interest in contributing something back to social world of gangs or to the communities in which they gathered data. Social scientist Mark Fleisher commented upon the emotional toll he encountered while discovering and observing the lives and experiences of marginalized youth, a toll that led him to pursue the development of solutions instead of just conducting research:

> It's our moral obligation to engage fully in the arguments over how to remedy poverty, repair neighborhoods, and improve the lives of the youngest people who inhabit the poorest households. To hide behind the white coat of science is immoral and irresponsible, and it contributes to social injustice and oppression in America. If we aren't actively engaged in reconstructing our poorest neighborhoods, who is?[26]

Fleisher outlined the importance of ethnography to criminology, but he warned that such investment can cause personal damage to the researcher because he or she observes the suffering of others. In addition, Fleisher cautioned that ethnography can be like "pimping" (i.e., capitalist exploitation), in that the data obtained primary serves the needs of the researcher rather than the interviewee, and the knowledge produced primarily resides in the "company store" for other academics rather than being available to the community at large.[27]

Pioneers who were members of underrepresented groups, such as W.E.B. Du Bois, helped create new spaces (i.e., institutions, departments, journals, etc.) for developing minority perspectives.[28] Many of these researchers were not interested simply in detached data collection, but also in scholarly activism. These researchers, possibly due to marginalized backgrounds, felt pressure to not only use research to correct assumptions and biases, but also to improve the social standing of their families, children, and members of a similar background. Sociologist Aldon Morris captures this point perfectly in the following quote by Du Bois: "I returned ready and eager to begin a life-work, leading to the emancipation of the American Negro. History and the other social sciences were to be my weapons, to be sharpened and applied by research and writing."[29] Thus research could be used as a tool to shape policy, but getting people to listen often required ensuring you were first considered a human worthy of inclusion. The dominant ideology has often used propaganda to dehumanize marginalized groups in society.[30]

Political scientist Charles V. Hamilton, one of the contributors to Joyce A. Ladner's book, *The Death of White Sociology*, stated:

> If this society is to change in any viable way, black people will, of necessity, have to play a leading role. It will be, in large measure, the

new values, new insights, and new alternatives proposed by black people that will have the considerable legitimacy. It will not be without intense political struggle, which, again, one assumes from the outset. And neither will it be without the kinds of hard work started by our giants of social science scholarship many decades ago.[31]

So too must the indigenous and Mexican voices of this area be included. To this end, I will now share the solutions put forth by members of the community, local practitioners, student researchers, and finally my own reflections.

Student-Perceived Solutions

Anna, one of the students from my first class I taught in 2008 regarding the study of gangs, was very passionate about her research. She and a friend drove all over the city of Las Cruces, taking pictures of graffiti and talking with members of the community. Below is an excerpt from her write-up of the gang situation:

> In conducting an informal interview with a man in his 40's who still has ties to a local gang, it is survival. Not only as a person needing protection from others, but for one's self and well-being as a person. To have someone teach you how to take care of yourself and others. This man was left at home at age 9 while his mother went to work and did other things. He had to learn to fend for himself when it came to food, warmth, and sometimes even shelter. I had pointed out that I could not work with juveniles because I would want to help them all. According to this gentleman, if he had to help one, he would pick out the meanest, the worst offender in the room, take that one under his wing. Why? Because, that would be the one that needed the most. The most love and understanding. From that point on in life, whatever, whenever anything was needed, he would be provided for, no matter what.

Anna's interview highlights an approach that runs counter to most criminal justice policies, which are designed to punish more harshly those who were considered the worst of the worst. Suggesting that these individuals may instead need the most love and understanding aligns more closely with the approach advocated by Father Greg Boyle, an approach that appears to offer many positive success stories. Father Greg has written a book and has had a book written about his efforts to provide alternatives to gangs through employment.[32]

Robert, a Hispanic male from the class of 2012 in the Anthony group, described the need to reach out to youth:

> My solution for the gangs in this area would be to give more attention to the youngsters. I believe that the way a person grows up starts at home. The home is where the foundation of the individual's personality begins to form. The way a person is raised says a lot on how they will be in the future. I believe that the children need more attention, care, and affection at home. They need positive feedback on the questions that they have. Ignoring the children makes them want to look for other places where they will not get ignored. However, a solid foundation at home may not always be available. There are factors such as single-parent homes, living with grandparents, or being in foster care. In my opinion, no matter where the child is, a grown-up has to be around to motivate the child to strive for a good and healthy life. Another solution would be to offer more recreational activities in the community. Kids get bored easily and something that is both fun and positive for the kids to do would be an amazing asset to them. Kids need to stay away from gangs, period. Of course, they should know what a gang is to stay away from them, but they shouldn't feel the need to go looking to join in one.

This matched Daniella's account of how the community needed more recreational activities, which in this region of the country have historically been one the strongest buffers to delinquent or criminal activity. Gabriel, a Hispanic male from the class of 2012 from the Chaparral group, described how reaching youth required providing more support in the home and having available activities to engage youth. He wrote:

> I think the solution for problems such as this have to come from the home. Since the parents are struggling to put food on the table, they have no time to raise their kids. If the town would be able to create a better economy with better jobs for these people, so that they will make more and work less, they will have more time to spend with their kids and raise them. The schools are doing what they can with what

they have, but just the schools alone can't help all these kids. Also, what the city could do to help this problem is create more activities in the town such as boys and girls programs, sports leagues, parks, and even a community pool. I guess in general, these kids need an alternative to gangs and trouble in general.

Gabriel highlights one of the challenges of the geographic area, which included obtaining quality jobs. Even my students who had attained college degrees encountered difficulty in finding employment. The theme of emphasizing programs carried forward from several additional student researchers. Emilia, a Hispanic female from the class of 2010 from the Doña Ana group, emphasized the need for more programs for youth as a nationwide requirement:

Society needs to provide entertainment centers to keep our youths active and away from crime and misdemeanors. Many of these families are from poor homes and can barely make ends meet; therefore, they cannot afford to send their children to participate in activities that other families enjoy. They cannot afford to send their children to play football, baseball, basketball, tennis, golf, dance, and the list goes on and on. The government should provide funding for the future of America. This requires someone to care for the youth that are lonely, scared, unloved, unwanted, or simply just bored. Funding for all youth to have a choice to go play and stay away from trouble. People might inquire where this money will come from, but what we should be asking is, why Congress and other political parties are traveling in luxury, going from place to place on the tax payer's money. No one does anything about this. It is time for the American people to use their voice and stand up for the rights we all pay for. The youths are the future of America and they have been neglected for too long.

Emilia's point was clear: national priorities need to be altered to put the well-being of children at the forefront of our society. Ruby, a Hispanic female from the class of 2010 from the Anthony group, agreed that programs helped her when she was younger:

At one point the city did have prevention programs like boxing clubs, leadership academies, and police academies. Many sports were also offered and run by community members. Due to the lack of funds, programs were cut. Having those programs does help the community deter gang problems early on. Programs are needed because it provides the younger generation choices. When no choices are available, residents are left with only one choice, which is to join a group of people and commit crime. When I was growing up, having programs available helped me and my brother make better choices.

Raul, a Hispanic male from the class of 2008 from the El Paso group, believed a lot of institutions were needed to address issues impacting youth:

> Solutions can come in many forms. I think people alone can make an impact to inspire those that want to be helped. We were told when we interviewed a cop in El Paso about a cop who had such an impact with kids, that kids would look up to him and respect him. If kids have people to turn to that they feel they can trust when they need help, then at least someone is getting help. Schools also need to have available programs where kids can do constructive things; these programs can include athletic teams, or even academic teams like a math club or science club, or even a chess club. If a kid wants out of a gang, he should be able to turn to an adult for guidance, so schools should also have trained personnel that can handle an issue like that. Parents should also learn to identify if their child has a problem or needs help. Giving parents the knowledge to have the tools to help their kids could be valuable. Solutions for gangs in El Paso can start with helping the kids of El Paso. They need to have options growing up and alternatives they can choose from, not just gang life as a way out. If a kid feels the need to be part of a group to feel popular or safe, a gang doesn't have to be their only option, being part of the soccer team or any other athletic team could give him popularity and respect if a mind is set to accomplish a goal. If a kid learns to work hard for a good outcome, then they might learn to like to stay away from trouble and bad influence.

Positive role models were a theme emphasized by sociologist Victor Rios in his book *Human Targets*.[33] He emphasized how emotional intelligence and high-quality interactions were possible and provided several examples of leaders who have often been treated as outcasts or have been stigmatized within their institutions but how these individuals should become the norm.

Practitioner-Perceived Solutions

Practitioners were actively working in jobs my students desired. Through years of dealing with these institutions, they provided insight into what they perceived to be working well and what needed improvement. My objective with these officials was to first understand the issues they encountered in responding to juvenile delinquency, and then to learn whether there were any best practices that could be offered as solutions.

Several leading practitioners believed in the importance of different agencies working together to address youth issues involving schools, law enforcement, juvenile probation, parents, and youth leadership. Thus, quarterly session meetings included a member from juvenile detention, health care, juvenile probation, law enforcement, and schools, along with court, fiscal, parent, and student leaders. They discussed some of the current challenges. Working together was seen—and I'd agree—as one of the best opportunities to create change, but different philosophies and tools available to respond to issues made these collaborations challenging. The continued goal was to improve relationships with these local stakeholders.

Practitioners often emphasized not letting egos or traditional ways of doing things get in the way of implementing programs that might be more effective than current strategies. Some of the traditional forms of punishment included restitution and community service, but a more promising goal was to find more youth activities, which ranged from athletics such as midnight basketball, boxing, and karate classes to bringing in community members, peers, or respected professionals to serve as role models, such as cheerleaders, football players, and private business owners. Other ideas including moving past previous negative identities with tattoo removal; increasing youth involvement with formal institutions through police athletic leagues, junior deputy sheriffs, and the U.S. Customs and Border Protection Explorer Program; providing alternative activities beyond sports such as art programs or working together to create murals; making use of the area's geography by offering trust-building camps in the mountains; and bringing together different generations of the community by having a dance at a nursing home or participating in food and toy drives.

Chris, the county-city manager who grew up in the community as a young child, stated:

> As the fiscal agent that supervises legislative funds over the years. I help get the funding out to the various recreation programs. We funded a bicycle program with [the Juvenile Probation and Parole Office]. We provide a service where the kids build the bikes themselves and through their labor earn the money to buy the bike. We pay for youth to take swim lessons, join art programs, and participate in art camps. We have offered golf lessons. We get a lot of tourism in the summer, but a lot of kids having nothing to do. There are a broad range of kids and the ones who get in trouble are often the same kids over and over. In the summer, we hold a blues festival, a rodeo, and an international bike race that has been occurring here every year for the past twenty-five years.

My conversation with Chris highlighted the challenges that existed in a rural mining community in which strikes and temporary shutdowns left residents without employment. In such a situation, care givers were no longer able to provide necessities for their families, and the county attempted to compensate for this.

Another fiscal agent, a Hispanic male, reported how his community started an Advisory Committee for youth pride to discuss ways for collaboration.

> We found our community suffered in two main ways: First was pride. As facilitators we learned there was a negative image and perception of the town as dirty. So, we started better codes enforcement. There were no zoning laws at the time; only the city had this. Second were youth concerns. We needed their leadership and we met once a month. At first there were only four or five youth, now there are fifteen to twenty-two. There are still two elements missing: [the Juvenile Probation and Parole Office] and schools, and they are key to these needs. During the last two months, these agencies have been stepping up as they have new leadership.

Rural communities lacked resources that even the poor cities of Las Cruces and El Paso could provide, at least to some extent. One of the programs that was being conducted in Luna County was called Circles. According to Richard, the white male facilitator of these small groups, stated:

> The concept of Circles developed in the 1970s in Minnesota. They adopted a Native American concept built around sitting in a circle around a fire to resolve conflict. So, we establish sitting in a circle with nothing in between. If you have the stick you can talk, otherwise you remain silent. It also teaches self-control. We talk about bullying, self-control, and respect. I pose a question. "Who in your family do you look up to and respect? Why do you look up to this person?" As we lead the discussion, the issues resolve themselves. Deming is thirty miles from the border. I have been here seven years from California. Many kids have lost people to cartels or have parents in prison. We run age-appropriate circles, girl circles, boy circles, and even circles with grandparents. For example, we help to resolve conflict with kids. It's nine o'clock and it's time to be in bed. Whereas in the past you might have the parents or grandparents going to bed and the kids going out the door. We try and foster [the idea that] they are not alone. We try and teach respect. Luna County is 60 percent Hispanic. I don't teach, but rather facilitate.

According to the informational pamphlet, the program is a restorative-justice approach to facilitate communication, and the county offered five different formats that involved schools, girls, families, homes, and repeat delinquent offenders.

Another program that had been implemented in several of these counties was called Teen Court. Ramiro, a young Latino male, described how he ran these groups:

> In Teen Court the kids have already pled guilty, and so this part of the process is receiving a sentence from their peers. We have Teen Court on the third Thursday of every month in the conference room. Recently Judge [name omitted] allowed us to use his courthouse. We file paperwork, and we all agree on a time and a date. The jury is composed of volunteers. We put together a full jury panel, between twelve and eighteen youth. The Judge and I are over 18, but everyone else is 13 to 17. The youth is sworn in and it's all in private and not open to public. The youths tell their story and the jury decides what is fair.

I then sign the contract and make sure the sentence matches with the GRID offenses. Referrals include speeding tickets, no seatbelt, possession of paraphernalia, and so on. A lot of times they are given 10–120 hours of community service, which also makes up some of the [time volunteered as] jury members.

Most of the practitioners I talked to think the program that would be the most beneficial for many of these communities would be an adolescent drug and alcohol court or even a family drug court. They also desired to see increased mental health programs. Both programs were explained as more expensive to obtain.

Judge Roger, a white male who had been working in this community for a long time and saw some very common problems that often weren't being addressed, stated:

> We have been facing a fifty-year battle with drugs, mental health, and crimes committed by those with mental disabilities. We prosecute, but it's a waste of time and money. We should have a juvenile and adult mental health facility. People say "throw [them] in jail," but that's not the answer. We live in a rural community where we see some of the same family names for generations. Some of the family members I had contact with in the 1970s, and I know these families, but how do you break the cycle that's been going on for generations. Three generations of [surname omitted]. They all drop out of school by the eighth or ninth grade. Both parents are in prison. It's almost like they grow up pre-ordained. It's tough to break that. They don't grow up as kids with a mentality of how to work; they know drugs but don't know much else in life but to sit around the house. They often aren't even counted in the unemployment records. . . . Biggest challenge in the county is how New Mexico is a poor state. We don't have Texas oil. We don't have money even during good economic times.

A district attorney named Michelle, a white female, stated that youth needed to learn to respond to adversity in different ways:

> It's part of their culture to strike back. Adults can give bad advice. We try and create activities like lake fishing. A lot of kids don't know how to do these things without a drink or drugs. We try and teach backpacking. Some of the older families go hunting. We try and encourage

kids with swimming pools, parks and recreation programs, and to use the library. It's common that a lot of people grow up and live and die here. They often grow up with a sense of not knowing anything different. We have a lot of generational issues where we have had the grandparents, the parents, and now the kids.

Raquel, the senior Latina juvenile probation officer, stated:

I wish the state was more aware of what model they wanted to pursue. A lot of time it feels like tunnel vision with more paperwork. In the past we would scold a kid and then do the next one. Now we have more staff empathy. This is not just a job. We have commitment, and everyone here works well together. We offer a tutoring program in the summer. A student might be in tenth grade but you don't know how because they can't read. I've seen kids learn to read. The kids struggle because they don't want to be embarrassed at school. The more they learn they begin to feel excited because before they felt ashamed. Our tutoring program builds confidence and I've seen the rewards through the years.

The greatest challenge these formal institutions seemed to face was personality conflicts, differing philosophies, and maintaining resources to keep a lot of these programs running. Like Gonzalez Van Cleve's argument regarding courtroom actors involving judges, district attorneys, and defense attorneys, all these individuals were invested in doing their jobs professionally. Probably the biggest difference for my research was that most of these practitioners were also from these same communities and of similar backgrounds. Thus, this was a major difference from other communities where I had worked in the past. These practitioners were devoting a lot of their own time and resources into helping youth to have greater resources and opportunities. I believe that the cycle of enhancing punishment was reduced because most of the practitioners saw themselves in the youth they were helping. There were also clear racial divisions. Although supposedly no one saw race, the white practitioners seemed to hold more negative views of generational family members who were perceived as being unable to change. Their last names were not the same as these families, whereas some of the practitioners of Mexican descent did share this burden of being seen as never being able to overcome these forms of adversity.

Community-Perceived Solutions

Community-perceived solutions include those from community members interviewed along with documents regarding efforts that appeared to make significant progress. Father Rahm's writings from the 1950s are just one example:

> We at Our Lady's Youth Center stay reminded of the fact that our gang youngsters need help. We shall continue working with them, despite the fact that results are slow and often disheartening. We recognize some of the problems of these troubled youngsters, and we shall try to solve them as we can. It is here that our work lies. The breezes from the mountains still stir up the sandy dust; bits of newspaper, match sticks, and other debris continually protrude from open garbage disposal cans; frequently a lonely dog or a forlorn cat will cross one's path, but for me this is no longer a lonely sight—one knows that continued efforts, hard work, inspiration, and sweat will at long last fulfill a dream, the dream that social justice brings about decent living conditions in which people may dwell in dignity.[34]

Father Rahm's work was an interesting case in point because he understood the importance of helping the community. Colonization theories critique the view of a white savior. However, there does appear to be a lot of genuine community support and appreciation for the investment of Father Rahm. This pattern also seemed to be present with Father Greg Boyle, which might involve the interplay of umbrella legitimacy described by Cid Martinez in his book *The Neighborhood Has Its Own Rules*, which is an excellent account of South Central Los Angeles and how the formal institutions did not meet the needs of the community.[35] To bridge this gap, the community created its own sources of informal social control through the street but also through the church. The role of the church in the communities I studied is an important aspect that I failed to explore. Martinez even described counter-narratives to violence.

My Thoughts Regarding Solutions

Most of the energy and focus of these communities have focused on addressing problems on the surface, but the overall structure of inequality remains in place. The increasing diversity of the practitioners alleviates some of the conflicts that occur in other places, but it does not alter the institutions themselves, the way they operate, or how they continue to place practitioners at risk for problematic behavior. Observing youth from marginalized backgrounds grow up, attend college, and then work in a hierarchy-reinforcing institution was seen as an accomplishment. These individuals now had better incomes and benefits, and they could serve as role models to members of the community. I admired and respected these student for their drive to accomplish professional occupations, but what does it mean when youth of indigenous and Mexican descent have to rely on formal institutions of social control to receive services? Without entering the juvenile justice system, these youths do not receive attention or support through state and local funding. The juvenile justice programs provide more services, and juvenile probation is actively involved in working for rehabilitation; if this agency didn't exist, the extending punishment approach of law enforcement would prevail. District attorneys and judges, depending on the individual, varied between these extremes.

Similar to *Gang Life in Two Cities*, I still believe that educational consciousness and knowledge of self and culture are the most important avenues for altering generations of exclusion. Breaking the "colonial mentality" has been advocated by scholar activists.[36] However, the practice of this region of the country is to ignore and exclude this type of education. Altering these structures of inequalities will require challenging unequal practices and encounters involving school officials, law enforcement, and juvenile probation officers who methodically utilize the systems of social control to enhance levels of supervision and criminalization. Due to an ideology that embraces a belief in assimilation, many of these challenges will also require confronting fellow residents who have bought into the belief that settler colonialism will provide for the needs of the entire community. Altering formal institutions is an issue that needs to be resolved on a federal and ideological level. Altering generations of exclusion requires an enhanced educational consciousness that appreciates and builds upon the local identities that were created from colonization but have been portrayed as unfavorable by those in power. After this is established, efforts should be devoted to altering these institutions or providing alternative institutions as outlined by the scenario offered at the beginning of this chapter.

In addition, it must be recognized why the residents of primarily Mexican and indigenous descent are poor. Communal resources and wealth that existed prior to U.S. colonization have been stripped from residents to the point where the challenge of living day to day with little or no wealth and limited income puts a major strain on families. Thomas Shapiro, a professor of law and social policy, states in his book *Toxic Inequality*, "So long as we have entrenched wealth inequality intertwined with racial inequality, we cannot even begin to bend the arc toward equity."[37] He argues that the traditional view of inequality—that people are in this situation because their lack of work ethic, the decline of marriage, dependence on welfare, or their lack of education—is incorrect and that if we want to understand these issues we need to analyze wealth and income inequality along with racial inequality. The story of the border highlights how current inequalities will only increase with time without bold and transformative policy solutions.

This chapter summarizes the empirical miracles occurring along the U.S. border region and outlines success stories of individuals of marginalized backgrounds who have overcome obstacles. The greatest deficit that currently exists in this area is the lack of appreciation for the histories and identities of the residents who lived in this region of the country prior to when it became part of the United States, and prior to when it became a Spanish colony. Answering the questions of who we were and what does this mean in this political context holds important implications for the strategies of empowerment that are needed to attain human rights. While I agree that self-consciousness does not put food on the table, it does provide a more important emphasis on developing a species-being, collective effervescence, or *concientizacao*, in which the vice of capitalism no longer crushes opportunities.[38]

Conclusion

For the past four years, I've been working on writing up the findings of this research study. In June 2014, my family and I moved from Las Cruces, New Mexico, to Knoxville, Tennessee. We said goodbye to our friends and the area where we had become comfortable. We saw more opportunities to grow outside of our comfort zone. We had the opportunity to visit the Las Cruces area two years later during the summer. Each time we visit the area, it strikes me that Las Cruces is such a small city while El Paso is busy. There is hardly any rain, and the sun seems brighter along the border. The dry climate reminds me that these communities exist in a desert. When we visit, we see our friends, we eat at our favorite restaurants, and we reflect on what life would have been like if we had stayed here. We miss the people, the food, my barbers, and the green chile. We miss the time when my wife and all four of our children lived together. So much time has passed since I first began this project in a community center listening to David explain the patterns of local gang activity. I have better data now to make sense of many of the claims he made. I'm thankful he came to speak to my classes when I called.[1] Now I understand how his response to gangs was shaped by an ideology of settler colonialism.

My wife and I raised our four children through three elementary schools, three middle schools, and several high schools. I had the opportunity to speak to youth who were having the most trouble at schools, youth programs, detention centers, and jails. I had the privilege to meet excellent advocates on behalf of youth. Everywhere I went, I asked these questions to myself: Where are the gangs? Where is the violence? Where is the drug distribution? All I found were youth who wanted to grow up and accomplish things but were unsure about what that should look like.

I observed adults who were busy working, supporting their families, and taking their children to sports practices and games. I observed excellent attendance by families at school activities. All of this made me question how practitioners could say parents weren't involved or interested. Whatever form of gangs, violence, and drug dealing that existed in the community was occurring underground and at levels much lower than official accounts. What I saw was poverty, a lack of resources, and a lack of things for kids to do. I watched as kids dropped out or were pushed out of middle school and high school. I scolded my high school daughter as she wanted to hang out at bonfire parties until three in the morning. I watched kids run away from home. I saw kids having babies, getting into fights, and occasionally dying. Throughout all of these challenges of trying to grow up along the U.S.-Mexico border, I also saw a lot of hope to be included as citizens, to have human rights. I saw success stories as my college students continued to inspire me and defy the odds.

I think about that first phone call in 2006 when a local news reporter inquired about gangs in Las Cruces and along the U.S.-Mexico border. At the time, I didn't have any insight to provide and I referred him to criminologists Larry Mays and Tom Winfree, who were in my department and had studied Las Cruces gangs back in the 1990s. After eight years of lived experience and ethnographic observation, interviews, and analyses of various sources of data from juvenile probation, police departments, schools, and local community groups, this book is now that answer. Clearly the data in this book come from a very impoverished area, but based on my data sources I found lower levels of violence and gang involvement. For the small number of residents who did join gangs, membership was often transitory as youth joined different groups (hood hop) or left these groups in adulthood. Some even went to college and worked in various criminal justice or social justice fields to help others make different choices, which is reflective of my own career. Nevertheless, does this counter the overwhelmingly negative historical narrative that has been in place for more than 170 years?[2]

In Tennessee, I began my analysis of the border region in a different region of the country, one that reportedly did not have gangs. Nine months after moving here, I was contacted by a defense attorney attempting to put together a counter argument to the highly used conviction tool built around gang enhancements. Several additional attorney requests came afterwards. Thinking of my hypothesis of gang involvement being greater in areas of higher levels of racial divide, I looked at the DMC Web-Based Data Entry system, which showed a higher relative rate index between blacks and whites in Tennessee than in Denver, Ogden, El Paso, or Las Cruces. I looked at the photos of the young men who received a gang enhancement, and they were overwhelmingly black. I looked at census tract data and observed that the small black population lives in highly segregated communities. The level of violence is higher: in 2017, there were thirty-seven homicides. For a population of 456,132 residents that was a rate of .081 per 1,000 residents, which was three times greater than what El Paso had experienced in the past twenty years.[3] *I've read the stories of youth being killed and sentenced to prison. Public officials attribute many of these homicides to gang violence, drug distribution, and troubled relationships. Based on the scholarly literature, violence in black communities is much higher than in white and even Latino communities, but there isn't really anything written about gangs in the Southeast United States. I remember attending a community forum where community members, overwhelmingly African American, criticized public officials for blaming these activities on gangs as they inquired why there were no jobs available in the community. I wondered why most of the gang enhancement efforts were not geared toward the Ku Klux Klan or other white hate groups active in the area. So here I am, once again curious and working to provide a voice for the issues that may not be covered in the story of gangs.*

In the current political climate, I have observed the election of a new President of the United States. During the campaign and President Donald Trump's first year in office, I've heard increased rhetoric about the dangers of the U.S. border with Mexico, immigrants, and pressure to build a wall along the U.S.-Mexico border. I wonder what people who have never been or have never lived along the border think of this region of the country. In Tennessee, when people ask my family where we are from, we say New Mexico. They comment on how well we speak English, coming from Mexico. They know very little if anything about New Mexico or the border, and watching the news or popular television shows certainly can't help ease concerns. The director of Tennessee's Bureau of Investigation recently claimed that drug cartels were partnering with local gangs to distribute drugs.[4] *The director did not provide any supporting information, but his claim was enough to achieve a news headline and continue to promote a back story for Tennessee's anti-immigration policies.*[5] *On April 5, 2018, Immigration and Customs Enforcement agents along with the Tennessee Highway Patrol and the Internal*

Revenue Service arrested 97 residents, most of whom were from Mexico or Guatemala, in Morristown, Tennessee, while they were working at a slaughterhouse. In what has been considered the largest raid in ten years, families have been divided as those arrested were being detained in a Louisiana federal detention center and face possible deportation.

The border region is composed of hard-working citizens, many of whom have ancestral ties to the land long before it became part of the United States. It is home to immigrants who have historically contributed to making the United States safer and culturally enriched, and who have provided labor. However, one of the challenges I have faced in writing this book is whether such an examination of gangs, drugs, and violence may contribute to these fears. There is an analogy that describes the difference of perception: Do you see a cup as half full or half empty? The response is usually described as implying optimism or pessimism, but in this context the cup is mostly full of hard-working and law-abiding residents, but that smaller portion receives greater attention. Many communities nationwide experience higher rates of violence, and there are segments of the population that have often fallen off the social awareness radar because they are seen as incapable of doing any wrong. The border region experiences higher rates of poverty and when this is combined with a lack of resources, the challenges go beyond a particular neighborhood. Studies on urban poverty that use census tract data may not be using the best source of data to quantify information in rural locations or regional areas such as the U.S.-Mexico border. It is my hope that this work can further educate others about the issues that exist along the U.S.-Mexico border region of Southern New Mexico and West Texas.[6]

Thus, in conclusion, several findings are worth re-emphasizing to understand how the local context shapes gang membership, juvenile activity, and the alternatives for youth of Mexican descent who are often marginalized in society but are working to achieve positive outcomes despite a structure that reinforces generations of exclusion. *Gang Life in Two Cities* outlined how the cities of Ogden, Utah, and Denver, Colorado, experienced racialized oppression involving a process of socially constructed power differences as a result of excessive regulation and enhanced by separation and segregation. Group and individual resistance to such domination resulted in increased punishment. Denver's encouraged response was activist organizations that challenged the root cause of the inequality, whereas in Ogden suppression was enhanced by structural barriers to education and decreased representation in city, county, and local government. In this book, the data gathered leads to other insights. Structural patterns shape outcomes that manifest differently based on the local historical, political, and social context. The entire state and the region along the U.S.-Mexico border is a minority group. The more embattled communities, based on my research, continued to be those having significant levels of underrepresentation and overrepresentation based on race and ethnicity. Racial and ethnic disparity holds clues for myriad social issues worth addressing.

In this book, I sought to enhance the methodological contributions of ethnography to become more reflective through comparison and social justice. The journey for me began opportunistically as an insider from a population group that has experienced colonization of their homelands in the Southwest. Perfecting and building upon ethnographic research to accomplish improved reliability and validity has required an effort to obtain and analyze various sources of data. Such an effort was not realized through abstracted empiricism but through a critically conscious awareness of history and current oppression that continues to deport, criminalize, and ignore the struggles of the largest minority group in the United States, a struggle that overlaps in many ways with the black civil rights movement.[7]

Punishment Is Not a Solution

Each institution, law enforcement, schools, and juvenile probation, viewed themselves in a role of benevolence where they were "helping" youth. Police officers helped youth by issuing a referral so they could receive additional services from agencies beyond the home. Schools were helping youth receive an education in a safe environment by utilizing referrals and disciplinary policies. Juvenile probation officers were helping youth have opportunities for more programming and diverting youth from entering the juvenile justice system. However, the entire system of law enforcement, schools, and juvenile probation were in reality "helping" youth of Mexican descent have greater contact with institutions that, in addition to providing services, also had a structure for increasing punishment. Law enforcement came with a continuum of force that ranged from providing verbal guidance to deadly force. Schools maintained the ability to suspend and expel students, which heightened educational obstacles later in life. Juvenile probation extended surveillance, utilized detention, or recommended secure confinement. Although most youth do not fall further along the most negative forms of punishment, this supposed role of benevolence toward youth of Mexican descent contrasted with the hands-off approach taken with white youth. The result is racialized social control that serves to enhance inequality. Moreover, the curriculum and emphasis of these institutions were to blame youth for their thinking errors, and over time these ideologies became internalized to the point where the institutions themselves were absolved of any responsibility for perpetuating inequality.

Sociologist Victor Rios reported how law enforcement, juvenile probation, parents, and schools developed a youth control complex where each institution began to work contrary to juvenile interests and more toward criminalization.[8] Criminologist Geoff Ward historically outlined how the juvenile justice system and mass schooling emerged in the 1800s, at which time the authority of parenting shifted toward the state.[9] The language used was to "reform," "uplift," and "develop" children into worthy citizens. However, the state consistently treated black children differently from whites. Ward stated, "In the view of the dominant group, the antebellum black child was never expected to become an economically independent or politically equal participant in society but was instead a profitable beast of burden, raised to accommodate to a subordinate caste status within the racial order" (p. 36). Along the U.S.-Mexico border, we see many patterns that fit in a context for settler colonialism.[10]

Because most of this help was targeted at youth, it masked the cumulative disadvantage of these forms of punishment over time. Thus, when law enforcement officers, school officials, and juvenile probation officers complained about the disruption of families along the border region, it was in effect compounded by adulthood incarceration and deportation. The structural barriers of a lack of education and wealth extended itself into having to work two or three lower-level service jobs to sustain a family. The process of coping for some residents included alcohol and drug use or participating in underground economies to make more money. The data available from states that implemented three-strike laws (e.g., California), gang injunctions, and increased incarceration or use of the death penalty have been unable to establish these forms of punishment as a deterrent. Southern New Mexico and El Paso were fortunate to not have adopted some of these more extreme levels of punishment because they result in enhancing the level of structural inequalities.[11]

Propaganda Rhetoric Does Not Address the Structural Problems

Despite the negative characterizations by the media, television shows, various public officials, and the occasionally horrendous actions by individual gang members, for the most part gangs along the U.S.-Mexico border region of Southern New Mexico and West Texas do not exert a profound negative influence. Perception can often weigh more heavily than facts, however, and in a region of the country with a population group that has encountered centuries of negative propaganda, the result of public perception is a distorted vision. Philosopher Jeffrey Reiman examined how distorted visions of crime were similar to a carnival mirror in making society fear street crime more than white-collar crime.[12] Gang researchers have reported how the fear of gangs has been influenced by individual-level factors and fear of persons who are viewed as being different from the individual—in other words, not a consequence of an objective threat.[13] Herman and Chomsky emphasized how propaganda models operate through the media with the use of experts to make the data appear objective, but such models actually contribute to ideologies of worthy and unworthy victims.[14] Thus, throughout the past two hundred years since the colonization along the U.S.-Mexico border, we have observed moments of hysteria and panic. Gang members, drug dealers, and "illegal aliens" make easy scapegoats. The most marginalized were the easiest to blame and to use as a reason to enhance punishment.

Marginalized groups exist among dominant institutions, and in this area of structural inequality the marginalized groups fall victim to scandals, corruption, and problematic responses. Threats continue to exist in the form of state violence, and a lack of resources coupled with national propaganda has resulted in a level of neglect for services along with oversaturation toward militarization.[15] As cities such as El Paso work to create a safer city by reducing gang violence, they can no longer neglect how law enforcement officers have participated in a significant portion of the death and injury that has been left unaddressed and, in being ignored, has continued to allow the carnival mirror to remain in place. Although there wasn't a greater level of gang involvement along the U.S.-Mexico border of Southern New Mexico and West Texas compared to other areas of the country, the focus on these marginalized individuals hid the activities of other groups that were organizationally more capable in the trafficking of drugs. Trade routes will continue to exist and fluctuate as they have historically, and the demand for a product will result in continued production, whether this comes from within the United States or elsewhere.

Increased levels of border enforcement, deportation, walls, and the use of incarceration do not address the structural problems in these communities. The high levels of poverty along the border coincides with children who continue to encounter obstacles to their overall well-being when it comes to education, health care, and social services. Incarceration and deportation do not address these issues, instead heightening the very problems about which the practitioners complain. Thus, most of the challenges occurring along the U.S.-Mexico border and in Southern New Mexico were beyond the control of the institutions of law enforcement, education, and youth services. The internal problems in each of these institutions highlight a resource-deprived community that influences even the individuals who consider themselves as the helpers because they too occasionally become embroiled in situations that lead to unethical and criminal outcomes. Although many individuals, including youth, presume that institutions of social control present a united oppositional front, this study found significant conflict between these institutions. Moreover, there were divisions among these institutions that ensured that most of these agencies preferred working independently.

Why Is There a Gang Paradox Here?

Theorist Hubert M. Blalock outlined challenges that have existed for minority groups in settings where whites were a numerical majority, but in instances where these population patterns were reversed, we can still observe many patterns of institutionalized inequality.[16] Critical race scholar Laura Gómez's analysis of the impact of colonization on New Mexico residents encapsulates many of these challenges.[17] Although individuals of Mexican descent were categorized as having the opportunity to claim racial whiteness, this did not translate into improved treatment. Psychologists James Sidanius and Felicia Pratto remind us that hierarchy-reinforcing institutions do not work on behalf of members of subordinate groups, and despite friendships with participants of Mexican descent working in these institutions, it is hard to come to terms with such disparate outcomes when the attempts to provide aid only open the door to greater punitive measures that would not otherwise have been available.[18] An interest in benevolence may thus mask the root causes of inequality, and this can't be fixed by a program alone.

Researchers have questioned why Latino communities have lower rates of violence despite living in disadvantaged communities.[19] Explanations have emphasized the role of greater labor involvement and immigration. Based on my ethnographic research and various forms of data collection, I argue three primary factors occur in the geographic areas studied.

First is the intense desire for individuals of Mexican descent to fit in socially and to be accepted as first-class citizens. This is demonstrated by working hard, taking care of families, displaying the U.S. flag, joining the military, and supporting public education. The reported fears, paranoia, and nativism of individuals such as Patrick Buchanan and Samuel P. Huntington are incorrect.[20] Most residents work to attain the American Dream and, in this context, working for such success required accepting the ideology that racial inequality did not exist, that everyone is equal. This is reinforced in the public schools and even in higher education. Race and ethnicity courses and departments are not institutionalized. Some of these fears of increased consciousness of self, resulting in political contestation, were highlighted in the discussions that existed prior to New Mexico achieving statehood and prior to the marketing of the land of enchantment. Non-racialized thinking required maintaining institutions and belief systems built around color-blindness.[21] In addition, contrary to the findings of my friends Avelardo Valdez and Charles Kaplan, who emphasized the invitational edge, an argument which is empirically more similar to my data, the residents of this section of the U.S.-Mexico border did not have an open view of deviance.[22] Residents were very traditional, conservative in many ways, and religious in their thinking, and they worked hard to maintain a good social standing.

Second is the availability of alternative opportunities. In my previous research in Ogden, Utah, most avenues for educational opportunity and occupations were closed off from individuals of Mexican descent. There was no institutional pathway. New Mexico's institutional structure of providing a lottery program to provide youth who graduated from high school with funding for college was very important. This process increased the level of diversity in terms of race, ethnicity, and socioeconomic class. The educational exclusion that I observed in Colorado and Utah were better addressed in New Mexico. Educational opportunities allowed for greater beliefs of inclusion into U.S. society, along with increased opportunities to pursue careers. This created a chance for youth to have role models in the community who weren't gang members or convicts; they got to see that, with effort, they could be law enforcement officials, lawyers, judges, politicians, etc. This greater inclusion was likely attained through the presence of a majority minority in New Mexico.

A third factor that may reduce violence in terms of homicide is the significance of religion and sports in this region, which are coping mechanisms that provide hope. These institutions provide an outlet for youth and families. Pursuing higher education is challenging due to its closed atmosphere, which requires a certain level of education as well as avoidance of racialized social control, but attending church or putting together an athletic team allows greater forms of inclusion. These institutions help maintain family activities and, in the words of Karl Marx, serve as an "opium" for the masses to survive in a highly poor and structurally disadvantaged setting. Part of this belief system may have also been built on the idea that things were worse in other places. Violence, cartels, and corruption were worse in Juárez, whereas in the United States things were better. Youth could push themselves physically and mentally. They could develop teamwork and independence by becoming local success stories. This allowed parents and caregivers an opportunity to cheer and keep youth away from some of the more harmful activities.

Because most youth and adults were participating in one of these three avenues, the rates of violence were reduced. A small proportion of the population, however, continued to experience disrupted families and greater challenges, often with regard to employment, based on the system of punishment. These community members were the targets of criticism from practitioners. The coping patterns of alcohol and drug use enhanced interactions with formal institutions. These were the youth who seemed to become more involved with gangs. They became the most marginalized members of our society. They conflicted with other groups, yet the levels of violence were reduced by the three avenues described.[23] The formal methods of punishment directed youth toward arrest and subsequent incarceration.

Where Does This Leave Our Youth?

In the words of gang scholar James Diego Vigil, "As long as certain environmental and economic patterns persist, the gang subculture will continue to recruit new members, especially given the reinforcement the subculture receives from those who return from prison life."[24] Thus, there are gangs in this geographic area, but there are at least three primary alternatives to gang membership that effectively reduce these violence rates compared to other places around the country. However, even with such a miracle, where does this leave our youth? In *Gang Life in Two Cities*, one of my key partners named D-loc gave the following account for youth to get attention:

> So in all of our communities these people that are unrecognized found an avenue to be heard. And the gang movement made people be heard. It gave our children [a way] to be heard. It might not have been heard in the best way, but it was a cry for help. It was a cry for attention. It was a cry that there was a problem here in our community. And if it wasn't for our young people, our children killing and shooting and blastin' motherfuckers, our community wouldn't get heard, and we're only heard when these things happen.... Those kids don't know what they are, they don't know exactly why or how it is that they came to be in the position that they're in now—facin' prison, facin' their legs being cut off, facin' living in a wheelchair, having a colostomy bag hanging off the side of them that they take a shit in for the rest of their life. They don't know why all of these things are happening around them, they don't know why they're being pushed out of school, why they're dropping out of school, why they're getting pregnant, why they're using drugs.... They don't know why these things are the way they are in their community, but when they start shootin', and showing their fear and their hurt, and their pain and their depression, well then someone hears about it in our community.

Although I was thankful that the border region had lower rates of violence, there was still death that occurred due to violence. The community mourned and struggled to give voice to the victims of these crimes.[25] However, the greatest impact on the loss of life was problematic self-coping through the use of alcohol and drugs. Deaths that occurred through accidents, suicide, or liver disease didn't receive attention from the criminal justice system or increased calls for punishment or more law enforcement officers.[26] Instead it created a space in which the community struggled without attention. These were the inequalities that left children growing up in poverty, and left some having a family member dead, deported, or incarcerated. These were the small number of youth who weren't being channeled into the avenues of sports or religion or increased educational opportunities. Most youth in this region of the country will be okay because colonization worked to attain sustenance, but for the youth who are struggling, the "help" mechanism continues to filter them into increased levels of punishment that become the patterns described by officials as generational. These are the issues that continue to produce generations of exclusion for youth of Mexican descent.

In this setting, I'd ponder how Chicana/o leaders would assess this situation. I'd imagine they would argue how a perceived inclusion among the citizenry of the United States has not resulted in equality. The fear of and hate for Mexicans and the border have been enhanced by President Donald Trump, but they have existed historically, and both political parties have offered only token inclusion. Although the border region may have provided a bubble in which certain forms of attainment were possible, it did not change the lower level of resources or the broad forms of inequality that most citizens in the United States have not had to endure. My research demonstrates that individuals of Mexican descent share an experience similar to that of African Americans in terms of not being welcome in the United States, yet different in that Mexican Americans are not even perceived as a minority group. The national focus on black and white leaves Mexican Americans without a national political base. Justice as a people requires self-determination and acknowledgement that residents live in a broader society of settler colonialism. The activism of civil rights organizations has advocated on behalf of altering the system, and these efforts are needed along the border region to provide real change.

APPENDIX ONE

Methods

The biography and background of the researcher are important to ethnographic research. The researcher is the tool by which information is initiated, gathered, and analyzed.[1] *As a Chicano from a working-class background, with greater family predictions to enter an institution of incarceration rather than higher education (four of my five brothers have been imprisoned at some point in their lives), gangs and drug markets became a part of my young life. College provided an alternative, as did employment in juvenile justice and community advocacy groups, where I could begin to give back to the community and carve a path to mainstream respectability. Thus, the goal of trying to fit in with a society that has historically demonized a particular population (Mexicans) while simultaneously asserting that they should achieve equal participation in the United States is a contradictory challenge. Research data show improved inclusion, but things are definitely not equal, and thus as a Chicano I have attempted to utilize the investigatory tools of field work, interviews, archival research, juvenile probation files, and other forms of officially collected data to lay out the insights obtained.*

Fieldwork

One of the primary components of my research is fieldwork, or participant observation. Jorgensen states, "The methodology of participant observation seeks to uncover, make accessible, and reveal the meanings (realities) people use to make sense out of their daily lives."[2] The goal is to empirically observe what people do rather than what they say they do. While I was attentive to issues of social injustice, this form of research stresses maintaining emotional distance from the participants until after the study is completed. The presumption is that such closeness may damage the qualitative reliability and validity of the study. However, rather than distancing myself from my "key partners," I sought to use my insider status to enhance rapport. Professors Adler and Adler argued that there are many types of membership roles when conducting ethnographic research: the greatest level of commitment on the part of the researcher involves the complete membership role.[3] These scholars reported, "We believe that the native experience does not destroy but, rather, enhances the data-gathering process. Data gathering does not occur only through the detached observational role, but through the subjectively immersed role as well."[4] One variant of the complete membership role is gaining access opportunistically—in other words, using the sociological imagination and turning it inward to reflect upon the researcher's unique historical and biographical experiences.[5] These efforts merge into analytic autoethnography, which differs from evocative ethnography because the empirical world remains central to the data collection process.[6]

My ethnographic observations began in Doña Ana and El Paso in 2007 and continued throughout this project in 2014. I visited the various communities of Anthony, Berino, Chaparral, Deming, Doña Ana, El Paso, Hatch, Las Cruces, Lordsburg, Silver City, and Sunland Park as part of the research that coincided with my student courses focused on gangs and when I was invited to speak or learn more about various institutions in the region. My ethnographic observations were more intensive in District Six (Grant, Hidalgo, and Luna Counties) from September 2011 to August 2012. I also participated in a six-week Border Patrol Citizens Academy, where I learned more about border enforcement. Each week was organized into a particular theme, such as border observations, immigration detention centers, bike and dog patrols, SWAT, technology, and immigration and custom inspection laws, culminating in a graduation ceremony at the Border Patrol Museum. I also served as a volunteer member of the Wellness and Promotion Team at Gadsden Middle School located in Anthony, New Mexico. I had the opportunity to visit Southern Correctional Facility through a student connection and Rogelio Sanchez State Jail as a speaker in a scared-straight program. I visited schools, alternative schools, and detention centers. I felt welcomed by most the institutions I had the opportunity to visit, due primarily to my status as college professor in criminal justice and my family ancestry being from New Mexico.

Interviews

A second major component of my data-gathering efforts included conducting interviews.

Unstructured and semi-structured interviews along with several focus groups with practitioners began in 2007 and continued until 2014. Bernard stated that researchers should use unstructured interviews based on a clear plan but with the goal of getting individuals to share their thoughts, and with an opportunity to talk over an extended period.[7] Semi-structured interviews followed an interview guide and was based on the possibility of a one-time interview. I interviewed a total of seventy-six individuals, of whom nineteen were key members in the fields of law enforcement, sixteen worked in K–12 education, twelve worked in juvenile probation, and twenty-two were part of the overall juvenile services workgroups including district attorneys, judges, directors of prevention programs, city and county managers, social workers, and corrections personnel. In addition, I interviewed seven highly engaged, long-term community members. I took handwritten notes during each interview, and interviewees determined the use of a voice recorder. Interviews lasted anywhere from forty-five minutes to two hours. All handwritten notes and tape-recorded transcriptions were entered into a Microsoft Word document. The key participants were diverse in terms of race and ethnicity: forty-eight were Hispanic, twenty-seven were white, and one was black. In terms of gender, twenty-nine participants were female, and forty-seven were male. My interviews were conducted primarily in English, although I understand an intermediate level of Spanish, which allowed some conversations to occur in both languages. Observations and conversations with law enforcement involved federal, state, county, and local law enforcement officers. Formal interviews with juveniles did not receive institutional review board approval, thus field notes, informal conversations, and my parenting of several K–12 children captured some of these experiences.

Archival Research

Gathering historical information was made possible through libraries in Las Cruces and El Paso. The El Paso Library had several folders regarding the history of gangs in the area, and I supplemented this information with Newsbank Access World News for after the 1990s. The University of Texas at El Paso Institute of Oral History was also of great value.

Juvenile Probation Files

The random sample of eight-two juvenile probation cases consisted of sixty-six (80 percent) Hispanic/Latino juveniles, eight (10 percent) white juveniles, six (7 percent) other/mixed youth, one African American juvenile, and one Asian juvenile. Sixty-three (77 percent) were male; nineteen (23 percent) were female. The random sample of eighty-two cases was generated from a census of 412 probation case files using Microsoft Excel software. Due to one or two missing files, my colleague Carlos Posadas and I decided to generate additional random numbers to achieve the 20 percent quota of eighty-two probationers established for case reviews. This random sample consisted of 20 percent of the census of probation cases and is satisfactory for making applicable inferences. The referral history covered the years of 1999 to 2010 for a total of 716 referrals, of which 494 were separate incidents. The major characteristics analyzed included race and ethnicity, gender, gang affiliation, age at first offense, drug use or abuse, domestic violence and disruptive home, most serious offense, total charges, socio-economic status, police report, source of referral, and mental history.

The Juvenile Probation and Parole Office files for this report were primarily evaluated qualitatively by pulling specific themes from each file to create a complete family, social, and delinquency history of each probationer. With the assistance of the Juvenile Probation and Parole Office in Doña Ana County, researchers were granted a work area at the probation office to review the case files. Reliability was increased by comparing separately collected data sets of the same cases, noting discrepancies, resolving each discrepancy, and agreeing on the proper coding of each item. After completing the data collection, Carlos Posadas and I entered the data into a Microsoft Excel file. The data were scrubbed and verified through checks for data-entry errors and reliability by comparing the data entered by each of the two researchers. Frequencies were run on the variables identified as the most crucial, such as juvenile characteristics, family characteristics, delinquency history of the juvenile, referral patterns, and some characteristics of the juvenile justice system.

Other Sources of Data

Primary and secondary sources of data were obtained from law enforcement agencies, schools, state juvenile justice centers, technical reports, pamphlets, and the Neighborhood Change Database 1970–2010 Tract Data developed by Geolytics. I was given access to official statistics through the Family Automated Client Tracking System (FACTS) for the years of 2002 to 2008. The data were collected and housed in the state of New Mexico by the state's Children Youth and Families Department (CYFD) agency. I also accessed the DMC web-based data entry system.

APPENDIX TWO

Development of Gangs Timeline in the New Mexico/Texas Region

1915/1916	Perceived time period for the creation of El Paso gangs
1921	Creation of the Ku Klux Klan in El Paso
1924	Creation of the U.S. Border Patrol
1927	Roy Dickerson's account of El Paso gangs in Thrasher's 1927 book
1936	Article about South El Paso gangs
1942	War on gangs in El Paso
1950	X-2 gang
	7-11 gang
	Dukes
	Duchesses
	Dead End Kids
	Gas House Guys
	Old Fort Bliss gang
1952	Father Rahm arrives in El Paso
1956	7-X Estimate origination 1937 or 1942
1958	X-14s older aligned with 7-X younger
	Cypress Kids
	Little 9ers older aligned with Lucky 13 younger
	4-Fs—1940s
	Scorpions
	7-11
	Eagles
	Trampas
	Alley Cats

DEVELOPMENT OF GANGS TIMELINE IN THE NEW MEXICO/TEXAS REGION

	Crusaders
	Cougars
	Jokers
	Lucky Charms
	Shamrocks
1960	Lucky 14 rivalry with 7-X
1962	7-X
	Charms
	4-F
	Lucky 13
	Little 9s
	X-9
	LMs
	Terrengers
	DDTs
1972	Thunderbirds (T-Birds)
	Tecatos
1976	Flaming Angels
	Fonzies
	La Sana
	Chicanos in Action (CIA)
	Bandidos
1977	T-Birds
	Chicanos in Action (CIA)
	Blue Stars
	Los Demonios
	The Flaming Angels
	Mestizos
1979	Bandidos
	T-Birds (1965 origination)
1980s	45ers in Las Cruces, but also may be in 1975
	Barrio Azteca (formed in 1986 by members of X-14 gang in prison)
	North Side Doña Ana
	East Side Locos
	Meadow 13
	Varrio Anthony Locos
	Teners

DEVELOPMENT OF GANGS TIMELINE IN THE NEW MEXICO/TEXAS REGION

1990s	Fatherless Gang
	Diablos
	Chicos Tres
	Sunset Heights gangs
	Los Vatos de la Sana
	Mestizos
	T-Birds
	4,500 members
1992	5,000 members listed as ludicrous by reporter in El Paso
2003	Injunctions against Aztecas in Barrio Segundo
2006	4,000 members, more activity in 1990s
2007	5,000 members
2006–2014	

New Mexico

Anthony: Varrio Anthony Locos (VALs) Teners (TNS), and West Side Dukes

Chaparral: East Side Locos, North Side, West Side Lokos

Doña Ana: Brown Pride, East Side Locos, East Side Crips, LCK, North Side Doña Ana (NSDA), SSL, Queseros, Norteños, Sureños, and Zoe Pound

Las Cruces: Brown Pride, Chiva Town or 8-Ball Posse, Cruces Most Wanted, East Side Bloods, East Side Locos, Mesquiteros, North Siders (Norteños), Red Rag, South Side Crypts, South Siders (Sureños), South Side Royal Knights, Varrio Cruces Cartel, Varrio Mesquite Locos, and West Side

Silver City: China Town Locos, East Side Folk

Sunland Park: Anapra Homeboys, Barrio Azteca, Dukes, Meadow X3, Meadow Vista 13, Misfits, and Riverside Rockers

Prisons: Aryan Brotherhood, Barrio Azteca, MS-13, Los Carnales, Nuestra Familia, Syndicato de Nuevo Mexico

Texas

El Paso: List of potentially 500 gangs in El Paso

Barrio Azteca, Bloods, East Side Mob, Folks, Latin Kings, Latin Queens, Logan Heights, Lopez Maravilla, Los Midnight Locos, Mexican Mafia, and 19th Street

Horizon: Brown Dogs, BSA 13, D.C. Bloods, Sureño 13

Ciudad Juárez, Mexico

Artistas Asecinos, Juárez Cartel, Los Aztecas, Mexicles, Paisanos, Partido

Revoluncionario Mexicano (PRM), and Sinaloa Cartel

Notes

Acknowledgments

1. Telles and Ortiz wrote a powerful book in 2008 using this title to emphasize how a large part of the Mexican-American population has not been given the same opportunities as whites and how these disadvantages were often reproduced across generations.

Introduction

1. Deciding what term to use to identify the mixed population of Spanish and indigenous population in New Mexico is a difficult task. Chapter 1 will highlight this ancestral background and how race became socially constructed. For the purposes of this book, the term "Mexican" will be used interchangeably for people of Mexican descent. Most individuals living in these areas were native born, but there were foreign-born residents as well, which excluded citizenship as a criteria that could be determined by appearance. "Latino" will be used as the umbrella term to include individuals with a heritage from various Latin American countries as well as those colonized in the United States. Although the term "Hispanic" is used predominantly in the area, this federally created designation will be used when quoting or outlining the preferred terms used by respondents. Personally, my preferred term of "Chicana/o" to designate ancestry and political consciousness was not widely adopted in this region of the country but will be used when relevant to denote distinctions with the government-created terms "Latino" and "Hispanic." "White" will be used to denote non-Hispanic whites. For analysis purposes, all searches conducted focused specifically on non-Hispanic whites rather than the larger racial category of white because some Hispanics self-identify as this racial group. Chapters 1 and 2 will provide more background on this issue. In this region of the country, there were smaller levels of blacks and Native Americans.

2. Not mentioned in this discussion, in 2005 an alleged Aryan Brotherhood prison gang member was shot and killed by an Otero County Sheriff deputy.

3. Lopez 2017. Blaming parents or "poor parenting" was a popular reason cited, even used by the District Attorney and later Governor of New Mexico, Susana Martinez, at a gang-prevention seminar in Las Cruces. October 2, 2004. *Las Cruces Sun News.*

4. Brotherton and Barrios 2004; Hagedorn 1998; Moore 1978, 1991; Vigil 1988, 2007.

5. Klein 1995; Klein and Maxson 2006; Krohn and Thornberry 2008; Thornberry et al. 2003.

6. U.S. Department of Education 2012.

7. An excellent overview of the challenges existing at Hispanic Serving Institutions, particularly at New Mexico State University, can be found in the special edited *Journal of Latinos and Education* published in 2012, vol. 11, which was written by several of my colleagues.

8. Gómez 2007.

9. Perea 1995, 1997.

10. Rios 2011; Sidanius and Pratto 1999; Ward 2012.

11. Durán 2013. Currently the gang as criminal paradigm in criminology has grown beyond its original base with the help of departments in criminal justice and criminology. Although I too am interested in crime, a problem develops when researchers become consumed by illegal behavior and fail to notice all of the non-criminal behaviors. Moreover, they tend to neglect the criminality imposed by the state.

12. Morris 2015; Ladner 1973.

13. Adler and Adler 1987; Kirk and Miller 1986.

14. Anderson 1999; Contreras 2013; Jones 2010; Moore 1978, 1991; Rios 2011; Vigil 1988, 2002, 2007.

15. Becker 1967; Collins 2000; Gouldner 1968.

16. Atkinson et al. 2001:4.

17. Gellert and Shefner 2009:211.

18. Adler and Adler 1987; Deegan 2001; Morris 2015; Wright 2002.

19. Du Bois 1899.

20. Du Bois [1903] 1994:2. In relation to defining reflexivity, Hertz (1996:5) drew the following conclusion:

> The best definition of reflexivity I have found is Helen Callaway's (1992:33): 'Often condemned as apolitical, reflexivity, on the contrary can be seen as opening the way to a more radical consciousness of self in facing the political dimensions of fieldwork and constructing knowledge. Other factors intersecting with gender—such as nationality, race, ethnicity, class, and age—also affect the anthropologist's field interactions and textual strategies. Reflexivity becomes a continuing mode of self-analysis and political awareness.' Reflexivity, then, is ubiquitous. It permeates every aspect of the research process, challenging us to be more fully conscious of the ideology, culture, and politics of those we study and those whom we select as our audience.

21. Adler and Adler 1987; Gans 1999; Wright and Calhoun 2006.

22. Durán 2013; Contreras 2013; Rios 2011.
23. Brunsma, Brown, and Placier 2013.
24. Acuña 1998; Bonilla-Silva and Herring 1999; Bourgois 1996; Bracey, Meier, and Rudwick 1973; Contreras 2013; De la Luz Reyes and Halcón 1988; Rios 2011; Schneider and Segura 2014.
25. Collins 2000; Morris 2015; Wright 2002; and Wright and Calhoun 2006.
26. Thrasher [1927] 1963.
27. The ethnographic research on gangs that I admire the most includes the work of Joan Moore, James Diego Vigil, David Brotherton and Luis Barrios, Felix Padilla, John Hagedorn, Steven Cureton, Susan Phillips, and the new projects forthcoming by Avelardo Valdez and Alice Cepeda.
28. Brotherton 2015.
29. Mills [1959] 2000.
30. Mills [1959] 2000:147.
31. National Gang Center 2015.
32. Martinez 2002; Vélez 2006.
33. Martinez 2002, 2015.
34. Martinez 2015:162.
35. Telles and Ortiz 2008.
36. Dohan 2003.
37. Additional information on life chances can be found in the work of Max Weber outlined by Gerth and Mills 1946 and Dahrendorf 1979. For more on the concept of the Latino paradox, see Bock et al. 2005; Elder et al. 2005; Harrison and Kennedy 1996; McQueen et al. 2003; Morgan-Lopez et al. 2003; Parker et al. 1998; Phillip 2005; Sampson 2006; Vidrine et al. 2005.
38. Andreas 2000; Dunn 1996; Heyman 1999; Nevins [2002] 2010; United States-Mexico Border Health Commission 2010.
39. Dunn 2009; Nevins [2002] 2010.
40. Posadas and Medina 2012.
41. Holmes 1998; Rosas 2012.
42. Romo 2005.
43. Herman and Chomsky 2002.
44. Johnson [1995] 2000.
45. Bonilla-Silva [2003] 2018; Perea 1995, 1997.
46. Durán 2012; Martínez 2007; Weitzer 2014.
47. Compare insights from Brunson and Miller 2006; Durán 2012; Escobar 1999; Goldsmith et al. 2009; Holmes 1998, 2000; Mirandé 1987; Romero 2006; Solis, Portillos, and Brunson 2009; Urbina 2012.
48. There were a number of sensational books (Buchanan 2002; Diaz 2009; Dougherty 2004; Huntington 2004), federal agency reports, and congressional testimonies that have made this argument (United States Congress, House Committee on Homeland Security 2012). Although academics for the most part do a better job covering these issues, I still had a personal concern about whether the effort to cover violence and drug trafficking contributed to the general climate of fear of Mexican immigrants and Mexican Americans in the United States (Bowden 2010; Campbell 2009; Muehlmann 2014). Staudt (2008) rightfully

argues how we must keep from distancing the "other" as is often done to residents in Mexico. This book explores how U.S. policies have shaped historical obstacles in Mexico.

49. Bell 1992: xi; Delgado and Stefancic [2001] 2017
50. Haney-López 2003.
51. Haney-López 1996.
52. Delgado 1995, 1996, 1999; Bell 1992; Mirandé 2011.
53. Blalock 1967.
54. Acuña 1972; Almaguer 1971; Barrera 1979; Barrera, Muñoz, and Ornelas 1972; Blauner 1972; Hernández 2017; Murguía 1975; Navarro 2005.
55. Acuña 1972; Almaguer 1971; Barrera 1979; Blauner 1972; Murguía 1975; Navarro 2005.
56. Murguía 1975.
57. Hernández 2017:9.
58. Mirandé 1987.
59. Haney-López 2006.
60. Gómez 2007.
61. Sidanius and Pratto 1999.
62. Sidanius et al. 1994.
63. My favorite work consists of liberation theology.
64. Laurentin 1982.
65. I actually believe that all three of these themes were occurring in the geographic area that I was studying, and I hope that future research can build upon these themes. Unfortunately, none of my students followed up on these leads. See Boyle 2010; Flores 2014; Fremon 1995; Martinez 2016; Rahm and Weber 1958.
66. Martinez 2016.
67. Radley Balko (2009) wrote a similar article in *Reason Magazine* titled "The El Paso Miracle," which focused on how communities with a greater proportion of immigrants were safer.
68. Bock et al. 2005; Elder et al. 2005; Harrison and Kennedy 1996; McQueen et al. 2003; Morgan-Lopez et al. 2003; Parker et al. 1998; Phillip 2005; Sampson 2006; Vidrine et al. 2005.

Part One: A Revisionist History

1. Delgado and Stefancic 2017:25.

1. The Context for the Origination of Gangs: Double Colonization

1. Wagley and Harris 1958. An interesting overview of the work of Charles Wagley can be found in Hay 2014.
2. Gutiérrez 1991.
3. Calloway 1999.
4. Stannard 1992.

5. Bentley and Ziegler 2008.
6. Gutiérrez 1991.
7. Hall 1989:81.
8. Liebmann 2012.
9. White 1991.
10. Montgomery 2002.
11. Gómez 2007.
12. Gutiérrez 1991:103.
13. Gutiérrez 1991:193.
14. Gutiérrez 1991.
15. Montgomery 2002.
16. Gutiérrez 1991.
17. Hall 1989.
18. Owen 2005.
19. Foos 2002.
20. Gómez 2007; Montgomery 2002; Nieto-Phillips 2004. This is in contrast to the one-drop rule used against blacks for socially constructing an individual as nonwhite.
21. Hall 1989.
22. McWilliams [1948] 1990.
23. Nieto-Phillips 2004. Martinez (1975) estimated a New Mexico population of 75,000 and a Southwest population estimate of 86,000 to 116,000. Gonzales (2015) has used the term "Hispano" to refer to nuevomexicanos, whereas opposition to "Mexican" was due to it being used pejoratively.
24. Martinez 1980; Timmons 1990.
25. Gómez 2007.
26. Montgomery 2002.
27. Carrigan and Webb 2013; Gómez 2007; Montgomery 2002; Nieto-Phillips 2004.
28. Montgomery 2002:10.
29. McWilliams [1948] 1990.
30. García 1981.
31. Moorehead [1958] 1995.
32. Moorehead [1958] 1995; Jackson 2006; Perales 2010.
33. García 1981.
34. Lay 1985.
35. García 1981; Lay 1985.
36. Perales 2010:23.
37. Romo 2005:215.
38. Levario 2012.
39. Romo 2005:216.
40. Timmons 1990:162.
41. Dowling 2010:71, Dissertation.
42. Lay 1985.
43. Dowling 2010, Dissertation; Gabbert 2003.
44. November 30, 1925. *El Paso Times.*

45. June 17, 1933. *El Paso Herald-Post.*
46. Bryson 1980:60.
47. Stover, June 25, 1933. *El Paso Times.*
48. Rosen 1995.
49. Nieto-Phillips 2004.
50. Holtby 2012:4.
51. Ellis 1978; Montgomery 2002; Nieto-Phillips 2004.
52. Gonzales 2015.
53. Lay 1985.
54. Wasserman 1993.
55. Romo 2005.
56. Robinson 2002, Dissertation.
57. Jamieson 1980.
58. Lay 1985; Romo 2005; Timmons 1990. The trafficking of guns became an issue of central concern as Mexican cartel violence increased from 2006 to 2011. It was reported that a significant portion of guns were smuggled into Mexico from the United States.
59. Romo 2005.
60. Horne 2005.
61. Horne 2005:50.
62. Dyson 2011.
63. Carrigan and Webb 2013; Roberts 1993.
64. Day 1980.
65. Mottier 2009.
66. July 16, 1976. *El Paso Herald-Post.*
67. Robinson 2002, Dissertation.
68. Levario 2012:37.
69. Lay 1985.
70. Along with Levario (2012), Romo 2005 also wrote about this topic.
71. García 1981; Lay 1985; Timmons 1990.
72. Romo 2005:229.
73. Martin and Midgley 1999, 2006.
74. Lay 1985:62.
75. Romo 2005; Timmons 1990.
76. Robinson 2002, Dissertation.
77. Langston 1974, Dissertation.
78. Horne 2005; Timmons 1990.
79. Katz 1998.
80. Timmons 1990.

2. The Formation of Gangs in El Chuco

1. It appears that "ethnographic update" may be the preferred term over "ethnographic revisit," given that Burawoy (2003) seems to have something different in mind.

2. Romo provides a revolutionary walking tour map in his 2005 book.
3. Juaráz, Farah, and Burciaga 1997.
4. Vigil 1988.
5. Vigil 1988:9.
6. Thrasher [1927] 1963:264.
7. Tovares 2002.
8. Dickerson 1919:297.
9. García 1981:147.
10. Levario 2012.
11. García 1981.
12. Perales (2010) also supports these criticisms of schools in *Smeltertown: Making and Remembering a Southwest Border Community*.
13. Part of the challenge was due to the El Paso Public Library only having themes completed after 1970. They did have a thematic folder on gangs, but most leads required skimming various dates on microfiche. Future research could benefit from systematically indexing the files from El Paso newspapers from 1900 to 1940. Additional insights could be obtained by reviewing newspaper and technical reports in Ciudad Juárez to see if there were any overlaps with the different gangs listed.
14. March 8–9, 1919. "Oh Skinnay! The Gangs All Up in Court!" *El Paso Herald*.
15. I reviewed microfiche of each new article from March 1, 1919, to April 22, 1919, in the *El Paso Herald* and then from April 17, 1920, to June 14, 1920, from the *El Paso Times*. This was a slow process, and it did not feel very productive.
16. Interview no. 195, p. 29. UTEP Institute of Oral History, July 3, 1975.
17. Durán 2013; Moore 1978; Vigil 1988.
18. Vigil 1988:39–40.
19. Barker 1950; Cummings 2009; Escobar 1999; Griffith 1947, 1948; Licón 2009 Dissertation; Macías 2008; Mazón 1984; Ornstein 1951; Ornstein-Galicia 1987; Obregón-Pagan 2003.
20. Barker 1950; Cummings 2009; Griffith 1947, 1948.
21. Cummings 2009.
22. See also Ramírez 2009.
23. Lay 1985.
24. Durán 2013; Goodstein 2006.
25. Cunningham 2013.
26. Sonnichsen and McKinney 1971.
27. August 10, 1923. *Frontier Klansman*.
28. August 10, 1923:1. *Frontier Klansman*.
29. Robinson 2002. Dissertation.
30. Dunn 1996; Hernández 2010; McWilliams [1948] 1990.
31. Hernández 2010.
32. Interview no. 135. UTEP Institute of Oral History, June 25, 1974.
33. Levario 2012:3.
34. Sonnichesen and McKinney 1971.

35. Langston 1974. Dissertation.
36. Hernández 2010.
37. Langston 1974.
38. Hernández 2010.
39. *Frontier Klansman* 1923:4.
40. An *El Paso Times* newspaper article written on August 19, 1979, alleges that an Edward F. Sherman paper on the Klan from 1958 and housed at UTEP provides names of members. This news article also supported the argument that the Klan was originated by some southern soldiers and their secret practices appealed to the masons. This paper states that although the Klan came to dominate the school board, three newspapers opposed the organization.
41. Lay 1985.
42. Fullerton Gerould 1925:204. *Harpers Monthly Magazine*.
43. Fulleteron Gerould 1925:206. *Harpers Monthly Magazine*.
44. Ellis 1978.
45. García 1981; Montejano 1987, Levario 2012.
46. June 6, 1929. *El Paso Herald*.
47. Carrigan and Webb 2013.
48. Wasserman 1993.
49. Robinson 2002. Dissertation.
50. In addition to the dissertation research by Robinson (2002), Perales (2010) also emphasizes the point of many U.S. based companies present in Mexico and extracting its resources and financial capital.
51. Robinson 2002:69. Dissertation.
52. Mottier 2009.
53. Mottier 2009.
54. Abadinsky 2010; Brotherton and Barrios 2004; Hagedorn 1998; Klein 1995, 2004; Klein and Maxson 2006.
55. Abadinsky 2010:61.
56. Thrasher 1927.
57. Langston 1974. Dissertation. It would be of interest to see what role major U.S. businesses played in supporting the trafficking of alcohol or drugs. For instance, the Guggenheim family was reported to have many financial interests in Mexico.
58. Robinson 2002:303. Dissertation.
59. Dowling 2010; Langston 1974. Dissertations.
60. Langston 1974. Dissertation.
61. Campbell 2009.
62. Wasserman 1993.
63. Robinson 2002. Dissertation.
64. Although attempting to provide an objective scientific account, a lot of this information sounds prejudicial and closed off from the group he is interested in writing about.
65. Vigil 1988.
66. García 1994.
67. Cummings 2009; Licón 2009.
68. Macias 2008.

69. Barker 1950.
70. "Analyzing the Delinquent Situation." No date. No author. Reports.
71. Montgomery 2002.
72. Montgomery 2002.
73. Dowling 2010. Dissertation.
74. May 27, 1936. *El Paso Herald-Post*.
75. García 1981. It has been reported that the first mass at Sacred Heart Church was celebrated in 1893. The cover of this book emphasizes the central role of this church.
76. Cisneros, Ramirez, and Granado 1971. Reports.
77. March 12, 1940. *El Paso Herald-Post*.
78. July 21, 1941. *El Paso Herald-Post*.
79. April 20, 1942, and August 14, 1942. *El Paso Herald-Post*.
80. Torres 2010.
81. Durán 2013.
82. Licón 2009. Dissertation.
83. Bogardus 1943.
84. McWilliams [1948] 1990.
85. McWilliams [1948] 1990:231.
86. Macías 2008.
87. Dowling 2010. Dissertation.
88. Rivas-Rodriguez 2005.
89. Dowling 2010. Dissertation.
90. Dowling 2010. Dissertation.
91. Dowling 2010:223. Dissertation.
92. Ramos 1998.
93. June 22–23, 1950. *El Paso Herald-Post*.
94. June 24, 1950. *El Paso Herald-Post*.
95. June 24, 1950. *El Paso Herald-Post*. June 24, 1950. *El Paso Times*.
96. June 26, 1950. *El Paso Herald-Post*.
97. June 27, 1950. *El Paso Herald-Post*.
98. February 16, 1981. *El Paso Times*.
99. Fernando Lujan was the individual who was shot and killed.
100. Although Father Gregory Boyle has received a lot of contemporary acclaim for working to reduce gang violence, his actions were not alone (Boyle 2010; Fremon 1995).
101. Rahm and Weber 1958. Reports.
102. Perales (2010) reported how many upper-middle class Mexicans had moved to Sunset Heights but still did not receive equal treatment at the schools or churches, or in the broader community.
103. Vigil 1988.
104. Cisneros, Ramirez, and Granado (1971 Reports) and Jurado (1976 Master's Thesis) both noted how the Our Lady's Youth Center was known by the community as K.C. because it was the previous building of the Knights of Columbus.
105. Joan Moore reached a similar finding for those who did not join gangs in Los Angeles.

106. Klein 1995:40, made a similar argument in his book on gangs.
107. February 4, 1954. *El Paso Times.*
108. October 20, 1956. *El Paso Herald-Post.*
109. Torres 2010.
110. García 1989.
111. García 1989:139.
112. September 16, 1957. *El Paso Herald-Post.*
113. This origination date of 1937–1942 conflicts with one of Barker's (1950) respondents.
114. November 12, 1957. *El Paso Herald-Post.*
115. Murdered was Humberto Salazar.
116. Zinn 1959.
117. September 19, 1958. *El Paso Herald-Post.*
118. Murdered was Julio Duran.
119. Murdered was Manual Silva. September 17, 1958. *El Paso Herald-Post.*
120. June 3, 1959. *El Paso Times.* This is the article I'm referring to about not encountering any harassment during my walk at the beginning of this chapter.
121. September 20, 1976. *El Paso Times.*
122. Interview no. 610. UTEP Institute of Oral History, May 24, 1979.
123. Mr. Rodriguez passed away in 2008.
124. July 21, 2000. *El Paso Times.*
125. Murdered was Trinidad Mora. February 16, 1960. *El Paso Herald-Post.*
126. December 3, 1962. *El Paso Times.*
127. February 16, 1981. *El Paso Times.* The OK Nines controlled 9th Avenue Oregon and Kansas, 7-X controlled Virginia Street near the Alamita housing project, and the 4-Fs were on 4th Avenue and Florence. Other gangs in the city included the Lucky 13s and Little Nines.
128. Interview no. 211. UTEP Institute of Oral History, August 28, 1975.
129. Interview no. 846. UTEP Institute of Oral History, March 21, 1994.
130. April 25, 2006. *El Paso Times.*
131. Jurado 1976 Master's Thesis.
132. September 20, 1976. *El Paso Times.*
133. Martin and Midgley 1999, 2006.
134. Johnson 2007.
135. September 19, 1976. *El Paso Times.*
136. Cisneros, Ramirez, and Granado 1971. Reports.
137. April 6, 1972. *El Paso Times.*
138. April 12, 1972. *El Paso Times.*
139. April 13, 1972. *Prospector.*
140. April 24, 1972. *El Paso Times.*
141. April 26, 1972. *El Paso Times.*
142. April 24, 1972. *El Paso Times.* Clubs or gangs? These groups differed from those 15 years ago such as the 7-X, Little Nines, and 7-11. The gangs include Noble Lords (Tornillo and Paisano), Santanas (Campbell and Fifth), Alley Cats (Oregon and Fifth), Dare-Devils (Virginia and Eighth), Royal Knights (Park and Sixth), Ochoa Saints (Ochoa and Seventh), Cougars (Chihuahua Street), Thunderbirds (Armijo Center), Trampas (St. Vrain and Fifth), Oregon

Eagles (Oregon and Seventh), Shamrocks (Mesa and Fourth), Blue Stars (El Paso and Fifth), and Allstars (Florence and Fourth).

143. January 29, 1976 *El Paso Times*; May 19, 1976. *El Paso Herald-Post*.
144. August 19, 1976. *El Paso Times*.
145. August 26, 1976. *El Paso Herald-Post*.
146. Murdered was 18-year-old Jose Manuel Urquidez (September 19, 1976 and September 21, 1976 *El Paso Times*).
147. April 2, 1977. *El Paso Herald-Post*.
148. October 30, 1977. *El Paso Times*.
149. Murdered was Emilio Dill. October 23, 1976. *El Paso Times*.
150. November 7, 1976. *El Paso Times*.
151. November 4, 1976. *El Paso Times*.
152. Murdered was Adrian Ruiz. Charged were Albert Carrillo, 17, and Antonio Marquez (March 9, 1977, *El Paso Herald-Post*).
153. Jurado 1976. Master's Thesis.
154. Durán 2013; Montejano 2010; Navarro 1998.

3. Moral Panic Under a Research Microscope: The Organizational Scene Prior to Arrival

1. In undergraduate school, the formative books that were assigned to me in sociological theory were Ritzer's *Classical Sociological Theory* (1996), and for research methods Earl Babbie's *The Practice of Social Research* (1998).
2. In his book *The Barrio Gangs of San Antonio*, Mike Tapia (2017) faced a similar challenge. One of his successes was being able to interview previous members from the 1950s.
3. February 16, 1981. *El Paso Times*.
4. Murdered was Carlos Gandara Patino.
5. December 18, 1981. *El Paso Herald-Post*.
6. January 16, 1989. *El Paso Times*.
7. Texas Office of the Attorney General 1992. Report.
8. April 24, 1992. *El Paso Times*.
9. Texas Office of the Attorney General 1992. Report, p. 25. Fort Worth was also mentioned.
10. April 24, 1992. *El Paso Times*.
11. April 24, 1992. *El Paso Times*.
12. November 28, 1992. *El Paso Herald-Post*.
13. August 25, 1996. *El Paso Times*.
14. March 2, 1996. *El Paso Herald-Post*.
15. Manuel Almeraz, 23, was killed in 1996. One of the men accused was found innocent and two juveniles, who were 16 and 14 at the time, were given probation (Alfredo Martinez and Armando Martinez). After violating probation and picking up new offenses, Alfredo was sentenced to prison and Armando to a Restitution Center. January 16, 1999. *El Paso Times*; May 10, 1999. *El Paso Times*. In another instance, 16-year-old Jake Aguirre was killed and one of offenders was sentenced to 40 years in prison. November 2, 1999. *El Paso Times*.

16. Martinez 2015.
17. Tapia 2017.
18. January 8, 1992. *El Paso Herald-Post*.
19. January 8, 1992. *El Paso Times*.
20. The officers involved were Dirk Hiltl, 32, and Salvador Vega, 27.
21. Murdered was Nicholas Huerta. June 3, 1999. *El Paso Times*; November 10, 1999. *El Paso Times*.
22. June 13, 1999. *El Paso Times*.
23. October 28, 1999. *El Paso Times*.
24. October 30, 1999. The recommendation to fire came from Commander Cerjio Martinez of the Central Regional Command Center.
25. May 5, 2000. *El Paso Times*.
26. I have ongoing research on this topic. More will be explored on this topic in chapter 7 and in an upcoming dossier in *Aztlan* edited by Alfredo Mirandé.
27. September 19, 1999. *El Paso Times*.
28. January 28, 2001. *El Paso Times*.
29. November 23, 2003. *El Paso Times*.
30. Murdered was David Rivera. October 19, 1999. *El Paso Times*.
31. December 15, 1999. *El Paso Times*.
32. March 29, 2006. *El Paso Times*.
33. Both Uniform Crime Report data and National Crime Victimization Survey data support the empirical finding of a decreasing violent crime rate since the early 1990s. For property crime it has been a downward trajectory since the 1970s.
34. Governor's Organized Crime Prevention Commission 1991:2.
35. New Mexico Department of Public Safety 1994. Report.
36. Katz and Webb 2006.
37. City of Las Cruces Gang Task Force 1992.
38. It became effective in August 1992
39. Franco 1992. Report; Lobato and Tafoya 1993. Report; Sandoval-Monnét 1996. Master's thesis.
40. Mays, Winfree, and Jackson 1993.
41. Winfree et al. 1992.
42. Mays, Fuller, and Winfree 1994.
43. Mays, Fuller, and Winfree 1994:27.
44. Winfree and Bernat 1998; Winfree, Bernat, and Esbensen 2001.
45. Picacho, Sierra, and Lynn Middle Schools in Las Cruces.
46. Winfree, Bernat, and Esbensen 2001:114.
47. Winfree and Bernat 1998.
48. Moorhead-Nord 1994. Master's Thesis; Sandoval-Monnét 1996. Master's Thesis; Vigil-Bäckström 1992. Master's Thesis.
49. Jackson 1993. Master's Thesis.
50. Delgado 2001. Master's Thesis.
51. Arevalo Becerril 2000. Master's Thesis.
52. December 14, 1999. *El Paso Times*.
53. October 9, 1999. *El Paso Times*.

54. December 8, 2004. *Las Cruces Sun-News*.
55. January 15, 2006. *Las Cruces Sun-News*.
56. It is unclear the reason for the higher number of reported rapes in Las Cruces compared to the national average. Every semester I asked this question of my students, and we continued to be surprised by this number. The region is religious yet patriarchal, but it is not clear why rape would occur at rates higher than many other places in the country.
57. March 6, 2004. *Las Cruces Sun-News*; February 29, 2004. *Las Cruces Sun-News*. Jorge Olivas was the first murder of the year. Based on their records, he was the first teen in Las Cruces killed since 19-year-old Alex Medina, who was shot to death on December 16, 2000.
58. October 28, 2004. *Las Cruces Sun-News*.
59. December 10, 2005. *Las Cruces Sun-News*.
60. March 24, 2002. *El Paso Times*.
61. Durán 2013.
62. Pyrooz and Sweeten 2015.
63. Tapia 2017.
64. Decker and Van Winkle 1996; Durán 2013; Klein and Maxson 2006; Thornberry et al. 2003.
65. Klein and Maxson 2006.
66. June 21, 1973. *El Paso Times*.
67. August 1, 1974. *El Paso Herald-Post*.
68. March 2, 1979. *El Paso Times*.
69. September 7, 1988. *Chicago Tribune*.
70. March 7, 1977. *Los Angeles Times*.
71. For additional information on Mexico's Operation Condor, see Craig 1980.
72. February 27, 1979. *El Paso Herald-Post*.
73. Rather than only negative stories, Joe Renteria was later released from prison and continued his successful career. According to an *El Paso Times* article from May 10, 2011, Mr. Renteria had accumulated more than 200 national and international feature film, television, and commercial credits. He was currently working as a screenwriter and producer.
74. May 19, 1978. *El Paso Times*.
75. August 6, 1978. *El Paso Times*.
76. Chambers v. State 508 S.W. 2nd 348. Tex Crim App. 1974.
77. January 26, 1979. *El Paso Times*.
78. January 22, 1979. *Washington Post*; June 17, 1979. *New York Times*; August 4, 1979. *Boston Globe*.
79. October 14, 1979. *El Paso Times*; October 15, 1979. *El Paso Times*.
80. In 1967, Leopoldo Morales, Jr., was given the death penalty for shooting and killing an 18-year-old bride and her soldier husband.
81. April 16, 1982. *Chicago Tribune*. Additional readings on the Chagra family can be found in Cartwright [1984] 1998 and Chagra 2015.
82. Adler 1993.
83. Durán 2013; Fleetwood 2014.

84. Valdez and Kaplan 2007:900.
85. Campbell 2009.
86. December 26, 1972. *Hartford Courant*.
87. April 2007. *Texas Monthly*.
88. An internet website titled onepercenterbikers.com stated that Donald Eugene Chambers was paroled in 1983, and that he later died from cancer on July 18, 1999, and was buried in Houston, Texas.
89. November 11, 1976. *El Paso Herald-Post*. Chico 30-year-old Robert V. Lujan died.
90. Arrested were Donald Chambers, 46, Raymond Barriett, 39, and Jesse Fain Deal, 43. October 30, 1976. *El Paso Herald-Post*. Murdered were George Lyman Jones, 27, Jimmie Retha Brown, and Dana Thompson. December 16, 1977. *El Paso Herald-Post*.
91. February 12, 1979, and February 13, 1979. *El Paso Herald-Post*.
92. February 22, 1979. *El Paso Herald-Post*.
93. May 23, 1979. *El Paso Herald-Post*.
94. October 10, 1979. *El Paso Herald-Post*.
95. Moore 1978, 1991.
96. Moore 1991.
97. April 12, 1996. *El Paso Times*. There were some parolees who may have simply been attempting to start a new life. For example, in 1979 federal authorities, city police, and deputy sheriffs from Bakersfield, California, participated in the arrest of 31-year-old man who was described as a lieutenant of La Nuestra Familia prison gang. Arrested was Richard Lujan Hernandez, alias Frank Villobos.
98. September 29, 1997. *El Paso Times*. Death of Richard Bracknell, 26, an alleged member of the Mexican Mafia who was found hanging on shower curtain rod. It was debated whether it was a suicide or whether he had been killed by Richard Morales Castillo and six other members of the prison gang who were later charged with the death of Bracknell. January 11, 1999, March 26, 1999, and March 27, 1999. *El Paso Times*.
99. January 11, 1999. *El Paso Times*.
100. January 21, 2001. *El Paso Times*.
101. November 16, 2001. *El Paso Times*.
102. Camp and Camp 1985. Report.
103. Fong 1990; Fong and Buentello 1991; Marquart and Crouch 1985; Ralph and Marquart 1991; Tapia et al. 2014.
104. Another news story stated that Barrio Azteca was created by five El Paso residents serving time in an East Texas Prison.
105. June 5, 1999. *El Paso Times*.
106. December 22, 2006. *El Paso Times*.
107. April 15, 2003, May 3, 2003, May 12, 2003, May 15, 2003. *El Paso Times*.
108. September 5, 2005. *El Paso Times*.
109. City of Chicago v. Morales, , 527 U.S. 41 (1999).
110. Camp and Camp 1985. Report; Fong 1990; Fong and Buentello 1991; Marquart and Crouch 1985; Ralph and Marquart 1991; Tapia et al. 2014.

111. August 2, 2005. *El Paso Times*.
112. Operation Community Shield, Fact Sheet, 2008. Report.
113. Chacón 2007.
114. Cole 2003.
115. May 9, 2004. *El Paso Times*.
116. March 12, 2006. *El Paso Times*.
117. December 12, 1999. *El Paso Times*.
118. July 28, 1999. *El Paso Times*.
119. October 10, 1999. *El Paso Times*.
120. Fregoso and Bejarano 2010; Staudt 2008.
121. Timmons 1990.
122. January 28, 2004. *El Paso Times*.
123. August 17, 2004. *El Paso Times*.
124. September 18, 2002. *El Paso Times*.
125. July 11, 2003. *El Paso Times*.
126. January 5, 2004. *El Paso Times*.
127. September 20, 2002. *El Paso Times*.

Part Two: An Ethnographic Foundation

1. Baca Zinn 1979; Bourgois 1996; Collins 2000; Contreras 2013; Cureton 2008; Hagedorn 1990; Mirandé 1985; Morris 2015; Riessman 1987; Rios 2011. An excellent overview of intersectionality and its roots can be found in Potter (2013).

4. How Youth of Mexican Descent Encounter Criminalization

1. I remember a conversation with a colleague and friend, Ramiro Martinez, about data patterns based on my research on officer-involved shootings. I told him Denver had a high rate of shootings. He asked, compared to what? He went on to elaborate on how everything is relative, and our conversation turned to how one could answer this question. Although this was not my intention at the beginning, most of my research has focused on comparison, and I thank him for pushing me to become more reflexive of how my local research compared to other locations.
2. Peterson and Krivo 2012; Telles and Ortiz 2008.
3. Kupchik 2010; Peguero and Shaffer 2015; Portillos, González, and Peguero 2012; Rios 2011.
4. The Office of Juvenile Justice and Delinquency Prevention—OJJDP DMC website.
5. Pope and Feyerherm 1990; Pope, Lovell, and Hsia 2002.
6. Pope, Lovell, and Hsia 2002.
7. National Council on Crime and Delinquency 2007.
8. Kempf-Leonard 2007.
9. Carmichael, Whitten, and Voloudakis 2005. Report.

10. Menon and Jordan 1997. Report. This study provides a great historical overview of these early efforts.
11. Carmichael, Whitten, and Voloudakis 2005. Report.
12. Carmichael, Whitten, and Voloudakis 2005:62. Report.
13. Members of TARC included Lisa Bond Maupin, James Maupin, Dana Greene, Carlos Posadas, Julian Lapeyre, and myself.
14. Benekos, Merlo, and Puzzanchera 2011; National Center for Juvenile Justice 2010. Report.
15. In New Mexico an arrest and referral are treated as the same, whereas in some other states they are separate forms of decision-making.
16. Other groups analyzed in our data included Native American youth, who accounted for 12 percent of all youth aged 10 to 17, and black youth, who accounted for 2 percent of all youth. However, both racial groups were an even smaller proportion of residents along the U.S.-Mexico border. Readers interested in these patterns for other racial and ethnic groups for the entire state should consult the original article by Durán and Posadas 2013.
17. Durán and Posadas 2013.
18. See Pope, Lovell, and Hsia 2002 and Piquero 2008 for more information regarding this empirical question.
19. Based on census tract data, Luna County was the exception to this rule in terms of neighborhood segregation. However, the county continued to experience segregation by occupation as highlighted by a city governmental room containing photographs of its elected leaders and newspapers chronicling the history and current townspeople. I would still like to do additional analysis of El Paso census tract data.
20. This includes Doña Ana County, Hidalgo County, Grant County, and Luna County.
21. This observation may merge with Bonilla-Silva's ([2003] 2018) argument of race relations in the United States moving toward triracial stratification, which he argues was found more frequently in Latin American and Caribbean nations. However, in this book the data show that individuals of Mexican descent have received fewer social advantages despite being characterized as white. Part of this region's effort to destroy the concept of race appears to have been intended to reduce conflict with a majority minority population. Local whites seemed fearful to boast about their superior positioning in society.
22. Wilson 1996.
23. Bond-Maupin and Maupin 1998.
24. Willging, Quintero, and Lilliott 2014.
25. Kubrin, Zatz, and Martínez 2012; Martínez 2015; Martínez and Valenzuela 2006.
26. Government Accountability Study 2013.
27. Bejarano 2005:49.
28. Menjívar and Bejarano 2004:122.
29. Katz and Schnebly 2011.
30. Looking across the border from El Paso into Ciudad Juárez provides a view of how the high degree of poverty in El Paso pales in comparison to

the higher levels of poverty in Mexico. Based on interviews, respondents have described a decrease in local gangs in the State of Chihuahua, Mexico, due to the cartels taking over.

31. Kupchik 2010.
32. U.S. Department of Education 2012; New Mexico Voices for Children 2012; Annie E. Casey Foundation 2013, 2014.
33. New Mexico Public Education Department 2010; U.S. Chamber of Commerce 2012.
34. Kupchik 2016.
35. See also Flores 2016; Noguera 2003.
36. Rios 2017.
37. Peguero et al 2015.
38. Peguero and Shaffer 2015.
39. Portillos, González, and Peguero 2012.
40. Key among these leaders were my friends and professors, Rudolfo Chávez Chávez and Hermán García.
41. March 14, 2009. *Las Cruces Sun News*.
42. Kupchik 2016.
43. Full coverage of these data and various analyses involving informal referrals, probation cases, and number of repeat offenders can be found in previous technical reports completed by Durán and co-authors Posadas and Mata.
44. Lopez 2017.
45. Mata, Durán, and Posadas 2008. Report.
46. The use of detention data deserve greater research attention in a separate study.
47. For the state as a whole, majority minority status for Mexican Americans did not prevent overrepresentation in outcomes. The data for Native Americans were mixed, and blacks were overrepresented in New Mexico regardless of whether Mexican Americans or whites were in numerical control (as demonstrated by county data).
48. Bejarano 2005; Hirschfield 2009; Nicholson-Crotty, Birchmeier, and Valentine 2009; Peguero and Shaffer 2015; Peguero et al. 2015; Portillos, González, and Peguero 2012.

5. Contradictions in Law Enforcement

1. The *Washington Post* published an article by Lyndsey Layton about youth living in Mexican border communities on September 20, 2013, titled "Children Cross Mexican Border to Receive U.S. Education." The author points out how these youths were U.S. citizens living in Mexico.
2. Timmons 1990: xvi.
3. Disproportionate Minority Contact Technical Assistance Manual 2006. The terms arrest and referral were used interchangeably in New Mexico.
4. Davis and Sorensen 2012; Pope and Feyerherm 1995; Pope, Lovell, and Hsia 2002.

5. Pope and Feyerherm 1995:10.
6. Dillard 2013.
7. El Paso Police Department 2015. "Dedicated to Serve." Annual Report. El Paso County Sheriff's Office. 2015 Annual Report.
8. Alex 1969; Dulaney 1996; Durán 2015; Heyman 2002; Urbina and Álvarez 2015.
9. There was still a significant shortage of female officers, who only comprised anywhere from 3 to 12 percent of the force.
10. Dulaney 1996; Ruiz 1997; Sklansky 2006.
11. Heyman 2002.
12. Van Cleve 2016.
13. Sapp 2011. Report.
14. Sapp 2011. Report.
15. Sapp 2011. Report.
16. Andreas 2000, 2003; Dunn 1996; Kubrin, Zatz, and Martínez 2012.
17. Heyman 2008.
18. Andreas 2000, 2003; Dunn 1996; Goldsmith et al. 2009; Romero 2006.
19. Dunn 1996.
20. Hacker and Pierson 2010.
21. U.S. Immigration and Customs Enforcement, Fiscal Year 2016. Report.
22. May 16, 2012. KVIA.
23. Fox, Levin, and Quinet 2008; Hamm and Spaaij 2017; Newman et al. 2004.
24. January 23, 2018. *Las Cruces Sun-News*.
25. My colleague and friend Carlos Posadas and I were very interested in learning more about U.S. Border Patrol agents. Unfortunately, our application to conduct research on this organization was denied by our university's institutional review board. They requested we obtain approval from the director of Homeland Security.
26. September 26, 2017. *Las Cruces Sun-News*.
27. Vera Lopez's (2017) research on system-involved girls also found that practitioners blamed parents.
28. Presentation by the Las Cruces Police Department Gang Unit on March 14, 2008.
29. Syndicato Nuevo Mexico also had a History Channel "Gangland" episode that focused on this prison gang under the name "Hell House."
30. Katz and Webb 2006; Klein 2004.
31. National Institute of Corrections.
32. Hernandez v. Mesa, 582 U.S. (2017). No. 15-118.
33. June 26, 2017. *Univision*.
34. This section does not provide an exhaustive review of the number of problematic cases involving law enforcement officers. These were some of the cases that caught my attention, but further research should be devoted to providing a more systematic analysis with the purpose of improving these law enforcement agencies and the structural challenges they experience.
35. August 25, 2011. *Las Cruces Sun-News*; June 14, 2012. *Las Cruces Sun-News*.

36. November 9, 2003. *El Paso Times*.
37. July 21, 2016. *The Texas Tribune*.
38. January 29, 2009. *Las Cruces Sun-News*; October 7, 2009. *Albuquerque Journal*.
39. Davis and Sorensen 2012; Dillard 2013; Durán and Posadas 2013; Kempf-Leonard 2007; Leiber and Rodriguez 2011; Pope and Feyerherm 1995; Pope, Lovell, and Hsia 2002.
40. Vera Sanchez and Rosenbaum 2012.

6. Participatory Action Research Teams at a Minority-Serving Institution

1. According to a pamphlet, the Legislative Lottery Scholarships were created in 1996 and pay 100 percent of tuition. To qualify, students need to be a New Mexico resident, graduate from New Mexico public high school, enroll full-time in public college or university, and obtain and maintain a 2.5 grade-point average.
2. Moore 1978.
3. See the work of Appadurai (2006) for the "right to research" concept and how it is tied to "the capacity to aspire." Also see Lather (1986) for "research as praxis" and Delgado Bernal (2002) for "recognizing students of color as holders and creators of knowledge."
4. For more on PAR, see Fine 2009; Fine et al. 2003, 2007; Payne 2013; Stoudt, Fox, and Fine 2012.
5. Payne 2013. Report.
6. Brotherton and Barrios 2004; Moore 1978, 1991; Hagedorn 1998, 2015.
7. Burgess 1991.
8. Acuña 1998; Bracey, Meier, and Rudwick 1973; Bonilla-Silva and Herring 1999; De la Luz Reyes and Halcón 1988; Schneider and Segura 2014.
9. Bonilla-Silva and Herring 1999:6. Bonilla-Silva (2017) argues that this pattern still exists today.
10. De la Luz Reyes and Halcón 1988.
11. Bracey, Meier, and Rudwick 1973; Buckler 2008; Chilungu 1976; Collins 2000; Hayano 1979; Jones 1970; Morris 2015.
12. Acuña 1998; Collins 2000; Hooks [2000] 2015; Morris 2015.
13. Blauner and Wellman 1973; Chilungu 1976; Durán 2013.
14. Due to space limitations, the graduate students' work could not be incorporated because they were written as ten-page papers with a literature review, methods section, findings, and conclusion. However, their insights were incorporated into this larger book project.
15. To give credit but also to provide a level of anonymity, only the students' first names will be used. The full reports and the pictures that students and I have taken can be seen on my department website: http://rjduran.utk.edu/gang-updates. I am also using the preferred ethnic term of the area, which was Hispanic.

16. A Google search of the term "Fort Bliss solider arrested" brought up several news stories regarding this topic, which would require a more thorough examination before I could speculate about the number of these incidents.

17. December 3, 2008. *El Paso Times.* July 20, 2017. *El Paso Times.* This group had also been featured on the History Channel's "Gangland" under the title of Barrio Azteca.

18. August 13, 2013. *Albuquerque Journal.*

19. January 12, 2017. *El Paso Times.*

20. January 4, 2018. KVIA.

7. Empirical Miracles and Where Do We Go from Here?

1. Ernesto Vigil was a key partner in my first book *Gang Life in Two Cities* and is the author of *The Crusade for Justice: Chicano Militancy and the Government's War on Dissent.*

2. A good background of these events can be found in Armando Navarro's (1998) *The Cristal Experiment: A Chicano Struggle for Community Control*, José Angel Gutiérrez's (1998) *The Making of a Chicano Militant: Lessons from Cristal*, Ernesto Vigil's (1999) *The Crusade for Justice: Chicano Militancy and the Government's War on Dissent*, and Reies López Tijerina's (2000) *They Called Me "King Tiger": My Struggle for the Land and Our Rights*, translated from Spanish and edited by José Angel Gutiérrez.

3. Another reference to Telles and Ortiz 2008.

4. Bowden 2010; Campbell 2009; Correa-Cabrera 2017; Poppa 1998.

5. New Mexico Department of Health 2013. Report.

6. Cohen [1972] 2002.

7. National Drug Threat Assessment 2011; National Gang Intelligence Center 2011:39.

8. More on the problems of police and gang lists can be found in my previous book, *Gang Life in Two Cities* (Durán 2013).

9. Bjerregaard 2002; Hagedorn [1988] 1998.

10. Rios 2017.

11. Pyrooz and Sweeten 2015.

12. Vigil 1988.

13. Tapia 2017.

14. Esbensen et al. 2001.

15. Decker 1996; Vigil 1988.

16. Moore 1991, 2000.

17. In future research, I would like to obtain and analyze these data with a goal of creating a study similar to Valdez, Cepeda, and Kaplan 2009.

18. Maxson, Gordon, and Klein 1985.

19. Tita and Abrahamse 2004.

20. Bogardus 1943; Cook and Ludwig 2000; Moore 1991; Vigil 2007; Durán 2013. Report.

21. Papachristos 2009.

22. December 15, 2010. CNN.
23. Mirandé 1987.
24. Davies and Holz 1992.
25. The title for this section comes from a book written by Dr. Martin Luther King Jr. and published in 1967.
26. Fleisher 1998b:250.
27. Fleisher 1998a.
28. Baca Zinn 1979; Delgado and Stefancic 2001; Mirandé 2011; Morris 2015; Phillips and Bowlings 2003; Takagi 1981; Wright 2002; Wright and Calhoun 2006.
29. Morris 2015:134.
30. Acuña 1998; Bonilla-Silva [2003] 2018; Mirandé 1987.
31. Hamilton 1973.
32. Boyle 2010; Fremon 1995.
33. Rios 2017.
34. Rahm and Weber 1958:66. Report.
35. Martinez 2016.
36. Barrera 1979; Fanon 1963; Memmi 1965.
37. Shapiro 2017:18.
38. Maybe Karl Marx, Emile Durkheim, or Paulo Freire pondered the possibility of a better reality.

Conclusion

1. Rest in peace to the individual who first provoked me into researching gangs along the U.S.–Mexico border.
2. The starting point used is the signing of the Treaty of Guadalupe Hidalgo, which added 525,000 square miles to the United States and removed half of Mexico's territory.
3. December 30, 2017. *USA Today Network*.
4. November 22, 2017. *USA Today Network*.
5. Amada Armenta (2017) has a new book titled *Protect, Serve, and Deport: The Rise of Policing as Immigration Enforcement*, which is centered in Nashville, Tennessee.
6. Although my perceived future included staying in Tennessee, I have accepted a job offer that involves moving to East Central Texas in August 2018.
7. Mills [1959] 2000.
8. Rios 2011.
9. Ward 2012.
10. Hernández 2017.
11. In Carrigan and Webb's (2013) book, these authors reported how the common justifications for lynchings were based on perceived criminality or a lack of justice in frontier courts. However, these authors found they were more inspired by economic competition and racial prejudice. Thus, in my work, increased calls for enhanced punishment often do not entail a desire for empirical

validation that such a level of punishment will be effective, but only a prejudicial belief that punishment will remove perceived wrongdoers rather than the structural sources of strain.

12. Reiman 2001.
13. Katz, Webb, and Armstrong 2003; Lane and Meeker 2000.
14. Herman and Chomsky 2002.
15. Andreas, 2000; Dunn, 1996; Heyman, 1999, Nevins [2002] 2010; United States Government. Accountability Office 2013.
16. Blalock 1967.
17. Gómez 2007.
18. Sidanius and Pratto 1999.
19. Peterson and Krivo 2012; Martinez 2015; Vélez 2006.
20. Buchanan 2002; Huntington 2004.
21. Bonilla-Silva [2003] 2018.
22. Valdez and Kaplan 2007.
23. Criminologist John Hagedorn outlined a possible fourth explanation in his book *The Insane Chicago Way*; I did not acquire data to support this but I thought it was worthy to mention in a footnote. In his book, Hagedorn described how local gangs in Chicago came together to create the Spanish Growth and Development that could organize crime and control violence. He mentioned this as a possibility in El Paso when providing possible comparisons with the data he acquired in Chicago.
24. Vigil 1988:175.
25. Rest in peace to residents in Doña Ana whose lives were taken too soon, including Baby Brianna (2002); Katie Sepich (2003); Ashley Wax, Dana Joseph Grauke, and Luther Garcia (2005); Gerardo Baltazar and Alberto Soto (2007); Bobby Zertuche (2008); Adam Espinoza (2010); Jerry Zamarripa (2011); and Jocelyn Marrie Trujillo (2017). Condolences to the families and friends of loved ones whom I missed in recognizing. For historical purposes, it would be empowering to have the names of everyone taken too soon by violence.
26. The New Mexico Department of Health analyzed the youth suicide rate in New Mexico from 2002 to 2007 and found that the New Mexico rate was more than double the rate of the United States overall; New Mexico Department of Health 2008. Report. For more on the challenges that exist in the border region, see U.S.-Mexico Border Health Commission 2010. Report.

Appendix 1. Methods

1. Adler and Adler 1987; Lofland and Lofland 1995; Punch 1986.
2. Jorgensen 1989:15.
3. Adler and Adler 1987.
4. Adler and Adler 1987:84.
5. Reimer 1977.
6. Anderson 2006.
7. Bernard 2006.

References

Abadinsky, Howard. 2010. *Organized Crime.* Belmont, CA: Wadsworth.
Acuña, Rodolfo. 1972. *Occupied America: The Chicano's Struggle Toward Liberation.* San Francisco: Canfield Press.
———. 1998. *Sometimes There Is No Other Side: Chicanos and the Myth of Equality.* Notre Dame, IN: University of Notre Dame Press.
Adler, Patricia A. 1993. *Wheeling and Dealing: An Ethnography of an Upper-Level Drug Smuggling Community.* New York: Columbia University Press.
Adler, Patricia A., and Peter Adler. 1987. *Membership Roles in Field Research.* Newbury Park, CA: Sage.
Alex, Nicholas. 1969. *Black in Blue: A Study of the Negro Policeman.* New York: Appleton-Century-Crofts.
Almaguer, Tomás. 1971. "Toward the Study of Chicano Colonialism." *Aztlan* 2:7–21.
Anderson, Elijah. 1999. *Code of the Street: Decency, Violence, and the Moral Life of the Inner City.* New York: W. W. Norton.
Anderson, Leon. 2006. "Analytic Autoethnography." *Journal of Contemporary Ethnography* 35(4):373–95.
Andreas, Peter. 2000. *Border Games: Policing the U.S.-Mexico Divide.* Ithaca, NY: Cornell University Press.
———. 2003. "A Tale of Two Borders: The U.S.-Mexico and U.S-Canada Lines after 9/11." Working Papers, Center for Comparative Immigration Studies, University of California–San Diego.
Appadurai, Arjun. 2006. "The Right to Research." *Globalisation, Societies and Education* 4(2): 167–77.
Armenta, Amada. 2017. *Protect, Serve, and Deport: The Rise of Policing as Immigration Enforcement.* Oakland: University of California Press.
Atkinson, Paul, Amanda Coffey, Sara Delamont, John Lofland, and Lyn Lofland, eds. 2001. *Handbook of Ethnography.* Thousand Oaks, CA: Sage.
Babbie, Earl. 1998. *The Practice of Social Research.* 8th Ed. Belmont, CA: Wadsworth.
Baca Zinn, Maxine. 1979. "Field Research in Minority Communities: Ethical, Methodological and Political Observations by an Insider." *Social Problems*, 27(2):209–19.

Barker, George C. 1950. *Pachuco: An American-Spanish Argot and Its Social Functions in Tucson, Arizona*. University of Arizona Bulletin: Social Science Bulletin no 18(1). Tucson: University of Arizona Press.

Barrera, Mario. 1979. *Race and Class in the Southwest: A Theory of Racial Inequality*. Notre Dame, IN: University of Notre Dame Press.

Barrera, Mario, Carlos Muñoz, and Charles Ornelas. 1972. "The Barrio as an Internal Colony." *Urban Affairs Annual Review* 6:465–98.

Becker, Howard S. 1967. "Whose Side Are We On?" *Social Problems*, 14(3):239–47.

Bejarano, Cynthia L. 2005. *Que Onda? Urban Youth Culture and Border Identity*. Tucson: University of Arizona Press.

Bell, Derrick. 1992. *Faces at the Bottom of the Well: The Permanence of Racism*. New York: Basic Books.

Benekos, Peter J., Alida V. Merlo, and Charles M. Puzzanchera. 2011. "Youth, Race, and Serious Crime: Examining Trends and Critiquing Policy." *International Journal of Police Science & Management*, 13(2):132–48.

Bentley, Jerry H., and Herbert F. Ziegler. 2008. *Traditions and Encounters: A Global Perspective of the Past*. New York: McGraw-Hill.

Bernard, Russell H. 2006. *Research Methods in Cultural Anthropology: Qualitative and Quantitative Approaches*. Lanham, MD: Alta Mira Press.

Bjerregaard, Beth. 2002. "Self-Definitions of Gang Membership and Involvement in Delinquent Activities." *Youth and Society* 34(1):31–54.

Blalock, Hubert M. 1967. *Toward a Theory of Minority-Group Relations*. New York: Capricorn Books.

Blauner, Robert. 1972. *Racial Oppression in America*. New York: Harper & Row.

Blauner, Robert, and David Wellman. 1973. "Toward the Decolonization of Social Research," pp. 310–30, in *The Death of White Sociology*, edited by J. A. Ladner. New York: Vintage Books.

Bock, Beth C., Raymond S. Niaura, Charles J. Neighbors, Rosa Carmona-Barros, and Munawar Azam. 2005. "Differences between Latino and non-Latino White Smokers in Cognitive and Behavioral Characteristics Relevant to Smoking Cessation." *Addictive Behaviors* 30(4):711–24.

Bogardus, Emory S. 1943. "Gangs of Mexican-American Youth." *Sociology and Social Research* 28(1):55–66.

Bond-Maupin, Lisa J., and James R. Maupin. 1998. "Juvenile Justice Decision Making in a Rural Hispanic Community." *Journal of Criminal Justice*, 26(5):373–84.

Bonilla-Silva, Eduardo. [2003] 2018. *Racism Without Racists: Color-Blind Racism and the Persistence of Racial Inequality in the United States*. Boulder, CO: Rowman and Littlefield.

———. 2017. "What We Were, What We Are, and What We Should Be: The Racial Problem of American Sociology." *Social Problems* 64:179–87.

Bonilla-Silva, Eduardo, and Cedric Herring. 1999. "We'd Love to Hire Them, But . . . The Underrepresentation of Sociologists of Color and Its Implications." *ASA Footnotes* 27(3): 6.

Bourgois, Philippe. 1996. "Confronting Anthropology, Education, and Inner-City Apartheid." *American Anthropologist* 98(2):249–58.
Bowden, Charles. 2010. *Murder City: Ciudad Juárez and the Global Economy's New Killing Fields.* New York: Nation Books.
Boyle, Gregory. 2010. *Tattoos on the Heart: The Power of Boundless Compassion.* New York: Free Press.
Bracey, John, August Meier, and Elliott Rudwick. 1973. "The Black Sociologists: The First Half Century," pp. 3–22, in *The Death of White Sociology*, edited by J. A. Ladner. New York: Vintage Books.
Brotherton, David C. 2015. *Youth Street Gangs: A Critical Appraisal.* New York: Routledge.
Brotherton, David C., and Luis Barrios. 2004. *The Almighty Latin King and Queen Nation: Street Politics and the Transformation of a New York City Gang.* New York: Columbia University Press.
Brunsma, David L., Eric S. Brown, and Peggy Placier. 2013. "Teaching Race at Historically White Colleges and Universities: Identifying and Dismantling the Walls of Whiteness." *Critical Sociology* 39(5):717–38.
Brunson, Rod K., and Jody Miller. 2006. "Young Black Men and Urban Policing in the United States." *British Journal of Criminology* 46(4):613–40.
Bryson, Conrey. 1980. "El Paso, Texas—U.S.A.," pp. 48–62, in *Four Centuries at the Pass: A New History of El Paso on its 400th Birthday*, edited by W. H. Timmons. El Paso, TX: 4 Centuries 81 Foundation.
Buchanan, Patrick J. 2002. *The Death of the West: How Dying Populations and Immigrant Invasions Imperil Our Country and Civilization.* New York: St. Martin's Press.
Buckler, Kevin. 2008. "The Quantitative/Qualitative Divide Revisited: A Study of Published Research, Doctoral Program Curricula, and Journal Editor Perceptions." *Journal of Criminal Justice Education* 19(3):383–403.
Burawoy, Michael. 2003. "Revisits: An Outline of a Theory of Reflexive Ethnography." *American Sociological Review* 68(5):645–79.
Burgess, Robert G. 1991. "Sponsors, Gatekeepers, Members and Friends: Access in Educational Settings," pp. 43–52, in *Experiencing Fieldwork: An Inside View of Qualitative Research*, edited by W. B. Shaffir and R. A. Stebbins. Newbury Park, CA: Sage.
Calloway, Colin G. 1999. *First Peoples: A Documentary Survey of American Indian History.* Boston: Bedford/St. Martin's Press.
Campbell, Howard. 2009. *Drug War Zone: Frontline Dispatches from the Streets of El Paso and Juárez.* Austin: University of Texas Press.
Carrigan, William D., and Clive Webb. 2013. *Mob Violence against Mexicans in the United States, 1848–1928.* New York: Oxford University Press.
Cartwright, Gary. [1984] 1998. *Dirty Dealing: Drug Smuggling on the Mexican Border and the Assassination of a Federal Judge.* El Paso, TX: Cinco Puntos Press.
Chacón, Jennifer M. 2007. "Whose Community Shield? Examining the Removal of the 'Criminal Street Gang Member.'" *University of Chicago Legal Forum* 317–57.

Chagra, Catherine. 2015. *Dirty Darlings: A Story of Big Shots, Free-Falling, and a Texas-Sized Return to Grace*. Castroville, TX: Black Rose Writing.

Chilungu, Simeon W. 1976. "Issues in the Ethics of Research Method: An Interpretation of the Anglo-American Perspective." *Current Anthropology* 17(3):457–67.

Cohen, Stanley. [1972] 2002. *Folk Devils and Moral Panics: The Creation of the Mods and the Rockers*. New York: St. Martin's Press.

Cole, David. 2003. *Enemy Aliens: Double Standards and Constitutional Freedoms in the War on Terrorism*. New York: New Press.

Collins, Patricia Hill. 2000. *Black Feminist Thought: Knowledge, Consciousness, and the Politics of Empowerment*. New York: Routledge.

Contreras, Randol. 2013. *The Stickup Kids: Race, Drugs, Violence, and the American Dream*. Berkeley: University of California Press.

Cook, Philip J., and Jens Ludwig. 2000. *Gun Violence: The Real Costs*. New York: Oxford University Press.

Correa-Cabrera, Guadalupe. 2017. *Los Zetas Inc.: Criminal Corporations, Energy, and Civil War in Mexico*. Austin: University of Texas Press.

Craig, Richard. 1980. "Operation Condor: Mexico's Antidrug Campaign Enters a New Era." *Journal of Interamerican Studies and World Affairs* 22(3):345–63.

Cummings, Laura L. 2009. *Pachucas and Pachucos in Tucson: Situated Border Lives*. Tucson: University of Arizona Press.

Cunningham, David. 2013. *Klansville, U.S.A.: The Rise and Fall of the Civil Rights-Era Ku Klux Klan*. New York: Oxford University Press.

Cureton, Steven R. 2008. *Hoover Crips: When Cripin' Becomes a Way of Life*. Lanham, MD: University Press of America.

Dahrendorf, Ralf. 1979. *Life Chances: Approaches to Social and Political Theory*. Chicago: University of Chicago Press.

Davies, Christopher S., and Robert K. Holz. 1992. "Settlement Evolution of 'Colonias' along the U.S.-Mexico Border: The Case of the Lower Rio Grande Valley of Texas." *Habitat International* 16(4):119–42.

Davis, Jaya, and Jon R. Sorensen. 2012. "Disproportionate Juvenile Minority Confinement: A State-Level Assessment of Racial Threat." *Youth Violence and Juvenile Justice* 11(4):296–312.

Day, James M. 1980. "The Building of a City, 1900–1940," pp. 64–78, in *Four Centuries at the Pass: A New History of El Paso on its 400th Birthday*, edited by W. H. Timmons. El Paso, TX: 4 Centuries 81 Foundation.

Decker, Scott H. 1996. "Collective and Normative Features of Gang Violence." *Justice Quarterly* 13(2):243–64.

Decker, Scott H., and Barrik Van Winkle. 1996. *Life in the Gang: Family, Friends, and Violence*. New York: Cambridge University Press.

Deegan, Mary Jo. 2001. "The Chicago School of Ethnography," pp. 11–25, in *Handbook of Ethnography*, edited by P. Atkinson, A. Coffey, S. Delamont, J. Lofland, and L. Lofland. Thousand Oaks, CA: Sage.

De la Luz Reyes, María, and John J. Halcón. 1988. "Racism in Academia: The Old Wolf Revisited." *Harvard Educational Review* 58(3):299–314.

Delgado, Richard. 1995. *The Rodrigo Chronicles: Conversations About America and Race*. New York: New York University Press.

———. 1996. *The Coming Race War? And Other Apocalyptic Tales of America After Affirmative Action and Welfare.* New York: New York University Press.

———. 1999. *When Equality Ends: Stories About Race and Resistance.* Boulder, CO: Westview Press.

Delgado, Richard, and Jean Stefancic. [2001] 2017. *Critical Race Theory: An Introduction.* New York: New York University Press.

Delgado Bernal, Dolores. 2002. "Critical Race Theory, Latino Critical Theory, and Critical Raced-Gendered Epistemologies: Recognizing Students of Color as Holders and Creators of Knowledge." *Qualitative Inquiry* 8(1):105–26.

Diaz, Tom. 2009. *No Boundaries: Transnational Latino Gangs and American Law Enforcement.* Ann Arbor: University of Michigan Press.

Dickerson, Roy E. 1919. "Some Suggestive Problems in the Americanization of Mexicans." *The Pedagogical Seminary* 26(3):288–97.

Dillard, Dorothy. 2013. "Limited Disproportionate Minority Contact Discourse May Explain Limited Progress in Reducing Minority Over-representation in the US Juvenile Justice System." *Youth Justice* 13(3):207–17.

Dohan, Daniel. 2003. *The Price of Poverty: Money, Work, and Culture in the Mexican American Barrio.* Berkeley, University of California Press.

Dougherty, Jon E. 2004. *Illegals: The Imminent Threat Posed by Our Unsecured U.S.-Mexico Border.* Nashville, TN: WND Books.

Du Bois, W.E.B. [1899] 1996. *The Philadelphia Negro: A Social Study.* Philadelphia: University of Pennsylvania Press.

———. [1903] 1994. *The Souls of Black Folk.* Mineola, NY: Dover.

Dulaney, Marvin W. 1996. *Black Police in America.* Bloomington: Indiana University Press.

Dunn, Timothy J. 1996. *The Militarization of the U.S.-Mexico Border 1978–1992: Low-Intensity Conflict Doctrine Comes Home.* Austin: University of Texas Press.

———. 2009. *Blockading the Border and Human Rights: The El Paso Operation that Remade Immigration Enforcement.* Austin, Texas: University of Texas Press.

Durán, Robert J. 2012. "Policing the Barrios: Exposing the Shadows to the Brightness of a New Day," pp. 42–62, in *Hispanics in the U.S. Criminal Justice System: The New American Demography*, edited by M. G. Urbina. Springfield, IL: Charles C. Thomas.

———. 2013. *Gang Life in Two Cities: An Insider's Journey.* New York: Columbia University Press.

———. 2015. "Mexican American Law Enforcement Officers: Comparing the Creation of Change Versus the Reinforcement of Structural Hierarchies," pp. 128–47 in *Latino Police Officers in the United States: An Examination of Emerging Trends and Issues*, edited by M. G. Urbina and S. E. Álvarez. Springfield, IL: Charles C. Thomas.

Durán, Robert J., and Carlos E. Posadas. 2013. "Disproportionate Minority Contact in the Land of Enchantment: Juvenile Justice Disparities as a Reflection of White-over-Color Ascendancy." *Journal of Ethnicity in Criminal Justice* 11(1–2):93–111.

Dyson, Rick. 2011. "Buffalo Soldiers." In *The Encyclopedia of North American Indian Wars 1607–1890: A Political, Social, and Military History*. Santa Barbara, CA: ABC-CLIO.
Elder, John P., Shelia L. Broyles, Jesse J. Brennan, Maria Luisa Zuniga de Nuncio, and Philip R. Nader. 2005. "Acculturation, Parent-Child Acculturation Differential, and Chronic Disease Risk Factors in a Mexican-American Population." *Journal of Immigrant Health* 7(1):1–9.
Ellis, Richard N. 1978. "Hispanic Americans and Indians in New Mexico State Politics." *New Mexico Historical Review* 53(4):361–64.
Esbensen, Finn-Aage, L. Thomas Winfree, Jr., Ni He, and Terrance J. Taylor. 2001. "Youth Gangs and Definitional Issues: When Is a Gang a Gang, and Why Does It Matter." *Crime and Delinquency* 47(1):105–30.
Escobar, Edward J. 1999. *Race, Police, and the Making of a Political Identity: Mexican Americans and the Los Angeles Police Department 1900–1945*. Los Angeles: University of California Press.
Fanon, Frantz. 1963. *The Wretched of the Earth*. New York: Grove Press.
Fine, Michelle. 2009. "Postcards from Metro America: Reflections on Youth Participatory Action Research for Urban Justice." *Urban Review* 41(1):1–6.
Fine, Michelle, Nick Freudenberg, Yasser Payne, Tiffany Perkins, Kersha Smith, and Katya Wanzer. 2003. " 'Anything Can Happen with Police Around': Urban Youth Evaluate Strategies of Surveillance in Public Places." *Journal of Social Issues* 59(1):141–58.
Fine, Michelle, María Elena Torre, April Burns, and Yasser A. Payne. 2007. "Youth Research/Participatory Methods for Reform," pp. 805–28, in *International Handbook of Student Experience in Elementary and Secondary School*, edited by D. Thiessen and A. Cook-Sather. Springer.
Fleetwood, Jennifer. 2014. *Drug Mules: Women in the International Cocaine Trade*. New York: Palgrave Macmillan.
Fleisher, Mark S. 1998a. "Ethnographers, Pimps, and the Company Store," pp. 44–64, in *Ethnography at the Edge: Crime, Deviance, and Field Research*, edited by J. Ferrell and M. S. Hamm. Boston: Northeastern University Press.
———. 1998b. *Dead End Kids: Gang Girls and the Boys They Know*. Madison: University of Wisconsin Press.
Flores, Edward Orozco. 2014. *God's Gangs: Barrio Ministry, Masculinity, and Gang Recovery*. New York: New York University Press.
Flores, Jerry. 2016. *Caught Up: Girls, Surveillance, and Wraparound Incarceration*. Oakland: University of California Press.
Fong, Robert S. 1990. "The Organizational Structure of Prison Gangs: A Texas Case." *Federal Probation* 54(1):36–44.
Fong, Robert S., and Salvador Buentello. 1991. "The Detection of Prison Gang Development: An Empirical Assessment." *Federal Probation* 55(1):66–70.
Foos, Paul. 2002. *A Short, Offhand, Killing Affair*. Chapel Hill: University of North Carolina Press.
Fox, James Alan, Jack Levin, and Kenna Quinet. 2008. *The Will to Kill: Making Sense of Senseless Murder*. New York: Pearson.

Fregoso, Rosa-Linda, and Cynthia Bejarano, Eds. 2010. *Terrorizing Women: Feminicide in the Américas*. Durham, NC: Duke University Press.
Fremon, Celeste. 1995. *Father Greg and the Homeboys: The Extraordinary Journey of Father Greg Boyle and His Work with Latino Gangs of East L.A.* New York: Hyperion.
Gabbert, Ann R. 2003. "Prostitution and Moral Reform in the Borderlands: El Paso, 1890–1920." *Journal of the History of Sexuality* 12(4):575–604.
Gans, Herbert J. 1999. Participant Observation in the Era of 'Ethnography.' " *Journal of Contemporary Ethnography* 28(5):540–48.
García, Mario T. 1981. *Desert Immigrants: The Mexicans of El Paso, 1880–1920*. New Haven, CT: Yale University Press.
———. 1989. *Mexican Americans: Leadership, Ideology, and Identity, 1930–1960*. New Haven, CT: Yale University Press.
———. 1994. *Memories of Chicano History: The Life and Narrative of Bert Corona*. Los Angeles: University of California Press.
Gellert, Paul K., and Jon Shefner. 2009. "People, Place and Time: How Structural Fieldwork Helps World-Systems Analysis." *Journal of World-Systems Research* 15(2):193–218.
Gerth, Hans H., and C. Wright Mills. 1946. *From Max Weber: Essays in Sociology*. New York: Oxford University Press.
Goldsmith, Pat Rubio, Mary Romero, Raquel Rubio-Goldsmith, Manuel Escobedo, and Laura Khoury. 2009. "Ethno-Racial Profiling and State Violence in a Southwest Barrio." *Aztlán: A Journal of Chicano Studies* 34(1):93–123.
Gómez, Laura E. 2007. *Manifest Destinies: The Making of the Mexican American Race*. New York: New York University Press.
Gonzales, Phillip B. 2015. "New Mexico Statehood and Political Inequality: The Case of Nuevomexicanos." *New Mexico Historical Review* 90(1):31–52.
Goodstein, Phil. 2006. *In the Shadow of the Klan: When the KKK Ruled Denver, 1920–1926*. Denver: New Social Publications.
Gouldner, Alvin W. 1968. "The Sociologist as Partisan: Sociology and the Welfare State." *American Sociologist* 3(2):103–16.
Griffith, Beatrice. 1947. "The Pachuco Patois." *Common Ground* 7(4):77–84.
———. 1948. *American Me*. Cambridge, MA: Riverside Press.
Gutiérrez, José Angel. 1998. *The Making of a Chicano Militant: Lessons from Cristal*. Madison: University of Wisconsin Press.
Gutiérrez, Ramon A. 1991. *When Jesus Came, the Corn Mothers Went Away: Marriage, Sexuality, and Power in New Mexico, 1500–1846*. Stanford, CA: Stanford University Press.
Hacker, Jacob S., and Paul Pierson. 2010. *Winner-Take-All Politics: How Washington Made the Rich Richer—And Turned Its Back on the Middle Class*. New York: Simon and Schuster.
———. 1990. "Back in the Field Again: Gang Research in the Nineties," pp. 240–59, in *Gangs in America*, edited by C. R. Huff. Newbury Park, CA: Sage.
Hagedorn, John M. [1988] 1998. *People and Folks: Gangs, Crime, and the Underclass in a Rustbelt City*. Chicago: Lakeview Press.

———. 2015. *The Insane Chicago Way: The Daring Plan by Chicago Gangs to Create a Spanish Mafia.* Chicago: University of Chicago Press.
Hall, Thomas D. 1989. *Social Change in the Southwest, 1350–1880.* Lawrence: University Press of Kansas.
Hamilton, Charles V. 1973. "Black Social Scientists: Contributions and Problems," pp. 471–76, in *The Death of White Sociology*, edited by J. A. Ladner. New York: Vintage Books.
Hamm, Mark S., and Ramón Spaaij. 2017. *The Age of Lone Wolf Terrorism.* New York: Columbia University Press.
Haney-López, Ian F. [1996] 2006. *White by Law: The Legal Construction of Race.* New York: New York University Press.
———. 2003. *Racism on Trial: The Chicano Fight for Justice.* Cambridge, MA: Belknap Press of Harvard University.
Harrison, Lana D., and Nancy Kennedy. 1996. "Drug Use in the High-Intensity Drug-Trafficking Area of the U.S. Southwest Border." *Addiction* 91(1):47–61.
Hay, Fred. 2014. "Race, Culture, and History: Charles Wagley and the Anthropology of the African Diaspora in the Americas." *Boletim de Museu Paraense Emilio Goeldi. Ciencas Humanas* 9(3):695–705.
Hayano, David M. 1979. "Auto-Ethnography: Paradigms, Problems, and Prospects." *Human Organization* 38(1):99–104.
Herman, Edward S., and Noam Chomsky. 2002. *Manufacturing Consent: The Political Economy of the Mass Media.* New York: Pantheon Books.
Hernández, Kelly Lytle. 2010. *Migra: A History of the U.S. Border Patrol.* Berkeley: University of California Press.
———. 2017. *City of Inmates: Conquest, Rebellion, and the Rise of Human Caging in Los Angeles, 1771–1965.* Chapel Hill: University of North Carolina Press.
Hertz, Rosanna. 1996. "Introduction: Ethic, Reflexivity and Voice." *Qualitative Sociology* 19(1):3–9.
Heyman, Josiah McC. 1999. "Why Interdiction? Immigration Control at the United States-Mexico Border." *Regional Studies*, 33(7):619–30.
———. 2002. "U.S. Immigration Officers of Mexican Ancestry as Mexican Americans, Citizens, and Immigration Police." *Current Anthropology* 43(3):479–507.
———. 2008. "Constructing a Virtual Wall: Race and Citizenship in U.S.-Mexico Border Policing." *Journal of the Southwest* 50(3):305–34.
Hirschfield, Paul. 2009. "Another Way Out: The Impact of Juvenile Arrests on High School Dropout." *Sociology of Education* 82(4):368–93.
Holmes, Malcolm D. 1998. "Perceptions of Abusive Police Practices in a U.S.-Mexico Border Community." *The Social Science Journal* 35(1):107–18.
———. 2000. "Minority Threat and Police Brutality: Determinants of Civil Rights Criminal Complaints in U.S. Municipalities." *Criminology* 38(2):343–67.
Holtby, David V. 2012. *Forty-Seventh Star: New Mexico's Struggle for Statehood.* Norman: University of Oklahoma Press.
Hooks, Bell. [2000] 2015. *Feminism Is for Everybody: Passionate Politics.* New York: Routledge.

Horne, Gerald. 2005. *Black and Brown: African Americans and the Mexican Revolution, 1910–1920*. New York: New York University Press.
Huntington, Samuel P. 2004. *Who Are We? The Challenges to America's National Identity*. New York: Simon and Schuster.
Jackson, Hal. 2006. *Following the Royal Road: A Guide to the Historic Camino Real de Tierra Adentro*. Albuquerque: University of New Mexico Press.
Jamieson, Perry D. 1980. "A Survey History of Fort Bliss," pp. 80–90, in *Four Centuries at the Pass: A New History of El Paso on its 400th Birthday*, edited by W. H. Timmons. El Paso, TX: 4 Centuries 81 Foundation.
Johnson, Allan G. [1995] 2000. *The Blackwell Dictionary of Sociology: A User's Guide to Sociological Language*. Malden, MA: Blackwell.
Johnson, Kevin R. 2007. *Opening the Floodgates: Why America Needs to Rethink Its Borders and Immigration Laws*. New York: New York University Press.
Jones, Delmos J. 1970. "Towards a Native Anthropology." *Human Organization* 29(4):251–59.
Jones, Nikki. 2010. *Between Good and Ghetto: African American Girls and Inner-City Violence*. New Brunswick, NJ: Rutgers University Press.
Jorgensen, Danny L. 1989. *Participant Observation: A Methodology for Human Studies*. Thousand Oaks, CA: Sage.
Juaráz, Miguel, Cynthia Weber Farah, and José Antonio Burciaga. 1997. *Colors on Desert Walls: The Murals of El Paso*. El Paso, TX: Texas Western Press.
Katz, Charles M., and Stephen M. Schnebly. 2011. "Neighborhood Variation in Gang Member Concentrations." *Crime and Delinquency* 57(3):377–407.
Katz, Charles M., and Vincent J. Webb. 2006. *Policing Gangs in America*. New York: Cambridge University Press.
Katz, Charles M., Vincent J. Webb, and Todd A. Armstrong. 2003. "Fear of Gangs: A Test of Alternative Theoretical Models." *Justice Quarterly* 20(1):95–130.
Katz, Friedrich. 1998. *The Life and Times of Pancho Villa*. Stanford, CA: Stanford University Press.
Kempf-Leonard, Kimberly. 2007. "Minority Youths and Juvenile Justice: Disproportionate Minority Contact after Nearly 20 years of Reform Efforts." *Youth Violence and Juvenile Justice* 5(1):71–87.
Kirk, Jerome, and Marc L. Miller. 1986. *Reliability and Validity in Qualitative Research*. Beverly Hills, CA: Sage.
Klein, Malcolm W. 1995. *The American Street Gang: Its Nature, Prevalence, and Control*. New York: Oxford University Press.
———. 2004. *Gang Cop: The Words and Ways of Officer Paco Domingo*. Walnut Creek, CA: AltaMira.
Klein, Malcolm W., and Cheryl L. Maxson. 2006. *Street Gang Patterns and Policies*. New York: Oxford University Press.
Krohn, Marvin D., and Terence P. Thornberry. 2008. "Longitudinal Perspectives on Adolescent Street Gangs," pp. 138–47, in *The Long View of Crime: A Synthesis of Longitudinal Research*, edited A. Liberman. New York: Springer-Verlag.

Kubrin, Charis E., Marjorie S. Zatz, and Ramiro Martínez. 2012. *Punishing Immigrants: Policy, Politics, and Injustice*. New York: New York University Press.

Kupchik, Aaron. 2010. *Homeroom Security: School Discipline in an Age of Fear*. New York: New York University Press.

———. 2016. *The Real School Safety Problem: The Long-Term Consequences of Harsh School Punishment*. Oakland: University of California Press.

Ladner, Joyce. 1973. *The Death of White Sociology*. New York: Random House.

Lane, Jodi and James W. Meeker. 2000. "Subcultural Diversity and the Fear of Crime and Gangs." *Crime and Delinquency* 46(4):497–521.

Lather, Patti. 1986. "Research as Praxis." *Harvard Educational Review* 56(3):257–77.

Laurentin, René. 1982. *Miracles in El Paso? The Amazing Story of God's Work among the Poor of El Paso-Juarez*. Ann Arbor, MI: Servant Books.

Lay, Shawn. 1985. *War, Revolution, and the Ku Klux Klan: A Study of Intolerance in a Border City*. El Paso, TX: Texas Western Press.

Leiber, Michael, and Nancy Rodriguez. 2011. "The Implementation of the Disproportionate Minority Confinement/Contact (DMC) Mandate: A Failure or Success?" *Race and Justice* 1(1):103–24.

Levario, Miguel Antonio. 2012. *Militarizing the Border: When Mexicans Became the Enemy*. College Station: Texas A&M Press.

Liebmann, Mathew. 2012. *Revolt: An Archeological History of Pueblo Resistance and Revitalization in 17th Century New Mexico*. Tucson: University of Arizona Press.

Lofland, John and Lyn H. Lofland. 1995. *Analyzing Social Settings: A Guide to Qualitative Observation and Analysis*. New York: Wadsworth.

Lopez, Vera. 2017. *Complicated Lives: Girls, Parents, Drugs, and Juvenile Justice*. New Brunswick, NJ: Rutgers University Press.

Macías, Anthony. 2008. *Mexican American Mojo: Popular Music, Dance, and Urban Culture in Los Angeles, 1935–1968*. Durham, NC: Duke University Press.

Marquart, James W., and Ben M. Crouch. 1985. "Judicial Reform and Prisoner Control: The Impact of Ruiz v. Estelle on a Texas Penitentiary." *Law and Society Review* 19(4):557–86.

Martin, Philip, and Elizabeth Midgley. 1999. "Immigration to the United States." *Population Reference Bureau. Population Bulletin* 54(2):1–44.

———. 2006. "Immigration: Shaping and Reshaping America." Revised and updated 2nd ed. *Population Reference Bureau. Population Bulletin* 61(4):1–30.

Martinez, Cid Gregory. 2016. *The Neighborhood Has Its Own Rules: Latinos and African Americans in South Los Angeles*. New York: New York University Press.

Martínez, Oscar J. 1975. "On the Size of the Chicano Population: New Estimates, 1850–1900. *Aztlán* 6(1):43–59.

———. 1980. "El Paso and Juarez," pp. 92–103, in *Four Centuries at the Pass: A New History of El Paso on its 400th Birthday*, edited by W. H. Timmons. El Paso, TX: 4 Centuries 81 Foundation.

Martinez, Ramiro. 2002. *Latino Homicide: Immigration, Violence, and Community.* 1st ed. New York: Routledge.
———. 2007. "Incorporating Latinos and Immigrants into Policing Research." *Criminology and Public Policy* 6(1):57–64.
———. 2015. *Latino Homicide: Immigration, Violence, and Community.* 2nd ed. New York: Routledge.
Martinez, Ramiro, and Abel Valenzuela. 2006. *Immigration and Crime: Race, Ethnicity, and Violence.* New York: New York University Press.
Maxson, Cheryl L., Margaret A. Gordon, and Malcolm W. Klein. 1985. "Differences Between Gang and Nongang Homicides." *Criminology* 23(2):209–22.
Mays, Larry G., Kathy Fuller, and L. Thomas Winfree. 1994. "Gangs and Gang Activity in Southern New Mexico: A Descriptive Look at a Growing Rural Problem." *Journal of Crime and Justice* 17(1):25–44.
Mays, Larry G., L. Thomas Winfree, and Stacey Jackson. 1993. "Youth Gangs in Southern New Mexico: A Qualitative Analysis." *Journal of Contemporary Criminal Justice.* 9(2):134–45.
Mazón, Mauricio. 1984. *The Zoot-Suit Riots: The Psychology of Symbolic Annihilation.* Austin: University of Texas Press.
McQueen, Amy, J. Greg Getz, and James H. Bray. 2003. "Acculturation, Substance Use, and Deviant Behavior: Examining Separation and Family Conflict as Mediators." *Child Development* 74(6):1737–50.
McWilliams, Carey. [1948] 1990. *North from Mexico: The Spanish-Speaking People of the United States.* Westport, CT: Praeger.
Memmi, Albert. 1965. *The Colonizer and the Colonized.* Translated by Howard Greenfield. New York: Orion Press.
Menjívar, Cecilia and Cynthia Bejarano. 2004. "Latino Immigrants' Perceptions of Crime and Police Authorities in the United States: A Case Study from the Phoenix Metropolitan Area." *Ethnic and Racial Studies* 27(1):120–48.
Mills, C. Wright. [1959] 2000. *The Sociological Imagination.* New York: Oxford University Press.
Mirandé, Alfredo. 1985. *The Chicano Experience: An Alternative Perspective.* Notre Dame, IN: University of Notre Dame Press.
———. 1987. *Gringo Justice.* Notre Dame, IN: University of Notre Dame Press.
———. 2011. *Rascuache Lawyer: Toward a Theory of Ordinary Litigation.* Tucson: University of Arizona Press.
Montejano, David. 1987. "The Demise of 'Jim Crow' for Texas Mexicans, 1940–1970. *Aztlán* 16(1–2):27–69.
———. 2010. *Quixote's Soldiers: A Local History of the Chicano Movement, 1966–1981.* Austin: University of Texas Press.
Montgomery, Charles. 2002. *The Spanish Redemption: Heritage, Power, and Loss of New Mexico's Upper Rio Grande.* Los Angeles: University of California.
Moore, Joan W. 1978. *Homeboys: Gangs, Drugs and Prison in the Barrios of Los Angeles.* Philadelphia: Temple University Press.
———. 1991. *Going Down to the Barrio: Homeboys and Homegirls in Change.* Philadelphia. PA: Temple University Press.

———. 2000. "Latino Gangs: A Question of Change." *Justice Professional* 13:7–18.
Moorhead, Max L. [1958] 1995. *New Mexico's Royal Road: Trade and Travel on the Chihuahua Trail*. Norman: University of Oklahoma Press.
Morgan-Lopez, Antonio A., Felipe Gonzalez Castro, Laurie Chassin, David P. MacKinnon. 2003. "A Mediated Moderation Model of Cigarette Use among Mexican American Youth." *Addictive Behaviors* 28(3):583–89.
Morris, Aldon D. 2015. *The Scholar Denied: W.E.B. Du Bois and the Birth of Modern Sociology*. Oakland: University of California Press.
Mottier, Nicole. 2009. "Drug Gangs and Politics in Ciudad Juárez: 1928–1936." *Mexican Studies/Estudios Mexicanos*, 25(1):19–46.
Muehlmann, Shaylih. 2014. *When I Wear My Alligator Boots: Narco-Culture in the U.S.-Mexico Borderlands*. Berkeley: University of California Press.
Murgía, Edward. 1975. *Assimilation, Colonialism, and the Mexican American People*. Austin: University of Texas Press.
Navarro, Armando. 1998. *The Cristal Experiment: A Chicano Struggle for Community Control*. Madison: University of Wisconsin Press.
———. 2005. *Mexicano Political Experience in Occupied Aztlán*. Walnut Creek, CA: Alta Mira Press.
Nevins, Joseph. [2002] 2010. *Operation Gatekeeper and Beyond: The War on "Illegals" and the Remaking of the U.S.-Mexico Boundary*. New York: Routledge.
Newman, Katherine S., Cybelle Fox, David Harding, Jal Mehta, and Wendy Roth. 2004. *Rampage: The Social Roots of School Shootings*. New York: Basic Books.
Nicholson-Crotty, Sean, Zachary Birchmeier, and David Valentine. 2009. "Exploring the Impact of School Discipline on Racial Disproportion in the Juvenile Justice System." *Social Science Quarterly* 90(4):1003–18.
Nieto-Phillips, John M. 2004. *Language of Blood: The Making of Spanish-American Identity in New Mexico, 1880s–1930s*. Albuquerque University of New Mexico Press.
Noguera, Pedro A. 2003. Schools, Prisons, and Social Implications of Punishment: Rethinking Disciplinary Practices. *Theory into Practice* 42(4):341–50.
Obregón Pagán, Eduardo. 2003. *Murder at the Sleepy Lagoon: Zoot Suits, Race, and Riot in Wartime L.A.* Chapel Hill: University of North Carolina Press.
Ornstein, Jacob. 1951. "The Archaic and the Modern in the Spanish of New Mexico." *Hispania* 34(2):137–42.
Ornstein-Galicia, Jacob L. 1987. "Chicano Caló: Description and Review of a Border Variety." *Hispanic Journal of Behavioral Sciences* 9(4):359–73.
Owen, Gordon. [1999] 2005. *Las Cruces, New Mexico: Multi-Cultural Crossroads*. Las Cruces, NM: Doña Ana County Historical Society.
Papachristos, Andrew V. 2009. "Murder by Structure: Dominance Relations and the Social Structure of Gang Homicide." *American Journal of Sociology* 115(1):74–128.
Parker, Vanessa, Steve Sussman, David Crippens, Pam Elder, and Donna Scholl. 1998. "The Relation of Ethnic Identification with Cigarette Smoking among

U.S. Urban African American and Latino Youth: A Pilot Study." *Ethnicity and Health* 3(1–2):135–44.

Peguero, Anthony A., and Kelsey Shaffer. 2015. Academic Self-Efficacy, Dropping Out, and the Significance of Inequality. *Sociological Spectrum* 35(1):46–64.

Peguero, Anthony A., Zahra Shekarkhar, Ann Marie Popp, and Dixie J. Koo. 2015. "Punishing the Children of Immigrants: Race, Ethnicity, Generational Status, Student Misbehavior, and School Discipline." *Journal of Immigrant and Refugee Studies* 13(2):200–20.

Perales, Monica. 2010. *Smeltertown: Making and Remembering a Southwest Border Community.* Chapel Hill: University of North Carolina Press.

Perea, Juan F. 1995. "Ethnicity and the Constitution: Beyond the Black and White Binary Constitution." *William and Mary Law Review* 571(2):571–611.

———. 1997. "The Black/White Binary Paradigm of Race: The Normal Science of American Racial Thought." *California Law Review* 85(5):127–72.

Peterson, Ruth D., and Lauren J. Krivo. 2012. *Divergent Social Worlds: Neighborhood Crime and the Racial-Spatial Divide.* New York: Russell Sage Foundation.

Phillips, Coretta, and Benjamin Bowling. 2003. "Racism, Ethnicity and Criminology: Developing Minority Perspectives." *British Journal of Criminology* 43(2):269–90.

Piquero, Alex. 2008. "Disproportionate Minority Contact." *The Future of Children* 18(2):59–79.

Pope, Carl E., and William H. Feyerherm. 1990. "Minority Status and Juvenile Justice Processing: An Assessment of the Research Literature (Part I)." *Criminal Justice Abstracts* 22(2):327–35.

———. 1995. Minorities and the Juvenile Justice System: Research Summary. Washington, DC: U.S. Department of Justice, Office of Justice Programs, Office of Juvenile Justice and Delinquency Prevention.

Pope, Carl E., Rick Lovell, and Heidi Hsia. 2002. "Disproportionate Minority Confinement: A Review of the Research Literature from 1989 through 2001." Washington, DC: Office of Juvenile Justice and Delinquency Prevention.

Poppa, Terrence E. 1998. *Drug Lord: The Life and Death of a Mexican Kingpin.* Seattle: Demand Publications.

Portillos, Edwardo L., Juan Carlos González, and Anthony A. Peguero. 2012. Crime Control Strategies in School: Chicana'/os' Perceptions and Criminalization. *Urban Review* 44(2):171–88.

Posadas, Carlos E., and Christina Medina. 2012. "Immigration Lockdown: The Exclusion of Mexican Immigrants Through Legislation," pp. 80–93, in *Hispanics in the U.S. Criminal Justice System: The New American Demography*, edited by M. Urbina. Springfield, IL: Charles C. Thomas.

Potter, Hillary. 2013. "Intersectional Criminology: Interrogating Identity and Power in Criminological Research and Theory." *Critical Criminology* 21:305–18.

Punch, Maurice. 1986. *The Politics and Ethics of Fieldwork.* Beverly Hills, CA: Sage.

Pyrooz, David C., and Gary Sweeten. 2015. "Gang Membership Between Ages 5 and 17 years in the United States." *Journal of Adolescent Health* 56(4):414–19.

Ralph, Paige H., and James W. Marquart. 1991. "Gang Violence in Texas Prisons." *Prison Journal* 71(2):38–49.

Ramírez, Catherine S. 2009. *The Woman in the Zoot Suit: Gender, Nationalism, and the Cultural Politics of Memory.* Durham, NC: Duke University Press.

Ramos, Henry A. J. 1998. *The American GI Forum: In the Pursuit of the Dream, 1948–1983.* Houston: Arte Publico Press.

Reiman, Jeffrey. 2001. *The Rich Get Richer and the Poor Get Prison.* Boston: Allyn and Bacon.

Reimer, Jeffrey W. 1977. "Varieties of Opportunistic Research." *Urban Life* 5(4):467–77.

Riessman, Catherine Kohler. 1987. "When Gender Is Not Enough: Women Interviewing Women." *Gender and Society* 1(2):172–207.

Rios, Victor M. 2011. *Punished: Policing the Lives of Black and Latino Boys.* New York: New York University Press.

———. 2017. *Human Targets: Schools, Police, and the Criminalization of Latino Youth.* Chicago: University of Chicago Press.

Ritzer, George. [1992] 1996. *Classical Sociological Theory.* New York: McGraw-Hill.

Rivas-Rodriguez, Maggie, ed. 2005. *Mexican Americans and World War II.* Austin: University of Texas Press.

Roberts, David. 1993. *Once They Moved Like the Wind: Cochise, Geronimo, and the Apache Wars.* New York: Simon and Schuster.

Romero, Mary. 2006. "Racial Profiling and Immigration Law Enforcement: Rounding Up of Usual Suspects in the Latino Community." *Critical Sociology* 32(2–3):447–73.

Romo, David Dorado. 2005. *Ringside Seat to a Revolution: An Underground Cultural History of El Paso and Juárez: 1893–1923.* El Paso, TX: Cinco Puntos Press.

Rosas, Gilberto. 2012. *Barrio Libre: Criminalizing States and Delinquent Refusals of the New Frontier.* Durham, NC: Duke University Press.

Rosen, Lawrence. 1995. "The Creation of the Uniform Crime Report: The Role of Social Science." *Social Science History* 19(2):215–38.

Ruiz, Mona. 1997. *Two Badges: The Lives of Mona Ruiz.* Houston: Arte Público Press.

Schneider, Beth E., and Denise A. Segura. 2014. "From Affirmative Action to Diversity: Critical Reflections on Graduate Education in Sociology." *Sociology Compass* 8(2):157–71.

Shapiro, Thomas M. 2017. *Toxic Inequality: How America's Wealth Gap Destroys Mobility, Deepens the Racial Divide, and Threatens Our Future.* New York: Basic Books.

Sidanius, Jim, James H. Liu, John S. Shaw, and Felicia Pratto. 1994. "Social Dominance Orientation, Hierarchy Attenuators and Hierarchy Enhancers: Social Dominance Theory and the Criminal Justice System. *Journal of Applied Social Psychology* 24(4):338–66.

Sidanius, Jim, and Felicia Pratto. 1999. *Social Dominance: An Intergroup Theory of Social Hierarchy and Oppression.* New York: Cambridge University Press.

Sklansky, David Alan. 2006. "Not Your Father's Police Department: Making Sense of the New Demographics of Law Enforcement." *The Journal of Criminal Law and Criminology* 96(3):1209–43.

Solis, Carmen, Edwardo L. Portillos, and Rod K. Brunson. 2009. Latino Youths' Experiences with and Perceptions of Involuntary Police Encounters. *The Annals of the American Academy of Political and Social Science* 623(1):39–51.

Sonnichsen, C. L., and M. G. McKinney 1971. "El Paso-from War to Depression." *The Southwestern Historical Quarterly* 74(3):357–71.

Stannard, David E. 1992. *American Holocaust: The Conquest of the New World.* New York: Oxford University Press.

Staudt, Kathleen. 2008. *Violence and Activism at the Border: Gender, Fear, and Everyday Life in Ciudad Juárez.* Austin: University of Texas Press.

Stoudt, Brett G., Madeline Fox, and Michelle Fine. 2012. "Contesting Privilege with Critical Participatory Action Research." *Journal of Social Issues* 68(1):178–93.

Takagi, Paul. 1981. "Race, Crime, and Social Policy: A Minority Perspective." *Crime and Delinquency* 27(1):48–63.

Tapia, Mike. 2017. *The Barrio Gangs of San Antonio, 1915–2015.* Fort Worth, TX: TCU Press.

Tapia, Mike, Corey S. Sparks, and J. Mitchell Miller. 2014. "Texas Latino Prison Gangs: An Exploration of Generational Shift and Rebellion." *The Prison Journal* 94(2):159–79.

Telles, Edward E., and Vilma Ortiz. 2008. *Generations of Exclusion: Mexican Americans, Assimilation, and Race.* New York: Russell Sage Foundation.

Thornberry, Terence P., Marvin D. Krohn, Alan J. Lizotte, Carolyn A. Smith, and Kimberly Tobin. 2003. *Gangs and Delinquency in Developmental Perspective.* New York: Cambridge University Press.

Thrasher, Frederic M. [1927] 1963. *The Gang: A Study of 1,313 gangs in Chicago.* Chicago: University of Chicago.

Tijerina, Reies López. 2000. *They Called Me "King Tiger": My Struggle for the Land and Our Rights*, translated from Spanish and edited by José Angel Gutiérrez.

Timmons, W. H. 1990. *El Paso: A Borderlands History.* El Paso, TX: Texas Western Press.

Torres, Jaime F. 2010. *Pachuco: Out of El Segundo Barrio.* Bloomington, IN: Xlibris.

Tovares, Raúl Damcio. 2002. *Manufacturing the Gang: Mexican American Youth Gangs on Local Television News.* Westport, CT: Greenwood Press.

Urbina, Martin Guevara. 2012. *Hispanics in the U.S. Criminal Justice System: The New American Demography.* Springfield, IL: Charles C. Thomas.

Urbina, Martin Guevara, and Sofía Espinoza Álvarez. 2015. *Latino Police Officers in the United States: An Examination of Emerging Trends and Issues.* Springfield, IL: Charles C. Thomas.

Valdez, Avelardo, Alice Cepeda, and Charles Kaplan. 2009. "Homicidal Events Among Mexican American Street Gangs: A Situational Analysis." *Homicide Studies* 13(3):288–306.

Valdez, Avelardo, and Charles Kaplan. 2007. "Conditions that Increase Drug Market Involvement: The Invitational Edge and the Case of Mexicans in South Texas." *Journal of Drug Issues* 7(4):893–918.

Van Cleve, Nicole Gonzalez. 2016. *Crook County: Racism and Injustice in America's Largest Criminal Court*. Stanford, CA: Stanford University Press.

Vélez, María B. 2006. "Toward an Understanding of the Lower Rates of Homicide in Latino versus Black Neighborhoods," pp. 91–107, in *The Many Colors Crime: Inequalities of Race, Ethnicity, and Crime in America*, edited by R. D. Peterson, L. Krivo, and J. Hagan. New York: New York University Press.

Vera Sanchez, Claudio G., and Dennis P. Rosenbaum. 2012. "Racialized Policing: Officers' Voices on Policing Latino and African American Neighborhoods," pp. 23–40, in *Voices from Criminal Justice: Thinking and Reflecting on the System*, edited by H. Copes and M. R. Pogrebin. New York: Routledge.

Vidrine, Jennifer Irvin, Cheryl B., Anderson, Kathryn I. Poliak, and David W. Wetter. 2005. "Race/Ethnicity, Smoking Status, and Self-Generated Expected Outcomes from Smoking among Adolescents." *Cancer Control* 12(4 Suppl): 51–57.

Vigil, Ernesto B. 1999. *The Crusade for Justice: Chicano Militancy and the Government's War on Dissent*. Madison: University of Wisconsin Press.

Vigil, James Diego. 1988. *Barrio Gangs: Street Life and Identity in Southern California*. Austin: University of Texas Press.

———. 2002. *A Rainbow of Gangs: Street Cultures in the Mega-City*. Austin: University of Texas Press.

———. 2007. *The Projects: Gang and Non-Gang Families in East Los Angeles*. Austin: University of Texas Press.

Wagley, Charles, and Marvin Harris. 1958. *Minorities in the New World: Six Case Studies*. New York: Columbia University Press.

Ward, Geoff K. 2012. *The Black Child-Savers: Racial Democracy and Juvenile Justice*. Chicago: University of Chicago Press.

Wasserman, Mark. 1993. *Persistent Oligarchs: Elites and Politics in Chihuahua, Mexico 1910–1940*. Durham, NC: Duke University Press.

Weitzer, Ronald. 2014. The Puzzling Neglect of Hispanic Americans in Research on Police-Citizen Relations. *Ethnic and Racial Studies* 37(11):1995–2013.

White, Richard. 1991. *It's Your Misfortune and None of My Own: A New History of the American West*. Norman: University of Oklahoma Press.

Willging, Cathleen E., Gilbert A. Quintero, and Elizabeth A. Lilliott. 2014. "Hitting the Wall: Youth Perspectives on Boredom, Trouble, and Drug Use Dynamics in Rural New Mexico." *Youth and Society* 46(1):3–29.

Wilson, William J. 1996. *When Work Disappears: The World of the New Urban Poor*. New York: Vintage.

Winfree, L. Thomas, Jr., and Frances P. Bernat. 1998. "Social Learning, Self-Control, and Substance Abuse by Eighth Grade Students: A Tale of Two Cities." *Journal of Drug Issues* 28(2):539–558.

Winfree, L. Thomas, Jr., Frances P. Bernat, and Finn-Aage Esbensen. 2001. "Hispanic and Anglo Gang Membership in Two Southwestern Cities." *Social Science Journal* 38(1):105–117.

Winfree, L. Thomas, Jr., Kathy Fuller, Teresa Vigil, and G. Larry Mays. 1992. "The Definition and Measurement of 'Gang Status': Policy Implications for Juvenile Justice." *Juvenile and Family Court Journal* 43(1):29–38.

Wright, Earl. 2002. "The Atlanta Sociological Laboratory 1896–1924: A Historical Account for the First American School of Sociology." *The Western Journal of Black Studies* 26(3):165–74.

Wright. Earl, and Thomas C. Calhoun. 2006. "Jim Crow Sociology: Toward an Understanding of the Origin and Principles of Black Sociology via the Atlanta Sociological Laboratory." *Sociological Focus* 39(1):1–18.

Zinn, Elizabeth. 1959. "He Begged that Gang Violence End with His Death." *Federal Probation* 23(3):24–30.

Other Sources

Master's Theses

Arevalo Becerril, Jaime. 2000. "Self-Constitution and Gang Affiliation: The Preferred Realities of Three Latinos in the Southwest." New Mexico State University.

Delgado, Sonya Lynn. 2001. "Our Middle-School Youth in Trouble with Gangs?" New Mexico State University.

Jackson, Stacey Lynn. 1993. "Media Influence on Public Perceptions of Crime: A Look at Youth Gangs in a Southwestern Community." New Mexico State University.

Jurado, Pete. 1976. "The Chicano Aggregation: A Barrio Gang." University of Texas at El Paso.

Moorhead-Nord, Tamera. 1994. "An Evaluation of the Gang Resistance Education (GREAT) Program. A Model for Success?" New Mexico State University.

Sandoval-Monnét, Danette M. 1996. "Understanding Youth Gangs and Youthful Behavior: A Preliminary Test of Social Learning Theory with the Perspective of Multiple Marginality." New Mexico State University.

Vigil-Bäckström, Teresa A. 1992. "Youth Gangs in New Mexico: A Social Learning Perspective." New Mexico State University.

Dissertations

Dowling, Winifred B. 2010. "The Border at War: World War II Along the United States–Mexico Border." University of Texas at El Paso. UMI No. 3433544.

Langston, Edward Lonnie. 1974. "The Impact of Prohibition on the Mexican–United States Border: The El Paso–Ciudad Juarez Case." Texas Tech University.

Licón, Gerardo. 2009. "Pachucas, Pachucos, and Their Culture: Mexican American Youth Culture of the Southwest, 1910–1955." University of Southern California. UMI No. 3389512.
Robinson, Robin E. 2002. "Vice and Tourism on the U.S.-Mexico Border: A Comparison of Three Communities in the Era of U.S. Prohibition." Arizona State University. UMI No. 3054654.

Oral Histories

Interview no. 135. University of Texas at El Paso Institute of Oral History, June 25, 1974.
Interview no. 195, p. 29. University of Texas at El Paso Institute of Oral History, July 3, 1975.
Interview no. 211. University of Texas at El Paso Institute of Oral History, August 28, 1975.
Interview no. 610. University of Texas at El Paso Institute of Oral History, May 24, 1979.
Interview no. 846. University of Texas at El Paso Institute of Oral History, March 21, 1994.

Reports

"Analyzing the Delinquent Situation." Obtained from El Paso Public Library. Border Heritage Section. File on Gangs.
Annie E. Casey Foundation. 2013. "The 2013 Kids Count Data Book: State Trends in Child Well-Being." http://datacenter.kidscount.org/publications/databook/2013
———. 2014. "The 2014 Kids Count Data Book: State Trends in Child Well-Being." http://www.aecf.org/resources/the-2014-kids-count-data-book
Camp, George M., and Camille G. Camp. 1985. "Prison Gangs: Their Extent, Nature, and Impact on Prisons." Washington, DC: U.S. Department of Justice.
Carmichael, Dottie, Guy Whitten, and Michael Voloudakis. 2005. "Study of Minority Over-Representation in the Texas Juvenile Justice System." Final Report. Submitted to the Office of the Governor Criminal Justice Division. Public Policy Research Institute. Texas A&M University.
Cisneros, John, Salvador Ramirez, and Jesus Granado. 1971. "*South El Paso: El Segundo Barrio* by Los Atrevidos." Boulder: University of Colorado.
City of Las Cruces. City Council. Gang Task Force. Work Session. February 10, 1992.
Department of Public Safety, Special Investigations Division, Criminal Information Analysis Bureau. 1993. "Street Gang Update."
"Disproportionate Minority Contact Technical Assistant Manual." 2006. 3rd ed. Washington, DC: U.S. Department of Justice.

Durán, Robert J. 2013. "Tenure Track Faculty and Race/Ethnicity at New Mexico State University." Hispanic Faculty and Staff Caucus. New Mexico State University.
El Paso County Sheriff's Office. 2015. Annual Report.
El Paso Police Department 2015. "Dedicated to Serve." Annual Report.
Franco, Charles. 1992. "Gang Activity Update." Las Cruces: New Mexico Police Department.
Governor's Organized Crime Prevention Commission. 1991. "New Mexico Street Gangs."
Lobato, Dennis, and Genno Tafoya. 1993. "Las Cruces Police Department Gang Assessment." Las Cruces: New Mexico Police Department.
Las Cruces Task Force on Gangs and the Las Cruces Interagency Team. November 1992. Draft.
———. February 1993. Final Report.
Mata, Jonás O., Robert J. Durán, and Carlos E. Posadas. 2008. "Juvenile Justice Project Las Cruces, New Mexico: Disproportionate Minority Contact Assessment Study." Third Judicial District, City of Las Cruces, New Mexico.
Menon, Ramdas, and Jeffrey A. Jordan. 1997. "Juvenile Justice in Texas: Factors Correlated with Processing Decisions." Public Policy Research Institute. Texas A&M University.
National Center for Juvenile Justice. 2010. "RRI Calculations." Office of Juvenile Justice and Delinquency Prevention. Office of Justice Programs. http://ojjdp.ncjrs.gov/ojstatbb/dmcdb/asp/whatis.asp
National Council on Crime and Delinquency. 2007. "And Justice for Some: Differential Treatment of Youth of Color in the Justice System." Oakland, CA: Author.
National Drug Threat Assessment. 2011.
National Gang Center. "National Youth Gang Survey Analysis." http://www.nationalgangcenter.gov/Survey-Analysis/Demographics#anchorregm
National Gang Intelligence Center. 2011. "National Gang Threat Assessment: Emerging Trends."
New Mexico Department of Health. 2008. "Racial and Ethnic Health Disparities Report Card."
New Mexico Department of Health. 2013. "The State of Health in New Mexico."
New Mexico Department of Public Safety. 1994. New Mexico Street Gangs: Update.
New Mexico Public Education Department. 2009–2010. "2010SY 40D Enrollment by District." http://www.ped.state.nm.us/IT/fs/05/09.10.enroll.dist.pdf
New Mexico Voices for Children. 2012. "Kids Count in New Mexico."
Operation Community Shield Fact Sheet. 2008." Targeting Violent Transnational Street Gangs." Washington, DC: U.S. Immigration and Customs Enforcement.
Payne, Yasser Arafat. 2013. "The People's Report: The Link Between Structural Violence and Crime in Wilmington, Delaware." Newark: University of Delaware. http://www.thepeoplesreport.com/images/pdf/The_Peoples_Report_final_draft_9-12-13.pdf

Rahm, Father Harold J., and J. Robert Weber. 1958. "Office in the Alley: Report on a Project with Gang Youngsters." Bert Kruger Smith, Editor. Hogg Foundation for Mental Health.

Sapp, Lesley. 2011. "Apprehensions by the U.S. Border Patrol, 2005–2010." Fact Sheet. Washington, DC: Office of Immigration Statistics.

Texas Office of the Attorney General. "The 1992 Texas Attorney General's Gang Report." Dan Morales, Texas Attorney General. Jeanie R. Stanley, Director. Elizabeth T. Buhmann, Research Specialist.

Tita, G., and A. Abrahamse. 2004. "Gang Homicide in L.A., 1981–2001." *At the Local Level: Perspectives on Violence Prevention* 3:1–20. Sacramento: California State Attorney General's Office.

U.S. Chamber of Commerce. 2012. "Breaking the Monopoly of Mediocrity: Just the Facts." El Paso, TX: U.S. Chamber Foundation.

U.S. Congress. 2012. "On the Border and In the Line of Fire: U.S. Law Enforcement, Homeland Security, and Drug Cartel Violence." Subcommittee on Oversight, Investigations, and Management of the Committee on Homeland Security House of Representatives. Washington, DC: U.S. Government Printing Office.

U.S. Department of Education. 2012. "Provisional Data File: SY2010–11 Four-Year Regulatory Adjusted Cohort Graduation Rates."

U.S. Department of Education, National Center for Education Statistics. 2012. "The Condition of Education 2012." https://nces.ed.gov/fastfacts/display.asp?id=72

U.S. Government Accountability Office. 2013. "Southwest Border Security: Data Are Limited and Concerns Vary About Spillover Crime Along the Southwest Border."

U.S. Immigration and Customs Enforcement. 2016. "ICE Enforcement and Removal Operations."

U.S.-Mexico Border Health Commission. 2010. "Health Disparities and the U.S.-Mexico Border: Challenges and Opportunities."

Court Cases

Chambers v. State 508 S.W. 2nd 348. Tex Crim App. 1974.
City of Chicago v. Morales, 527 U.S. 41 (1999).
Hernandez v. Mesa, 582 U.S. (2017).

Newspapers and Media

Albuquerque Journal

October 7, 2009. Rene Romo. "Ex-Border Agent Admits Aiding Drug Trafficking"
August 13, 2013. "N.M. High Court Upholds Conviction in Rest-Stop Murder."

Boston Globe

August 4, 1979. Robert Levey. "The Lure of Drugs in El Paso."

Chicago Tribune

April 16, 1982. "5 Charged in Federal Judge's Murder."
September 7, 1988. Robert Blau. "Tunnels Carry Mexican Bandits Into Border City."

CNN

December 15, 2010. Nick Valencia. "Juarez Counts 3,000th Homicide of 2010."

El Paso Herald

March 8–9, 1919. "Oh Skinnay! The Gangs All Up in Court!"
June 6, 1929. "El Paso's History Unstained by Lynching Officer Recalls."
October 24, 1931. "Detective Chief Claims Hectic Days of 1916 Were Worst in City's History."

El Paso Herald-Post

June 17, 1933. "Early Day Officer Killed Man Who Broke Pipe."
May 27, 1936. "South El Paso Gang Scored."
March 12, 1940. "12 Arrested in Gang Cleanup."
July 21, 1941. "Deputy Sheriffs Round up Gangs in South El Paso."
April 20, 1942. "Police Continue to Rid Streets of Roaming Thugs."
August 14, 1942. "City Detectives War on Gangs; 13 Arrested."
June 22, 1950. "Grand Jury Probes 'Rat Packs.'
June 23, 1950. "Grand Jury Investigates Reported Juvenile Gangs."
June 24, 1950. "Gang Throws Rock Through Window of Grocery Store."
June 24, 1950. "Probation Chief Urges Conference on 'Rat Packs.' "
June 26, 1950. " 'Rat Pack' Beats Up Small Fry Initiate."
June 27, 1950. "Police, Judge, Warns Parents to Curb Delinquents."
February 4, 1954. "Officer Move to 'Wrap Up' Gang Inquiry."
September 16, 1957. "Mayor Warns Teenage Gangs."
September 16, 1957. "Parents Face Grand Jury Gang Inquiry."
November 12, 1957. "Gang Breaks Vow, Beats, Kicks Man."
September 17, 1958. "Youth Gang Wars Claim Second Life in 16 Days."
September 19, 1958. "Youth Gangs Scorn 'Soft' Police Policy."
February 16, 1960. "Gang Beats, Stabs Youth to Death."

August 1, 1974. Jane Pemberton. "Does E.P. Have 'Organized' Crime?"
May 19, 1976. "EPPD to Launch Youth Division Monday with Many-Faceted Purposes."
July 16, 1976. "E.P. Law Enforcement Evolves From 'Watch' to Complicated Unit."
August 26, 1976. " 'Police not the Answer,' Residents Say."
October 30, 1976. "Bandidos Lose Appeal."
November 11, 1976. Bill Thompson. "Bandido Funeral: Chico Goes Out in Style."
March 9, 1977. Frank Ahlegren. "Two Arrested in Youth's Murder."
April 2, 1977. Jane Pemberton. "Dares Make Statistics Out of Youths."
December 16, 1977. Al Duitman. "Bandidos Linked to 3 Murders."
February 12, 1979. Peter Brock. "Officers link Bandidos raid, attack on Kerr."
February 13, 1979. Peter Brock. "Bandido Leader Indicted."
February 22, 1979. Peter Brock. "2 More Hooded Witnesses Testify."
February 27, 1979. "Renteria Gets 30-Year Term."
May 23, 1979. Bill Kidel. "Jury Convicts Local Bandido Leader."
October 10, 1979. Peter Brock. "Bandidos Blamed for Trio of Unsolved Murders."
December 18, 1981. Frank Ahlgren. "T-Birds Complain of Harassment."
January 8, 1992. Leon Lynn. "Cops on the Campuses: Police Making Their Presence Known at Middle Schools."
November 28, 1992. Raul Hernandez. "Police Call 8-Year-Olds Gangsters: List of 5,000 Lumps Musicians, Inmates."
March 2, 1996. Juan A. Lozano. "Kids and Gangs."
November 10, 1999. Christina Ramirez. "Supervisor Says Teen Shot by Police."

El Paso Times

November 30, 1925. "History of Police Force Full of Romance."
June 25, 1933. Raymond J. Stover. "Early El Paso Peace Officers Were Quick on the Draw, Veteran Member of Department Recalls."
June 24, 1950. "10 Boys in Zavala Gang Rifles, 'Zip' Guns Seized."
October 20, 1956. Bill Montgomery. "Juvenile Authorities Say 50 Teen-Age Gangs Active."
June 3, 1959. Jim McVicar. "EP Juvenile Gang Wars Exist But Underground."
December 3, 1962. Bill Birge. "Charms Fought Their Way Up."
April 6, 1972. "Armijo Center Charged as 'Shooting' Gallery."
April 12, 1972. "Thunderbird Club Members Meet with Mayor Williams."
April 24, 1972. Bert Salazar. "Area Respects Unwritten 'Law.' "
April 26, 1972. Bert Salazar. "Can Hindsight Help Now."
June 21, 1973. Charles Kreher. "DA Says Organized Crime Active in EP."
January 29, 1976. "Beefed-up EP Juvenile Squad Not Just Additional Manpower."
August 19, 1976. "Baby Faced 'El Raton' Terrorizing Elderly in South El Paso." By Ramon Villalobos.

September 19, 1976. Bill Moore and Ramon Renteria. "Gang Wars in El Paso? Views Vary."
September 20, 1976. Bill Moore. "20 Years Ago Southside was a Battleground."
September 21, 1976. Ramon Renteria. "Mourning for Son Began Before He Died."
October 23, 1976. "Youth Charged with Murder in South EP Slaying."
November 4, 1976. Ed Curda. "Gang Strife, EP Housing Violence Bring Planning for Security Force."
November 7, 1976. Bill Moore. "EP Social Agencies Face Gang Problems with Cluster Effect."
October 30, 1977. "Gang Brotherhood Lacks Toys."
May 19, 1978. Ron Dusek and Ed Kimble. "Feds Allege EP Singer in Conspiracy."
August 6, 1978. Ron Dusek. "DEA Thinks Major Blow Dealt Smuggling Ring."
January 26, 1979. Ed Curda. "FBI Joins List of Chagra Probers."
March 2, 1979. Ron Dusek. "El Paso Businessmen in Crime—Big Time—FBI Chief Says."
August 19, 1979. Barbara Funkhouser. "KKK Had El Paso Day."
October 14, 1979. Karen Gorham. "Wallace Guilty in Lee Chagra Murder."
October 15, 1979. Karen Gorham. "Wallace Gets Death for Chagra Murder."
February 16, 1981. "Gang Warfare Erupted in El Paso 50s Scene."
February 16, 1981. "Waning Attention Doesn't Curb Gangs."
January 16, 1989. Julian Resendiz. "Gang Violence Top Concern."
January 8, 1992. Leon Lynn. "Cops on the Campuses: Police Making Their Presence Known at Middle Schools."
April 24, 1992. "Gangs Claim Turf in Every Part of Town."
April 24, 1992. Sito Negron. "California Connection Can Be Tough to Pin Down."
April 12, 1996. "Reno on Right Track to Control Gangs in Prisons, on Streets."
August 25, 1996. Betsy McArthur. "El Paso Shows Slight Increase in Gang Activity."
September 29, 1997. Raul Hernandez. "Mexican Mafia Murder Trial Begins."
January 11, 1999. Laura Smitherman. "Legal Errors, Bickering Hamper Trial, Lawyers Say."
January 16, 1999. "Jury Acquits Man Charged in Death."
March 26, 1999. Laura Smitherman. "Jury Ponders Fate of Man Accused of Hanging Inmate."
March 27, 1999. Laura Smitherman. "Inmate Trial Ends in Hung Jury."
May 10, 1999. Laura Smitherman. "2 Convicted Teens Violate Their Probation."
June 3, 1999. Christina Ramírez. "Officers Fired Over Killing."
June 5, 1999. Laura Smitherman. "Inmate Found Guilty in County Jail Murder."
June 13, 1999. Christina Ramírez. "Police, Mother Debate Facts of Teen's Death."
July 28, 1999. Diana Washington Valdez. "Kidnapping Suspects Arrested in Mexico."
September 19, 1999. Christina Ramírez. "Crackdown Produces 20 Gang Arrests."

October 9, 1999. Sharon Simonson. "Armed Students Interrupt Las Cruces Class."
October 10, 1999. Diana Washington Valdez. "Homicide Suspects in Juarez are Getting Younger."
October 19, 1999. "Man Gets 30 Years in Killing."
October 28, 1999. Laura Smitherman. "Scientist Contends Evidence Doesn't Match Fired Officers' Story."
October 30, 1999. Christina Ramirez. "Leon: Firings Reflected New Philosophy."
November 2, 1999. "Gang-beating Case."
November 10, 1999. Christina Ramírez. "Supervisor Says Teen Shot by Police Was Gang Member."
December 12, 1999. Opinion. "Dismantle the Cartel.
December 14, 1999. "Gangs Queried in Gadsden Threat Case."
December 15, 1999. Ken Flynn. "El Paso Could Get $200,000 in Federal Crime-fighting Cash."
May 5, 2000. Christina Pino-Marina. "Fired Police Officers Are Back in Uniform."
July 21, 2000. Guadalupe Silva. "Happy Anniversary, Father Rahm."
January 21, 2001. "Man Gets Life Term in County Jail Killing."
January 28, 2001. Jennifer Shubinski. "Killing Won't Alter Plans to Disband Gang Unit."
November 16, 2001. Louie Gilot. "62 Charged in Alleged Prison Gang."
March 24, 2002. Donna Lynn Dennis. "In the News."
September 18, 2002. Diana Washington Valdez. "Officials Link 2 Charged in FBI Beating with Gang."
September 20, 2002. Jennifer Shubinski and Daniel Borunda. "13 Indicted in FBI Beatings, Train Theft."
April 15, 2003. Tammy Fonce-Olivas. "Limits Set on South Side Gang to Make Neighborhood Safer."
May 3, 2003. Daniel Borunda. "2 Arrested for Alleged Defiance of Court Order."
May 12, 2003. Daniel Borunda. "Police Unit Expands to Downtown."
May 15, 2003. Daniel Borunda. "Police Wield New Tool Against Gangs."
July 11, 2003. Louie Gilot. "FBI Agent Describes Gang Attack in Anapra."
November 9, 2003. Diana Washington Valdez. "City's FBI Chief Out."
November 23, 2003. Daniel Borunda. "El Paso Units Combine in Tactical Teams."
January 5, 2004. Daniel Borunda. "Anapra Gang Linked to Thefts."
January 28, 2004. Louie Gilot. "11 Bodies Found."
May 9, 2004. Louie Gilot. "Gang Fight Responsible for Deadly Prison Riot."
August 17, 2004. Louie Gilot. "Cartel Killings Sweep Juárez."
August 2, 2005. Daniel Borunda. "582 Arrested in Gang Roundup, Including Three in El Paso Area."
September 5, 2005. Opinion. "Our Views: El Paso Shows Way."
March 12, 2006. Adriana M. Chávez. "Eight Cereso Prison Inmates Killed in Riot."
March 26, 2006. Reveles Acosta, Gustavo, and Tammy Fonce-Olivas. "Gangs in Schools—West Side High Schools Have Most Gang Activity."

March 29, 2006. Daniel Borunda. "EP to Get Anti-Gang Prosecutor."
April 25, 2006. Ramón Renteria. "El Paso was Integrated City Before Most of U.S."
December 22, 2006. Daniel Borunda. "Drug Sales Dispute Led to Slaying, Report Says."
December 3, 2008. Daniel Borunda and Erica Molina-Johnson. "6 in Barrio Azteca Guilty."
May 10, 2011. Ramón Rentería. "Back to His Roots: Performer Joe Renteria Boosts Boys and Girls Club."
January 12, 2017. Daniel Borunda. "Man Gets Prison in Fatal Horizon Cartel Kidnap."
July 20, 2017. Daniel Borunda. "Barrio Azteca Gets 3 Life Terms in Consulate Case."

Frontier Klansman

August 10, 1923. Vol 1. No. 45.

Harper's Monthly Magazine

July 1925. Katherine Fullerton Gerould.

Hartford Courant

December 26, 1972. "2 Bodies Found; Police Arrest 12 in Cycle Gang."

KVIA

May 16, 2012. Angela Kucherga. "Cartels Use Students to Smuggle Drugs Through Busy Border Crossing."
January 4, 2018. Stephanie Guadian. "Expert: 'El Chapo' Vacuum Tied to Rising Juarez Violence."

Las Cruces Sun-News

February 29, 2004.
March 6, 2004. Gabriela C Guzman. "Two Arrested in Teen's Death."
October 2, 2004. T. S. Hopkins. "Seminar Explores Gang Problem."
October 28, 2004. T. S. Hopkins. "Stats Show Drop in Violent Crime Last Year."
December 8, 2004. "Taking Aim at Gangs."
December 10, 2005. Steve Ramirez. "City, County to Get $475,000 for Gang Prevention."

January 15, 2006. Walter Rubel. "Money Issues to Dominate This Year's Legislative Meet."
January 29, 2009. Kevin Buey. "Deming Border Agent Arrested."
March 14, 2009. Michael Hays. Opinion. "A Tale of Two Cities."
August 25, 2011. Ashley Meeks. "Vega Pleads Guilty on Gun Ring Charges."
June 14, 2012. Brian Fraga. "Former Columbus Mayor Sentenced in Gun-Smuggling Case."
September 26, 2017. Diana Alba Soular. "Doña Ana County to Accept Federal Border-Security Funds through Operation Stonegarden."
January 23, 2018. "Lordsburg Border Agents Seize $1.6M in Marijuana."

Los Angeles Times

March 7, 1977. Leonard Greenwood. "A New, Ruthless Breed: Mexican Gangs Pouring Narcotics Across Border."

New York Times

June 17, 1979. John M. Crewdson. "El Paso Is Called a Major New Hub of Drug Traffic."
March 11, 2006. Robert J. Sampson. "Open Doors Don't Invite Criminals: Is Increased Immigration Behind the Drop in Crime?" p. A27 (OP-ED).

Prospector

April 13, 1972. Chuck Emerson. "Gang Warfare?"

Reason Magazine

July 6, 2009. Radley Balko. "The El Paso Miracle."

Texas Monthly

April 2007. Skip Hollandsworth. "The Gang's All Here."

Texas Tribune

July 21, 2016. Julián Aguilar. "U.S. Citizen Receives Settlement over Body Cavity Search at Border."

Univision

June 26, 2017. Damiá Bonmatí. "Supreme Court Sends Case of Sergio Adrian Hernández, shot on Mexican Territory by U.S. Border Agent, Back to Lower Court."

USA Today Network

November 22, 2017. Adam Tamburin. "Gangs and Cartels are Teaming Up to Bring Drugs into Rural Tennessee, TBI Director Says."
December 30, 2017. Travis Dorman. "Homicide Tracker: A list of 37 Killings in Knoxville, Knox County in 2017."

Washington Post

January 22, 1979. Lou Cannon. "Lawyer Slain: Flamboyant Figure's Death Shocks Border Underworld."
September 20, 2013. Lyndsey Layton. "Children Cross Mexican Border to Receive U.S. Education."

Index

Abadinksy, Howard, 50
Abrahamse, Allan, 194
African Americans: culture of, 6, 204–5; in double colonization, 34–35; Latin Americans compared to, 10–11; law enforcement for, 102–3; slavery and, 36–37. *See also* minority groups
America. *See* United States
American Me (film), 90
American Smelting and Refining Company (ASARCO), 30–31
anecdotes. *See* narratives
Anthony (New Mexico): culture of, 187, 189; juvenile gangs in, 206–7, 230; narratives from, 1–3, 145–47, 173–78, 198–201; policy in, 139–41
Anthony (Texas). *See* Texas
Arizona: gangs in, 192; poverty in, 109; research from, 81–82
Armijo, Marcos B., 64
ASARCO. *See* American Smelting and Refining Company
Atkinson, Paul, 7

Barker, David, 44, 52
Barrios, Luis, 158
Becerril, Arevalo, 82
Bell, Derrick, 12–13
BIP. *See* Border Industrialization Program

Blalock, Hubert M., 13, 224
Bogardus, Emory, 51–52
Bond-Maupin, Lisa, 107
Border Industrialization Program (BIP), 92–93
border patrol. *See* immigration
Boyle, Greg, 205–6, 214
Bracknell, Richard, 90–91
Brotherton, David, 8–9, 158
Buchanan, Patrick, 225

California: culture of, 150; gangs in, 77–78, 175–76; immigration for, 72; Mexico and, 90; organized crime in, 145–46; Zoot Suit Riots in, 54
Campbell, Howard, 88
Cárdenas, Lázaro, 51
Carrigan, William, 48
Carrillo, Mary Lou, 75
Castillo, Richard Morales, 90–91
Chacón, Jennifer M., 92
Chagra, Lee, 87–88
Chambers, Donald, 87–89
Chaparral (New Mexico). *See* rural New Mexico
El Chapo, 185–87
Chicanos. *See* Mexican-Americans
Children, Youth, Families Department (CYFD), 136
Chomsky, Noam, 12
El Chuco. *See* El Paso (Texas)

Ciudad Juárez (Mexico), 17; communities in, 203; culture of, 135–36; *Drug War Zone: Frontline Dispatches from the Streets of El Paso and Juárez* (Campbell), 88; economics in, 45–46; El Paso (Texas) and, 34–36, 40–41, 153–54; for gangs, 109; narratives from, 184–87; organized crime in, 173, 180; PAR teams in, 184–87; research from, 92–93; U.S. and, 48–51; violence in, 163–64, 194–96, 196, 226
Civil Rights Movement, 63–64
clubs, 86–94
Cole, David, 92
colonialism, 13–14, 19, 25, 26, 27. *See also* double colonization
Columbus, Christopher, 25
communities: in Ciudad Juárez (Mexico), 203; economics and, 108–9; empirical miracles for, 214; family issues for, 200–201, 207–8; gangs and, 145–51; graffiti for, 181–82; history and, 9–10; JPPOs for, 148–49; for Latin Americans, 14–15, 225–26; media and, 227; narratives from, 152, 154–55; in New Mexico, 23–24, 52–53, 95, 205–6; policy for, 17, 169–70, 206–7, 214; poverty for, 210–11; practitioners for, 214–15; referrals for, 144–45; religion for, 16, 68; in rural New Mexico, 109–10; in Sunland Park, 140; in Texas, 109–10; violence for, 10, 60–62, 160, 182–83, 227–28
Complicated Lives (Lopez), 118
Cordero, Gaspar, 43
Corrales, Arturo, 64, 67
Cortés, Hernán, 25
crime. *See* gangs; organized crime; research; violence
critical race theory: colonialism in, 25, 26, 27; identity in, 12–15, 37; research and, 18; revisionist history in, 21, 38–39
Crook County (Van Cleve), 133–34
culture: of African Americans, 6, 204–5; of Anthony (New Mexico), 187, 189; of California, 150; of Ciudad Juárez (Mexico), 135–36; *Divergent Social Worlds* (Peterson/Krivo), 10–11; of El Paso (Texas), 34–36, 38–39, 41–44, 125–226, 132–33; family issues and, 212–13; of gangs, 51–55, 167–68; of Latin Americans, 57–58, 135–37; of law enforcement, 137–42; of Mexican-Americans, 225–26; of Mexico, 146; of minority groups, 44–45, 74, 220–21, 223–24; of Native Americans, 24–25, 26, 27; of New Mexico, 29–30, 117–25, 139–42, 144–45, 152–53, 192–93; of pachuquismo, 17, 41–48; of politics, 215–16; of poverty, 107–10, 116, 142–44, 178, 199, 216; of prison, 168; of religion, 35; research and, 9–12; Vigil on, 226–27
Cummings, Laura L., 44
CYFD. *See* Children, Youth, Families Department

Death of White Sociology, The (Ladner), 204–5
Delgado, Abelardo, 12–13, 63–64
Delgado, Richard, 13, 21
Department of Education, U.S., 110–11
Department of Justice, U.S., 166
detention. *See* prison
Dickerson, Roy, 41–43
discrimination: law enforcement and, 72–73; as policy, 63
Disproportionate Minority Contact (DMC), 218–19; gangs and, 125–28; history of, 97–101; immigration for, 132; for juvenile

gangs, 117–21; research from, 155–56; in schools, 110–16
Divergent Social Worlds (Peterson/Krivo), 10–11
Dobbs, O. Leon, 86
domestic family issues, 142–51
Doña Ana (New Mexico). *See* rural New Mexico
double colonization: African Americans in, 34–35; El Paso (Texas) in, 30–32, *31*; Mexico in, 27, *28*, 33–39; narratives from, 23–24; for Native Americans, 24–25, *26*, *27*; in New Mexico, 32–33; prohibition and, 33–39; Spain in, 24–25, *26*, *27*; U.S. in, 29–30
drugs. *See* organized crime
Drug War Zone: Frontline Dispatches from the Streets of El Paso and Juárez (Campbell), 88
Drummond, Ronald Paul (Frankenstein), 89
Du Bois, W. E. B., 7–9, 204

economics: in Ciudad Juárez (Mexico), 45–46; communities and, 108–9; of gangs, 48–51, 67–68; of law enforcement, 86–88, 91, 207; of organized crime, 52–55; politics and, 77–78; of rural New Mexico, 178–79, 210–11; of U.S., 50–51
education. *See* schools
El Paso (Texas), 191–93; Ciudad Juárez (Mexico) and, 34–36, 40–41, 153–54; culture of, 34–36, 38–39, 41–44, 125–226, 132–33; in double colonization, 30–32, *31*; *Drug War Zone: Frontline Dispatches from the Streets of El Paso and Juárez* (Campbell), 88; gangs in, 17, 55–58, 59, 60–64, 65, 66–68; immigration for, 196–97; KKK and, 44–48, 68; for Latin Americans, *106*, 107–9; *Miracles in El Paso?* (Laurentin), 15–16; narratives from, 40–41, 160–66; New Mexico compared to, 93–94; organized crime and, 48–51, 85; PAR teams in, 160–66; poverty in, 51–55; in research, 70–76; violence in, 89–92, 194–95, *195*
empirical miracles, 188–90, 215–16; for communities, 214; in labor, 197–203; for policy, 203–5; for practitioners, 209–13; in rural New Mexico, 191–93; in schools, 197–203; in violence, 193–97, *195*–96
enhanced border enforcement zone, *131*
ethnographic analysis: *The Handbook of Ethnography* (Atkinson), 7; for policy, 221; for research, 6–7; in research, 95, 101, 102–4, 104–5; theory of, 7–9

familial drug networks, 86–88
family issues: for communities, 200–201, 207–8; culture and, 212–13; CYFD for, 136; domestic family issues, 142–51; gangs and, 169; for law enforcement, 142–45; from organized crime, 135–37
Federal Racketeer Influenced and Corrupt Organizations Act (RICO), 91
Fernández, Enrique, 49, 51
Fine, Michelle, 158
Fleisher, Mark, 203–4
Forgotten Dead (Carrigan/Webb, C.), 48
Franco, Juan, 32

Gallardo, Rob, 162
Gang Cop (Klein), 150
gangs: in Arizona, 192; in California, 77–78, 175–76; Ciudad Juárez (Mexico) for, 109; communities and, 145–51; culture of, 51–55, 167–68; DMC and,

gangs (continued)
  125–28; economics of, 48–51, 67–68; in El Paso (Texas), 17, 55–58, 59, 60–64, 65, 66–68; familial drug networks and, 86–88; family issues and, 169; graffiti for, 164–66, 171–74, 198–99; Hispanics and, 160–63, 183–84; identity for, 17–18, 80–81; for law enforcement, 145–51; in media, 8–9, 70–73, 187; for Mexican-Americans, 11, 41; from Mexico, 150–51; military and, 162–63; minority groups and, 84–85, 224–26; motorcycle clubs and, 89–94; narratives about, 1–3; narratives on, 217–20; NGIC on, 191; *Policing Gangs in America* (Katz/Webb, V.), 78, 150; politics of, 188–90; prison for, 165; prison gangs, 90–94; religion for, 62–63; students and, 175–77; tagging for, 177–78, 181–82; terminology for, 83–85, 84, 165–66, 193; in Texas, 139–41, 145–47; theory of, 2–3; in U.S., 172–73; violence and, 79–80, 160–61, 179. *See also* double colonization; juvenile gangs; minority groups; organized crime; research; social groups
Garcia, Bill, 87–88
García, Mario T., 30, 43, 53, 60
Generations of Exclusion (Telles, E./Ortiz), 11
Gerould, Katherine Fullerton, 47
Gómez, Laura, 14, 25, 27, 224
González, Ignacia Jasso (La Nacha), 49–50
Gordon, Linda, 34–35
graffiti: for communities, 181–82; for gangs, 164–66, 171–74, 198–99; tagging as, 177–78, 181–82
Guerrero, Lalo, 52
Gutiérrez, Ramón, 24–25, 27
Guzmán, Joaquín (El Chapo), 185–87

Hagedorn, John, 158
Hall, Thomas, 25, 27
Hamilton, Charles V., 204–5
The Handbook of Ethnography (Atkinson), 7
Haney-López, Ian, 13–14
Harrelson, Charles V., 88
Harris, Marvin, 24
Harrison Narcotics Act (1914), 35
Herman, Edward, 12
Hernández, Kelly, 14, 46–47
Hernandez, Raul, 72–73
Hernández Güereca, Sergio Adrián, 153
Heyman, Josiah, 133
HIDTA program. *See* High Intensity Drug Trafficking Areas Program
higher education, 197–203
High Intensity Drug Trafficking Areas (HIDTA) Program, 138–42
Hispanics: gangs and, 160–63, 183–84; in media, 170–71; in New Mexico, 170–71, 174–76. *See also* Latin Americans; minority groups
historical trade route map, 31
history: communities and, 9–10; of DMC, 97–101; of immigration, 5–7, 16, 36–37, 63, 129–34; of juvenile gangs, 55–58, 59, 60–62; of labor, 51–52; of Mexican-Americans, 32–39; of minority groups, 34–35; of organized crime, 37–38; of pachuquismo, 51–55, 67–68; of trade routes, 30–32, 31; of U.S., 216; of violence, 43–48. *See also* revisionist history
Holtby, David, 33
Homeroom Security (Kupchik), 110
homicide. *See* violence
Horizon City (Texas), 179–80
Horne, Gerald, 34–35
Human Targets (Rios), 208–9
Huntington, Samuel P., 225

ICE. *See* Immigration and Customs Enforcement, U.S.

identity, 42–43, 55; colonialism in, 13–14; in critical race theory, 12–15, 37; for gangs, 17–18, 80–81; for Mexican-Americans, 2–3, 16, 18–19, 62, 188–90; for minority groups, 4, 29–32, 57–58; in New Mexico, 47; racism and, 13–15; research and, 193; from slavery, 36–37; in U.S., 32–33
immigration, 42–43, 55; BIP for, 92–93; for California, 72; for DMC, 132; for El Paso (Texas), 196–97; enhanced border enforcement zone for, *131*; history of, 5–7, 16, 36–37, 63, 129–34; in labor, 140–42; law enforcement and, 134–42, 219–20; maps of, *131*; for Mexico, 184–87; narratives on, 188–90; National Origins Act (1924) for, 46; for New Mexico, 180–84; organized crime and, 134–42, 153–54; politics of, 18–19, 87, 91–92, 129–30, 190; research on, 126–28, 158–59; from South America, 134–35; for U.S., 18, 209–10; violence and, 12, 163–64, 217–20. *See also* double colonization
Immigration and Customs Enforcement, U.S. (ICE), 91–92
Immigration and Naturalization Service (INS), 133
intelligence, for law enforcement, 89–90

Jackson, Stacey, 80–82
JJDP Act (1974). *See* Juvenile Justice and Delinquency Prevention Act
JPPOs. *See* Juvenile Probation and Parole Officers
Juárez. *See* Ciudad Juárez
Jurado, Pete, 67
juvenile gangs: in Anthony (New Mexico), 206–7, 230; DMC for, 117–21; *Gang Cop* (Klein), 150; history of, 55–58, *59*, 60–62; JPPOs and, 117–25; law enforcement and, 17–18, 62–64, 65, 66–67, 71–73, 123–28, 143–44; in media, 83, 211–12; from Mexico, 135–37; organized crime and, 115–16, 154–56; policy for, 74–76, 206, 226–28; in U.S., 84, *84*; *Youth Street Gangs: A Critical Appraisal* (Brotherton), 9
Juvenile Justice and Delinquency Prevention (JJDP) Act (1974), 98–99
Juvenile Probation and Parole Officers (JPPOs), 117–25, 135–36, 221–22, 226–27; for communities, 148–49; policy for, 151–56

Kaplan, Charles, 88, 225
Katz, Charles, 78, 109, 150
Kempf-Leonard, Kimberly, 99
KKK. *See* Ku Klux Klan
Klein, Malcolm, 150
Kocherga, Angela, 120
Krivo, Lauren, 10–11
Ku Klux Klan (KKK), 17, 44–48, 68, 219
Kupchik, Aaron, 110, 112

labor: BIP for, 92–93; empirical miracles in, 197–203; history of, 51–52; immigration in, 140–42; from Mexico, 55; organized crime and, 207
Ladner, Joyce A., 204–5
La Nacha. *See* González, Ignacia Jasso
Langston, Edward, 46–47
Las Cruces. *See* New Mexico
Latin Americans, *102–4*, 119–23; African Americans compared to, 10–11; communities for, 14–15, 225–26; culture of, 57–58, 135–37; El Paso (Texas) for, *106*, 107–9; New Mexico for, 14, 105, *106*, 107–10; in U.S., 113–14. *See also* minority groups

Laurentin, René, 15–16
law enforcement: for African Americans, 102–3; BIP as, 92–93; culture of, 137–42; discrimination and, 72–73; economics of, 86–88, 91, 207; family issues for, 142–45; gangs for, 145–51; ICE for, 91–92; immigration and, 134–42, 219–20; intelligence for, 89–90; juvenile gangs and, 17–18, 62–64, 65, 66–67, 71–73, 123–28, 143–44; juvenile probation in, 117–25; in media, 74–76, 151–56, 167, 169–70; for Mexican-Americans, 101, 102–4, 104–5; for minority groups, 221–22; narratives from, 129–30, 142–51; for Native Americans, 102–3; organized crime and, 212–13; *Policing Gangs in America* (Katz/Webb, V.), 78, 150; policy for, 10–12, 15, 18, 56–58, 60–62, 69–70, 77–83, 162–63, 172–73, 205–6, 221–22; politics of, 53–55, 75–76, 130–34, 131, 184; research and, 125–28, 161–62, 170–71; RICO for, 91; in rural New Mexico, 139–40, 147–48; in schools, 114–16; SROs and, 111–13; for students, 166–67; terminology for, 83–85, 84; violence and, 66. *See also* research
Lay, Shawn, 36–37
Leon, Carlos, 75–76
Levario, Miguel Antonio, 35–36, 43, 46
Lopez, Vera, 118

Maio, Rudolph James (Shakey), 89–90
Manufacturing Consent (Chomsky/Herman), 12
Manufacturing the Gang: Mexican American Youth Gangs on Local Television (Tovares), 42–43
maps: of El Paso gangs, 59, 65; enhanced border enforcement zone, 131; historical trade route, 31; of immigration, 131; of New Spain, 26; of U.S., 28
Martinez, Cid, 15–16, 214
Martinez, Ramiro, 10, 73–74, 194
Marx, Karl, 226
Maupin, James, 107
MAYA. *See* Mexican American Youth Association
Mays, Larry, 80–82, 218
McWilliams, Carey, 54
media: communities and, 227; gangs in, 8–9, 70–73, 187; Hispanics in, 170–71; juvenile gangs in, 83, 211–12; law enforcement in, 74–76, 151–56, 167, 169–70; policy and, 86–87; politics of, 11–12, 168–69; propaganda and, 223–24; research for, 166, 179–80; Sunland Park in, 93; in U.S., 161–62; violence and, 162–63, 174–75, 195–96
Mexican-Americans: culture of, 225–26; gangs for, 11, 41; history of, 32–39; identity for, 2–3, 16, 18–19, 62, 188–90; INS for, 133; JPPOs and, 117–25; law enforcement for, 101, 102–4, 104–5; Mexico for, 105, 106, 107–10; as minority groups, 98–101; narratives from, 97–98, 197–203; in New Mexico, 110–16; organized crime and, 97–98; in politics, 60–61; racism for, 132–33; schools for, 5. *See also* minority groups
Mexican American Youth Association (MAYA), 63
Mexican revolution, 33–39, 41–42
Mexico: California and, 90; culture of, 146; in double colonization, 27, 28, 33–39; gangs from, 150–51; immigration for, 184–87; juvenile gangs from, 135–37; labor from, 55; for Mexican-Americans, 105, 106, 107–10; New Mexico

and, 27, 28, 30–31; organized crime and, 183–84, 201, 203; U.S. and, 4–5, 11–12, 35–38, 88, 92–94, 105, 106, 107–10, 129–30, 155–56, 158, 163–64, 184–87, 223–24; U.S.-Mexican War, 29; violence in, 202. *See also* Ciudad Juárez
military, 162–63
Mills, C. Wright, 9–10
minority groups: ASARCO for, 30–31; Civil Rights Movement for, 63–64; culture of, 44–45, 74, 220–21, 223–24; gangs and, 84–85, 224–26; higher education for, 197–203; history of, 34–35; identity for, 4, 29–32, 57–58; law enforcement for, 221–22; Mexican-Americans as, 98–101; music for, 52; narratives from, 97–98; NMSU for, 197–98; poverty for, 117–21; in prison, 90–91; racism and, 1–2, 155–56; research on, 100–101; in revisionist history, 24; in schools, 7–9, 159–60; segregation for, 110; in U.S., 228. *See also specific minority groups*
minority-serving institutions. *See* participatory action research teams
Miracles in El Paso? (Laurentin), 15–16
Mirandé, Alfredo, 14, 197
Montgomery, Daniel, 29–30
Moore, Joan, 90, 158
Morales, Fred, 62–63
Morales, Manual, 43
Mottier, Nicole, 35, 49
Murgúia, Edward, 14–15
music, 52

narratives: from Anthony (New Mexico), 1–3, 145–47, 173–78, 198–201; from Ciudad Juárez (Mexico), 184–87; from communities, 152, 154–55; from double colonization, 23–24; from El Paso (Texas), 40–41, 160–66; about gangs, 1–3; on gangs, 217–20; on immigration, 188–90; from law enforcement, 129–30, 142–51; from Mexican-Americans, 97–98, 197–203; from minority groups, 97–98; from New Mexico, 166–73; from PAR teams, 157–58; from research, 69–70; from rural New Mexico, 3, 90–91, 97–98, 173–79; from students, 18; from Sunland Park (New Mexico), 180–84; from Texas, 179–80
National Drug Intelligence Center (NDIC), 191
National Drug Threat Assessment (2011), 145
National Gang Intelligence Center (NGIC), 191
National Institute of Corrections, 151
National Origins Act (1924), 46
Native Americans: culture of, 24–25, 26, 27; double colonization for, 24–25, 26, 27; law enforcement for, 102–3; U.S. and, 34. *See also* minority groups
NDIC. *See* National Drug Intelligence Center
Neighborhood Has Its Own Rules, The (Martinez, C.), 214
The Neighborhood Has Its Own Rules (Martinez, C.), 15–16
New Mexico: children's code in, 117; communities in, 23–24, 52–53, 95, 205–6; culture of, 29–30, 117–25, 139–42, 144–45, 152–53, 192–93; double colonization in, 32–33; El Paso (Texas) compared to, 93–94; Hispanics in, 170–71, 174–76; identity in, 47; immigration for, 180–84; JPPOs in, 135–36; juvenile gangs in, 148–50; for Latin Americans, 14, 105, 106, 107–10; Mexican-Americans in, 110–16; Mexico and, 27, 28, 30–31; narratives from, 166–73;

New Mexico (*continued*)
National Institute of Corrections on, 151; PAR teams in, 166–73; policy in, 225–26; politics of, 130–33, *131*; prison in, 121–23; in research, 77–83; schools in, 114, 174–76; Sunland Park, 93, *131*, 140, 180–84; TARC for, 100–101; Texas compared to, 38–39, 99–101, 173–74, 180–81; for U.S. Department of Education, 110–11; violence in, 85, 194–95, *196*. *See also* Anthony (New Mexico)

New Mexico, rural, 111, 117; communities in, 109–10; economics of, 178–79, 210–11; empirical miracles in, 191–93; law enforcement in, 139–40, 147–48; narratives from, 3, 90–91, 97–98, 173–79; PAR teams in, 173–79; research from, 125–26, 136–37. *See also* Anthony (New Mexico)

New Mexico State University (NMSU), 157–59, 187, 197–98

New Spain, 26

NGIC. *See* National Gang Intelligence Center

NMSU. *See* New Mexico State University

Oñate, Don Juan de, 25

organized crime: in California, 145–46; in Ciudad Juárez (Mexico), 173, 180; *Drug War Zone: Frontline Dispatches from the Streets of El Paso and Juárez* (Campbell), 88; economics of, 52–55; El Paso (Texas) and, 48–51, 85; family issues from, 135–37; history of, 37–38; immigration and, 134–42, 153–54; juvenile gangs and, 115–16, 154–56; labor and, 207; law enforcement and, 212–13; Mexican-Americans and, 97–98; Mexico and, 183–84, 201, 203; poverty and, 142–44; research on, 86–94; for students, 147–50; in Texas, 88, 151; in U.S., 184–85; violence and, 184–87

Ortiz, Vilma, 11

"Pachuco Boogie" (Tosti), 52

pachuquismo: culture of, 17, 41–48; history of, 51–55, 67–68; violence and, 62–63

participatory action research (PAR) teams: in Ciudad Juárez (Mexico), 184–87; in El Paso (Texas), 160–66; narratives from, 157–58; in New Mexico, 166–73; politics of, 158–59; in rural New Mexico, 173–79; in Sunland Park (New Mexico), 180–84; in Texas, 179–80

Payne, Yasser, 158

Peguero, Anthony, 113

Perales, Monica, 30–31

Peterson, Ruth, 10–11

Phoenix. *See* Arizona

police. *See* law enforcement

Policing Gangs in America (Katz/Webb, V.), 78, 150

policy, 209–13; in Anthony (New Mexico), 139–41; for communities, 17, 169–70, 206–7, 214; discrimination as, 63; empirical miracles for, 203–5; ethnographic analysis for, 221; for JPPOs, 151–56; for juvenile gangs, 74–76, 206, 226–28; for law enforcement, 10–12, 15, 18, 56–58, 60–62, 69–70, 77–83, 162–63, 172–73, 205–6, 221–22; media and, 86–87; in New Mexico, 225–26; for poverty, 64, 66–68, 204

politics, 209–13; culture of, 215–16; economics and, 77–78; of gangs, 188–90; of immigration, 18–19, 87, 91–92, 129–30, 190; of law enforcement, 53–55, 75–76,

130–34, 131, 184; *Manufacturing Consent* (Chomsky/Herman), 12; of media, 11–12, 168–69; Mexican-Americans in, 60–61; of New Mexico, 130–33, 131; of PAR teams, 158–59; of poverty, 14–15, 208–9; in U.S., 19, 151–56, 219–20
Pope, Carl E., 99
Posadas, Carlos, 117, 181–82
poverty: in Arizona, 109; for communities, 210–11; culture of, 107–10, 116, 142–44, 178, 199, 216; in El Paso, 51–55; for minority groups, 117–21; organized crime and, 142–44; policy for, 64, 66–68, 204; politics of, 14–15, 208–9; research on, 220; for students, 111–12; violence and, 4, 73–74
practitioners, 209–13, 214–15. *See also* Juvenile Probation and Parole Officers; law enforcement
Pratto, Felicia, 5, 14–15, 224–25
prison: culture of, 168; for gangs, 165; minority groups in, 90–91; in New Mexico, 121–23; prison gangs, 90–94; in Texas, 46; violence in, 92–93, 165
prohibition (U.S.), 33–39, 48–51. *See also* organized crime
propaganda, 223–24
Pueblo Indians, 24–25, 47
punishment. *See* law enforcement
Pyrooz, David, 84

racism: discrimination and, 63; identity and, 13–15; for Mexican-Americans, 132–33; minority groups and, 1–2, 155–56; segregation and, 110; sexism compared to, 201–2; slavery and, 36–37; in Texas, 48; in U.S., 34–39; Vigil on, 57; violence and, 38–39, 58, 60. *See also* critical race theory

Rahm, Harold J., S.J., 57–58, 61–62, 214
Real School Safety Problem, The (Kupchik), 112
Reeves, Edwin M., 46
referrals, for communities, 144–45
Relative Rate Index (RRI), 100–101, 104, 104–5, 117, 125–26
religion, 205–6, 214; for communities, 16, 68; culture of, 35; for gangs, 62–63
Renteria, Joe, 87–88
research, 63–64; from Arizona, 81–82; from Ciudad Juárez (Mexico), 92–93; critical race theory and, 18; culture and, 9–12; from CYFD, 136; from DMC, 155–56; El Paso (Texas) in, 70–76; ethnographic analysis for, 6–7; ethnographic analysis in, 95, 101, 102–4, 104–5; identity and, 193; on immigration, 126–28, 158–59; law enforcement and, 125–28, 161–62, 170–71; for media, 166, 179–80; on minority groups, 100–101; narratives from, 69–70; from National Drug Threat Assessment (2011), 145; from National Institute of Corrections, 151; New Mexico in, 77–83; on organized crime, 86–94; on poverty, 220; RRI for, 100–101, 104, 104–5, 117, 125–26; from rural New Mexico, 125–26, 136–37; for social groups, 21, 113–14; for students, 157–59, 184; terminology for, 83–85, 84; in U.S., 98–101; on violence, 164. *See also* empirical miracles; participatory action research teams
revisionist history, 63–64; in critical race theory, 21, 38–39; minority groups in, 24; U.S. in, 21
RICO. *See* Federal Racketeer Influenced and Corrupt Organizations Act

Rios, Victor, 5, 192, 208–9, 222
Robinson, Robin, 49–51
Rodriguez, Bill, 62
Romo, David, 11–12, 31–32
RRI. See Relative Rate Index
rural New Mexico. See New Mexico, rural

Schnebly, Stephen, 109
School Resource Officers (SROs), 111–13
schools: DMC in, 110–16; empirical miracles in, 197–203; *Homeroom Security* (Kupchik), 110; law enforcement in, 114–16; for Mexican-Americans, 5; minority groups in, 7–9, 159–60; in New Mexico, 114, 174–76; *The Real School Safety Problem* (Kupchik), 112
segregation, 110
sexism, 201–2
Sidanius, James, 5, 14–15, 224–25
slavery, 36–37
social dominance theory, 14–15
social groups, 21, 113–14
South America, 134–35
Southern New Mexico. See New Mexico
Spain, 24–25, 26, 27. See also double colonization
SROs. See School Resource Officers
Stannard, David, 25
Stefancic, Jean, 12–13, 21
students: empirical miracles for, 205–9; gangs and, 175–77; law enforcement for, 166–67; narratives from, 18; organized crime for, 147–50; poverty for, 111–12; research for, 157–59, 184; violence for, 168–69, 200. See also schools
Sunland Park (New Mexico), 180–84; communities in, 140; enhanced border enforcement zone, 131; in media, 93. See also New Mexico, rural
Sweeten, Gary, 84

tagging, 177–78, 181–82
Tapia, Mike, 192
TARC. See Technical Assistance and Resource Center
Technical Assistance and Resource Center (TARC), 100–101
Telles, Edward, 11
Telles, Raymond, 60–61
terminology, 83–85, 84, 165–66, 193
Texas: communities in, 109–10; gangs in, 139–41, 145–47; Horizon City in, 179–80; narratives from, 179–80; New Mexico compared to, 38–39, 99–101, 173–74, 180–81; organized crime in, 88, 151; PAR teams in, 179–80; prison in, 46; racism in, 48; violence in, 32, 179–80. See also El Paso
theory: of ethnographic analysis, 7–9; of gangs, 2–3; social dominance theory, 14–15. See critical race theory
Thrasher, Frederic, 8–9, 41–42, 98–99
Timmons, Wilbert H., 21, 131
Tita, George, 194
Torre, Rick de la, 87–88
Torres, Jamie F., 53–54
Tosti, Don, 52
Tovares, Raúl, 42–43
trade routes, 30–32, 31
Trump, Donald, 228
Tyack, David, 110

underrepresented groups. See minority groups
United States (U.S.): *American Me* (film), 90; Ciudad Juárez (Mexico) and, 48–51; Department of Education in, 110–11; Department of Justice in, 166; in double colonization, 29–30; economics of, 50–51; gangs in, 172–73;

Harrison Narcotics Act (1914) in, 35; HIDTA Program for, 138–42; history of, 216; ICE for, 91–92; identity in, 32–33; immigration for, 18, 209–10; INS for, 133; JJDP Act (1974) in, 98–99; juvenile gangs in, 84, *84*; Latin Americans in, 113–14; maps of, *28*; MAYA in, 63; media in, 161–62; Mexican revolution for, 41–42; Mexico and, 4–5, 11–12, 35–38, 88, 92–94, 105, *106*, 107–10, 129–30, 155–56, *158*, 163–64, 184–87, 223–24; minority groups in, 228; National Drug Threat Assessment (2011) for, 145; National Institute of Corrections in, 151; National Origins Act (1924) in, 46; Native Americans and, 34; NDIC in, 191; NGIC in, 191; organized crime in, 184–85; *Policing Gangs in America* (Katz/Webb, V.), 78, 150; politics in, 19, 151–56, 219–20; prohibition in, 33–39, 48–51; racism in, 34–39; research in, 98–101; in revisionist history, 21; RICO for, 91; U.S.-Mexican War, 29; violence in, 76, 193–95, *195–96*. *See also* Mexican-Americans

Valdez, Avelardo, 88, 225
Van Cleve, Nicole Gonzalez, 133–34
Vélez, María, 10–11
Vigil, James Diego, 41, 44, 52, 192; on culture, 226–27; on racism, 57
Villa, Pancho, 36, 38, 43

violence: in Ciudad Juárez (Mexico), 163–64, 194–96, *196*, 226; for communities, 10, 60–62, 160, 182–83, 227–28; in El Paso (Texas), 89–92, 194–95, *195*; empirical miracles in, 193–97, *195–96*; gangs and, 79–80, 160–61, 179; history of, 43–48; immigration and, 12, 163–64, 217–20; law enforcement and, 66; media and, 162–63, 174–75, 195–96; in Mexico, 202; in New Mexico, 85, 194–95, *196*; organized crime and, 184–87; pachuquismo and, 62–63; poverty and, 4, 73–74; in prison, 92–93, 165; racism and, 38–39, 58, 60; research on, 164; for students, 168–69, 200; in Texas, 32, 179–80; in U.S., 76, 193–95, *195–96*

Wagley, Charles, 24
Wallace, David Leon, 87–88
Ward, Geoff, 5, 222
Webb, Clive, 48
Webb, Vincent, 78, 150
Webster, Daniel, 33
White, Don, 87–88
Wilson, Woodrow, 36
Winfree, Thomas, 80–82, 119, 192, 218
Wood, John H., Jr., 88
Wood, William E., 63

Youth Street Gangs: A Critical Appraisal (Brotherton), 9

Zoot Suit Riots, 54

GPSR Authorized Representative: Easy Access System Europe, Mustamäe tee 50, 10621 Tallinn, Estonia, gpsr.requests@easproject.com

www.ingramcontent.com/pod-product-compliance
Lightning Source LLC
Chambersburg PA
CBHW021936290426
44108CB00012B/853